THE EARLY DEVELOPMENT OF HENRY JAMES

THE EARLY DEVELOPMENT OF HENRY JAMES

BY CORNELIA PULSIFER KELLEY

WITH AN INTRODUCTION BY LYON N. RICHARDSON

REVISED EDITION

UNIVERSITY OF ILLINOIS PRESS, URBANA, 1965

Originally published as Vol. 15, Nos. 1-2, in the Illinois Studies in Language and Literature.

INTRODUCTION

HENRY JAMES: FROM 1930 TO 1964

I

When Cornelia Pulsifer Kelley's *The Early Development of Henry James* appeared in 1930 in the fifteenth volume of the *University of Illinois Studies in Language and Literature*, one of the most basic and perceptive contributions to Jamesian scholarship lay open to scholars and students. Happily, there had been for her Le Roy Phillips' first edition of his scholarly work, *A Bibliography of the Writings of Henry James* (1906), and, as Miss Kelley noted, with it in hand she had traced James chronologically in the books he had read and in his essays, reviews, critical articles, and fiction from 1864, the year of his first published pieces,[1] to 1881, the year of *The Portrait of a Lady*. She had allowed nothing of later years to divert her steady gaze on the developing novelist as she placed his literary commentaries alongside his tales and novels. Thus she had followed the current of his thoughts on realism, romanticism, truth, style, and technical methodology; and she had recognized them in his progressive practice of fiction, watching him imitate, adopt, and change the patterns of his literary sources until he could rise above adaptation and by enlarged powers of observation and perception create a technique and a world quite deeply his own.

During this period 1864-1881 sixteen volumes of his tales, sketches, critical works, and novels were published, among the novels being *Roderick Hudson* (1875), *The American* (1877), *The Europeans* (1878), *Daisy Miller* (1878), *An International Episode* (1879), *Washington Square* (1880), and *The Portrait of a Lady* (1881).

Let us for a moment riffle the pages of Miss Kelley's book, packed with literary associations; and for the purpose of introduction let three short comments suffice as a preview or recollection, whichever it may be for the reader.

In James's earliest years of self-apprenticeship to his craft, he

---

[1] Leon Edel, in *Henry James: The Untried Years* (1953), dethroned a James review, mentioned in Phillips as being first, and identified a preceding unsigned short story, "A Tragedy of Error," published in the same year.

profited by studying themes, methodology, and portrayal of character in the works of Balzac, Flaubert, Gautier, Mérimée, Musset and others; and even later, Balzac's *Eugénie Grandet* served as a partial prototype for James's Catherine Sloper in *Washington Square*. But he came to believe that the French had allowed their minds to drift too far toward the grotesque, that a fundamental sense of the moral was missing, and he drew away from them.

Also, his earliest years of apprenticeship were leavened by the friendship and counsel of William Dean Howells, who was his elder by six years and assistant editor of *The Atlantic Monthly* when they first met. It was Howells who opened *The Atlantic* to James; and it was Howells, the great advocate of realism, who suggested to the young James that he might achieve better control and higher artistry if he would weave some Hawthornesque romance into the pattern of some of his stories. Later, James reviewed Howells' *A Chance Acquaintance* (1873) and *A Foregone Conclusion* (1875), which may have drawn him more strongly to doing portraits of the American Girl himself, as in *Daisy Miller* (1878) and *An International Episode* (1879).

But throughout the years there were two novelists whom James held above all others. One was Turgénieff, who taught him that the most interesting characters were the moral failures, not the moral victors, and who, as James said in an essay on Turgénieff, "cared for more things in life than any novelist save George Eliot." George Eliot was James's other idol, truly great, of high moral worth and deep understanding. These two novelists did much toward developing James's art, and their influence may be found, for example, in *The Portrait of a Lady*, with richness of substance and treatment, with Turgénieff's sense of the greater glory in loss, and with Eliot's Gwendolen Harleth of *Daniel Deronda* used in some part in creating Isabel Archer. Gwendolen remains as a partial prototype of Isabel, and only when later biographical knowledge of James became available could scholars also recognize that the dominant image of James's cousin, Mary Temple, enabled him to create in large part not only Isabel Archer but other heroines, especially Milly Theale of *The Wings of the Dove*.

II

As one rereads *The Early Development of Henry James* thirty-four years after publication, the discoveries, associations, recognitions, judgments, and tracings of literary development remain basic and vital. They have become common property in the mass of critical knowledge, so long have they been used: most of them accepted, some modified or supplemented, but seldom wholly rejected in the flood of critical opinion and insight published in the last two decades. The amount of scholarly work has grown tremendously, and one sees in it, here and there, where *The Early Development of Henry James* has played its part in informing later scholars working in the same area.

I recall the real satisfaction I felt in having so sound a study as Miss Kelley's before me when doing *Henry James: Representative Selections* (1941). F. O. Matthiessen, in *Henry James: The Major Phase* (1944), recorded the value of her work as a base for any study of James "in terms of his relation to the evolution of the nineteenth century novel," and he further remarked that since Miss Kelley's "painstaking" study had presented James's "many reviews and essays about Hawthorne, George Eliot, Balzac, Turgénieff, and other masters of fiction to whom he was indebted, and related them to all the stages of his own work up to *The Portrait of a Lady*, I have not felt it necessary to take the reader over that ground again." Bruce R. McElderry, Jr. acknowledged her "useful" study in "The Uncollected Stories of Henry James" (*American Literature*, November, 1949). Frederick W. Dupee, in *Henry James* (1951), accounted her work "helpful on the subject of James's early stories and reviews," and so did Robert Le Clair in *The Young Henry James: 1843-1870* (1955). Quentin Anderson, in *The American Henry James* (1955), referred especially to her remarks on James's "emancipated" female characters. Richard Poirier directed attention to Miss Kelley several times in *The Comic Sense of Henry James: A Study of the Early Novels* (1960), finding himself in agreement with reference to *Roderick Hudson* and Hawthorne, though taking issue with her opinion that *The American* is not at all autobiographic. Let the roll call be closed with Oscar Cargill's extraordinarily close and detailed study, *The Novels of Henry James* (1961). Professor Cargill incorporated his own analyses and recognized and evaluated the points of view of many scholars, and he mentioned Miss Kelley on fifteen occasions, fourteen of which he listed in the index. Among the topics discussed, Professor Cargill added points of view relative to *Watch and Ward* and George Sand, supported Miss Kelley's belief in James's knowledge of the *ancien régime* over that of his critics, considered her evaluation of *The Europeans* too low in the light of later judgments, and extended the literary ancestry of Isabel Archer and Gilbert Osmond of *The Portrait of a Lady*.

III

The year 1930—the date of Miss Kelley's *The Early Development of Henry James*—is a critical point in time in Jamesian scholarship. Not many major studies lie behind 1930, and in the immediate years ahead his reputation was to fall to its lowest point, thereafter to rise to phenomenal heights. This dramatic course has been traced by Robert E. Spiller in *Eight American Authors: A Review of Research and Criticism* (1956, rev. 1962), edited by Floyd Stovall.

During the latter quarter of the nineteenth century and the earlier decades of the twentieth, James's reputation had not fared too well with the critics who were blindly dedicated to any one of several warring camps. James was both a romantic and a realist, or a realist who used the devices of romance; and he revolted against naturalism—in an essay on Zola, for example, describing him as never able to rise above the "malodorous Common." In this position James's true stature was recognized by only a limited number of readers. Yet before 1930 there were several perceptive books about him. In addition to his autobiographical volumes may be added such studies described by Professor Spiller as F. M. Hueffer's *Henry James: A Critical Study* (1916), Joseph Warren Beach's *The Method of Henry James* (1918), Percy Lubbock's two-volume edition of *The Letters of Henry James* (1920) and his critical study of James, *The Craft of Fiction* (1921), Pelham Edgar's biographical *Henry James: Man and Author* (1927); and Morris Roberts' Harvard dissertation (1928), *Henry James's Literary Criticism*.

Against these discerning critics were others who ignored James or deemed him a literary snob writing an ostentatious style yielding little or no substance. As an internationalist, writing of Americans in Europe and of Europeans in America, James was ill regarded by the nationalist critics. Van Wyck Brooks, in *The Pilgrimage of Henry James* (1925), saw him as a troubled man without a country, and Vernon Louis Parrington, in his third volume of *Main Currents in American Thought* (1930) saw him only as "a self-deceived romantic . . . who fell in love with culture and never realized how poor a thing he worshiped."

But low though James's general reputation was in certain quarters, worse was to follow. When Miss Kelley's study of the growth of James as artist and humanist appeared, he stood at the brink of a sharp decline. In Professor Spiller's words, it was "in the early thirties when James's stock reached what was perhaps its all-time low with the application of the Marxian formula to literary history."

Since then, during somewhat over two decades, James has risen to the heights; and he probably has attracted more scholars to critical literary endeavors than any other novelist of his time. The Freudians found in the tales and novels of James a nigh inexhaustible vein of psychological ore for their spades. With the surge of aesthetic criticism on texts and on the art of the novel, James's critical dicta and fiction have supplied rich and abundant substance, and critics and scholars have found in his prefaces, essays, tales, and novels a most exciting source for structuring their own sense of artistry. Lately large designs have developed. There is the definitive *A Bibliography of Henry James* (1959, revised 1961) by Leon Edel and Dan Laurence, and the republication of James's works under the editorship of Leon Edel. There are such continuing studies as Oscar Cargill's exhaustive interpretations of James's fiction, already represented by *The Novels of Henry James* (1961), and Leon Edel's masterpiece of biography, *Henry James*, the first volume of which appeared in 1953, the second and third in 1962, and the fourth is yet to come.

But Jamesian scholarship stands still in need of Miss Kelley's *The Early Development of Henry James*, and the need has brought about this new printing, very slightly revised, for wider distribution.

LYON N. RICHARDSON

PREFATORY NOTE

This study of the early development of Henry James is the out-growth of two things: remotely, of an interest in the comparative study of literature which was aroused in me by Professor Babbitt at Radcliffe, and directly, of an interest in the field of fiction which was stimulated and furthered by Professor Bernbaum of the University of Illinois, under whose helpful direction and guidance the study has been written.

Practically all the research has been done in the library of the University of Illinois, the resources of which have been supplemented by loans from other libraries. I have investigated the card catalogues in many city and college libraries, and during the summer of 1928, I spent some time in Cambridge, Massachusetts, in an endeavor to find new biographical material. None was to be obtained, but the contact with people who had known or studied or written upon James was most helpful. Throughout my investigation of the early period, I have been dependent upon the *Bibliography of the Writings of Henry James*, compiled by LeRoy Phillips and published in 1906. Without this valuable book, which Mr. Phillips is now bringing up to date, my study would not have been possible.

To the many people who have assisted me with advice and suggestions, especially to Professor Bernbaum whose patient aid has been unlimited and most valuable, and to the members of the committee on the University of Illinois Studies in Language and Literature who have made possible the publication of my study, I wish to express my gratitude and thanks.

CORNELIA PULSIFER KELLEY

URBANA, ILLINOIS, March 1, 1930

TABLE OF CONTENTS

THE EARLY DEVELOPMENT OF HENRY JAMES

CHAPTER I

THE PURPOSE AND THE METHOD OF THIS STUDY

1. *The Problem*

It is doubtful if any American novelist of recent years has stimulated more interest than Henry James. I write American hesitantly, for Englishmen sometimes claim him as their own on the grounds of his gesture of loyalty in 1915 when he became an English citizen, early critics dubbed him European, and others, more broadly minded, have called him variously international, cosmopolitan, or the man without a country. As it is, critics and novelists and short-story writers of both Europe and America have read his stories with interest, albeit with praise and censure, as lofty in one case as it is bitter in the other, have dissected and analyzed, and attempted to synthesize again these marvellous works, have endeavored to write psychological studies along his model, or have, casting aside these stories of James except for the biographical revelations of them, attempted to explain not James the novelist, but James the man, American, English, or what you will. There have been books[1] on the subject, breezy, well-written, sometimes not quite serious enough, considering the seriousness of James, and articles in other books, chapters treating James as one of the forces to be reckoned with in the development of the short story or the trend of the novel, or trying to settle one of the many moot questions about his very individual method and style, or merely commenting upon the facts of his life, interesting and unusual as they were, or occasionally, following James's own clue, disregarding the facts in the interest of the impressions or the ideas of the man. Magazines have been full of articles upon James, as one critic after another has restated the perplexing points about this interesting novelist and his works. But most of these articles and books have approached James from the end instead of the beginning of his development. The authors have read his autobiographi-

[1] See Bibliography at the end of this thesis.

cal volumes, *A Small Boy and Others, Notes of a Son and Brother, The Middle Years*,[2] all written in the later years of his life when the past had become rosecolored to the successful writer, and his prefaces to the Definitive Edition of his Novels and Tales,[3] which were intended to be autobiographical expositions of how he wrote certain of his stories, but the more or less gauzy and filmy material of memory, James dipped in such a riot of colors and hues that the result, except for the very astute, is difficult to grasp and understand. James, too, in these books dealing with his early years, gives us his mature self rather than his younger. In his development he had gone so far that he could not get back to a contemporary view of himself nor did he want to, for the productions of those formative years were afterwards hideous to him, even though the period otherwise was so bright. The developed man rebelled at the crudities and outspokenness of youth, and of those early works he wished to salvage but few. Yet James is such a distinct figure in the development of the modern novel that it is most important to study his own development and in this especially to see how he got started in the method which was so peculiarly his until it has since been adopted by many novelists.

Critics have been altogether too prone to respect James's wishes. They have approached him going from 1916, the date of his death, or from 1907–09, the dates of his prefaces, backwards, rather than coming from 1864, his first published review, downwards. To be sure, they have often prefixed their critical conclusions with biographical sketches or have even treated the development of his work from *Roderick Hudson*—rarely from an earlier work—chronologically, but almost without exception in the light of what James said in his lengthy prefaces rather than in the light of what he was thinking and saying at the time the short story or novel under consideration was being written. Rebecca West confesses frankly that she has no concern about the early stories, and says next to nothing of the reviews.[4] Beach makes a careful study of James's method, but he is interested almost solely in its evolved state, and studies only the prefaces and late critical works in an endeavor to understand the result; though he considers some of the early stories, it is

[2] *A Small Boy and Others*, New York, 1913. *Notes of a Son and Brother*, New York, 1914. *The Middle Years*, New York, 1917.

[3] Scribner's, New York, 1907–09, 24 volumes.

[4] West, R.: *Henry James*, Boston and New York, 1916 (see especially p. 24).

in the light of the conclusions reached from the later works.[5] Van
Wyck Brooks's interest is wholly autobiographical, but even in this
he ignores the sources of information furnished by the travel
sketches.[6] Ford Madox Hueffer claims to have a great admiration
for James, but shows no interest in any work but the novels of the
Definitive Edition and the major works of criticism and autobiography.[7] Pelham Edgar brushes the early period very lightly
and inadequately.[8] One has little idea from any of these books upon
James that he put in a period of long, laborious apprenticeship to
the masters of his craft before he became successful. One has no
conception that he distinguished himself as a reviewer unless perchance one opens the very useful bibliography compiled by LeRoy
Phillips in 1906.[9] Then if one turns to the third section entitled
Contributions to Periodicals, one will suddenly see how much
James did in the first seventeen years of his production that has never
been noticed by critics. The first review appeared in October, 1864;
fifteen reviews and a short story followed during the next year;
twelve reviews and two stories the next, and so on in varying ratio,
increasing rapidly through the seventies with notes on art, on travel,
on the theatre running the reviews a close race while the original
fiction often trailed far in the rear. James was apparently a very
prolific writer. One marvels at the way he jumped from American
shores to the English, then fearlessly crossed the channel to France,
having his say on novels good and bad, on poetry, on criticism, on
drama, on travel, on art in general; and one wishes, perhaps, to see
the young mind in action.

The earliest reviews, so neglected often from sheer perversity
by critics, were collected, with one most unfortunate omission, by
Pierre de Chaignon la Rose in 1921,[10] while a few were published
during James's lifetime, edited in 1908 by LeRoy Phillips.[11] The
only printed criticism directly bearing upon them is that in the
general prefaces appended by la Rose and Phillips to their collections, a review or two, and the first chapter of a thin volume by

[5] Beach, J. W.: *The Method of Henry James*, Yale University Press, 1918.
[6] Brooks, V. W.: *The Pilgrimage of Henry James*, New York, 1925.
[7] Hueffer, F. M.: *Henry James: A Critical Study*, New York, 1916.
[8] Edgar, P.: *Henry James: Man and Author*, London, 1927.
[9] Phillips, L.: *Bibliography of the Writings of Henry James*, New York, 1906.
[10] *Notes and Reviews*, Cambridge, Massachusetts, 1921. Omits an important
review of Goethe's *Wilhelm Meister*.
[11] *Views and Reviews*, Boston, 1908.

Morris Roberts which considers James's criticism independently of his fictional interests and thus fails to see the interplay of the two.[12] Occasionally a critic has referred to the reviews devoted to books by George Eliot, but without discerning the steadily increasing influence of the English novelist upon the young American, and no critic has gone to all the early reviews, uncollected as well as reprinted, in order to understand James's development in the writing of fiction and the many influences which entered it. *French Poets and Novelists*,[13] a collection of some of the critical articles written during the seventies and assembled by James in 1878, has fared better—or is it worse?—with the critics, its existence at least being recognized by them, but this book comprises but a small part of the critical work which James was writing during his early period, and for the most part shows the ideas after they were formed rather than in the process of formation. A critic who approaches James only through this book as representing his early views, will fail to understand the way in which James was in the beginning influenced by Balzac and will quite miss the fact that George Sand at one time so strongly affected James that there was danger of his following her lead, though there are essays upon both writers in the book. Nor have critics who have referred in passing to this book noticed the specific clues to the influence of Turgénieff upon James which are given in the review first printed in 1874 and later reprinted in the volume. Most critics depend rather upon James's preface to *The Portrait of a Lady* for the treatment of this influence and miss its full significance.

Some of the travel sketches were brought out by James in *Transatlantic Sketches*, 1875,[14] and *Portraits of Places*, 1883,[15] but these have been quite overlooked by recent writers on James, and the only criticism of them is in some brief contemporary reviews or notices which consider them quite independently of their place in James's development as a novelist. The question of the influence of other writers of travel sketches, Gautier, for instance, whose reports fascinated James, has never been considered, and the influence of Italy upon James has been slighted or overlooked.

Practically all the short stories, however, have been repub-

---

[12] *Henry James's Criticism*, Cambridge, Massachusetts, 1929.
[13] London, Macmillan and Company, 1878.
[14] Boston, James R. Osgood and Company, 1875.
[15] London, Macmillan and Company, 1883.

lished at one time or another, but many of the scattered volumes are difficult of access, and it is easier for the reader to find the story in the place of its original appearance, using Phillips's *Bibliography* as a guide. James himself supervised the republishing of some of the better ones during his early period.[16] He chose to preserve in their rewritten form in the Definitive Edition, only nine prior to *The Portrait of a Lady* in 1881. These nine, *A Passionate Pilgrim*, 1871; *The Madonna of the Future*, 1873; *Madame de Mauves*, 1874; *Roderick Hudson*, 1875; *The American*, 1876; *Four Meetings*, 1877; *Daisy Miller*, 1878; *An International Episode*, 1878; and *A Bundle of Letters*, 1879, have been freely criticised and often very well, but usually independently of the many other things James was doing at the same time. Since James's death, New York companies have brought out four volumes reprinting some of the early tales, but with brief, incompetent prefaces.[17] Although not recognized by James as worthy of resurrection—no doubt he would greatly deprecate the fact that they have been republished—these stories are interesting and important for the light they throw upon his early tendencies, and together with the reviews show the evolution of James as a novelist. Only by studying them can one understand the evolution of his method. For the many other youthful attempts, some three hundred and more articles of many kinds, one must go, Phillips in hand, to the *Nations* and *Atlantics* and *North American Reviews* of those years, and in these dusty volumes discover the young man, Henry James, plainly outspoken as he thought and wrote in that formative period from 1864 to 1881.

2. *The Purpose and the Method of This Study*

It is for this purpose that the present dissertation has been undertaken. The approach will be chronological. The later works, the few prefaces which deal with the early novels and tales, will be used only as they may give a fact or two about the occasion of composi-

[16] See Phillips, Part I for the various publications.

[17] a. *Gabriel de Bergerac*, Boni and Liveright, New York, 1918. b. *Travelling Companions*, Boni and Liveright, New York, 1918 (contains also "The Sweetheart of M. Briseux," "Professor Fargo," "At Isella," "Guest's Confession," "Adina," "De Grey"). c. *A Landscape Painter*, Scott and Seltzer, New York, 1919 (contains also "A Day of Days," "Poor Richard," "A Most Extraordinary Case." d. *Master Eustace*, T. Seltzer, New York, 1920 (contains also "Longstaff's Marriage," "Theodolinde," "A Light Man," "Benvolio"). Macmillan and Co., Ltd. of London publish a thirty-five volume edition of *The Novels and Tales of Henry James* which includes many of these early tales.

tion, but Mr. Gosse has already pointed out how disappointing they are in this respect;[18] or as I may realize that something in an early work is pointing with an emphatic index finger to something in a later, or as I may see a tendency in an early work or two which suddenly disappears never again to come to the surface, search as one may for it. Nor will the autobiographical volumes be used except for the facts they supply. This may seem to some an oversight, and I hasten to add that the volumes have been continually borne in mind as furnishing all the direct information, if it may, indeed, be called direct, that is available on James's early training. This information is often of the haziest kind, conveyed in a still hazier way. Occasionally a fact can be detached, and these I have collected in a preliminary chapter, but it would be presumptuous and futile for an alien pen to try to interpret these years. Except in a few cases, James did not tell us exactly what books he read—exactly how they affected him. Probably he could not. Having no specific data, no boyish letters nor early scribblings from the pen of James, I have felt even more than he did the impossibility of discovering the significance of his earliest reading. The critic can conclude only that he read widely and avidly, and that out of this was born the desire to become a novelist. What it had all come to mean to him by 1864, however, begins to become apparent with the first of his reviews. It is at this point, when contemporary evidence is first available, that I have begun my study, and in a way, then, the early reading is considered by means of the imprint which it left. From 1864, James can be easily understood from the many things of all sorts that he was writing, often going into things deeply, analyzing them thoroughly but expressing them as plainly as one expresses an arithmetical addition or subtraction and never in the unknown x and y of algebra. His reading and background appear in the reviews. His ideas and demands emerge giving one a yardstick by which to measure him, to smile perhaps as one discovers the often thought infallible James doing just what he condemned in others, then to sympathize as one realizes how hard, how extraordinarily difficult, how well-nigh impossible even, it was for James to write fiction in the beginning. One understands why James was later ashamed of some of his early work, why he wished it to remain hidden. One rejoices when James with a flash did something remarkably good after another something abominably bad. One sees in the early period that James as a critic outweighed James as a writer of original fiction in bulk and often in idea and expression. One notices James as a lover of art and of travel and observes how this influenced his stories. One observes finally James really and conclusively emerging as a novelist in *The Portrait of a Lady* in 1881, and understands then how he had *made* himself into a writer of tales and novels. His only genius was that which is the most dependable of all—a genius for work.

The scheme of treatment followed in this study was suggested by an article of Sir Edmund Gosse's on Henry James where he complains that it is difficult to decipher from James's prefaces or from his autobiographical volumes the facts of James's life and suggests that the latter especially should be edited by someone who would preface them with "a skeleton chronicle of actual facts and dates."[19] In writing the dissertation I have resorted to the use of interchapters to give these facts and serve as a background, and have followed these with chapters containing a detailed study of the internal development of James, of necessity often repeating the facts but endeavoring to focus the attention upon the writer. The seventeen years covered in the study fall into three distinct phases in the early development—from 1864 to 1869, from 1869 to 1875, and from 1875 to 1881. The first of these phases has been treated even more intensively than the subsequent ones. James developed slowly at first and each review that he wrote represented much thought and reflection. Later his development increased in momentum, and by 1875 he was able to dash off reviews and critical articles almost without effort. The articles still are of interest for the expression of James's ideas, but the stories and novels assume the lead in explaining the development of the writer. In this study, accordingly, the treatment has been determined by James's own development, and an attempt has been made to reflect the nature and the pace of it.

[19] *Ibid.*, p. 20.

INTERCHAPTER A

THE LIFE OF JAMES, 1843–1869

1. *Childhood and Youth, 1843–1864*

Henry James, novelist, was born April 15, 1843, at 2 Washington Place, New York City.[1] He was the second son of Henry James, philosopher and man of letters—but not "pasteur" as French critics frequently call him— and of Mary Walsh. Both parents were from families which had lived a generation or two in New York state, the paternal ancestors coming originally from Ireland, the maternal from Scotland. To the couple were born four other children: William, the eldest, Wilky, Robertson, and Alice.

When Henry James was but a year and a half old, his parents took him and his elder brother to Europe, where even the younger child saw the Place Vendôme vividly enough to recognize it later when he saw it for a second time. Upon the return to America Henry's earliest years were divided between living in New York City and visiting in Albany where the grandparents and numerous aunts, uncles, and cousins lived.. Of this early New York life, *A Small Boy and Others* gives a most charming picture.

James's schooling was somewhat desultory. There was a rapid succession of different small private schools where the female teachers apparently made more impression upon the lad than the facts of instruction. And more than from teachers or from text books, James began very early to pick up an education from novels—Hawthorne and many magazines, and especially, English books. In fact, James concluded later, "All our books in that age were English."[2] He was evidently an avid reader from an early age. Then there were the theatres to which he was occasionally taken to see Shakespeare, or stage arrangements of the novels of Dickens, or popular shows of the day. The female teachers gave way to male as he grew older, and the schools became slightly larger— the Institution Vergnes, and then Mr. Jenk's school—but school still meant little to the boy. He was often engaged, he remembered,

[1] *A Small Boy and Others, Notes of a Son and Brother*, and the Biographical Sketch appended by Lubbock to the edition of James's letters have been used for the facts of these early years.
[2] *A Small Boy and Others*, p. 81.

in "dramatic, accompanied by pictorial composition," writing a page of dialogue and capping it off with a picture, and he sought in this fact, an explanation of his later preoccupation with scene.[3]

In 1855, the parents took their children to Europe for three years, hoping to give them the opportunity of as broad an education as possible. They landed at Liverpool, stopped in London till Henry could recover from an attack of malaria sufficiently to move on to Paris, and then came a journey from Lyons to Nantes which marked a crucial hour in James's life when he saw his first old castle and first peasant—"Supremely, in that ecstatic vision, was 'Europe,' sublime synthesis, expressed and guaranteed to me."[4]

The family settled for a time in Geneva, putting William and Wilky in a boarding school, but Henry, because of his delicate health, had to stay with his parents. The winter and spring were spent in London, where William and Henry were tutored by Robert Thompson, who afterwards taught Stevenson, and London was enjoyed as the scene of the stories of Dickens and Thackeray. The streets and the people, the picture galleries and the theatres all played a part in opening England to the lads. Then in the summer of 1856, the family moved back to Paris for two years. Here a succession of French tutors and a liberal dose of French literature and drama and art—Henry's interest directed to the latter by his brother's early desire to be an artist—stimulated the interest in France and things French which was to have such a lasting effect upon Henry. For a time, the children attended the Institution Fezandié, a French school then experimenting with the educational ideas of Fourier. It was during these two years of "picking up an education" in Paris and breathing the artistic atmosphere of the place, vaguely but lovingly treated by James in his reminiscences, that he believed he must first have fumbled with "the aesthetic clue."[5] Once each year, probably during the summer months, the family moved from Paris to Boulogne-sur-mer, and here, on the occasion of the second visit, Henry became violently ill with typhus fever.

In 1858, the family came back to America for a year at Newport, but by the winter of 1859 they had returned to Geneva, and this time Henry, along with this brothers, was sent for an unhappy

[3] *Ibid.*, pp. 260 f.
[4] *Ibid.*, p. 284.
[5] *Ibid.*, p. 354.

few months to the Institution Rochette, a scientific school, and then, the error discovered, to the Academy where he was allowed to take a literary course. Here under M. Toeppfer, he read "French literature," under M. Verchère he "worried out" Virgil and "Tite-Live," and under a noisy little professor of German, he struggled with Schiller and Lessing.[6] Of more importance, however, as James recalled it in later years, was the English literature which came to the family through the pages of the *Cornhill Magazine* and the *Once a Week* where the latest productions of Dickens, Thackeray, George Eliot, Meredith, Reade, Trollope, and du Maurier were to be enjoyed.[7] Trollope's *Framely Parsonage* and Thackeray's *Roundabout Papers* and *The Newcomes* began there, while *Adam Bede* was lent to the family by some English friends.[8] During a summer at Bonn, James "rioted" among other things, on "the supreme German classics"—what they were, he does not say.[9] From all this, treated most generally and vaguely in *Notes of a Son and Brother,* he believed began the "impressions" that were going to cause him eventually to turn novelist,[10] and it is the effects of this and the subsequent greedy devouring of fiction which, we shall see later, formed the background for James's reviews.[11]

In the fall of 1860 the family returned to America and settled at Newport in order that William might study art with William Hunt whose studio was there. Here Henry, when not at Mr. Leverett's school, dawdled, quite unsuccessful as far as painting went, but enjoying his first really close connection with art. La Farge was there also, and revealed Browning and Mérimée and, "most of all," Balzac, especially *Eugénie Grandet* to James,[12] who now that he had lived in France, found French literature the most absorbing of all literatures. The *Revue des Deux Mondes* coming twice a month kept up the connection, and James was led to translate Musset's *Lorenzaccio* and Mérimée's *La Venus d'Ille* and send them to New York magazines which cruelly ignored them.[13]

[6] *Notes of a Son and Brother*, pp. 7 f.

[7] *Ibid.*, pp. 20 f.

[8] *Ibid.*, p. 19.

[9] *Ibid.*, p. 24.

[10] *Ibid.*, pp. 24 f.

[11] Into the autobiographical volumes touching lightly and broadly on the reading of his youth, the critic must not read too much. James's view of his education in literature is widely comprehensive rather than deep or analytical.

[12] *Notes of a Son and Brother*, pp. 93 f.

[13] For the fact that James translated *Lorenzaccio* we are dependent upon a

Then suddenly William's interest in painting ceased and the days at the studio stopped. William went to Harvard to study science. Wilky and Bob were sent to a school in Concord, and Henry remained in Newport reading. The Civil War broke out and the younger brothers enlisted. Henry was kept from this because of an accident to his back, and evidently in order to do something, entered Harvard Law School in 1862. In Cambridge he seems to have obtained more from Miss Upham's boarding house, "a translation into American terms of Balzac's Maison Vauquer,"[14] and from William's friends, than from the class rooms. According to his later view, what he " 'wanted to want' to be was, all intimately, just literary,"[15] and failing that directly, he took to looking around at life and "taking in" New England—to how little real purpose, however, will soon be apparent. The muse, he felt, even then was "the muse of prose fiction."[16] Henry's course in law was never completed, hardly even begun, but the years from 1862 to '64 were filled in somehow, with the shadow of the war and Wilky's and Bob's service in it falling over the scene. Gradually in some way which will ever remain a mystery, unless some early notebooks or letters of Henry James are discovered and published, he advanced toward his literary debut, and at last, summoning up his courage, he boldly stepped into the profession of literature.

These are the facts of the first twenty-one years. For the atmosphere one must go to the autobiographical volumes, discounting for the fact that they are memories recalled later in life, remembering that James then inclined to see everything as it had tended away from America toward Europe. Presently, as we are able to approach James through what he was writing from 1864 on, we shall see that he was American in point of view much longer and more loyally than has generally been believed.

2. *The Boston-Cambridge Scene, 1864–1869*

It was in 1864 then that "the plot began most to thicken" for Henry James.[17] The parents realizing their elder sons' interests in

---

statement by T. S. Perry, quoted by Lubbock in the edition of the letters (I, 8). Perry says also that James wrote stories where the heroines were lambs and the heroes villains. James confessed to the translation of *La Venus d'Ille* in *Notes of a Son and Brother*, p. 94.

[14] *Ibid.*, p. 306.
[15] *Ibid.*, p. 294.
[16] *Ibid.*, p. 342.
[17] *Notes of a Son and Brother*, p. 402. It is unfortunate that the only account of

the Boston and Cambridge scenes and feeling themselves the pull
and urge of the new cultural awakening there led by their friends,
Norton, Lowell, Fields, moved in the spring of that year to Ashburton Place and then two years later to Cambridge itself. As
James recalled later, they were busy, throbbing years, "a period
bristling . . . . with an unprecedented number of simultaneous
particulars"[18]—the close of the war, Lincoln's "unforgettable death,"
and the irony of the succession of Johnson. More moving for an aspirant to literature was the death of Hawthorne, to which James found
it difficult to reconcile himself, all grateful as he was for the earlier
American's literary example,

for the moral of it was that an American could be an artist, one of the
finest, without 'going outside' about it, as I liked to say; quite in fact as
if Hawthorne had become one just by being American enough.[19]

And then there was Dickens's visit to America, touching James
directly and deeply yet briefly as he was allowed with Arthur
Sedgwick to slip in after the Norton's dinner in honor of the celebrity
in November '67 and be introduced. There was no shaking of hands,
no exchanging of words, just the look and felt presence of the master
in the short confrontation, but to "the already dreaming and yearning dabbler in the mystery" that was much.[20] James's health continued to be rather uncertain, sometimes stopping his activity
altogether, but in the main his life was that of the usual young man
of his day, filled with "coming and going."[21] There were trips to
the White Mountains, and "sittings" to John La Farge during
James's tea-drinking visits in Newport, "winter attempts, a little
weak, but still more or less achieved, upon New York,"[22] the long
summer of 1866 when the family moved to "the rural retreat of

---

these years which we have from James's own pen is that in Chapter XII and a few
references in the chapters dealing with his father. The letters which later reveal
many interesting sidelights, as edited by Percy Lubbock, do not begin till the
European trip in 1869. Regarding these years, James confesses the difficulty of
treating them, "in the first place everything was in some degree an adventure, and
in the second any difference of degree guiding my selection would be imperceptible
at this end of time to the cold eye of criticism," (p. 414) and the result is that the
period is treated for the most part generally and inadequately.

[18] *Notes of a Son and Brother*, p. 402.
[19] *Ibid.*, p. 411.
[20] *Ibid.*, p. 254.
[21] *Ibid.*, p. 413.
[22] *Ibid.*, p. 413.

Swampscott,"[23] but the all-pervading, unifying atmosphere was the literary one of Boston and Cambridge. The presence of his father, the reestablishment of the home life of the family,[24] meant much in a protective and still more in an encouraging way to the second son. Henry was suddenly lifted up, as it were, into a group of older men, of men who had done things; as the son of Henry James, Senior, he was recognized, and as his own abilities, stimulated by the kind words of these men, began to assert themselves, he was accepted by the cultural fraternity as one of its most promising neophytes. Before this time he had been a younger brother, outshone by William. Now, and perhaps aided in part by William's long absences, he stepped out of the enveloping haze a distinct, emphatic figure, fired with youthful ardor, with gratitude and joy that at last he could play a part with older men. His "deeply reserved but quite unabashed design of becoming as 'literary' as might be," aided by their "whole new medium of existence"[25] became at last a fact.

It is noteworthy that Boston was the setting for this development, Boston with its lofty ideals of government, literature, and life kindled into flame by the war. Here Lowell and Norton had but recently taken over the editorship of the *North American Review* with high cultural aims; Godkin was frequently here as he prepared to break new ground with the *Nation*, published, to be sure, in New York, but with many of its assistants recruited from Boston, while the *Atlantic Monthly* was flourishing under Fields with Howells soon to be added to the staff, and the doors of all three publications were opened wide to James. There was something especially auspicious in being a young man at this time, in being able to start existence for one's self, if such a phrase is permissible, just as existence collectively was becoming intense and earnest and future-facing with a new lease on life. For nearly five years, 1864 to the end of 1868, Henry James devoted himself seriously yet thrillingly to the cause of literature in America. He was not resignedly trying to console himself for the fact that he had had to be but an onlooker in that other cause, the Civil War, while Wilky and Robertson achieved wounds and a kind of glistening glory, as Rebecca West would have

---

[23] *Ibid.*, p. 437.

[24] A glimpse of the happy trend of the family life is given in *The Life of E. L. Godkin*, New York, 1907, II, 118, with reference to the lively arguments at meal times upon morals and literature.

[25] *Notes of a Son and Brother*, p. 403.

us believe,[26] nor was he then devoured with a nostalgia for Europe, as Van Wyck Brooks[27] makes out. He realized the weight and values of European literature not enviously, but gratefully, as an example which American literature might notice and profit by, and he was filled with the ardor and zeal of a patriot in the literary civil war which he saw must be waged in America. Under the generalship of Norton and Godkin, he rose quickly from awkward, gawky private to polished lieutenant. It is the history of this change which the following chapters will trace.

That was the course of his outer development, but there was an inner development as well. It made him, more than a critic of the literature of others, a critic of himself. He wished to help the cause of American literature by practice as well as by precept, and that, he was to find, was difficult. Thus, as James improved in one way quickly, brilliantly, we shall observe him slowly, arduously, at times a bit frantically trying to improve in the other way, and we shall recognize that at the end of 1868 he was really but just beginning in the craft which was ultimately to be almost his sole interest in life.

[26] *Henry James*, London, 1916, p. 21.
[27] *Pilgrimage of Henry James*, New York, 1925, Chapter II.

CHAPTER II

JAMES'S DEBUT AS A WRITER: THE STORY ELEMENT

1. *The Time and the Place*

The date which was to stand out ever after for Henry James as the beginning of recognized literary activity was October 1864, the place, the *North American Review*, the occasion, a review of Senior's *Essays on Fiction*, lately collected and published in book form.

I had addressed in trembling hope my first fond attempt at literary criticism to Charles Eliot Norton, who had lately, and with the highest, brightest competence, come to the rescue of the North American Review, submerged in a stale tradition and gasping for life, and he had not only published it in his very next number—the interval for me of breathless brevity—but had expressed the liveliest further hospitality, the gage of which was thus at once his welcome to me at home. I was to grow fond of regarding as a positive consecration to letters that half-hour in the long library at Shady Hill, where the winter sunshine touched serene bookcases and arrayed pictures, the whole embrowned composition of objects in my view, with I know not what golden light of promise, what assurance of things to come.[1]

The elder Henry James had already written occasionally for the *Review* on the subject of Swedenborgianism and his allied interests, but it was not simply because of the father that the son was immediately recognized and welcomed by Norton. The review itself was a reason, not so much for what it said about Senior's book, for it was but scantily concerned with that, as for its general tenor and aims, its digressions about the novel-reading, story-loving public, its carefully differentiated analysis of Scott's place in English literature, which called the attention of the editors to a young man who knew the field of fiction and desired to "write stories for weary lawyers and school-masters."[2] Norton probably smiled at the somewhat naive way of thinking and manner of expression of James; he very likely frowned at the review *as* a review, ill proportioned and clumsily put together; but he saw that here was a young man

---

[1] *Notes of a Son and Brother*, p. 405.
[2] *Notes and Reviews*, Cambridge, Mass., 1921, p. 3.

whose *ideals* about fiction coincided with those of the editors of the *North American Review* and who could be of service to it.

When Lowell and Norton had taken over the magazine in 1863, it had been with the purpose of lifting it from the mediocrity into which it had fallen, especially of improving the section which dealt with recent books, of changing criticism, which had consisted of perhaps but a sentence or two of general comment, to something thought out, developed, yet expressed attractively and lightly, to serve as a guide to worth-while literature.[3] Almost immediately the reviews had lengthened and improved in value, but it was difficult to find cultured men who would write for the few dollars it could afford to pay them, and so it was, we may imagine, with a sense of a stroke of sudden good fortune that Norton invited Henry James to become a regular contributor. The young man had the rare combination of cultural background and felicity of expression, the lightness of touch so desired if the magazine was to be popular and achieve its end of reaching the people. He was peculiarly adapted to put American literature on the right track, to lift it from dripping sentimentality or crude realism to the plane of European literature, to point out ways and means and models to the many writers of the day—Miss Prescott, Miss Alcott, Mrs. Seemuller, Mrs. Rebecca Harding Davis—all popular writers but with none of the qualities which make literature that will endure. For all these editors, Lowell, Norton, to a certain extent, Fields of the *Atlantic* and presently Godkin of the *Nation*, reviewing and criticism was but a means to two desired, interdependent ends—the improvement of the literary output of American writers and the improvement of literary taste on the part of the reader. To be engaged with such earnest men in such an undertaking, does not this explain in part the ardor, the

[3] The letters of Lowell and Norton reveal these purposes. (a) *Letters of J. R. Lowell*, ed. C. E. Norton, New York, 1894, I, 334 f. Lowell writes to J. L. Motley: "It wanted three chief elements to be successful. It wasn't thoroughly, that is, thickly and thinly, loyal, it wasn't lively, and it had no particular opinions on any particular subject;" Lowell asks Motley to write "on anything that may be solemn in topic and entertaining in treatment." (b) *Letters of C. E. Norton*, ed. Norton and DeWolf Howe, Boston and New York, 1913, see pages 266, 272 and 281; the last reveals that the editors undertook to affect public opinion and to raise the standard of criticism and scholarship in America; on p. 272, in a letter to Lowell, written July 7, 1864, Norton writes, "The July North American seems to me good but too heavy. How can we make it lighter? People will write on heavy subjects; and all our authors are destitute of humor." It was in the next issue that James's first review appeared.

productivity, the quick success of twenty-one-year-old James? But in the midst of all this, James's individuality was preserved; he was allowed to speak his own ideas upon fiction, and it is these ideas which are valuable to us for the insight which they afford into the art of which he was to become a master. Though his criticism was directed at others, we find that underneath it all there was the quest of a young man for the ways and means to make himself into a writer.

2. *A Young Mind Stocked with Ideas*

James seems to have had at first many ideas which were in rather an unregulated state. In his omnivorous reading of all kinds of fiction and literature he had picked up thoughts here and there which he had not stopped to arrange, discarding some which might clash with others, working out for himself a definition of fiction, reducing it to a formula. But James had his likes and his dislikes. He knew the kind of fiction which held him—Scott's, Reade's, Mérimée's, Balzac's—and the kind which repelled—Richardson's, rather surprisingly, Fielding's, Smollett's—and it was from these likes and dislikes that his first reviews got under way.

Senior's volume with its chapter upon Scott offered James a starting point. James knew the field of English fiction and saw that Scott had performed a great service for it; he had rescued it from the didactic, moralistic trend of the 18th century writers.[4] He was a novelist in the highest sense, writing to *please* and *amuse* the public, not a preacher or a moralist.

"Waverley" was the first novel which was self-forgetful. It proposed simply to amuse the reader, as an old English ballad amused him. It undertook to prove nothing but facts. It was the novel irresponsible.[5]

He had, moreover, imagination.

Before him no prose-writer had exhibited so vast and rich an imagination. . . . . Since Shakespeare, no writer had created so immense a gallery of portraits, nor, on the whole, had any portraits been so lifelike. Men and women, for almost the first time out of poetry, were presented in their habits as they lived.[6]

And accordingly James attractively concluded:

[4] *Notes and Reviews*, p. 10.
[5] *Ibid.*, p. 11.
[6] *Ibid.*, p. 11.

Scott was a born story-teller: we can give him no higher praise. Surveying his works, his character, his method, as a whole, we can liken him to
nothing better than to a strong and kindly elder brother, who gathers his
juvenile public about him at eventide, and pours out a stream of wondrous
improvisation. Who cannot remember an experience like this? On no
occasion are the delights of fiction so intense. Fiction? These are the triumphs of fact. In the richness of his invention and memory, in the in-
finitude of his knowledge, in his improvidence for the future, in the skill
with which he answers, or rather parries, sudden questions, in his low-
voiced pathos and his resounding merriment, he is identical with the ideal
fireside chronicler. And thoroughly to enjoy him, we must again become
as credulous as children at twilight.[7]

It would seem from this review that Scott was one of James's
favorite novelists, that he delighted in his spell and enjoyed nothing
more than his "wondrous improvisation." Yet this first review is
unique among the reviews of James considered as a whole, for in
no other does he more than mention the great novelist. There is,
in fact, a suggestion here and there in the review, even in the last
sentence quoted, that being a story-teller, diverting the reader is not
all. And this suggestion, we shall presently see, gradually becoming
the key-note of James's reviews as he saw the necessity that a writer
tell the truth and realized that the imagination often leads a writer
and thus his readers astray. Then the hint assumes shape—the
novelist must instruct and instruct truly. But because Scott, though
he was "tender of the past,"[8] did not violate it or distort it to such
an extent that his readers were harmed, and because he in general
used his imagination in the interest of truth, James gloried in him
and praised him. James's first stated thought about the novelist's
problem was accordingly—the novelist should tell a story to amuse
the reader.

But immediately the modification of this thought began, brought
about by the kind of fiction which James was given to review. He
had volunteered this first review. Norton accepted it, and summoned him to his study. And in that half hour at Shady Hill not
only did the older man welcome the younger as a contributor to the
North American Review but he probably gently and kindly suggested
to him what the editors, Lowell and himself, most desired in the way
of criticism. That this had to do with the improvement of American

[7] *Ibid.*, p. 14.
[8] *Ibid.*, p. 12.

fiction, we may be sure, for in the next issue of the *Review* there appeared from the pen of James, two long attacks upon two American women novelists—one a popular author with many novels and stories published in the *Atlantic* and then in book-form, to her credit, the other a newcomer in the ranks.[9]

James forgot Scott, forgot the course of English fiction, and took up his pen with but one thought about these two writers—Miss Prescott and Mrs. Seemuller—that they were bad, pernicious elements to literature in America. He was marching into the thick of the fray. The popularity of Miss Prescott did not deter him in the least; quite possibly it whetted his weapon; it caused him not only to attack but to give long constructive paragraphs, venturing to tell her and her ilk—"for, alas, there is a school!"[10]—how to improve. The great flaw was her style, elaborate, extravagant, picturesque, which sinned heavily against truth. She had taken a plot in *Azarian*, the novel which called forth the review,[11] which needed few incidents but much feeling for its development and then had proceeded by means of—words! Miss Prescott mixed her figures and dressed up her descriptions to such an extent that the whole book was cloyed.

What we want is Passion's self,—her language, her ringing voice, her gait, the presentment of her deeds. What do we care about the beauty of a man or woman in comparison with their humanity? In a novel we crave the spectacle of that of which we may feel that we *know* it. The only lasting fictions are those which have spoken to the reader's heart, and not to his eye. .... "Azarian" is true to nothing.[12]

How shall the writer proceed to get this truth? Let her follow Mérimée, "he seldom or never describes; he conveys,"[13] or better, Balzac, since he does describe but keeps his description subordinate. Let her read his *Eugénie Grandet*.

Balzac does not *paint*, does not copy, objects; his chosen instrument being a pen, he is content to *write* them. He is literally real; he presents

---

[9] Reviews of *Azarian* by Miss Prescott and of *Emily Chester* by Mrs. Seemuller. Both appeared in the *North American Review* for January, 1865. Between them was a review of Trollope's *Lindisfarn Chase*, also by James.

[10] *Notes and Reviews*, p. 20.

[11] Professor Pattee, *Development of the American Short Story*, New York, 1923, p. 162, wrongly attributes to James a review of Miss Prescott's *Amber Gods*, published in the *North American Review* in October, 1863, which is by C. G. Smith; see General Index of the *Review*, 1815–1878, p. 102. Professor Pattee touches upon *Azarian*, pp. 197–98.

[12] *Notes and Reviews*, p. 22.

[13] *Ibid.*, p. 23.

objects as they are. The scenes and persons of his drama are minutely described. Grandet's house, his sitting-room, his habits, his appearance, his dress, are all reproduced with the fidelity of a photograph. The same with Madame Grandet and Eugénie. . . . . We almost see the musty little sitting-room in which so much of the action goes forward. We are familiar with the gray *boiserie*, the faded curtains, the rickety card-tables, the framed samplers on the walls, Madam Grandet's footwarmer, and the table set for the meagre dinner. And yet our sense of the human interest of the story is never lost. Why is this? It is because these things are all described *only in so far as they bear upon the action*, and not in the least for themselves . . . . as the soul of a novel is its action, you should only describe those things which are accessory to the action. . . . .

. . . . There is a reason latent in every one of Balzac's tales *why* such things should appear thus, and such persons so,—a clear, well-defined reason, easily discoverable by the observing and sympathetic eye. Each separate part is conducive to the general effect, and this general effect has been studied, pondered, analyzed: in the end it is produced. Balzac lays his stage, sets his scene, and introduces his puppets. He describes them once for all; this done, the story marches.[14]

From his demand for truth, which meant to him here the careful recording of the facts as a setting, James indirectly worked up to another important canon about fiction, one which was so evident in Scott it had not been necessary to note it, but which was so lacking in *Azarian* that James emphasized it strongly—that its soul is *action*. Description is subordinate, something to be done carefully and thoroughly but in the sense of getting it out of the way so that the story can march. But what did James mean by action? Remembering his praise of Scott, we are apt to think, that he might have meant a mass of incidents, a great many exciting happenings, thrilling deeds, and glamorous episodes, but we see that his statement here grew out of praise of Balzac and meant, not a profusion of events, but development, growth, often slow and moderate, of whatever it is with which the story is concerned. Some novels, *Azarian* for instance, need comparatively few incidents for the telling. Others may need many. But all novels need action—a sustained progression instead of a static non-progression or standing still. This early distinction between incident and action is important in understanding James, for it was to grow more pronounced instead of less.

There is another important conclusion about action to be drawn

14 *Ibid.*, pp. 24 and 25.

from this review and that is its relation to character. Read again the quotations given above, especially the last two sentences: "Balzac lays his stage, sets his scene, and introduces his puppets. He describes them once for all; this done, the story marches." Action is the main thing, the "soul" of the novel; characters are but puppets secondary to it. James had failed to grasp the interdependence of character and action, the fact that action may illustrate character, and thus become secondary to it, a means rather than an end. He had not, in fact, really understood Balzac; he had perceived but part of the lesson of the master. This review, however, his second published work, marks the beginning of James's avowed discipleship of the French novelist. It reveals how carefully James had considered him, how well he had seen into his method of approach and development though the initial conception of many of his stories in character he had not grasped. That lesson was to be called to his attention shortly by an English novelist. We must remember, however, that *Azarian* challenged James to attack it from the standpoint of development and not of conception.

The state of literature in America was indeed discouraging. There was Mrs. Seemuller, for instance, with her first novel, *Emily Chester*, well-meaning, no doubt, but unconsciously immoral and dull. It is a question whether its immorality or its dullness affected James the more. Its dullness, however, was easily discernible. Mrs. Seemuller had

. . . . told a story of character in a would-be psychological mode; not of everyday character, such as is employed by Mr. Trollope and Miss Austen, but of character which she must allow us to term exceptional. She has brought together three persons . . . . and during three hundred and fifty close pages, we are invited to watch the moral operations of this romantic trio. What a chance for dullness is here![15]

But its "questionable moral tendency"[16] was less apparent to the average reader, and James, discerning youth of twenty-one, proceeded to point it out. Mrs. Seemuller's three persons bear the rather trite relationship of husband, wife, and lover to each other, not an improbable situation except for the characters involved. Max is repulsive, horribly so; Emily is outwardly a cold, statuesque, supposedly noble and perfect specimen of womanhood, yet inwardly

[15] *Ibid.*, p. 38.
[16] *Ibid.*, p. 37.

she burns with passion; while Dr. Hastings is a mild, unconvincing sort of charmer. James saw that the novel belonged to that dangerously growing class of "novels of temperament" where the authors built up figures "minus the soul."[17] And its immorality was most flagrant just at the point where the author probably felt herself to be most moral—at the end, where Emily droops and dies— "Passion was indeed conquered by duty, but life was conquered by passion. The true victory of mind would have been, not perhaps in a happy, but at least in a peaceful life."[18] The author should have worked out a conclusion. It was an evasion rather than a meeting and solving of the state of affairs. Thus early James glimpsed that true morality demands a solution by the characters involved, an idea which he was shortly to develop more extensively.[19] The present day reader of the book will discern how closely this criticism is connected with what James thought about action. There are incidents, many of them, but *not any developing action*. It is, throughout, a static exposition of love and hate which always remain in the same superlative degree, and the book is finally stopped simply because the author has exhausted her means of repetition.[20]

Between these two long attacks upon tendencies in American fiction, James inserted a brief one upon T. Adolphus Trollope. James had cited Anthony Trollope to both Miss Prescott and Mrs. Seemuller[21] for his "delicate perception of the actual,"[22] but when he came to review *Lindisfarn Chase*, he took the author to task as a second rate novelist quite as strongly as the American writers. Much of his impatience was due to the fact that he felt Trollope with the material he selected for his novel might have done something first rate, but he seemed to James to have shirked his task, writing his novels by an easy recipe.

[17] *Ibid.*, p. 42.

[18] *Ibid.*, p. 44.

[19] See Chapter V.

[20] In view of the fact that James later wrote novels of a psychological nature, these remarks are doubly interesting. One must note, however, what aspect of them James was attacking here—that they neglected the *soul* of man—and this unanalyzable aspect is one which he never failed to take into account though he often analyzed motives with scientific detail and thoroughness. The often quoted remark that Henry James wrote novels like a scientist while William James wrote psychology like a novelist is a most dangerous epigramatic halftruth, from the standpoint of both writers.

[21] *Notes and Reviews*, pp. 32 and 38.

[22] *Ibid.*, p. 32.

The first requisite is to collect a large number of persons, so many that you have no space to refine upon individuals . . . . to give these persons pleasant, expressive names, and to scatter among them a few handfuls of clever description. The next step is to make a fair distribution of what may be called prehistoric facts,—facts which are referred to periods prior to the opening of the tale, and which serve, as it were, as your base of supplies during its progress. According as these facts are natural or common-place, or improbable and surprising, your story is an ordinary novel of manners, a sober photograph of common life or a romance. Their great virtue is to relieve the writer of all analysis of character, to enable him to forge his interest out of the exhibition of circumstance rather than out of the examination of motive.[23]

He collected people and he gathered facts, but he did not analyze character. He forged "his interest out of the exhibition of circum-stance rather than out of the examination of motive." This last sentence almost hidden in the short review devoted to Trollope is yet far more important in regarding James than his carefully differ-entiated account of action or his statement of morality. It is a statement of what is presently to emerge under the influence of another author as the guiding motive of James's fiction—the analysis of character. Here, however, it is just suggested, a possibility rather than a principle which must be followed.

From these first four reviews many intelligently grasped and strongly expressed ideas stand out. James had flung out one idea after another as the novel in question seemed to call it forth. We realize that he had a head stocked with ideas, something to say on any case which might come up. But we realize too, that, though he was interested in method because of his own purpose to write, he had not grasped the relative importance and interdependence of his ideas; each existed in a superlative form. A story must have action—if one had not the imaginative ability of a Scott to *make* things happen, one must have the perceiving life of a Balzac to *see* them happen in life and then report them—it must have character; it must have truth; it must amuse the reader; it must be moral— not obviously so, as in the case of the 18th century writers, but inherently so. The problem was to get all in and reconcile all, and this was going to mean for James the neglecting of some and the promotion of others till eventually each came to fit into its place. Fiction *is* made up of many diverse elements, but not each in the

[23] *Ibid.*, p. 34.

same proportion. It takes a scientist to measure the ingredients carefully and exactly with much of this and but a dash of that, and an artist to combine them. James's reviewing was to help him get things straight; as he put his ideas upon paper, they were to assume comparative and relative values.

3. *The Story Writer*

James plunged into his original fiction writing in much the same confident way that he had plunged into his reviewing. He would write a story which had action and character analysis and truth and amuse the reader and be moral—and so he wrote *The Story of a Year* which appeared in the *Atlantic Monthly* the following March. It did indeed attempt all five; it was well intentioned, and one can, like Professor Pattee, find the germs here of the later work of James,[24] but it achieved no one in any distinctive way. James was over ambitious. Still it is surprisingly good for a first story; but one must judge James by his own emphatically stated standards, and then the verdict becomes almost as negative as James's own verdicts.

The title, "The Story of a Year," gives some idea of its ambitious scope and of its emphasis upon action, the "story." The plot gives more. John Ford, a high-principled, educated young man, asks Lizzie Crowe, a weak, shallow girl who has been brought up by his mother, to become engaged to him just before he leaves for the war. He tells her, however, that should he be killed, she is to "beware of that tawdry sentiment which enjoins you to be 'constant to my memory,' "[25] dangerous advice to give a weak creature, but the clue to the rest of the story is in his advice and her shallowness. James's task was to make a story out of it. He employed two developments. First, Lizzie, subject to his will, tries to make herself worthy of John on his return by study and "the delicious companionship of thought"[26] becoming "deeply enamored of what a French book calls her *aises intellectualles.*"[27] This first development proceeds with no incidents to speak of but with a suggestion of analysis as James commented upon his heroine, and is brought to an end with a melodramatic flourish: "John Ford became a veteran down by the

[24] F. L. Pattee, *History of American Literature since 1870*, New York, 1915, pp. 189 f.

[25] *Atlantic Monthly*, March, 1865, p. 259.

[26] *Ibid.*, p. 264.

[27] *Ibid.*, p. 265.

Potomac. And truth to tell, Lizzie became a veteran at home. That is, her love and hope grew to be an old story. She gave way, as the strongest must, as the wisest will, to time."[28] How proud James must have been of that flourish!

But the year is not up; there has not been enough *action*, and James decided to add another development, a relapse on the part of Lizzie. Perhaps he discerned, with a flash of insight into human nature, that given the shallow character with which he first endowed her, a sudden deepening of it could not be lasting. Mrs. Ford is now brought into an active part in the story, to help him manage Lizzie. She is endowed with a mother's protective jealousy for her son and made to desire to get Lizzie safely married to someone else before John returns. She becomes all kindness outside, makes Lizzie fine clothes, and sends her to a neighboring town where she will forget studies and thought and John in a social whirl. Lizzie is introduced to Mr. Bruce, made to order with a French accent, and her heart flutters. But things do not happen too quickly. Her visit comes to an end, and she is saddened by her farewell to Mr. Bruce when she hears that John has been severely wounded. Her mind now is rudely torn, but she is relieved on reaching home to find that Mrs. Ford is going to him and forbids her to. "And now it was a relief to have responsibility denied her. Like most weak persons, she was glad to step out of the current of life, now that it had begun to quicken into action."[29]

Gradually she comes to believe that John is going to die. Mr. Bruce appears upon the scene, proposes, and she accepts him. But suddenly John is brought home, and it looks as if he may get well. Lizzie promises to care for him. Now at last we expect a real complication which Lizzie will *have* to solve for herself, but James, seeing the difficulty, again took responsibility from her, by making John die, magnanimously repeating his first advice, that she forget him and marry. He then tacked on a French ending; Lizzie suddenly becomes strong—for a moment—and refuses to let Mr. Bruce enter when he comes to call, but "for all that, he went in,"[30] and the reader knows the rest.

James had material enough here for a novel but he brought it into the scope of twenty-five pages. His initial conception, his idea,

[28] *Ibid.*, p. 266.
[29] *Ibid.*, p. 271.
[30] *Ibid.*, p. 281.

as he would later have called it—the shallow nature of Lizzie—
around which he built his story, is not bad; it offers possibilities,
especially in the wartime setting which he chose for it. One is not
sure, however, whether the initial conception *was* Lizzie's character
or the plot, the action. But either was overambitious for a young
writer, and James's execution, as a result, was full of flaws. The
story does not *march*. It has been driven, with frequent pokings
and proddings. Lizzie is, indeed, a weak individual; she is entirely
James's creature. There is action of a sort, but not in the sense of
connected development; each separate part is not conducive to the
general effect, for this general effect was not sufficiently "studied,
pondered, analyzed" to be "produced" in the end. This part of
Balzac's lesson, so. plainly understood, has proved to be difficult
to put into practice.

There are several other discrepancies between theory and practice which must alarm us even more than this. The ending of the
story cannot be considered satisfactory or wholly moral, according
to the ideas advanced in the review of *Emily Chester*, for it is an
evasion by means of the death of one member of the triangle rather
than a solution. The fact that James's characters are not yet
married, while Mrs. Seemuller's are, does not materially change
the situation; if anything, it should have facilitated a solution in
terms of character. Then, too, James used words,—thought for
Lizzie was a "pensive ecstacy"[31]—figures of speech,—the sky becomes a battlefield as James and Lizzie plight their troth[32]—extravagances of expression which though always more pertinent to the
story than Miss Prescott's flowery effusions, are amateurish and
awkward. It was the beginning of a practice, however, which was
to enable James to use words naturally and beautifully later, but
now he seems to be striving for effect. And the suggestion of analysis
which we noted in the first development is more a desire to comment cleverly and somewhat facetiously upon his characters, Lizzie
in particular, rejoicing in the opportunity it gave him to use words,
than any "examination of motive," such as he suggested might
be desirable in the review of Trollope. Moreover, it shows no insight
into character.

However, *The Story of a Year* is, with all its flaws, slightly better
than the other stories which were being written in the sixties and

[31] *Ibid.*, p. 265.
[32] *Ibid.*, p. 258.

published in the *Atlantic*. It is better than those by Miss Phelps or Miss Terry or Mrs. Davis, certainly better than those by Miss Prescott. It is not as sentimental, not as emotional, not as sensational, not as melodramatically realistic, not as "Dickensonian," the trait which distinguishes these early *Atlantic* tales to Professor Pattee.[33] There is in this story the detached way of looking at a story which was to remain, of visualizing it scientifically and artistically, not of merely feeling it. Even the awkwardnesses of execution which we noted, were due to James's over-eager endeavor to make the story do as he thought it should.

James had made his debut! He was a writer! He was one of the literary profession! His life path must have stretched before him alluringly. Poor William was still undecided, uneasily trying to find himself, wondering if perhaps a trip to South America with the great Agassiz might not solve his problem for him, hesitating reluctantly as he considered the expense for his parents who had already expended so much on the education of their eldest son, at length deciding to go. Henry, however, was jingling a few coins of his own in his pocket, smoothing out lovingly a few greenbacks, walking the streets of Boston with a tiny swagger as he realized that *his* problem was solved, for so it must have seemed at that time. The difficulties, though they are apparent to us in the discrepancies of theory and practice, were not then apparent to him in all their intensity. It was simply a matter of a little time and a little practice and he would be the Balzac of America. And American literature with its writers following the waving of his flashing sword would march on, becoming equal to the greatest elsewhere. So far as we know there were no rejected manuscripts. There may, of course, have been some; but except for that translation of *Lorenzaccio* long before,[34] and that other of *La Venus d'Ille*,[35] we are told of none. Acceptance and success of a sort seem to have been instantaneous.

[33] *Development of the American Short Story*, New York, 1923, p. 169.
[34] See Interchapter A, also Chapter XI.
[35] *Ibid.*

CHAPTER III

RECOGNITION, RESPONSIBILITY, REFLECTION

1. *Recognition and Responsibility*

To have one's first attempts accepted by two of the leading magazines of the time was surely an honor, but a greater one was to follow, and it was to be grasped not only as an honor but as a responsibility. E. L. Godkin seeing the need of the time for magazines which would frequently and concisely put before the people the state of post-war affairs of the country in a true, impartial way, was spending the spring of 1865 building up a competent body of editors for his project. The prospectus which announced this, listed six points, all bearing upon the civic and national life of the day. There was a seventh, however, more important for us—"Sound and impartial criticism of books and works of art."[1] An anonymous article in the first issue of the *Nation*, July 6, 1865, was to expand upon this, giving a statement of the condition of criticism in America:

One principal object of the Nation is to promote and develop a higher standard of criticism.[2]

In a new country like ours, the public mind passes through three stages before it is fully prepared to furnish or appreciate complete and well-balanced criticism. First, there is the chaotic or embryo period, when the whole energy of the people is employed in overcoming physical obstacles. Literature and art are then rare exotics, and their votaries run the risk of being considered very eccentric, if not absolutely mad. . . . . Then succeeds the childish age, or that of promiscuous and often silly admiration. The last stage before reaching the day of true criticism is a reaction from this, a period of indiscriminate censure. In art-criticism we seem to have arrived at the third stage or at least be very near it. In literature we are not well out of the second, though many spirited attempts have been made at intervals for thirty years or more to push us out of it. . . . . We really think that before our criticism comes to merit the name, it will have to pass through this stormy and belligerent stage, a period like that of English criticism during the first quarter of the century.[3]

James's reviews of *Azarian* and of *Emily Chester* had shown Godkin that he was capable of saying "This will never do!" to

[1] The Prospectus is given in *The Life of E. L. Godkin*, New York, 1907, I, 238.
[2] *Nation*, July 6, 1865, p. 10.
[3] *Ibid.*, p. 11.

literature in America; he could inaugurate criticism in its "stormy and belligerent stage." Thus it was as Henry James writes,

. . . . having commenced critic under Charles Norton's weighty protection, I was to find myself, on all but the very morrow, invited to the high glory, as I felt it, of aiding to launch, though on the obscurer side of the enterprise, a weekly journal which, putting forth its first leaves in the summer of '65 and under the highest auspices, was soon to enjoy a fortune and achieve an authority and a dignity of which neither newspaper nor critical review among us had hitherto so much as hinted the possibility. The New York Nation had from the first, to the enlivening of several persons consciously and ruefully astray in our desert, made no secret of a literary leaning; and indeed its few foremost months shine for me in the light of their bestowal of one of the longest and happiest friendships of my life, a relation with Edwin Lawrence Godkin, the Nation incarnate as he was to become, which bore fruit of affection for years after it ceased to involve the comparatively poorer exercise. Godkin's paper, Godkin's occasional presence and interesting history and vivid ability and, above all, admirably aggressive and ironic editorial humor, of a quality and authority new in the air of journalism that had meant for the most part the heavy hand alone, these things, with the sweet discovery that I might for my own part acceptedly stammer a style, are so many shades and shifting tints in the positive historic iridescence that flings itself for my memory . . . . over the 'period' of Ashburton place.[4]

All this did not turn the young lad's head. On the contrary, it wakened him to the responsibility of his position; he had got to prove worthy of the trust that had been placed in him. And if he was expected to keep his belligerent position, it was all the more reason why he should be just. He must think out more carefully this business of reviewing and this problem of fiction.

2. Reflection—Arnold and Goethe

There were two other very important things which happily came to James's attention in the spring or early summer of 1865. One was Matthew Arnold's Essays of Criticism. The other was Carlyle's translation of Wilhelm Meister. Both must have caused James to stop a moment and ponder, though not with any abatement of ardor, before he reviewed them for the July North American Review. One was to affect his ideas of criticism; the other, wonderful experience, was to perplex him at first, and then, unrecognized, was to influence him.

[4] Notes of a Son and Brother, pp. 425–26.

With the emphasis of the group of editors among whom James found himself upon higher standards in criticism it was inevitable that he should be most interested and alert to criticism in foreign countries. He did not conceive of himself as a lowly reviewer to be distinguished from the more general but infinitely higher denomination, critic; he thought of both reviewer and critic as one, actuated by one ideal, working for one end—Truth. Arnold's *Essays in Criticism* spoke then with some quiet insistence to the young American who was facing a literary life with two parallel roads—the critical and the fictional. As a critic, the proud young hope of older men, he must make good; he must justify their confidence. As a critic, his responsibility, indeed, was greater than as a writer on his own accord; he must put people on the right track, get them to enlist on the right side. When he came then to the reading of Arnold's essays, essays on criticism by a critic, he was interested in analyzing what the critic was, how he could accomplish the greatest good. Though James felt that the English school of criticism as a whole was inferior to the French, Arnold's voice was one to be reckoned with. There was perhaps a lesson to be learned if both schools were considered. The French school had intelligence, clear, cold perception of facts, upon which they based their judgments. Arnold had feeling: "Hundreds of other critics have stronger heads; few, in England at least, have more delicate perceptions."[5] But Arnold had been influenced by the French; it was an "intelligent sensibility,"[6] that he had. James would, however, have changed the emphasis for an ideal critic to feeling intelligence.

It is hard to say whether the literary critic is more called upon to understand or to feel. It is certain that he will accomplish little unless he can feel acutely; although it is perhaps equally certain that he will become weak the moment he begins to 'work,' as we may say, his natural sensibilities. The best critic is probably he who leaves his feelings out of account, and relies upon reason for success. . . . . One of the chief duties of criticism is to exalt the importance of the ideal.[7]

And further on, James, still seeking *la verité vraie* which the English were so prone to overlook,[8] proceeding cautiously in an attempt to get *at* his ideas, and then to say just what he meant with all the

[5] *North American Review*, July, 1865, p. 208.
[6] *Ibid.*, p. 207.
[7] *Ibid.*, p. 208.
[8] *Ibid.*, p. 210.

shades of meaning to which he had been indifferent in his confident
reviews on fiction, changed "ideal" to "intellectual." The critic
must exalt the importance of the "intellectual," "that is, the principle of understanding things."[9] He aims at the truth and therefore
must proceed first by reason, and second by feeling.

James worked out a critical article of his own, meeting Arnold on
his ground with some really weighty conclusions. Throughout the
essay are strong evidences that French influence upon judgment,
rationality in criticism, had been acting upon James. He referred to
the French school and the French type of mind often. He had, no
doubt, been reading the *Revue des Deux Mondes* with its careful,
thoughtful criticism, and a few months later he was to review
Scherer's essays,[10] betraying then a thorough acquaintance with
Sainte-Beuve, Taine, and a German critic greater than all, Goethe.

But another book was to cause James more pondering, more
bewilderment than Arnold's. He could *get at* what he thought and
wanted to say after he read the essays. Arnold did not mystify him;
he helped him, a bit negatively perhaps, to a clearer perception and
grasp of criticism; James could at length see through Arnold and beyond him. The case was different when he read Goethe's *Wilhelm
Meister* in Carlyle's translation. Goethe, great novelist, was not a
novelist in any sense as James had thought of novelists. His *Wilhelm
Meister* threatened to upset most of the youth's most prized ideas
about the craft of fiction.

James probably read and felt and reflected before he attempted
to write his review of *Wilhelm Meister* for the July *North American*.[11]
"To read 'Wilhelm Meister' for the first time" was "an enviable
and almost a unique sensation. Few other books . . . so steadily
and gradually *dawn* upon the intelligence. In few other works is
so profound a meaning enveloped in so common a form."[12]

Here was philosophy masquerading under the guise of a novel,

___

[9] *Ibid.*, p. 211.

[10] Appeared in *Nation*, Oct. 12, 1865. Taine, however, is but scantily referred
to for he seemed to James a philosopher and historian rather than a critic. (*Notes
and Reviews*, p. 106.)

[11] Strange to say this review was omitted from Phillips's *Bibliography* and probably because of this from la Rose's collection of early reviews. It follows a review,
also by James, of Miss Alcott's *Moods* in the July, 1865, *North American Review*
The earmarks of James's style are very pronounced. Then too the General Index
of the *North American Review* attributes it to Henry James, Junior.

[12] *North American Review*, July, 1865, p. 281.

and James may well have felt taken in. It was not clever but dull unless seriously read. It was written not to entertain but to edify," exhibiting "a sublime indifference to the reader,"[13] but the reader James could not remain wholly indifferent to it. A few months before he had demanded that a novel should amuse, divert, delight the reader. Now suddenly he found that he was *held* from beginning to end by a work which did not amuse him at all; it forced him to think and to think hard. Strangely enough—or perhaps consistently enough considering his one engrossing interest at that time—James did not think long about its philosophical meaning as most readers and critics of the great work are forced to. He perceived that it had such a meaning, a thing which he had not associated with novels before, but he perceived even more what it did not have from the standpoint of fiction, and he turned to a consideration of this. It had no plot. There were many, many incidents of various kinds, but no plot. Still a kind of unity was achieved by its hero, its central figure—"By him, through him, the tale is unfolded."[14] It is the account of his quest for happiness, "that happiness which, as he is never weary of repeating, can be found only in the subject's perfect harmony with himself."[15] But it differed from "last month's successful novel" in its figures. "Goethe's persons are not lifelike; that is the mark of our fashionable photographic heroes and heroines; they are life itself. We know neither their costume, nor their stature, nor the indispensable color of their eyes; and yet, for all that, they *live*."[16] This was most disturbing. Balzac had taught James that novels should record the details of their character's lives, their appearance, their homes, with all minuteness, as a necessary antecedent of the action. In the review of *Azarian* James had taken a roundabout way to say that Balzac was the historian of his age—the fortunate epithet was not borrowed from the French novelist till later.[17] Now Goethe was in no way the historian of his; he was the philosopher who dealt with no one age of man but with all ages. Goethe's idea of sending Wilhelm on a quest for happiness made it possible for him to have him

[13] *Ibid.*, p. 282.

[14] *Ibid.*, p. 282. Much later the smoldering remains of this idea are to appear as one of the guiding principles of James's novels, brought about, however, as the result of his own experimentation rather than by direct influence of Goethe. See Chapter on *Roderick Hudson*.

[15] *Ibid.*, p. 283.

[16] *Ibid.*, p. 283.

[17] *Review of Historial Novels, Nation*, Aug. 15, 1867.

meet people of all sorts, each a perfect example of his kind—"the lighthearted coquette," Philena, "the irretrievable sentimentalist," Aurelia, the "practical, sensible, reasonable" Teresa, with her "air of solid truth."[18] And these people live, exist before us despite their lack of physical make-up. Even Wilhelm as a physical being is shadowy. It was all greatly perplexing to James.

Although incidentally dramatic, therefore, it will be seen that, as a whole *Wilhelm Meister* is anything but a novel, as we have grown to understand the word. As a whole, it has, in fact, no very definite character, and, were we not vaguely convinced that its greatness as a work of art resides in this very absence of form, we should say that, as a work of art, it is lamentably defective. A modern novelist, taking the same subject in hand, would restrict himself to showing the sensations of his hero during the process of his education; that is, his hero would be the broad end, and the aggregate of circumstances the narrow end, of the glass through which we were invited to look; and we should so have a comedy or a tragedy, as the case might be. But Goethe, taking a single individual as pretext for looking into the world, becomes so absorbed in the spectacle before him, that, while still clinging to his hero as a pretext, he quite forgets him as a subject. It may be here objected that the true artist never forgets either himself or anything else. However that may be, each reader becomes his own Wilhelm Meister, an apprentice, a traveller, on his own account; and as his understanding is large or small, will Wilhelm and the whole work be real or the contrary. It is, indeed, to the understanding exclusively, and never, except in the episode of Mignon, to the imagination, that the author appeals. For what, as we read on, strikes us as his dominant quality? His love of the real.[19]

The bearing of Wilhelm Meister is eminently practical.[20]

It shows us how to make the most of life. It is, however, cold-blooded, calm. "It is hard to say which is truer, that his (Goethe's) mind is without haste or without rest."[21] There is no humor. Goethe's plan was "'non flere, non indignari, sed intelligere.'"[22]

Goethe had written a book which was both less than a novel and more than a novel. Was it, indeed, a novel at all? Was there, in fact, any lesson for the beginning novelist to learn from it? James seems in this review to have perceived none of any practical value. Goethe was so far above the ordinary tribe, his book in its way was

[18] *Ibid.*, pp. 283 f.
[19] *Ibid.*, p. 284.
[20] *Ibid.*, p. 284.
[21] *Ibid.*, p. 285.
[22] *Ibid.*, p. 285.

so great that it could not be imitated or followed or even approached. Goethe was sublime; he had a mind which soared aloft, surveyed all, grasped the eternal aspects of the transient facts of existence; he was beyond the need and the reach of rules. The average novelist was a pedestrian creature, dwelling among men, forced by his limited vision to present only the facts which surrounded him, the external aspects of life; he could proceed only along well-defined roads; directions, rules were necessary to him. James was incapable of reconciling philosopher and novelist. The bewilderment which seized James did not resolve itself into despair, however; it strengthened his purpose the more; it started him on a more enthusiastic search for the means and the methods which would help *him* become a novelist. His character was such that he could come away from a reading of this great work a more earnest, determined person along the lines which seemed to him possible without being daunted by any desire to do the impossible. And, though his immediate reaction was to differ with it, to dash off his review, and as he thought to cast it aside, subtly, silently, unrecognized, it was to affect him, a slow working, stimulating virus injected into his veins, and to influence permanently, as we shall presently see, one of his ideas about the novelist's craft.

CHAPTER IV

THE BATTLECRY OF TRUTH!

1. *The Two Kinds of Truth*

The summer of 1865 saw James well under way, ready to write reviews on any book which was handed to him. During the next three and a half years some fifty reviews and ten short stories were to come from his pen. For the first year, reviews of fiction continued to predominate but gradually some on poetry, on biography and journals, on philosophy, on books of travel and art, on science even, began to appear as the editors realized that James with his breadth of culture and point of view could handle all kinds of literature. His scope was extended, especially in the pages of the *Nation*, to include literature of England and of France. He became its spokesman as well as its belligerent critic in America. Occasionally a review with high praise broke the adverse tenor of the majority, but in general James was carrying out a conviction which he expressed in a review of Scherer's essays in October that the critic "is in the nature of his function *opposed* to his author" but that he finds a guiding "unit of sincerity and consistency" in his conscience.[1] He tried—though not always as successfully as one wishes—to be like Scherer whom he praised for having theories and standards but no rigid doctrine nor obtrusive morality, such as critics too frequently had. He found it difficult, however, to maintain a fairly objective stand for the demands of his editors, on one side, and his own fictional interests, on the other, necessarily affected his critical integrity. His warfare, though it remained civil in its effect, for it is doubtful if his words had any influence upon foreign writers or were indeed even noticed by them, was directed, nevertheless, often at them—the peckings of a young writer who meant to make himself felt sooner of later. Then too, of course, though it might not in any way be noticed *there*, it would help to rouse his countrymen *here* to high standards and ideals.

Many of James's critics believe he was so under the influence of Europe that he thought it could do no wrong. On the contrary, he did not consider it infallible in spite of the fact that it had certain guiding elements, chiefly in the near past, the ripened fruit of cen-

[1] *Notes and Reviews*, p. 102.

turies of endeavor, which America did not have except as she borrowed them from Europe. The great danger of literature was that it would fall behind in the march of progress, that instead of taking things at the developed stage which the past had brought about, it would neglect these things and stumble along blindly by itself. Few writers even thought of making the most of their inheritance. Hence it is that James used as his tangential points Balzac and Mérimée and their contemporaries, his immediate predecessors of the first half of the 19th century rather than earlier writers. They represented development. Hence it is, also, that later, when James came to supplement his reviews with critical articles and essays, he still chose to write upon his immediate predecessors in the craft of fiction rather than upon Richardson or Fielding or Sterne or Smollett or Cervantes, a fact which Brownell deplores and wonders at.[2] He need not have wondered had he stopped to consider that fiction for James was a developed thing, an evolved product, the art which was latest of all arts perhaps, to reach its height.

Now it is very likely that James saw that the literature of the past which *had* survived, be it fiction or poetry, all had one quality. It was true. The reader could accept it and believe it. Truth was the common denominator. And it was true usually not only to the external facts of the time which it chose to depict but to the inherent facts of human nature. Truth was thus of two sorts. In his second review James had revealed that Balzac had brought his attention to the former kind in the care with which he handled his settings and characters—the details of appearance. And the moral for the novelist was: Watch life. "Take note of what is."[3] Record its aspects truly. Then let your story march. Balzac had, of course, the second kind of truth, truth to human nature, but he kept it in the background. His emphasis was upon what he saw, the external aspects of men, as they bore upon the action. Accordingly, for James, the novelist was primarily concerned with such things—he was to write a pictorial story. As for truth to human nature, it was a base of supplies from which the author occasionally drew but which he kept as much as possible behind the scenes. The business of the novelist was not to display his knowledge of man. But James had realized too that Trollope who depicted the details of appearance might have been greater had he analyzed character and examined motive. Then

[2] Brownell, W. C., *American Prose Masters*, New York, 1909, p. 384.
[3] *Notes and Reviews*, p. 32.

he had read *Wilhelm Meister* where the author *had* done this, and
had upbraided Goethe harshly for not telling him how his characters
looked. Now what was the novelist to do? Where was the emphasis
to fall?

It was noted in the preceding chapter that Goethe the novelist
had had no immediate or direct effect upon James's ideas of fiction.
He had been able to extract nothing of a practical nature for the
aspirant of fiction from him. But Goethe the philosopher must have
exerted more pressure upon the sensitive brain of young James than
he gives us any idea of in his review. As he found that Goethe told
him nothing of the physical aspects of his characters, that he located
them in no special time or place, and discovered that, in spite of
that, they *lived*, he must have asked why? and have found the answer
in their truth to human nature, as revealed by the analysis of character which the author brought in. Though James had been unable to
reconcile philosopher and novelist when he wrote the review of
Wilhelm Meister, he was coming unconsciously to reconcile one
of the two, in his mind at least. Not until much later did James
refer in his reviews of fiction to Goethe,[4] but from July 1865 the
demand for truth becomes increasingly emphatic and tends to drown
out all other demands till it in turn resolves itself into a plea for
characterization. And the demand for truth to human nature, to be
gained by the study of man, to be revealed by analysis, is louder
than the request for truth to external appearances.

The distinction between these two is to be observed most closely
in the reviews James continued to write upon the Trollopes. More
than any other writers of the time, these pleasant English novelists
were flayed and lashed by the impatient American youth. He
hesitantly suggested in reviewing *Lindisfarn Chase* that T. Adolphus
should analyze motive. Now he demanded it, but he doubted
whether Anthony could do it or not, whether he knew any but the
external aspects of man. A series of reviews—of *Miss Mackenzie* in
July,[5] of *Can You Forgive Her?*,[6] in September, of *The Belton Estate*,[7]
the following January—bring out his stand.

Anthony Trollope had good characteristics; he wrote easily

[4] The first reference I have found in such a review occurs in a review of *Meta
Holdenis* by Cherbuliez, *North American Review*, Oct., 1873. There he implies the
advantage to a novelist of an early acquaintance with Goethe. See Chapter XII.

[5] Appeared in *Nation*, July 13, 1865.

[6] Appeared in *Nation*, Sept., 28, 1865.

[7] Appeared in *Nation*, Jan. 4, 1866.

and well; he observed the external aspects of life—but that was all he did. Never once did he go *into* a subject, get beneath the surface. He seemed to see, in fact, only the surface; he did not know the undercurrents of life, human nature. His characters were commonplace and stupid. James said in July, the same month he reviewed *Wilhelm Meister*:

Literally, then, Mr. Trollope accomplishes his purpose of being true to common life. But in reading his pages, we were constantly induced to ask ourselves whether he is equally true to nature; that is, whether in this multitude of real things, of uncompromisingly real circumstances, the persons put before us are equally real. Mr. Trollope has proposed to himself to describe those facts which are so close under every one's nose that no one notices them. Life is vulgar, but we know not how vulgar it is till we see it set down in his pages. . . . . Mr. Trollope has, we conceive, simply wished to interest us in ordinary mortals: it has not been his intention to introduce us to a company of imbeciles. But, seriously, we do not consider these people to be much better. Detach them from their circumstances, reduce them to their essences, and what do they amount to? They are but halves of men and women. . . . . If the truth is not so black as she is sometimes painted, neither is she so pale![8]

It was an error in judgment, coupled with his lack of imagination that caused Trollope to misuse his talents.

He is an excellent, an admirable observer; and such an one may accomplish much. But why does he not observe great things as well as little ones? . . . . He deals wholly in small effects. His manner, like most literary manners of the day, is a small manner.[9]

And James continued, repeating for emphasis, always lamenting the bad because of the good elements of his style. He has the "virtue of the photograph" but "the photograph lacks the supreme virtue of possessing a character."[10] And look at the kind of people he photographed! Commonplace, ordinary. "Why should we stop to gather nettles when there are roses blooming under our hands?"[11]

Though *Can You Forgive Her?* and *The Belton Estate* were somewhat better than *Miss Mackenzie*, James was still more vehement; it was as if he were trying to arouse Trollope to do something worth while. The idea of treating the natural flutterings and vacillations of

[8] *Notes and Reviews*, pp. 70 f.
[9] *Ibid.*, pp. 72 f.
[10] *Ibid.*, p. 74.
[11] *Ibid.*, p. 75.

a young girl's heart as major sins and submitting them to the judgment of a reader for decision. Trollope overdid the small things of
life; he evaded the great and the result was a general mediocrity.

To Mr. Trollope all the possible incidents of society seem to be of equal importance and of equal interest. He has the same treatment, the same tone,
for them all.[12]

His characters were sometimes pleasant and agreeable but he was
"simply unable to depict a mind in any liberal sense of the word."[13]
His villains were quite as mild as his virtuous characters. "Mr.
Trollope is never guilty of an excess in any direction."[14] And the
result of all this was " 'The Belton Estate' is a *stupid* book," "a work
prepared for minds unable to think."[15]

It is essentially, organically, consistently stupid; stupid in direct proportion to its strength. It is without a single idea. It is utterly incompetent to the primary functions of a book, of whatever a nature, namely—
to suggest thought. . . . . Mr. Trollope is a good observer, but he is
literally nothing else. He is apparently as incapable of disengaging an idea
as of drawing an inference. All his incidents are, if we may so express it,
empirical. He has seen and heard every act and every speech that appears
in his pages.[16]

He is "a good observer; but he is literally nothing else." This was
the key to James's antipathy and impatience, for Trollope observed
simply the obvious; he did not get at the inherent facts of human
nature which can be grasped only by reflection though their effects
may sometimes be seen by the eye if prompted beforehand by
thought. He was *not* a philosopher.[17] On every page of the reviews
of Trollope's novels from July to January can be discerned the influence of the German novel which James had just read and tried to
cast aside as no novel at all. Never once did James bring in the name
of Goethe, but the reader easily discerns that the omissions for which
James, increasingly vehement, takes Trollope to task, are the qualities which are most salient in *Wilhelm Meister*.

[12] *Ibid.*, p. 88.
[13] *Ibid.*, p. 127.
[14] *Ibid.*, p. 128.
[15] *Ibid.*, p. 130.
[16] *Ibid.*, pp. 130 f.
[17] It should be noticed that later James modified his attack upon Trollope to
an appreciation for what he *did* do; see an article published *Century Magazine*, July,
1883; James is also somewhat less bitter in a review of *Linda Tressel*, *Nation*,
June 18, 1868; see Chapter VII.

Trollope, at least, however, had no prejudice in favor of or against human nature. He simply did not see into it, did not realize its possibilities, its great moments of passion and feeling. He was, without, perhaps, intending to be or thinking at all about it, objective. But there were other writers who were not. They saw human nature as a glorified thing. They were quite overcome by the courage and the nobility of man, especially man of past ages, and by the goodness and wisdom of children. They were influenced by their feelings when they looked upon life. Chief of the sinners of this sort were the Kingsleys. A review called forth by Henry Kingsley's *The Hillyars and the Burtons*[18] took the form of a general attack upon the "muscular system of morality" of the two brothers, for Henry Kingsley was but a "reduced copy" of Charles[19] who had "exercised his powerful and perverse imagination upon the Greeks of the fifth century and the Englishmen of the sixteenth,"[20] in such a way as to impugn the writer's fidelity and lead the readers astray. He had in fact written history with a "prejudice in favor of human nature,"[21] just as Carlyle had one against it. Then when he and his brother came to write of contemporary life, they talked much about "human nobleness" without devising incidents which revealed it.

Human nobleness, when we come across it in life, is a very fine thing; but it quite loses its flavor when it is made so cheap as it is made in these works. It is emphatically an occasional quality; it is not, and with all due respect for the stalwart Englishman of Queen Elizabeth's time and eke of Queen Victoria's, it never was the prime element of human life, nor were its headquarters at any time on the island of Great Britain. By saying it is an occasional quality, we simply mean that it is a great one, and is therefore manifested in great and exceptional moments. In the ordinary course of life it does not come into play; it is sufficiently represented by courage, modesty, industry. Let the novelist give us these virtues for what they are, and not for what no true lover of human nature would have them pretend to be, or else let him devise sublime opportunities, situations which really match the latent nobleness of the human soul.[22]

Six months later, after reading *Hereward, the Last of the English*[23] James recognized that it was a better book than Charles Kingsley's

[18] Appeared in the first issue of the *Nation*, July 6, 1865.
[19]*Notes and Reviews*, p. 59.
[20] *Ibid.*, p. 60.
[21] *Ibid.*, p. 60.
[22] *Ibid.*, pp. 63 f.
[23] Reviewed in *Nation*, Jan. 25, 1866.

previous ones because of "the absence of the old attempt at philosophy and at the writing of history"[24] and the "most grateful suppression of that aggressively *earnest* tone which has hitherto found his chief point of contact with Mr. Carlyle,"[25] and he praised Kingsley "in the first place, ... in his being a heaven-commissioned *raconteur;* and, in the second place, in his being a consummate Englishman."[26] James did not abate in this his demand for truth to human nature one jot, but he recognized that Kingsley was a man of genius in his way. It was not, however, the way James chose to follow.

Still more pernicious because they were by an inferior novelist were the novels in the form of "chronicles" and "diaries" which were coming in rapid succession from the pen of Mrs. E. R. Charles.[27] She, too, had a prejudice in favor of human nature. She wrote literature of the "Sunday reading" variety, usually of religious movements of the past, adapted to the tastes of the whole family, young and old, with an obvious moral lesson unduly emphasized. But she gave a false picture for she lacked "that vigorous imagination and that serious reflection which can stand on tiptoe and overlook three centuries of civilization."[28] Her whole tone was that "of the retrospective present."[29] She failed also in dealing with her own time. *Winifred Bertram*[30] depicted impossibly good and wise little girls in a world where sin and sorrow were made to assume "a roseate hue." There was no survival of romantic sentimentality in James.

We firmly believe that children in pinafores, however rich their natural promise, do not indulge in extemporaneous prayer, in the cogitation of Scripture texts, and in the visitation of the poor and needy, except in very conscious imitation of their elders. The best good they accomplish is effected through a compromise with their essentially immoral love of pleasure. To be disinterested is among the very latest lessons they learn, and we should look with suspicion upon a little girl whose life was devoted

[24] *Notes and Reviews*, p. 143.

[25] *Ibid.*, p. 144.

[26] *Ibid.*, p. 145.

[27] In *Nation*, Sept. 14, 1865, James reviewed *Hearthstone Series: Chronicles of the Schönberg-Cotta Family; The Early Dawn: Sketches of Christian Life in England in the Olden Time; Sketches of the United Brethren of Bohemia and Moravia; Diary of Mrs. Kitty Trevylyan: A Story of the Time of Whitefield and the Wesleys.*

[28] *Notes and Reviews*, p. 81.

[29] *Ibid.*, p. 81.

[30] Reviewed in *Nation*, Feb. 1, 1866.

to the service of an idea. In other words, children grow positively good only as they grow wise, and they grow wise only as they grow old and leave childhood behind them.[31]

As a part of human nature, children have their place, but the novelist should know this place and keep them there. Mrs. Charles was not the only author to be criticized by James from this standpoint; Louisa Alcott[32] and Mrs. Whitney[33] had exalted ideas about childhood which the sagacious youth had already vehemently attacked.

Among the novelists who saw but one side of life was Miss Braddon,[34] descendant of Wilkie Collins and originator of the novel of domestic mystery. She did not have a prejudice in favor of human nature. Far from it! To her, human nature was characterized by bigamy, arson, murder, and insanity. Life as depicted in her novels accordingly was not good but evil. Possibly she wrote of that side because there was a demand for it by a certain small public just as another small public wished for Sunday School literature, but it was inexcusable even so. Miss Braddon's public was

. . . . that public which reads nothing but novels, and yet reads neither George Eliot, George Sand, Thackeray, nor Hawthorne. . . . . Their foremost desire is for something new. Now we all know that human nature is very nearly as old as the hills. But society is forever renewing itself. To society, accordingly, and not to life, Miss Braddon turns, and produces, not stories of passion, but stories of action.[35]

And her sin was the greater because she went "to work like an artist."

With a telling subject and a knowing style she proceeds to get up her photograph. These require shrewd observation and wide experience; Miss Braddon has both. Like all women, she has a turn for color; she knows how to paint. She overloads her canvas with detail. It is the peculiar characters of these details that constitute her chief force. They betray an intimate acquaintance with that disorderly half of society which becomes every day a greater object of interest to the orderly half. They intimate that to use an irresistible vulgarism, Miss Braddon "has been there."[36]

[31] *Ibid.*, pp. 149 f.
[32] Miss Alcott's *Moods* was reviewed in *North American Review*, July, 1865.
[33] Mrs. Whitney's *The Gayworthys*, was reviewed in *North American Review*, Oct., 1865.
[34] James reviewed *Aurora Floyd* in *Nation*, Nov. 9, 1865.
[35] *Notes and Reviews*, p. 114.
[36] *Ibid.*, p. 115.

Miss Braddon had thus misused truth of the first sort, truth to details, because she did not start with truth to human nature.

The subtle, deeply working influence of *Wilhelm Meister* upon James is revealed best of all in a review of Dickens's *Mutual Friend*.[37] Here James stated what he meant about truth to human nature with more shading and fine distinctions than in his other reviews. Probably he was more careful because he felt himself to be dealing with the most famous living novelist of the time, the man whom a short time later he was to meet at the Nortons and find himself speechless in the presence of the noted novelist. He had read Dickens from childhood, knew him intimately, and he realized that the *Mutual Friend* was not up to his standard; it revealed the "permanent exhaustion"[38] of the writer. "Seldom, we reflected, had we read a book so intensely *written*, so little seen, known, or felt,"[39] and he turned from a consideration of the novel to an appraisal of the author. Boldly, daringly, he pointed out that Dickens was not after all a truly great novelist; he knew men but not man.

It were, in our opinion, an offense against humanity to place Mr. Dickens among the greatest novelists. For . . . . he has created nothing but figure. He has added nothing to our understanding of human character. He is master of but two alternatives, he reconciles us to what is commonplace, and he reconciles us to what is odd. The value of the former service is questionable; and the manner in which Mr. Dickens performs it sometimes conveys a certain impression of charlatanism. The value of the latter service is incontestable, and here Mr. Dickens is an honest, an admirable artist. But what is the condition of the truly great novelist? For him there are no alternatives, for him there are no oddities, for him there is nothing outside of humanity. He cannot shirk it; it imposes itself upon him. For him alone, therefore, there is a true and a false; for him alone it is possible to be right, because it is possible to be wrong. Mr. Dickens is a great observer and a great humorist, but he is nothing of a philosopher. . . . . He must know *man* as well as *men*, and to know man is to be a philosopher. The writer who knows men alone, if he has Mr. Dickens's humor and fancy, will give us figures and pictures for which we cannot be too grateful, for he will enlarge our knowledge of the world. But when he introduces men and women whose interest is preconceived to lie not in the poverty, the weakness, the drollery of their natures, but in their complete and unconscious subjection to ordinary and healthy human emotions, all

---

[37] Appeared in *Nation*, Dec. 21, 1865.
[38] *Ibid.*, p. 786.
[39] *Ibid.*, p. 787.

his humor, all his fancy, will avail him nothing if, out of the fullness of his sympathy, he is unable to prosecute those generalizations in which alone consists the real greatness of a work of art. This may sound like very subtle talk about a very simple matter; it is rather very simple talk about a very subtle matter. A story based upon those elementary passions in which alone we seek the true and final manifestation of character must be told in a spirit of intellectual superiority to those passions. That is, the author must understand what he is talking about. The perusal of a story so told is one of the most elevating experiences within the reach of the human mind. The perusal of a story which is not so told is infinitely depressing and unprofitable.[40]

Does this not savor of Goethe? The novelist must know man as well as men. He must be a philosopher as well as an observer—a philosopher, the implication is, even more than an observer. The moral becomes: Study man. Know and understand him. Reveal in your novels that you are intellectually superior to the passions and the characters you treat. The emphasis has been shifted, due to the deficiencies of American fiction, due to the shortcomings of English fiction, due—is it not?—to the influence of a German novelist.

There is in *Wilhelm Meister* a remark of Wilhelm's which must have caused James some thought:

"From youth, I have been accustomed to direct the eyes of my spirit inwards rather than outwards; and hence it is very natural to a certain extent I should be acquainted with man, while of men I have not the smallest knowledge."[41]

Now James had always preferred to direct his gaze outwards; his autobiographical novels are replete with references to the joy he obtained from watching people, as he loitered to and from school, as he wandered through the streets of London, as he sat at Miss Upham's boarding table, always gazing, gaping, absorbing impressions. Balzac opened his eyes that he might the better observe; he increased his interest in men. But did not Goethe, perhaps, through the words of his youth cause our youth to see the even greater necessity for the novelist of directing his eyes inward and studying man? Of getting a basis? Did not this, in turn, cause James to emphasize the tendency to comment upon character and

---

[40] *Ibid.*, p. 787.
[41] Carlyle's translation, Standard Edition of Carlyle's Works, VIII, 215.

motive which we noted before and develop it into real analysis? A story should not only be true; its truth should be apparent.

It seems to me that Goethe more than any other early outside influence which can be traced from the reviews was responsible for the character which was gradually to shape and later to dominate the fiction of James, which was to give it the introspective, psychological nature since thought of as peculiarly Jamesian. Of course, it is not to be overlooked that James had been brought up in a home where the atmosphere was charged with philosophy. But this was an inner influence, and how little it had really affected him, except in a general way, he revealed in *Notes of a Son and Brother* when he confessed that the children of the household had had little comprehension of the meaning of "father's ideas."[42] They had lived in an atmosphere of philosophy without really absorbing it, though it had silently acted upon them and made them well disposed to thought when the outer influences began to press. Now to Henry the outer ones were coming. *Wilhelm Meister*, read at a time when the novels given him to review brought glaringly to his attention the fact that their authors knew nought of human nature, became the positive influence among the negatives. It sent him to studying the mind more than the body of man and this was to lead him later to bring philosophy, and its sister psychology, into the novel.

2. *Truth and Analysis in Practice*

James did not immediately become a philosopher. It takes time and thought, observation of the actions of men, and from that, by hypothetical reasoning, the derivation of the laws of life. Then, characters must be chosen by the novelist to illustrate these laws. Induction and deduction must go hand in hand. James realized when other authors were true or untrue, when they knew human nature. It was another thing to be philosophical one's self.

However, in the next two stories which James wrote, a different emphasis from that in the first is to be noted. *A Landscape Painter*[43] and *A Day of Days*,[44] both published in 1866, no longer have action as the main interest. In its place is character.

The former, *A Landscape Painter*, James cast into diary form in an effort, we may believe, to secure greater truth to life or make the

---

[42] *Notes of a Son and Brother*, pp. 156 f.
[43] Appeared in *Atlantic Monthly*, Feb., 1866.
[44] Appeared in *Galaxy*, June 15, 1866.

story *seem* more true by having its hero tell it, and with the purpose, too, of allowing him to bring in comment and analysis, which, in its turn, would also make the story appear true. But he was too avid in the cause of truth. It is improbable that any man, though he might reflect upon life, would reveal so minutely and outspokenly the many trivial details of his courtship and the words and actions of the object of his affections even to his diary; he might remember them stowed away in some dark corner of his brain but he would scarcely put all the small talk upon paper. However, this makes the story, and the plan and method were easier for a young writer than the less compact one of *The Story of a Year.* The author of the diary is a wealthy young painter who, to recover from a love affair which he had broken off when he discovered the mercenary motive of his betrothed, goes to a remote seashore village. His plan is to "abjure, for a while, my conventional self, and to assume a simple, natural character."[45] He becomes interested in a fisherman's daughter, "What a poetry there is after all in red hands."[46] He talks with her at great length, endeavoring to reconcile her to her lot in life, giving her to understand that he is very poor. But when he is ill, she, it develops later, reads this same diary and discovers he is wealthy. More strenuously she pursues her campaign, and he, nothing loath by this time, proposes. He worries, however, because he has deceived her about his wealth and fears her displeasure, but postpones telling her till after the wedding ceremony. Then she anticipates him and bluntly undeceives him, telling him she has read the diary. Angrily he accuses her:

"It was the act of a false woman" . . . . .

"A false woman? No,—simply a woman. I am a woman, sir! . . . . Come you be a man!"[47]

Human nature? Evidently James thought so, but surely not that of *all* women. This savors more of literature than of life, of certain scheming, treacherous, unscrupulous heroines of Thackeray and French literature. The label is unfortunate, and James seems, despite his demand for objectivity from other writers, to have a slight prejudice against womankind and not much respect for man.

One good point is to be noted. Though the author of the diary thinks and reflects upon life and the fisherman's daughter, James

---

[45] *Atlantic Monthly*, Feb., 1866, p. 184.
[46] *Ibid.*, p. 188.
[47] *Ibid.*, p. 202.

thought and reflected more. He analyzed her character to himself and then gave the results of the analysis in his story. It shows itself in the comments which the slightly perplexed suitor makes. James wisely took advantage of the fact that love is blind, though he endeavored not to be. The diary framework thus placed certain restrictions upon James which he observed, though he disregarded others.

In *A Day of Days*, however, he brought analysis more directly into the story. He reduced action to almost nothing and centered the interest upon the rapid development of the feeling of love in a rich young girl for a poor young man. It is thus the situation of *A Landscape Painter* reversed, a device frequently used by James. Adela Moore, tired of society, has sought the solitude of country life, withdrawing to her brother's country home. One afternoon a young man comes to see her brother. As he is absent, the visitor asks permission to wait. Adela talks with him somewhat cautiously, then commits the indiscretion of taking a walk with him, discovers he is to sail the next day for Europe to study, and finds herself suddenly in love with him. "She had pretty well unlearned the repose of the Veres de Vere. But she was to break with it still more completely."[48] She tries in vain to elicit a proposal from him, almost resorting to making one herself, but, though he catches a glimpse of her purpose, he leaves, and "The day was ended."[49]

James tried to make his incident probable by analyzing the character of Adela, stressing her boredom with society, and then of the man she falls in love with, making his egotistically humble statement of his situation the reason for her interest.

"I'm no man of genius. There's something I miss; some final distinctions I lack . . . . perhaps its humility. . . . . Perhaps it's patience—perhaps it's imagination. I'm vulgar . . . . the vulgar son of vulgar people."[50]

but the reader asks would this be reason enough for most women, are women generally so carried away by their fancies, is the story really true to human nature? To part of it, perhaps, but again surely not to all, and hardly, despite the attempt to make it seem so, to Adela Moore.

Analysis is prominent in these stories but analysis can not make an action seem true and probable unless it is in the beginning true

[48] *Galaxy*, June 15, 1866, p. 311.
[49] *Ibid.*, p. 312.
[50] *Ibid.*, p. 309.

and probable. These stories are possible; they might happen, but they are not the usual. James went out of his way for his people and his situations. He was not content to treat Adela, or Locksley, as they should have been treated, in their own setting, coming into connection with people of their own class, but he took them out of it, imagined people of a lower class, and brought the two awkwardly and stiffly together with the result that neither seems true to human nature. Of course not all human nature can be brought into a short story as Goethe so marvelously assembled it in *Wilhelm Meister*, but if a story is intended to be realistic and probable, if it is to be labeled at the end as generally true, the author must be more careful what phase of human nature he brings in. James was, however, trying to study man. He was reflecting upon it, though unfortunately, as he saw it revealed in books, especially in French books, and in the next chapter we shall see him putting forth some of the things which he had learned.

CHAPTER V

THE PHILOSOPHER APPEARS

1. *The Young Diogenes*

The spring of 1866 witnessed the first of those periods of despairing perplexity which were to lay hold of James off and on during his life and were to be the prelude to growth. Mentally disturbed by the problems of the novelist, he was, in addition, physically inconvenienced by the reappearance of certain bad aspects of his malady so that he could take little part in active life and was thus forced back upon himself to brood and reflect. He began to wonder if perhaps he had not been over hasty, over emphatic in regard to the matter of bringing truth to human nature, philosophy, into the novel. He had berated Dickens in no scant terms for not being a philosopher, and, before that, Goethe for not being a novelist. Had he been unjust? Had he demanded the impossible or the impracticable? Could not one strike a balance between philosopher and novelist so that one might be both? Had he been urging something upon novelists that was really not their business at all? The doubt assailed him. For a time he became less vehement in his demands and concerned himself when given a book to review with other aspects of the novelist's craft—method of treatment of a subject, truth to external aspects, and so on. Given Victor Hugo's *Les Travailleurs de la Mer*[1] he took up the space allotted him for the review by writing an ironical summary of the book, ending with an exhortation to the author to return to his former manner for which he expressed a great admiration. Slightly encouraged by Mrs. Gaskell's treatment of her women characters in *Wives and Daughters*,[2] he yet could extract nothing of a positive, constructive nature from the novel. And he was exasperated exceedingly by Henry Sedley's *Marian Rooke*,[3] false in even the external aspects of life—*could* the author be an American and write so blindly about it?—and by the weak sentimentality of Mrs. Craik's *A Noble Life*.[4] So far as we can judge from the reviews—or from the books themselves for that matter—Henry James was not helped at all by these novels

[1] Reviewed in *Nation*, Apr. 12, 1866.
[2] Reviewed in *Nation*, Feb. 22, 1866.
[3] Reviewed in *Nation*, Feb. 22, 1866.
[4] Reviewed in *Nation*, Mar. 1, 1866.

in his attempt to solve his problem. Very likely, indeed, they made him realize all the more the need of a firm basis of truth, a steady, straightforward gaze in looking at life, an understanding of it by the author, if books were to be worth the paper on which they were printed. Stubbornly, grimly, though more silently now, he clung to the idea which had tormented him ever since he read *Wilhelm Meister*. He wrote the two stories which we noted at the end of the last chapter, but found it difficult to proceed without a guide. He tested his ability to philosophize by giving a detailed statement of Epicureanism and a careful criticism of it when Higginson's edition of the philosophy of Epictetus came from the press[5] and happily surprised himself—or at least the reader—by his insight. He became a nineteenth century Diogenes turning over in his own mind for his own satisfaction the whole matter of truth to the laws of life in the novel, deaf to any popular Alexanders, but ready to hail the honest novelist when he, or she, appeared.

2. *The Search Rewarded—Felix Holt*

It was a great day then when in the midsummer of 1866 *Felix Holt*, hot from the press, arrived for him to review.[6] George Eliot! Here, indeed, was the philosophical novelist he sought, almost, it might be said, right under his very nose, for he had long been acquainted with her works, had eagerly read each novel as it had appeared. Why, the reader may ask, had he not thought of her before? Well, perhaps he had in a vague way. Perhaps some faint memory of *Adam Bede*, of *The Mill on the Floss*, of *Silas Marner*, as unrecognized as the virus implanted by *Wilhelm Meister*, had caused him to persist against discouragement in his demand that the novelist be in some degree also a philosopher. He had cited her briefly as a good writer in previous reviews.[7] But interested before in the craftsmanship of a novel, he had overlooked George Eliot's full strength, the way in which she could help *him*, till the epoch-making day when *Felix Holt* came to ease his bed of pain. He had sat up then, both literally and figuratively, to dash off his review and take a new lease upon life.[8]

[5] Reviewed in *North American Review*, Apr., 1866. La Rose in his Preface to *Notes and Reviews* is interested in this as James's one excursion into the field of Philosophy.

[6] Appeared in *Nation*, Aug. 16, 1866.

[7] See the reviews of *Azarian*, *The Gayworthys*, and *A Noble Life*.

[8] See *The Middle Years*, pp. 63 f. By comparing this account with the review

George Eliot was a philosophical novelist. What was more, she was approachable, understandable. Goethe had been too much for him. Intent upon form and method, James had not been able in 1865 to see how a writer so supremely great in one respect could be so poor, so negligent in another respect. A year later, intent upon thought, dealing, too, with a novelist who was not wholly disregardful of the mechanics of the craft, though she was oftentimes weak in them, James recognized at once in George Eliot his ideal of the philosophical novelist become real. The difference in emphasis of the reviews treating the two authors is striking and reveals how far James had progressed. In treating the German writer he had been almost wholly concerned with Goethe's discrepancies as a novelist—that he should write a novel to edify rather than to amuse, should snap his fingers at plot and form, should disregard completely the physical aspects of his characters. In treating the English writer he mentioned first of all her faults: "Her plots have always been artificial—clumsily artificial—the conduct of her story slow, and her style diffuse."[9] He was not blind to them but he could overlook them in large measure because

In compensation for these defects . . . . comes the firm and elaborate delineation of individual character. . . . . Then comes that extensive human sympathy, that easy understanding of character at large, that familiarity with man, from which a novelist borrows his real inspiration, from which he borrows all his ideal lines and hues, to which he appeals for a blessing on his fictitious process, and to which he owes it that, firm locked in the tissue of the most rigid prose, he is still more or less a poet. George Eliot's humanity colors all her other gifts—her humor, her morality, and her exquisite rhetoric.[10]

Because of his faults, Goethe had not been for James a great novelist. Despite her faults, George Eliot was. Their faults are not, to be sure, the same faults, but in each it is the craftsman who is weak, the thinker who is strong.

George Eliot's humanity, her sympathy for and understanding of character at large, as well as her "firm and elaborate delineation of individual character," was her great merit. She knew man as well as men. George Eliot, then, must be studied. With her ten years

---

written in 1866, James's tendency to embroider the past in his autobiographical volumes is apparent.

[9] *Notes and Reviews*, p. 200.
[10] *Ibid.*, p. 201.

start over him in this business of writing novels, James saw that she might help him. Accordingly he turned with a new eagerness to a reperusal of her works, followed by the writing of his first long critical article, *The Novels of George Eliot*.[11]

3. Lessons from George Eliot

Surveying her works as a whole and seeking a governing principle, James discovered that though George Eliot knew man, she was somewhat of a specialist in the class of men which she portrayed. She was a "painter of *bourgeois* life as Thackeray was a painter of the life of drawing rooms,"[12] giving her portraits such a "completeness, a rich density of detail"[13] that he felt she must have observed carefully the surroundings in which she herself had been brought up. Hetty and Adam, Felix and Esther, Tom and Maggie were just plain people, poor but honest. They might have been her neighbors, while near by lived rough country people or common working people. Occasionally their interests were brought into contact with those of the more remotely dwelling upper classes, as in *Felix Holt*, and it was then that James discerned how much better George Eliot was in her treatment of the lower classes and felt how wise she was to confine herself almost wholly to them. The first lesson for the novelist was then—observe your neighbors, the people who belong to your own class or among whom you have been brought up.

But George Eliot did more than observe her neighbors. She studied them. She looked into their hearts, into their minds, into their souls, and she discovered there the working of the laws of mankind. The thoughts and feelings and actions of her characters were such as belonged not to one class alone but to all classes. Here George Eliot was a philosopher. She did not attempt to bring all kinds and degrees of people into one book as Goethe had, but she did bring problems of life which must be met and solved by high as well as by low. She was, to be sure, viewing all her novels, rather narrow in the scope of the problems treated, a specialist here even as in the class of characters chosen. In all her novels she took the view of life first expressed in *Adam Bede*, " 'Our deeds determine us as much as we determine our deeds,' "[14] and kept it throughout

---

[11] Appeared in *Atlantic Monthly*, Oct., 1866.
[12] *Atlantic Monthly*, Oct., 1866, p. 480.
[13] *Ibid.*, p. 480.
[14] *Ibid.*, p. 491. James is quoting from *Adam Bede*.

revealing this " 'inexorable law of human souls, that we prepare ourselves for sudden deeds by the reiterated choice of good or evil that gradually determines character' "[15] most tremendously in *Romola*. The problems of behavior arising out of this law were universal; people of the upper classes as well as of the lower, people of today as well as of yesterday were confronted by them and had to reckon with them or be overcome by them. The second lesson for the novelist appeared—study your neighbor and thereby learn the problems of mankind.

Thus far George Eliot was merely proving to James the hypothesis he had already advanced about the necessity of the two kinds of truth—truth to external details and truth to internal, and thus, eternal aspects—in the novel. But she brought to his notice another important thing already grasped in the review when he spoke of her humanity, that gift which seemed to James to color all her other gifts. Out of her knowledge of human nature had been born a sympathy for it, and this was because she allowed her reflection to play around her characters and their problems, illuminating them and humanizing them.

. . . . it is to this union of the keenest observation with the ripest reflection, that her style owes its essential force. She is a thinker, not, perhaps, a passionate one, but at least a serious one; and the term can be applied with either adjective neither to Dickens nor Thackeray. The constant play of lively and vigorous thought about the objects furnished by her observation animates these latter with a surprising richness of color and a truly human interest. It gives to the author's style, moreover, that lingering, affectionate, comprehensive quality which is its chief distinction and perhaps occasionally it makes her tedious. George Eliot is so little tedious, however, because, if, on the one hand, her reflection never flags, so, on the other, her observation never ceases to supply it with material.[16]

Reflecting upon her characters, George Eliot came to care for them. Her understanding of them led her to feel for them and to sympathize with them. And the third lesson for the novelist appeared— do not be indifferent to your characters.

It was because of these three qualities, all of them connected with character, that George Eliot was great: she observed, she thought, she felt. Her plots were poor, disjointed things, clumsily artificial, not at all the dramatic wholes of the masterpieces of Bal-

---

[15] *Ibid.*, p. 491. James is quoting from *Romola*.
[16] *Ibid.*, p. 488

zac—"The author succeeds better in drawing attitudes of feeling than in drawing movements of feeling,"[17] but *The Mill on the Floss* had promise in its "dramatic continuity"[18] that some day she might succeed in drawing movements, while *Silas Marner* had something of the "simple, rounded, consummate aspect"[19] of a masterpiece. But plot, though essential, was no longer of primary importance to James; it was no longer the soul of the novel as he had written in his second review. In its place, out of the demand for truth, had come character. Character was now the soul of a novel. And character was, indeed, George Eliot's main concern. She began with character; she never forgot it, and her people remained with the reader after he closed the novel not because of what they did but because of what they were.

4. *The Problem of Morality—Conscience vs. Passion.*

But even as James grasped the greatness of George Eliot, he discerned also her shortcomings, and the emphasis of most of the critical article, in fact, falls upon a consideration of these.

George Eliot's mind, he felt, was both her strength and her weakness. She was great in a narrow way. She recognized that man was made up of two warring elements—passion and conscience —but in her novels conscience always proved the stronger, always won. Now did it always win in life? Should it always win? Was it better as far as the business of the novel was concerned that it should?

James did not look at life for his answers to these three questions, but he looked at what he had learned of life through books, in particular through French literature. He remembered the stories of Balzac where the passion of greed, of research, of fame, of social success, of love was the ruling force, the connecting link which made the stories "movements of feeling." There was Balthazar Claes and his passionate quest for the absolute. James thought especially, however, of another woman novelist whose stories appearing frequently in the *Revue des Deux Mondes* had for the last few years been repeatedly emphasizing the strength of passion and its imperative demand to be served. He thought of George Sand, of her *Valentine*, her *Lucrezia Floriani*, her *Consuelo*, her *Teverino*, and

[17] *Ibid.*, p. 487.
[18] *Ibid.*, p. 489.
[19] *Ibid.*, p. 482.

even of her more recent *Monsieur Sylvestre*, and *Le Dernier Amour*.
In all her stories, passion was the force which commanded obedience.
Love of man for woman and of woman for man—it was almost
always reciprocal—insisted upon having its way. Not always were
her stories happy ones; passion often brought pain at the same time
it brought bliss, but passion was the dominating force and the pain
as well as the bliss was born out of itself and never out of conscience
or any sense of "slighted obligations" as in George Eliot's characters.
Indeed, some of George Sand's characters, Felicie in *Le Dernier
Amour* and Lucrezia in the novel bearing her name knew not at all
about that other department of man; they were simply feeling;
while such characters as Valentine were restrained temporarily
from yielding to passion, not by conscience but by fear of mother
or husband, fear that is, of an outside force, not of an inside one.
Passion played from beginning to end in her novels carrying its
reader along in its copious flow till it spent itself or, more often,
spent its victims. Passion was the ruling force and the novels
caught from it a fire and a glow.

It was without doubt to George Sand that James referred when
he caught a glimpse of what he considered the limitation of George
Eliot in the review.

There is another great novelist who has often dealt with men and women
moved by exceptional opinions. Whatever these opinions may be, the
reader shares them for the time with the writer; he is thrilled by the contact of her passionate earnestness, and he is borne rapidly along upon the
floods of feeling which rush through her pages. The Radicalism of "Felix
Holt" is strangely remote from the reader; we do not say as Radicalism,
which we may have overtopped or undermined, but simply as feeling
entertained.[20]

And of her of whom he was thinking in the development of the idea
in the longer article when he wrote: "I profoundly doubt whether
the central object of a novel may be a passionless creature."[21] In
one book, where the passion of the hero should have burned like a
torch, she had smothered it, reduced it to a dim spark. In other
novels, she had tried to make her virtuous creatures, Dinah Morris,
for instance, stand out to hide and make the reader forget the
wrongdoing of the others. George Eliot's emphasis was wrong.
Though, and perhaps because, she had yielded to the demands of

[20] *Notes and Reviews*, p. 203.
[21] *Atlantic Monthly*, Oct., 1866, p. 487.

passion in her own life, her novels were an attempt to deny its right to be observed. She had chosen as her main characters and named her books for those people she wished to exalt, virtuous individuals, of whose deeds and manners she approved—Silas Marner, Adam Bede, Romola—but despite her precaution, her own and the reader's interest inevitably strayed to Godfrey Cass and Hetty and Tito. It strayed, however, only to be rudely jerked back. "Why not see things in their nakedness? the impatient reader is tempted to ask. Why not let passions and foibles play themselves out?"[22] In her endings, too, she was a conservative, trying to remedy any undue emphasis upon her passionate creatures. *Adam Bede* should have stopped "with Hetty's execution, or even with her reprieve."[23] Adam's marriage might follow in the course of time, but it was material for another novel in the manner of Balzac. And Romola's befriending Tessa was beside the point. In *The Mill on the Floss* there was nothing to warrant a tragic ending of an accidental nature, and James would have preferred one where Maggie and Stephen were brought together once more. Their passion should have been strong enough for that. But George Eliot was

. . . . in morals and aesthetics essentially a conservative. In morals her problems are still the old, passive problems. . . . . What moves her most is the idea of a conscience harassed by the memory of slighted observations. Unless in the case of Savonarola, she has made no attempt to depict a conscience taking upon itself great and novel responsibilities.[24]

But Savonarola was a secondary figure. And in no case did George Eliot recognize the right of a passion of any sort to dominate. It must be moderated or silenced. Was she, then, really true to human nature?

It was George Eliot's type of mind, the English type. The French type was different. Nowhere was this more to be observed than in the literature of the two countries. The writers across the channel were primarily interested in passion; it might be of love, of ambition, of greed, of hate. Whatever it was, it desired fulfillment and success in this world—the Church took care of the next—and because life is short and time fleeting, it poured all its energies into realizing itself in some way. It was active, even aggressive, and it

[22] *Ibid.*, p. 487.
[23] *Ibid.*, p. 485.
[24] *Ibid.*, p. 491. (This emphasis upon solution in terms of character is the development of the idea noted in regard to the review of *Emily Chester*, Chapter II.)

gave warmth and life to a book. . The English writers, on the other hand, were interested in the colder characteristics of man; courage, nobility of soul, renunciation, duty received far more attention at their hands than love, and when love was treated, it was scarcely ever as the "grand passion" of life consuming all others. It was, rather, consumed. Of course, courage, nobility, and duty might occasionally become active, might even be made into passions, but the English, except in a few rare instances, failed to do this. In their treatment of the nobler aspects of man, they observed a restraint, classical in its nature, engendered out of the aspects themselves. This made the result cold, detached from life. When James criticized English writers, as in this article upon George Eliot, he always deprecated the fact that the authors did not let themselves go, recognize the force of passion, and see whither it might lead them. He cried up the French to the English.

But a still more interesting thing is to be noted when James presently turned to criticize certain modern French novels. There was Dumas fils telling in his *Affaire Clemenceau* a story of passion of such an intense and horrible nature in its outcome that the reader was plunged into depression.[25]

To be completely great, a work of art must lift up the reader's heart; and it is the artist's secret to reconcile this condition with images of the barest and sternest reality. Life is dispiriting, art is inspiring; and a storyteller who aims at anything more than a fleeting success has no right to tell an ugly story unless he knows its beautiful counterpart.[26]

With George Eliot there had been no such depression; though her subjects were sometimes morally hideous, her reaction had always been one of moral beauty. She had seen the good beneath the evil, the hidden significance of things, and revealed it to the reader, and the effect of her books was inspiring. Her influence in this respect was to grow more and more upon Henry James, and in 1868 to ring as an undercurrent still more forcefully. James was then given Feydeau's *Comtesse de Chalis*[27] and Feuillet's *Camors*[28] to review. They were both immoral, repulsively so; the former gave odious pictures of passion and vice and produced no reaction except that

---

[25] Appeared in *Nation*, Oct. 11, 1866.
[26] *Notes and Reviews*, p. 225.
[27] Appeared in *Nation*, Jan. 23, 1868.
[28] Appeared in *Nation*, July 30, 1868.

of repulsion in the reader. In the latter, Feuillet tried to be moral, James believed, but was only thinly so.

Like most of the best French romancers, his works wear, morally, to American eyes, a decidedly thin and superficial look. Men and women, in our conception, are deeper, more substantial, more self-directing; they have, if not more virtue, at least more conscience; and when conscience comes into the game, human history ceases to be a perfectly simple tale.[29]

Men and women are thus dual creatures—creatures of passion and creatures of conscience—and it is the working of these two often oppositely directed instincts that complicates life into an interesting situation, far more interesting than when but one is active. Since the novelist's desire is for interesting situations, he may then find them in the conflict of these two elements. As to which element should receive the greater emphasis, however, James was not biased by any preformed opinions as George Eliot was restricted by her idea of morality or George Sand by her view of the importance of love. James was governed only by the demands of his art. And art had told him that it should *depend upon the characters chosen* and not upon the author's point of view whether one received more emphasis than the other. As the question arose out of the consideration of truth to human nature, so it was to be solved by thrusting it back. And the author, if he brought passion or conscience or, better, both, into his tale, must find his end, his final solution, in terms of the one which dominated the character under consideration. The more evenly balanced the two were, the greater the conflict and also the difficulty for the author, but he must understand his characters well enough to grasp the right solution. It was to confess defeat to evade it by death or accident as George Eliot had in *The Mill on the Floss.*

James's stand, thus, in the problem of morality was neither French nor English, nor was it American. One questions whether, indeed, the flexibility of his point of view, allowing itself to be regulated by the nature of the characters treated, never imposing itself, if, indeed, it had any opinion of its own, could really be called a stand at all. He could *see* both sides; moreover, he could *take* both sides, emphasizing whichever seemed to him to be most in accord with the characters which he was treating. For a while, we shall observe him writing tales in which passion is easily the dominat-

[29] *Ibid.*, pp. 92 f.

ing force. Later we shall see him bringing both elements into his stories in almost even balance, but his halting on the edge of the precipice, as in *Madame de Mauves*, as in *The Portrait of a Lady*, was due to his truth to human nature, to the type of American woman which he was picturing, and not to any prudery on his own part. His attitude was the attitude of the German philosopher—objective, indifferent.

5. *Stories of Passion*

Though James had discerned three important things in George Eliot's stories—observe your neighbor, study him, treat him with consideration—and knew that this was wise, true advice, he did not immediately follow it. Perhaps he felt that he knew mankind already. He watched his friends, no doubt, but when it came to writing stories, he carefully avoided them, loath to infringe in any way upon the limits of friendship. His characters he continued to manufacture or to borrow from other authors. The real influence of George Eliot upon his stories was delayed, though the question which she had brought up for him and George Sand had answered—that of the place of passion in a story—he proceeded to illustrate in his stories *My Friend Bingham*[30] and *Poor Richard*[31] which came out in 1867. In the article on George Eliot he had written, "I profoundly doubt whether the central object of a novel may successfully be a passionless creature,"[32] and the influence which is to be discerned in the stories, especially in the second, as we shall presently see, is that of George Sand rather than that of the English writer. It is not the question of passion itself, however, which must concern the critic as much as the two ways in which James dealt with it,—in the first instance, scantily, in the second, copiously,—as a result, defeating in both his honest intention of being true to human nature.

My Friend Bingham concerns itself with the love which an impoverished widow and a wealthy man come to have for each other after he has accidentally killed her little boy. Overcome with remorse, he wishes so passionately to help her that her sorrow turns to pity for him. Out of his remorse and her pity love is quickly, though somewhat unconvincingly, born, and "The proper conclu-

[30] Appeared in *Atlantic Monthly*, Mar., 1867.
[31] Appeared in *Atlantic Monthly*, June to Aug., 1867.
[32] *Atlantic Monthly*, Oct., 1866, p. 487.

sion of my story lies in the highly dramatic fact that out of the depths of her bereavement . . . . this richly gifted woman had emerged, responsive to the passion of him who had wronged her all but as deeply as he loved her."[33] Though the story is about passion, James did not deal with it directly and lost much intensity which he might otherwise have gained. He cast it into the narrative framework whereby a minor character, in this case a friend of the man, an observer, tells what the main characters do. This device, possibly borrowed from Mérimée, James was to use frequently in his stories.[34] It gave them, he probably felt, as in the case of the diary framework of *A Landscape Painter*, an authenticity, a reality to have someone connected with the characters vouch for them. However, it often caused him, as in this story, to shirk his own responsibility. The account of the birth of love under these somewhat unnatural circumstances should be lighted and warmed by some of the glow, at least, of that love. As handled by the narrator, it is told dispassionately, analyzed somewhat scientifically, and seems to the reader a "queer case," not convincingly nor typically true to human nature. James thus defeated his own purpose.

Perhaps he discerned this defect. Anyway when he came to write *Poor Richard* which ran through three issues of the *Atlantic Monthly*, he related the story directly, and the tale is quite as uncurbed in its nature and expression as *My Friend Bingham* is restrained. The opening scene where Richard, a dissolute country lad, pleads his cause in an outburst of passion with Gertrude, an orphaned heiress who lives on a neighboring farm, gives the tone to the whole story. She puts him off, magnanimously promising friendship as a palliative if he will give up drinking and become a man. Then she turns to consider Captain Severn and Major Luttrell, attracted by the glamour of their wartime exploits. She inclines toward the former but he is held back from making any definite advances by his poverty and pride. The independent Gertrude is capable of assuming the initiative, but at the impending moment Captain Severn is recalled to the front and prevented from bidding good-bye to her before he leaves, by an instinctive lie on the part of Richard. The farmer lad realizes his error, especially when he sees Gertrude's concern and then her grief at Severn's death which follows shortly, but instead of telling her, he relapses into his former de-

[33] *Atlantic Monthly*, Mar., 1867, p. 358.
[34] For the influence of Mérimée, see Chapters VIII and XI.

bauchery. Gertrude turns for consolation to the wily Luttrell who takes advantage of all this and much more. When Richard hears of Luttrell's success, he comes to his senses again, and, because of his love rather than of his conscience, tells Gertrude of Luttrell's baseness. She breaks the engagement, perceives Richard's true worth: " 'He has rescued me .... but his passion has perished in the tumult.' She felt that he was abundantly a man and she loved him,"[35] but it is too late. Richard leaves for the front and Gertrude seeks solace alone in Florence.

James called this story after Richard, but he seems to have been more concerned with Gertrude; like George Eliot his execution strayed from his intention. Gertrude is the pivotal point, and he found this "florid and vigorous dahlia"[36] and her three suitors not among his neighbors, not even in New England or in George Eliot but rather in the tales of passion of the French. The rich, independent heiress, living in the country attracting many admirers, among them a farmer lad, is reminiscent of George Sand, though, no doubt, unintentionally so. The situation thus is French, insufficiently localized in America by calling the heroine a Yankee and dressing two of the heroes in the uniform of the Civil War. The analysis of love by the author, the long discussions about it, often in the nature of soliloquies or asides, by the characters, is also reminiscent of such tales as *Lucrezia Floriani* or *Le Dernier Amour* though love, if not situation, bows to America and becomes the love which is to be sanctified by marriage and not an illicit passion.

James, however, did try to profit by the example of George Eliot. He looked into the minds of his characters and he allowed his "humanity," though it appears almost as sickly sentimentality, to play over what he found. But he found too much, the insignificant as well as the richly, surprisingly significant. And he told and commented upon everything that he found not realizing that some things are more effective when merely suggested or that some actions need no explaining or excusing. Then too, not only did he have insight into the minds of his characters, but they, uncannily, are also gifted with it. Richard and Gertrude understand themselves far too well to act and talk as they do. Either they should think less deeply or act more wisely to be true to the kind of people he has chosen to depict them as being. Again James defeated his purpose,

[35] *Atlantic Monthly*, Aug., 1867, p. 177.
[36] *Atlantic Monthly*, June, 1867, p. 698.

and this time because of his growing fondness for analysis. He allowed it to run away with him. The philosopher had already become the psychologist interested in the particular case rather than in the general, and the psychologist unfortunately predominated over the novelist. That was the rub.

But *Poor Richard*, though it does not strike the critic today as something especially promising—indeed most critics ignore it altogether along with the rest of the early stories—had an important part to play in 'James's early development. It was, as we shall see in the next chapter, the first story of Henry James's to come to the attention of William Dean Howells.

CHAPTER VI

EMERGENCE OF THE GREAT DESIRE

1. *The Meeting with Howells*

In the spring of 1866, William Dean Howells had come to Boston from New York, where he had been for a brief period in the office of the *Nation*, to act as assistant editor to Fields on the *Atlantic* staff. Aided and advised in his house hunting by Charles Eliot Norton, he had bought a house and settled in Cambridge and had immediately been welcomed by Longfellow, Lowell, Holmes, Child, Dana, the Wards, and many others who made Cambridge such an intellectual center at that time. These men, always interested in those they considered worthy, found the young man of twenty-nine with his active past, immensely interesting and promising. He had been earning his living since a boy; this in itself was enough to amaze many of them who considered work which brought financial returns more as an avocation than as a means of support. He had not been to college, but despite it had secured an education. He had edited papers and written poems and travel sketches. He had held the post of consul at Venice for four years. And now he had come to Boston, or more exactly Cambridge, to help Fields on the leading literary magazine of the time. They approved and asked him to their homes, to the meetings of their Dante club, and to their intellectual gatherings of all kinds.

And it was inevitable in the course of time, though probably not until the return of the Jameses from Swampscott in the fall that Howells should meet them, father and second son. The former was an important personage in the cultural gatherings; the latter was shyly venturing into them, hanging wistfully upon each word, hardly venturing to offer one of his own. But Howells noticed him; perhaps he had seen James's name on the list of contributors to the *Atlantic*, though from what he said some fifteen years later,[1] he apparently had not been called upon to judge the critical article on George Eliot or *My Friend Bingham*. However, he must have known of their existence at the time and have been led to take an interest in James as one of the contributors while James became interested

[1] See article in *Century*, Nov., 1882.

in him as an editor who in his position might have in his hands in no small measure his own trembling fate. Both were presently still more closely drawn together by the desire which one had admittedly and the other even then very likely cherished secretly, to become a great American novelist. By December the two were so well acquainted that Howells wrote to a friend:

Talking of talks: young Henry James and I had a famous one last evening, two or three hours long, in which we settled the true principles of literary art. He is a very earnest fellow, and I think extremely gifted— gifted enough to do better than any one has yet done toward making us a real American novel. We have in reserve from him a story for the *Atlantic*, which I'm sure you'll like.[2]

The story referred to was no doubt *Poor Richard* for James related long afterward in one of his autobiographical volumes, that that "most presuming as yet" of his "fictitional bids" had been addressed "at his positive invitation" to the "distinguished friend of a virtual lifetime as he was to become, William Dean Howells," whose "glittering response after perusal"—perhaps, indeed, the famous talk of the letter—had proved one of the distinct moments in the general confusion of the time.[3]

James, however, in his autobiographical reminiscences did not recover any more of the details of the friendship which sprang up between the two men, and it is not till several years later that his letters begin to trace intermittently its course. The letters of Howells occasionally refer to it. In August, 1867, he wrote to Norton, "I see the Jameses rather frequently,"[4] and he referred to Henry James's stories. In November, 1868, Howells again wrote to Norton:

Yesterday, it was the last favor of fortune to walk with Harry James to the Botanical Garden, and sit in the sun on the edge of a hotbed of violets, and think of the notices still to be written. What is better than to punch one's cane in a sandy path? You must have good company, of course.[5]

Except for such widely spaced remarks as these and occasional references to James's stories and later a letter or two to James, Howells's letters give little more satisfaction, while the often quoted

    [2] *Life and Letters of Wm. Dean Howells*, Garden City, 1928, I, 116, letter to Stedman, dated Dec. 5, 1866.
    [3] *Notes of a Son and Brother*, p. 437.
    [4] *Life and Letters*, I, 117.
    [5] *Ibid.*, p. 137.

article of his written fifteen years later treated the beginning of the friendship briefly and not always accurately as to facts.[6]

As a result, it is left to the biographer and critic to try to reconstruct or to indicate briefly in some way, the friendship of these two men and its meaning for American literature, a task neglected by writers on Howells as well as by those upon James. The early years from the standpoint of James will be treated in the course of this study, but there is a task awaiting the future historian of American literature to determine not only Howells's early influence upon James but James's influence upon Howells, for it seems that the friendship must have been productive of results in both directions. Up to this time, Howells had written extravagantly romantic poems, articles on travel, and editorial notes, but he had done nothing with prose fiction. Could James, by any chance, have suggested to Howells that he, Howells, write novels about American life so that Howells eventually, even more widely than James, became the historian of this time? Could he have turned Howells from romanticism to realism as Howells, as we shall presently see, probably influenced James to turn to romanticism? As the two most important figures in the American novel in the last quarter of the nineteenth century, the interrelations where certainly there were interrelations should be carefully considered.

2. *The Meaning of the Friendship to James*

As far as Henry James was concerned, the friendship struck up at this rather crucial moment in his development meant much. Howells became his first literary companion. Godkin, Norton, Fields, older men all, had given him advice, befriended him in a literary way, which had been that of genial godparents, interested in the son because of their fondness for the parent. Now Howells, but six years older than James, though considerably more experienced in life than those six years would indicate, was, like James, enthusiastically beginning a new adventure—the pursuit of literature and culture for its own sake. He was looking ahead and dreaming of great things

[6] *Century Magazine*, Nov., 1882, Howells refers to "Poor Richard" as the second story of Henry James to appear in the *Atlantic*. The reader of this study will realize that it was the fourth story to appear there, that another story had already appeared in the *Galaxy*, and that the article on George Eliot had appeared in the *Atlantic*. In two unfinished papers, written by Howells just before his death and published in *Life and Letters*, Vol. II, Howells refers to his early acquaintance with James.

which might be done in the cause. Though required to do a certain amount of office work—reading of manuscript, correction of proof—it was not irksome work, and he could see time enough ahead once he got fairly started, to write and further literature, as James was doing, by practice as well as by precept. Howells and James discovered at once that they had much in common, and there must have been many talks "two or three hours long" where the principles of literary art were "settled" and then re-settled.

What the principles were as far as James had formulated them we already know. Truth was the key word: truth to human nature which meant in practice analyzing it; truth to external details which meant faithful recording of facts. Everything else was secondary; everything else, passion versus conscience, action, or plot, was but a part of truth, regulated by it. What James desired to do, become an American Balzac, we also know, and this desire he must have expressed to Howells, telling him what being such meant in words which probably were not far different from those written in a review on historical novelists in August, 1867.

The novelist who of all novelists is certainly the most of one—Balzac—may be said, to a certain extent, to have done this, (i.e. curbed his imagination by truth to his time) and to have done it with excellent profit. . . . . He looked upon French society in the nineteenth century as a great whole, the character of which would be falsified if he made light of a single detail or episode. Although, therefore (if we except his "Contes Drolatiques") he wrote but a single tale of which the period lay beyond the memory of his own generation or that preceding it, he may yet in strictness be called a historical novelist, inasmuch as he was the historian of contemporary manners. . . . . The manners, the ideas, the tone of the *moment*, may always be seized by a genuine observer, even if the moment lasts but three months, and the writer who seizes them will possess an historical value for his descendants.[7]

James wished to catch the tone of his time; he thought it a comparatively easy thing for a man to do if he was a "genuine observer" and he had no doubt, unfortunately, about his own ability. He had clothed his heroes in the uniforms of the Civil War or sent them to Europe for polish, and this faithfulness to outer details he considered the means of getting tone, this and analysis of the motives and thoughts of his people.

Howells listened and agreed. It sounded well. He knew little

[7] *Nation*, Aug. 15, 1867, p. 126.

about realistic novels, but he thought of how he had enjoyed the plays of Goldoni which pictured Italian life.[8] However, he had not read Balzac.[9] Consequently he could not point out to James the discrepancies between intention and execution, the differences between student and master, which are so glaringly apparent to the reader of James and Balzac today. Balzac saw the general condition, caught the "tone of the moment," and depicted it as illustrated by specific individuals. The plot of each of his stories, the characters of each are clues to the general corruption of the society which he depicted. James, though he realized that each age had a "tone" of its own, had formulated as yet no definite theory about contemporary society. He saw only individuals and not outstanding ones. He understood the big eternal truths of human nature. But he did not see how human nature caught in the wheel of birth of any one age, took on a certain character which the individual illustrated. He was not able at twenty-three, nor, indeed, for some time, to apply the processes of inductive thought to life. It was unfortunate, however, that Howells could not have helped James more directly with this aspect of his problem, that he could not have discussed Balzac with James instead of simply listening to James's theories and intention and desire, and concluding, because of the young man's earnestness, that his must be a worthy aim, one which should be encouraged. It sounded well. To a great extent, he probably approved of James's principles, or he would not have written so enthusiastically to his friend about James, nor have praised *Poor Richard* so highly, nor have felt so keenly the negative criticism accorded it by the *Nation* on its publication.[10] This approval meant much to James; it encouraged and strengthened him. At the same time, however, it probably delayed his discovering for himself the real flaw of his stories from the standpoint of his intention.

Howells, however, must have taken some part in the conversations. It was not his way just to listen, any more than it was James's way to do all the talking. James quite preferred to listen. And Howells's ideas were different. If we glance at his autobiographical volumes, chiefly *My Literary Passions*, we shall see that he had leanings, decided ones, toward romanticism. As a boy, he had read

[8] See *My Literary Passions*, New York, 1895.

[9] At least Balzac does not appear in *My Literary Passions*, and "realism" generally was distasteful to him till about this time.

[10] *Life and Letters*, I, 117.

"Goldsmith and Cervantes and Irving, kindred spirits"[11] and found them wonderful and delightful. Then the "potent charm" of Dickens had thrilled him, made him "hot and cold."[12] Thackeray's "sentimentality" and "romanticism carried into the region of morals" had "dominated his love and fancy."[13] Heine had laid hold of him with his "potent spirit,"[14] and Hawthorne had, too, with his "potent spell."[15] Not a French author appears in his early likes and dislikes, and French literature never came to mean anything to him. The only author in whose praise he and James could have joined in 1866 was George Eliot, and she meant something quite different to both. From Howells, she elicited the "deepest respect, the highest honor," but he had no "passion" for her; her ability paled when compared— not with French writers as in the case of James—but with an American, Hawthorne.

He was always dealing with the problem of evil, too, and I found a more potent charm in his more artistic handling of it than I found in George Eliot. Of course, I then preferred the region of pure romance where he liked to place his action; but I did not find his instances the less veritable because they shone out in "The light that never was on sea or land" .... he held me by his potent spell and for a time he dominated me as completely as any author I have read. More truly than any other American author he has been a passion with me.[16]

If Hawthorne meant so much to Howells, if he was his favorite among American authors, Howells must have brought up the name of the earlier American frequently as he discussed literary art and its condition in America with James. He must have emphasized Hawthorne's "artistic handling" of his themes and his "potent charm" or "potent spell" as most desirable elements in fiction. James in his turn must have listened and agreed. This, too, sounded well. But perhaps it made James realize with a slight palpitation of the heart and a tightening of the cords of the throat that his stories could hardly be called "artistic," could not at all be said to have "potent charm" or "potent" anything unless analysis. And though he liked Scott and Mérimée and Gautier, who combined romantic

---

[11] Howells, *My Literary Passions*, New York, 1895, p. 33. Chapters II, III, IV deal with these authors praising them highly.

[12] *Ibid.*, p. 99, Chapter XV is devoted to Dickens.

[13] *Ibid.*, Chapter XX.

[14] *Ibid.*, p. 173, Chapter XXIV.

[15] *Ibid.*, p. 187, Chapter XXVI.

[16] *Ibid.*, pp. 186 f., Chapter XXVI.

and realistic elements—Howells, unfortunately, knew only Scott of these authors and somewhat inconsistently cared little for him[17]— James had looked askance at romanticism generally as not quite the thing for a young man who wished to make his fiction achieve a worthier purpose than that of mere entertainment. It was all right, perhaps, to amuse and beguile a reader temporarily, but realism, until now that Howells had begun to praise its opposite, had seemed so much more worthwhile. But was it? He began tentatively to wonder. Should a story please or instruct? He returned to the questions raised in his first reviews. The ideal would be, of course, for it to do both. Realism really could and should be handled so that it would please quite as much as romanticism. But how? He thought again of the distinction Howells had drawn between George Eliot and Hawthorne; in Howells's opinion the American writer was greater than the English because of a "more artistic handling" of the same problem. Was not the clue here? Artistry? That, James seems to have suddenly realized was the important thing. The novelist might be related to the philosopher or the historian, but he must *be*, as the painter or the sculptor or the poet was, an artist. He must pay attention to the handling of his themes—realistically or romantically, did it matter which, if the end achieved was artistic? He must strive for form and finish, perfection and beauty even more in a realistic story than in a romantic, since the latter possessed in itself what the other must abjure—imagination and atmosphere—to share the burden laid upon artistry of form.

James looked at his stories, those "concoctions" of which until now he had been so proud,[18] and saw at a glance how he had overlooked all the really important things. He had been careful of his diction, careful of his details, of all the little things, but as wholes, his stories were inartistic; plot had been made by the addition of elements and then progression had been sacrificed to analysis; strangely, both compactness of form and roundness of contour were lacking. The desire to be thorough as he proceeded had caused him to lose sight of the whole.

In an effort to correct his faults and learn the *art* of story-telling, James seems to have begun feverishly to experiment. Since little is revealed in the few reviews James wrote of novels, about the state of his mind at this time, it is necessary to turn to the stories them-

[17] *Ibid.*, Chapter VII.
[18] *Notes of a Son and Brother*, p. 436.

selves, six published during the first half of 1868 and two the following year after he had sailed for Europe, to see how James struggled
with his problem. Through it all, Howells advised and encouraged,
and it must be noted that three of the four stories which he accepted
for the *Atlantic* were romantic in tenor while those published in the
Galaxy were realistic. Howells, then, must have had no small part
to play in the entrance of romantic elements into James's work. Very
likely, indeed, he had suggested to James that it was quite as desirable to be an American Hawthorne as an American Balzac, for after
the publication of the last and best of the romantic stories Howells
wrote to James: " . . . when you've a fame as great as Hawthorne's,
you won't forget who was the first, warmest and truest of your admirers, will you?"[19]

3. *The Experimenter in Artistry*[20]

The first of the stories of 1868, *The Story of a Masterpiece*,[21] carries
on the realistic, analytic vein of the former ones, but James tried for
greater artistry in several ways, as we shall presently see, succeeding
in one, failing in others.

The story deals with the development and growth of jealousy in a
wealthy widower, Lennox, who learns that the second object of his
affections has known an artist whom he hires to paint her portrait,
before, and, it would appear, somewhat intimately. He tries to
overcome his suspicions and fears, but they mount gradually higher,
especially when the finished portrait ironically reveals to him a certain lightness of character in the maiden. "Marian's person was lightness—her charm was lightness; could it be that her soul was levity
too?"[22] He is gentleman enough, according to the code of 1868, not
to break the engagement, but the night before the ceremony he
relieves his feelings by destroying the picture. The ending is the
most effective part of the story. It reveals graphically the pent up
jealousy of Baxter. In one respect, James made his story artistic.

The story, however, as a whole does not proceed as directly as

[19] *Life and Letters of Wm. Dean Howells*, I, 144.
[20] Since there is no evidence as to the order of composition of the stories published in 1868 except the uncertain one of the order of their appearance in print, I
have followed this. Later research, if it has recourse to any notebooks of James,
may show that the two orders were not in agreement, but such a discovery should
not affect materially the interpretation.
[21] Appeared in *Galaxy*, Jan.–Feb., 1868.
[22] *Galaxy*, Feb., 1868, p. 135.

this synopsis would indicate. Up to this time James had proceeded from the present to the future in his tales; nothing connected with the action had happened prior to the beginning of the story. In *The Story of a Masterpiece*, however, the affair of Baxter and Marian had happened. It was, James felt, really part of the story since it was the cause of Lennox's jealousy and explained the character Baxter brought out in the picture. Instead of beginning with it, James wisely, in an attempt at compactness and unity of point of view, began much later, at the time when the widower has just honored the maid with his proposal and been accepted, and he obviously intended to keep the story that of the widower. However, he interrupted the story of Lennox in the middle, quite abandoned it for a while, and inserted several pages dealing with the previous affair of Baxter and Marian where a few hints skillfully managed would have been sufficient to enable an interested reader to reconstruct it for himself. Thus James defeated his purpose in several ways: he failed to keep Lennox as a central figure; he failed to secure compactness; he failed to hold the interest of the reader. As a whole then *The Story of a Masterpiece* is inartistic and belongs to the explanatory type of fiction which James had been writing up to this time.

The second of the stories published in 1868, *The Romance of Certain Old Clothes*,[23] is not analytic. James retained the theme of jealousy, but he treated it pictorially, showing throughout instead of just at the end, the *effect* of jealousy upon an individual. The story thus is the result of analysis, possibly of the reflection which went into *The Story of a Masterpiece*, but analysis itself James kept in the background.

The Romance of Certain Old Clothes opens with a brief, compact account of the setting, the characters, the preliminary action, and the situation: mid-eighteenth century, a widow with two marriageable daughters, Viola and Perdita, and a son, Bernard, who has studied in England and now returns to America, bringing with him an English friend, Lloyd. The girls bargain for Lloyd's attention, and he soon fixes it upon Perdita. The pictures now begin, a series of vivid and impressive scenes: Viola discovering the ring on Perdita's finger; Viola bitter and scornful while the women work upon the trousseau; Perdita finding Viola after the ceremony arrayed in the wedding gown which she has just removed; Perdita extracting a

[23] Appeared in *Atlantic Monthly*, Feb., 1868.

pledge from her husband, as she is dying after the birth of her daughter, that he will keep the clothes under lock and key for the infant to have when grown; Viola mothering Perdita's child in an attempt to impress Lloyd and succeeding; Viola seeking the key to the forbidden chest of clothes; and finally Viola found before the chest in the attic: "Her lips were parted in entreaty, in dismay, in agony; and on her bloodless brow and cheeks there glowed the marks of ten hideous wounds from two vengeful ghostly hands."[24]

These pictures, it should be apparent from the quotation if not from the rapid summary, are not photographs in neutral tones such as one expects after the previous stories of James, but are highly colored, impressionistic paintings, and the story is not realistic but romantic. If the talks of James and Howells are recalled, the reason is at once apparent. Howells had acclaimed romanticism; he had praised Hawthorne. James then turned to supply his editor-friend with a story as much as possible like Hawthorne's without being a direct imitation. He took his own theme, but he went back to the past, using his imagination to help him conjure up scenes and setting. This kept him from copying what he saw around him. He used a symbol—the wedding clothes—which he brought in repeatedly. This tied the parts together and allowed him to shift the point of view from Viola to Perdita and back again. He resorted to the impossible, the ghostly, to suggest figuratively and emphatically the way in which jealousy, if uncurbed, resulted in destruction—not of just a portrait—but of self. This made the meaning vivid without seeming too obviously to point a moral. And, in order definitely to debar analysis, he did the whole thing in terms of picture—this probably as much his own idea, deriving from his interest in the description of scene, as Hawthorne's. If the result seems extravagant in places, if the pictures are sometimes gaudy and garish, it must be remembered that this was the first time that James had tried romanticism and that it was natural for him in his desire to make the most of his materials, to go to extremes. The story as a whole is really not only effective but artistic, for the scenes move panoramically to the final one, each picture increasing the tone in much the same ominous manner as a heavy storm gathers and develops.

Howells read it, approved, called it "admirable" to Norton[25] and probably to James, and accepted it for publication. He had

[24] *Ibid.*, p. 220.
[25] *Life and Letters*, I, 117.

been nearly as disappointed as James at the cold reception given *Poor Richard*,[26] but he had hopes that this story, so different, would prove more acceptable to the readers of the *Atlantic*, and he urged James to do more like it.

But James's intention was not to keep on following the example of Hawthorne, and he turned back again to experiment variously in three realistic stories.

The first of these three, *A Most Extraordinary Case*,[27] retains the theme of jealousy—indeed all three retain it—but again James erred on the side of too much analysis. A wealthy widow, philanthropically inclined, discovers her dead husband's nephew in ill health from wounds received in the Civil War—"tone of the moment" attempted. She takes him to her home where her niece who has refused six men as proof of her charms, lives with her. She calls in a doctor. Both doctor and ex-soldier become suitors unknown to each other though they discuss and analyze the maiden's charms, and her short-comings as well, in lengthy conversations. The doctor wins the fair one and the colonel pines away and dies even though the widow is waiting to take him to Europe. James was too interested in analyzing and characterizing his people whom he did not care for but rather scorned; he was too anxious to say something clever or enigmatic about each, and quite forgot plot. The story makes all the more apparent James's need to get artistry of form.

In the next story, *A Problem*,[28] he more definitely tried for this. He conceived of the device of some fortunes told at the beginning of the story and then fulfilled to give him a framework and to keep him from overdoing analysis. The effect of a fortune upon an individual would allow him to bring in analysis, but the interest would be kept by the thought of whether or not the fortune was going to come true. David and Emma are on their honeymoon when an Indian tells them that they are to have a little girl who will die, and that they will both marry twice. The child comes, and Emma begins to worry not over its health but over the last part of the prophecy and becomes violently jealous. James confined his analysis to this but treated it rather too quickly for credulity. He wished to hurry on to the com-

[26] *Ibid.* See p. 117 for Howells's disappointment, and the *Nation*, May 30, 1867, p. 432; June 27, 1867, p. 516; and Aug. 1, 1867, for criticism of "Poor Richard."

[27] Appeared in *Atlantic Monthly*, Apr., 1868.

[28] Appeared in *Galaxy*, June, 1868.

pletion of the prophecy. Emma leaves David, taking the child with her. And the child, poor little victim sacrificed unfeelingly by the author on the altar of artistry, conveniently dies so that Emma can send for David. He comes; they are reconciled, and to complete the prophecy and remove all cause of jealousy from Emma, they are married again. James handled the device of the fortunes mechanically. He invoked no atmosphere to hover over the story as he was to shortly in a romantic story built on the framework of a curse and its fulfillment. He used no sympathy. He brought in no pathos. And again artistry was not secured. In this story, strangely, more instead of less analysis was needed.

Still another realistic story, dealing again with jealousy—the theme was almost threadbare by this time, but James did not perceive it—failed when James abused the artistic device of anticipation and suggestion of the outcome. *Osborne's Revenge*[29] begins with the suicide of Graham. His friend, Osborne, thinks it is because a certain young lady has jilted him and vows revenge. He seeks out the maiden, is somewhat disturbed to find her charming, and finds his hatred quickly and uncontrollably turning to love. She, however, it develops after some pages during which the action is practically at a standstill, has long been engaged to another man, has never cared for Graham, and cares not a whit for the arrogant Osborne. The end is divorced from the beginning. No revenge has been secured, if, indeed, any should have been, but the reader has been led to expect it and feels almost as tricked as the hero when nothing comes of his intention. In addition to this defect which is contrary to James's usual straightforward manner, analysis has clogged but has not made probable the story.

James's great trouble was, it will be realized, that he did not know and could not seem to learn how to reconcile artistry and analysis. He had been trying desperately in these last three stories and they are inferior to anything he had done up to this point. *The Romance of Certain Old Clothes*, just preceding, shines forth a vivid jewel, even though an imitation one, among pebbles. Unreal, imagined, it is yet far better than what he had tried to do by means of his intellect. The moral, then, was easy to grasp. Use your imagination. Write stories where you will *have* to use it. Turn romanticist again if necessary. Perfect your art, no matter how. The end will justify the means.

[29] Appeared in *Galaxy*, July, 1868.

Howells had reminded him of Hawthorne, but James now re-called another romanticist who might help him even more than the American writer—George Sand. She was, in fact, the very author who could most help him, for she both imagined and analyzed, and wrote artistic stories, and she already had helped him in the problem of passion. Probably he turned to reconsider her works, for in July a story which bears many marks of her influence was published, and the next month a review, called forth by *Mademoiselle Merquem* and surveying the whole field of her endeavor, appeared; then a year later another story testified to her influence. It is necessary to consider the review before the stories, though it may well have been written after the first one, for it gives a clew in what it emphasizes to the way in which George Sand really did influence James.

Never has a genius obtained a more complete and immediate mastery of its faculties. In the pages before us they seem to move not, as in common minds, at its express behest and injunction, but in harmony with its very instincts, and simultaneously with the art of inspiration.[30]

James's own difficulties are apparent here—his faculties would not move of their own accord, nor would they even obey him. He ad-mired and envied what George Sand had immediately and consist-ently done. He continued in his review to dwell upon her great ability which was so little his:

This perfect unity of the writer's intellectual character, the constant equilibrium of the powers reigning within its precinct, the confidence with which the imagination appeals to the faculty of utterance, and the radiant splendor which the latter reflects so gratefully from the imagination—these things, more than any great excellence of form in particular works, con-stitute the author's real claim to imagination and gratitude. . . . . The narrative gushes along copious and translucent as a deep and crystalline stream, rolling pebbles and boulders and reflecting all the convex vault of nature.[31]

George Sand's narrative gushed along. Though she analyzed love and motives of action, the analysis was always as in *Le Dernier Amour*, that "last word of narrative art," a *part* of the narrative. It was natural to it, belonged to it, and did not halt the action. She was far greater than Dickens or Thackeray.

The great difference between the author of "Consuelo" and "Made-moiselle Merquem" and the authors (let us say) of "The Newcomes" and

[30] *Nation*, July 16, 1868, p. 52.
[31] *Ibid.*

of "David Copperfield," is, that whereas the latter writers express in a satisfactory manner certain facts, certain ideas of a peculiar and limited order, Madame Sand expresses with equal facility and equal grace ideas and facts the most various and the most general. . . . . You do not feel that she looks in the world in any degree as a specialist. She handles men and women, the rich and the poor, the peasant and the noble, the passionate and the joyous, with equal sympathy and power.[32]

She was not a specialist in her attitude toward life, though she was in another respect. She dealt only with the passion of love, but she treated it thoroughly.

Madame Sand is said to have celebrated but a single passion—the passion of love. This is in a great measure true; but in depicting it she has incidentally portrayed so many others that she may be said to have pretty thoroughly explored the human soul.[33]

James suddenly became so enthusiastic that he thrust George Sand upon the pinnacle which Balzac had formerly held alone in his estimation. The two authors were different, one a romancer, the other a historian, but she was as great in her way as he was in his.

Balzac, we may say, if the distinction is not too technical, is a novelist, and George Sand a romancer. There is no reason why they should not subsist in harmony. A large portion of the works of both will eventually be swept into oblivion, but several of the best productions of each will, we imagine, survive for the delight of mankind. Let us softly add the expression of our belief that for Balzac, booked as he is for immortality or thereabouts, this is a very happy circumstance. You may read "Consuelo" and "Mauprat" and not be ashamed to raise your eyes from the book to the awful face of nature. But when you have been reading "Le Père Goriot" or "Un Ménage de Garçon," you emphatically need to graduate your return to life. Who at such a moment better than George Sand can beguile the remorseful journey, and with "Consuelo" and "Mauprat," or even with "L'Homme de Neige" and "Mademoiselle Merquem" reconcile you to your mortal lot?[34]

Hence it was no disparagement to write romantic tales. Scott, Mérimée, Hawthorne, Gautier, George Sand—there were as many big names on this side of the fence as on the other, if one stopped to count them, and they were quite as necessary, they filled as important a place. And Howells really preferred romance. He need have

[32] *Ibid.*
[33] *Ibid.*, p. 53.
[34] *Ibid.*

no hesitation then, in writing romantic stories. James felt, indeed, no compunction, but a glee and a freedom which are happily reflected in the tales when he turned to try again what he could do in an imaginative way.

Two stories, the first, *De Grey*, published in July, 1868, and the second, *Gabrielle de Bergerac*, not published till a year later, but probably written in the fall of 1868, are the result.[35] Both show decidedly the influence of George Sand. It is even more evident in these romantic tales than it was in the realistic stories considered in the last chapter, *My Friend Bingham* and *Poor Richard*, where the French writer had influenced James's idea of morality. George Sand was to influence not only the treatment of passion, but the entire story, —conception, material, atmosphere, and execution.

James located *De Grey*[36] in America, year uncertain though probably mid-nineteenth century. He called its characters Americans. Otherwise the entire story with its framework of a curse of death upon the first loves of the De Grey males because a remote crusading ancestor with the plague had disregarded a curse and married; with its Father Herbert, religious parasite in the household of the De Greys; with its doting mother and her young companion and confidante; with its miniatures, its passion, its attitude toward young men who must go out and let the world educate them while young women are guarded at home; with the death of its hero by being thrown from his horse—as George Sand's father had been thrown from his—and the resulting madness of its heroine, is decidedly French. It has throughout an old world atmosphere as though James, after steeping himself upon George Sand, had continued to sit at his desk and pour out his improvisation before he pulled himself from the spell. The story gushes along; it moves by itself and not at the command of the author; it is not hampered by any prejudice either for or against his characters on the part of the author; it deals with love and makes of it an overwhelming passion, and though its result is tragic, it does not overcome the reader for it is not reality, but romance. The story thus does the very things for which James praised George Sand in the review. In addition, the story has form; the curse provides it, but James's imagination and not his intellect, as in *The Problem*, presided at the task and supplied atmosphere.

[35] *Life and Letters*, I, 137. A letter of Howells, dated Nov. 15, 1868, undoubtedly refers to "Gabrielle de Bergerac."
[36] Appeared in *Atlantic Monthly*, July, 1868.

Even when James turned to analyze his characters and their state of mind as they feel themselves caught by the curse, atmosphere played over the analysis and kept him from being baldly psychological. And this state of mind, in turn, is part of the action; the victims challenge the curse and determine to thwart it if possible so that the interest of the reader is centered where it should be, upon whether their will power or the power of the curse is going to prove the stronger. The action gathers momentum; heightens to the climax:

She was to find, then, after her long passion, that the curse was absolute, inevitable, eternal. It could be shifted, but not eluded; in spite of the utmost striving of human activity, it insatiably claimed its victim. . . . . Deluded fool that she was, for a day, for an hour, to have concealed her sorrow from her lover! . . . . What neither might endure alone, they might have surely endured together. But she blindly, senselessly, remorselessly drained the life from his being. As she bloomed and prospered, he drooped and languished. While she was living for him, he was dying of her.[37]

It ends in a vivid and ghastly picture—the young man found dying at the foot of a tree after his horse has thrown him, and the young girl somewhat melodramatically lapsing into madness. If its tone is a trifle shrill at times, if its romance is a bit too wild and improbable, especially in its American setting, the reader must forgive the earnest youth, for it was quite as much his tendency to overdo here as it was in the analytic stories. He was so very earnest in his endeavor that he went too far, but here, at least, he achieved a certain degree of artistry.

In the next romantic story, *Gabrielle de Bergerac*,[38] however, James did not go too far. Glamour loses its high color and becomes charm, delicate but pervading, and makes this story the most delightful of those of the early period. The impossible gives way to the possible though not perhaps to the probable, and the story, though a romance, is not unreal. In fact, it seems quite real, laid as it is in France with its characters of the lower nobility of the time of the Revolution, and cast in the narrative framework where a descendant of Gabrielle's tells her story to a man who has become interested in her picture.

[37] *Ibid.*, p. 77. This same situation, though without a curse as a cause and less violent in its effect, James used later in *The Sacred Fount*, 1901, treating it then psychologically.

[38] Appeared in *Atlantic Monthly*, July–Sept., 1869.

The narrator, now advanced in years, had been born in 1789, the son of a poor baron who lived in the provinces on an estate which was rapidly falling to pieces because of the family poverty. He describes in detail the setting and the family life—his father, taciturn and proud; his mother, sickly, unhappy, longing for the gay life of the world which was denied her; M. de Treuil, a young cavalier, who came frequently from that world to amuse her with its anecdotes; Gabrielle, the sister of the baron, a young girl born for the happy things of life but with no dowry; himself, then in the impressive age when a child sees and takes in everything though it is often not till later that he comes to understand; and his tutor, M. Coquelin, a poor young man who suddenly arrived from nowhere and shortly was to become quite unintentionally the disturbing force in the situation. The Baron wished Gabrielle to marry M. de Treuil who sincerely cared for her and wished to marry her despite her lack of dowry, since he was expecting to inherit money at the death of a relative. Because there seemed to be no choice for a girl in her position, she resignedly promised to marry him when he should inherit the money. Then in that sudden, unaccountable way in which love sometimes operates, she found herself, during the three months while M. de Treuil was away dutifully waiting at the bedside of his benefactor for him to die, falling in love with Coquelin. The poor tutor had been in love with her from the beginning but with no intention of making known his love, but the two young people were constantly thrown together, and several occasions, chief among them the excursion of Gabrielle, Coquelin, and the child, to an old castle at Fossy where Gabrielle first realized the full import of her feeling for Coquelin while he hung in danger for a moment as he tried to descend from a high tower, revealed to them the love which each had for the other. They discussed love at length, analyzing it and the hopeless nature of theirs, Coquelin refusing to urge Gabrielle to give herself to him when that would mean poverty for her, Gabrielle gradually but surely coming to feel that she could not marry M. de Treuil. Before they had decided what to do, M. de Treuil returned, rich, to claim his bride, and she refused him. A terrific scene followed, M. de Treuil heartbroken and the baron enraged at what had gone on without his realizing it and still more angry that Gabrielle should continue to refuse to marry his friend, who still cared for her and would overlook everything. Gabrielle, at length the way clear to her, fled from the castle to join Coquelin, and together they left the estate, only to die some years later on the scaffold as Girondists.

The story might well have been made a realistic one, but the atmosphere with which James clothed it, the setting in the past, dealing as it does with an order of life which is no more, the details employed in developing it, the flow of imagination and improvisation, make it a romance. The summer breeze blows through its pages. The summer sun makes its days, especially the expedition to Fossy, despite its danger, so perfect that one realizes it can but be a prelude to disaster, but to the anomaly of happy disaster where one suffers for love.

This country setting and all its attributes, however, were influenced by, and possibly directly borrowed from, George Sand—from her novels of country life and the passion which may develop there between young girls of noble birth and poor young men. The situation, with the omission of minor complicating elements, is the situation found in *Valentine*—one girl, two lovers, and the parents who wish to dominate. Gabrielle has the independence of spirit, the intensity of passion of a George Sand heroine, and she is portrayed in the same gentle, understanding way, though some of the minor characters, notably the baron and the baroness, are because of the slight irony with which James handled them, more nearly related to the characters of Balzac's novels. The tale has the open air spirit of George Sand's novels; it is not a story of the city or the drawing room; it is a story of the out of doors. The passion which developed there is of the same strong, imperative kind as the passion treated by George Sand. And James employed the method of the French writer in treating it; he did not analyze it himself but allowed his characters to do it for him, in long, thoughtful, yet emotional conversations as lovers are wont to ponder, so that character is revealed and artistry is not sacrificed to analysis but gained by this new way of treating it. Many of the minor details and incidents employed in the development—the contrast of Gabrielle with her friend Marie de Chalais, the incident of the dying peasant and Gabrielle consoling the family, the long walks in the country, the way in which the danger of death may make the full force of one's love for the first time apparent—all these have frequent counterparts in the novels of the French writer. They are the trade marks of her style. Thus the story is not exactly Henry James's. It is more nearly George Sand's.

Gabrielle de Bergerac, however, neglected by most critics of James or considered simply as a romantic tale and thus of no account in James's ultimate development, is yet of great account. It came at the end of James's first period. It was his first success. It indicates, together with the silence which followed it, both what James might have been and why he was not. If James had followed the advice of Howells who praised his romantic tales and this one especially as "the best thing" he had yet done; if he had succumbed to the realization that *Gabrielle de Bergerac* was indeed, the best and should be followed by more of the same sort, he would have become simply another spinner of romances, delightful, entertaining, but of no lasting value. He would have considered the problem of writing fiction solved. All one had to do, all *he* had to do at least, to write entertaining stories was to read the stories of other writers, absorb their spirit, their atmosphere, even their material, and then squeeze himself dry as one would a sponge, but the water which came out— he saw it if Howells did not—was slightly less clear than that which had been taken in and might in time, if one continued to read the same authors, and added nothing of one's own, become quite muddy.

And James had no intention of being an imitator. He wanted to be an innovator. He wanted to start fiction on a new track. He saw what it needed—a man who would portray life as it was, who would seek out its meaning, analyze it so that the reader might gain not only amusement but knowledge and perhaps help in combatting his own problems from reading how others met and solved theirs or did not meet or solve them. Fiction might have a worthier motive than that of mere entertainment. And it was fiction of this sort that he wished to write. Otherwise, he would seek his livelihood in other fields—criticism for instance. *Gabrielle de Bergerac* sickened him by its very success; it mocked him, and made him all the more doggedly obstinate in his purpose. Rather despairingly he tried once more a realistic story, *A Light Man*,[39] where he attempted once again to treat analysis artistically by using the form of a diary for it, but even that framework did not make the impossible character he had chosen for his hero, real or even plausible, and then he closed his portfolio, laid aside his pen, and decided, as he should have long before, to go out and observe life, to let the problems of fiction rest for a while, to allow the muddle which he now had in his brain to readjust and untangle itself.

[39] Appeared in *Galaxy*, July, 1869.

CHAPTER VII

THE ALTERNATIVE—A CRITIC

During 1867 and 1868 while James was industriously experimenting with the short story, he still continued to write reviews for the
Nation and *The North American Review*. It was quite as much his
business in life at this time to attempt to improve literature by
attacking the inferior or praising the good as it was to try to improve
it by example. However, the novelty had somewhat palled. It was
no longer as much fun to lash and cut, and in fact sometimes, when
one was asked to review mediocre works which one could neither
censure severely nor praise highly, it was quite boring. The reviewing
of novels, especially, which he had taken to with so much zest in the
first of his critical endeavor, now seems to have annoyed him, making
him wonder if perhaps all this reading of inferior works and thinking
of them might not be hampering his own creative endeavor. At
least, this must have been one of the reasons why but eight of the
twenty-seven reviews were upon fiction, while the others were
concerned with poetry, criticism, travel, history, journals, painting,
and even anthropology. James had, possibly, appealed to Godkin
and Norton to let him fulfill his obligations to them by reviewng
other books than novels, and they, interested in the ambitious youth,
were glad to humor him. On the other hand, it may have been they
who had taken the initiative and had suggested to James that he
extend his scope and see what he could do in other directions. The
earlier reviews dealing with Matthew Arnold and with Edmund
Scherer had been promising; James knew the business of the critic,
and they had every reason to believe that he could wield his pen effectively in the cause of literature of all kinds.[1] Possibly they discerned—as Howells had seen something else—that there was in
James a critic in the making. America needed good critics quite as
much as good novelists. Why, then, should not James be given
every chance, be encouraged in every way? And James was. Reviews, good or inferior, reviews which were occasionally embryo
critical articles and other times but hasty synopses of the books in

[1] In addition to these two reviews upon critics, there had been a review of
Whitman's *Leaves of Grass*, one of Swinburne's *Chastelard*, two upon Eugénie de
Guèrin, and one upon Epictetus to give them further confidence.

question with little or no real critical discernment apparent, were printed side by side. However, the good outweighed the poor and the confidence of the two editors was thus not misplaced.

The eight reviews dealing with fiction are naturally the ones which most interest the reader of James today. Most important of these are the four already considered in the two chapters preceding this from the standpoint of what they reveal as to James's own fictional attempts and his theories in general about fiction: the review on historical novels,[2] that of George Sand's *Mademoiselle Merquem*,[3] that of Feydeau's *La Comtesse de Chalis*,[4] and that of Feuillet's *Camors*.[5] Of these, the last two, confined almost wholly to the novels in question, are simply reviews, pointed and pertinent, however, and though adverse, quite fair to the situations of vice and immorality with which the books abound. On the other hand, the review on historical novels which quite forgot the inferior novels it professed to be treating and put forth the cause of historical novels in general, and the one called forth by the publication of *Mademoiselle Merquem*, which surveyed the whole field of George Sand's writings, are not to be called reviews but miniature critical articles. They reveal a young man who knew what he was talking about, who thought deeply and sincerely about the craft of fiction, who weighed and pondered and analyzed, who could draw fine distinctions, who saw not one side of a question but all sides, those he disliked as well as those he liked, and gave a fair, unbiased judgment.[6] Enthusiasm is there, but it is rational enthusiasm.

The four other reviews dealing with novels are again simply reviews not especially noteworthy for the ideas advanced nor as indications of critical ability, but nevertheless of some interest—in one case, because James is to be discovered modifying an early opinion; in the other three, because he maintains his former antagonistic stand against inferior American fiction.

Linda Tressel, appearing anonymously, was given to James to review,[7] and he immediately discerned that it was by Trollope, but in treating it his former aversion changed even to slight praise of the English writer:

[2] See Chapter VI.
[3] See Chapter VI.
[4] See Chapter V.
[5] See Chapter V.
[6] This will be apparent if the quotations given in Chapter VI are reread.
[7] Appeared in *Nation*, June 18, 1868.

The whole force of the story lies just where, after all, it should—*in the story*, in its movement, its action, and the fidelity with which it reflects the little patch of human life which the author unrolls, heaven-wise, above it. When you can add nothing to the story in the telling, you must rest your claim to the reader's gratitude on your taking away as little as possible.[8]

The change in attitude was due to no greater merit which this novel has over *The Belton Estate* or *Can you Forgive Her?* If anything, it is not quite as good. Perhaps, however, James's own difficulties in writing fiction, in getting the force of the story where it should be, were making him less exacting and more appreciative of the good qualities of others, even if slight. As a parting thrust, however, James could not refrain from speaking of Trollope's "universal mediocrity."

Mediocrity, at least, was better than downright dullness such as one met in Anne Moncrure Crane, the former Mrs. Seemuller, author of the *Emily Chester* atrocity,[9] who now essayed another and even worse book, *Opportunity*.[10] It was better than slushy sentimentality such as Mrs. Rebecca Harding Davis indulged in in her *Waiting for the Verdict*[11] and *Dallas Galbraith*.[12] James, in his reviews of these three books, revealed himself as bitterly adverse to and despondent over American writers and American readers who seemed to like dullness and dripping sentiment, as he was in his first reviews. But his alert, antagonistic attitude had changed to one of bored and disgusted impatience with the whole situation.

Closely connected with James's reviews upon fiction were his reviews of poetic works, six in all, one of them insignificant and strangely mild and evasive upon a group of inferior American poets,[13] three of poems by William Morris, *The Life and Death of Jason*[14] and *The Earthly Paradise*,[15] and two of George Eliot's *The Spanish Gipsy*,[16] these last five of greater interest. It is significant that James

[8] *Ibid.*, p. 494.
[9] See Chapter II.
[10] Reviewed in *Nation*, Nov. 21, 1867.
[11] Reviewed in *Nation*, Dec. 5, 1867.
[12] Reviewed in *Nation*, Oct. 22, 1868.
[13] Review entitled "Recent Volumes of Poems," *North American Review*, Apr., 1867.
[14] Appeared in *North American Review*, Oct., 1867.
[15] Two were written of this appearing: (a) *North American Review*, July, 1868, and (b) *Nation*, July 9, 1868.
[16] Two were written appearing: (a) *Nation*, July 2, 1868, (b) *North American Review*, Oct., 1868.

concerned himself largely with matters of plot, dramatic effects, characterization, applying to the poems the standards he had evolved for stories and finding them on the whole satisfactory. Such purely poetic qualities as meter, verse, melody of expression, he spoke of but briefly. He did, however, make much of imagination. The quality of imagination which a writer possessed was the line of demarcation between novelist and poet. Poetry demanded a much greater degree of imagination. William Morris possessed this quality in abundance and was accordingly a great poet. James called *Jason* a "work of consummate art and genuine beauty"[17] and praised its successor no less highly. George Eliot, on the other hand, although she was a good poet, was not a great one. She lacked imagination. Her powers were intellectual, well suited to the writing of novels—James seemed to appreciate her genius as a novelist even more now than two years previously—but not to the production of poetry. *The Spanish Gipsy* was good, but "reflection, not imagination, had presided at the work,"[18] he said in his first review, and in his second: "Its great fault is simply that it is not a genuine poem. It lacks the hurrying quickness, the palpitating warmth, the bursting melody of such a creation. A genuine poem is a tree that breaks into blossom and shakes in the wind."[19] It was a "romance written by one who is emphatically a thinker."[20] Poetry, to James was something that tugs at its earthly bonds or breaks with them altogether and soars in the skies, while prose fiction was of a pedestrian nature, content to dwell among men. The second review of *The Spanish Gipsy* is, in reality, a critical article of greater length and thoroughness than the others, and appeared under the signature of James in the *North American Review*. It makes a fitting climax to James's critical ability at this time. Structurally it is far ahead of the more loosely-hung, unorganized, and ill-proportioned article of two years before.[21]

The other reviews of James are to be grouped as miscellaneous, though some are anticipations of later developments. Chief among these are two upon travel—the first upon Howells's *Italian Journeys*,[22] and the second upon Taine's *Italy*.[23] It was perhaps inevitable that

---

[17] *North American Review*, Oct., 1867, p. 691.
[18] *Nation*, July 2, 1868, p. 14.
[19] *North American Review*, Oct., 1868, p. 634.
[20] *Ibid.*, p. 635.
[21] See Chapter V.
[22] Appeared in *North American Review*, Jan., 1868.
[23] Appeared in *Nation*, May 7, 1868.

James should praise his friend's book exuberantly. He lauded Howells's keenness of observation and the vivacity of his sympathies; he called him variously a "man of the world," "a sentimental traveller," "a gentle moralist," "a humorist," and "a poet," and highest praise of all, since it was accorded to Howells, he named him the equal of Hawthorne as a descriptive writer. The praise given to Taine's *Italy* was more rational. James was almost wholly concerned with the powerful style of the French writer, his vigor of expression, and lamented with subtle yet gentle irony that it should not have been employed in the service of more worthy ideas.

The Journals of Maurice de Guèrin,[24] of Mme. Swetchine,[25] and *The Inner Life of Father Lacordaire*,[26] a biography, interested James as a student of human nature because of the people revealed in them, and his reviews of these books are to be noted because of this fact. They show once more that James's great interest was in people, and in the inner life and thought of individuals more than in the outer.

A review of Froude's *Short Studies of Great Subjects*[27] is sharply antagonistic. The infantile style and sentimental manner of thought of the author were distasteful to James. A review dealing with a collection of Sainte-Beuve's Portraits[28] is also adverse, not because of the French writer, however, but because the collector confined herself to the poorest of the portraits, resurrecting some that had been better forgotten. James fortunately was almost wholly concerned with this and treated Sainte-Beuve himself briefly and inadequately, confessing to his difficulty in judging him. "He contains a little of so many things in a degree that sadly puzzles the critic's mind and leads him to forswear the attempt to classify and label him. He is a little of a poet, a little of a moralist, a little of a historian, a little of a philosopher, a little of a romancer."[29]

A few other less noteworthy reviews on books of art, of science, and so on make up the twenty-seven, which reveal as a whole that James was growing tired of his task of criticism except when a great work stimulated him to exert himself. Then he could do something really worth while. Though he had taken the stand in his earliest reviews that a critic " is in the nature of his function *opposed* to the

[24] Reviewed in *Nation*, Mar. 7, 1867.
[25] Reviewed in *North American Review*, July, 1868.
[26] Reviewed in *Nation*, Jan. 16, 1868.
[27] Reviewed in *Nation*, Oct. 31, 1867.
[28] Reviewed in *Nation*, June 4, 1868.
[29] Reviewed in *Nation*, June 4, 1868, p. 455.

author,"[30] he was finding that he preferred to deal with writers whom he could praise, that he was far better when he could do that. His nature was a generous one, constituted to recognize the good rather than the bad. His best criticism was stimulated when he discerned merits and then set about carefully to consider how perhaps even those merits might have been made better. When there were no good points to be discerned, he attacked as formerly but with a somewhat less personal note, often preferring to evade real criticism of the book, giving in its place some remarks of a general nature. This attitude is to be noted in one of the last reviews of the period, that already mentioned of *Dallas Galbraith*, which, somewhat inadequate as a review, has a passage of much interest for the light it throws upon James's critical development.

The day of dogmatic criticism is over. . . . . The critic is simply a reader like all the others—a reader who prints his impressions. All he claims is, that they are honest; and when they are unfavorable, he esteems it quite as simple a matter that he should publish them as when they are the reverse. . . . . No writer pretends that he tells the whole truth; he knows that the whole truth is a synthesis of the great body of small partial truths. . . . . The critic reminds himself, then, that he must be before all things clear and emphatic. If he has properly mastered his profession, he will care only in a minor degree whether his relation to a particular work is one of praise or of censure. He will care chiefly whether he has detached from such a work any ideas or principles appreciable and available to the cultivated public judgment.[31]

This gives the course of James's own development as well as that of criticism in general. James had begun as a dogmatic critic. His "this will never do" had rung as a clarion note over American fiction. But American fiction had not heeded. It had not improved. The taste of its readers likewise had not been bettered. And James soon lost his youthful slash. He had then tried to print his impressions, striving that they be fair and honest. He was still doing this, for that was the business of the critic, and he could do it well when a poem by Morris or George Eliot, a novel by George Sand, stimulated him and he could extract from them worthwhile ideas. But when the book to be reviewed had nothing in it of good, when he could detach from it no "ideas and principles appreciable and available to the cultivated public judgment," he found it well nigh impossible to write

[30] See Chapter IV.
[31] *Nation*, Oct. 22, 1868, p. 330.

a worthwhile review. To be sure, he could always give a synopsis of the book, and this he often did, prefacing or affixing to it a few remarks of a critical or general nature. When he came to review books other than novels and the closely related genre, poetry, however, he had little of a general or critical nature to offer. The reviews accordingly were simply reviews, secondhand things, often without any real indication of whether James was for or against the book, whether he thought it should be read by the public or disregarded. It is more than ever evident in the reviews that though James could *say* something on any subject, he could *think* only upon one. His mind was the mind of the novelist.

And the novelist, we noted in the preceding chapter, was not getting along very well. He was finding that all the ideas which he had gathered and carefully formulated upon fiction were often difficult to apply, that it was one thing to *think* and another to *do*. Thus a certain impatience, a disappointment had come over him, and the young man who had started out so enthusiastically four years before was now quite baffled and perplexed. Four years had dutifully been given over to apprenticeship to his craft, but he was not even ready to write the novel that he so wished to. He was wearied with the spasm of his endeavor with the various kinds of the short story, and wondered whether he was ever going to be able to write good realistic ones or should have to content himself by following others in the romantic story. Looking at his own case, James became dogmatic and said to himself, "This will never do." He must bestir himself. If he could not solve his problem in the study, he must leave it for a while, get out into the world and live, and see if life would not solve it for him. He had been trying to force nature. Let nature hereafter take its course.

During the last year or so James had been looking with somewhat envious eyes every time a letter arrived from William who was, after his South American expedition with Agassiz, studying medicine and, incidentally, life in Europe. William often remarked of new novels to be had in Europe hot from the press, of the theatre, of art galleries, of the opportunity to observe life in an interesting aspect— the contrast of two civilizations, a new and an old.[32] William, in addition, wished generously that Henry might also have these ad-

[32] *Letters of William James*, Boston, 1920, Vol. I. See Section V covering years in Germany, his letters to his family, and also *Notes of a Son and Brother*, pp. 447–52, where one of William's letters is reprinted.

vantages. Then in November 1868 William came home, talking about Europe still more enthusiastically. It was then that the longing crept into the heart of Henry, that he decided to let the pen which he had recently flung down, remain where it was until he should have something to write about. His parents, perceiving his unrest, sensitive as always to the impulses and desires of their sons, determined that a way should be made so that Henry, as well as William, should have all the opportunities possible to become great. If Europe perchance had any to offer, then Europe must be visited. After a winter of productive inactivity but of much thought and conference with the family circle, Henry James set sail for Europe, landing the first of March, 1869, in Liverpool.

INTERCHAPTER B
THE BACKGROUND, 1869–1875

In contrast to the localized New England setting of the first four years of Henry James's productive activity, the next six years offered a varied, rapidly changing background. The period was his Wanderjahre. He went forth into the world to look, to listen, and to learn.

James, much later in the fragment of *The Middle Years*,[1] tried to recapture for us and for himself glowingly the sensations and experiences of the renewed contact with England. He saw the hotel at Liverpool with its "truth to type of the waiter, truth to history, to literature, to poetry, to Dickens, to Thackeray, positively to Smollett and Hogarth,"[2] and his rooms at No. 7 Half-Moon Street, London, and Mr. Lazarus Fox, his incomparable advice-giving landlord, and the breakfast parties—"association at a jump with the ghosts of Byron and Sheridan and Moore and Lockhart and Rogers and tutti quanti—"[3] and the National Gallery, where he had gazed and admired by the side of Swinburne, in the rosy glamour of reminiscence. Then there had been in April, '69, a Sunday call upon George Eliot, when he had been escorted there "by one of the kind door-opening Norton ladies."[4] And what a time it had been to call, when so great a celebrity was "quite humanly and familiarly agitated"[5] as one of her stepsons was writhing in excruciating pain and he, Henry James, had been of use on this very first encounter, posting off for Mr. Paget, the surgeon. Then all of this carried him rapidly in his book to other visits during the seventies, and there is a jumble of reminiscences of meetings with Tennyson, with Lowell, and with Mrs. Greville, herself, apparently, of as much help to him socially as the Nortons. It is all very interesting. But we must remember that *The Middle Years* was dictated during the autumn of 1914, was never completed, nor revised by James himself, and turn to the few letters edited by Percy Lubbock[6] and the Travel

---

[1] Dictated 1914, edited by Percy Lubbock, 1917; published by Charles Scribner's Sons.

[2] *Ibid.*, p. 6.

[3] *Ibid.*, p. 33.

[4] *Ibid.*, p. 61.

[5] *Ibid.*, p. 65.

[6] *Letters of Henry James*, Vols. I, II, Scribner's, New York, 1920.

Sketches[7] written by James himself for the facts in their order and the right atmosphere of 1868 to 1875. Then it appears that it was not so much England which furnished James with inspiration as Italy. With his successive returns to that country, each more important, more thrilling than the previous, with the influence of Italy upon his stories in setting and subject and atmosphere, this period might well be called his Italian one.

James landed at Liverpool the first of March, 1869. He then hurried to London and on the tenth wrote to his sister:

I really feel as if I had lived—I don't say a lifetime—but a year in this murky metropolis. . . . . Nevertheless, I may say that up to this time I have been crushed under a sense of the mere magnitude of London— its inconceivable immensity—in such a way as to paralyze my mind for any appreciation of details. This is gradually subsiding, but what does it leave behind it? An extraordinary intellectual depression, as I may say, and an indefinable flatness of mind. The place sits on you, broods on you, stamps on you, with the feet of its myriad bipeds and quadrupeds. In fine, it is anything but a cheerful or a charming city. Yet it is a very splendid one.[8]

Then he broke off to give an account of the first week, a dinner with Leslie Stephen and a trip to the Zoo, dinners with the Nortons, where he met one of Dickens's daughters, and a lecture by Ruskin, and most thrilling of all, a visit to Morris's home and shop with its mysterious pre-Raphaelite atmosphere.

And the second letter which is preserved for us, dated March 26, tells us more of the effect of England upon the sensitive youth and reveals to us far more truly than the enthusiasm of *The Middle Years* how he was "taking" it.

You have perhaps fancied that I have been rather stingy-minded towards this wondrous England, and that I was [not] taking things in quite the magnanimous intellectual manner that befits a youth of my birth and reading. The truth is that the face of things here throws a sensitive American back on himself—back on his prejudices and national passions, and benumbs for a while the faculty of appreciation and the sense of justice. But with time, if he is worth a copper, the characteristic beauty of the land dawns upon him . . . . and he feels he would fain plant his restless feet

[7] See Phillips's *Bibliography* for a complete list. Some of the American sketches were reprinted in *Portraits of Places*, Osgood, 1883, the European in *Transatlantic Sketches*, Osgood, 1875.

[8] *Letters*, I, 15.

into the rich old soil and absorb the burden of the misty air. If I were in anything like working order now, I should be very sorry to leave England.[9]

This certainly sounds like a loyal American somewhat dazed rather than excited and enthusiastic about England.

He did not hurry to leave, but according to Lubbock went to Malvern for three weeks for the cure,[10] and followed this with a tour of Oxford, Cambridge, and some of the Cathedral towns. Then he returned to London for a few weeks before going to Switzerland for the summer with the Nortons.

Around the first of September came the long-awaited descent into Italy, where we may imagine James's sentiments were similar to those of the young men whose pilgrimages he was shortly to record in two stories.[11] To him, Italy was the long dreamed of, the land of romance and love and passion, of art and culture and spiritual meanings. He seems, however, judging from the first letter which Lubbock prints, to have been most interested on this first trip in studying life, the people he met, especially his fellow countrymen whose historian he hoped some day to be. But he found them disappointing when transplanted to a European setting. A letter from Florence, dated October 13, 1869, reveals his conclusions:

A set of people less framed to provoke national self-complacency than the latter it would be hard to imagine. There is but one word to use in regard to them—vulgar, vulgar, vulgar. Their ignorance—their stingy, defiant, grudging attitude towards everything European—their perpetual reference of all things to some American standard or precedent which exists only in their own unscrupulous windbags—and then our unhappy poverty of voice, of speech, and of physiognomy—these things glare at you hideously. On the other hand, we seem a people of *character*, we seem to have energy, capacity and intellectual stuff in ample measure. What I have pointed at as our vices are the elements of modern man with *culture* quite left out. It's the absolute and incredible lack of *culture* that strikes you in common travelling Americans. The pleasantness of the English, on the other side, comes in a great measure from the fact of their each having been dipped into the crucible, which gives them a sort of coating of comely varnish and colour. They have been smoothed and polished by mutual social attrition. They have manners and a language. We lack both, but particularly the latter.[12]

[9] *Ibid.*, p. 19.
[10] Introduction to *Letters*, I, 11.
[11] See Chapter VIII.
[12] *Letters*, I, 22.

The international situation was beginning to impress itself upon him.

A week later he was in Rome! Analysis, criticism were forgotten as he gave himself up to the spell of the wonderful city.

From midday to dusk I have been roaming the streets. Que vous en dirai-je? At last—for the first time—I live! It beats everything: it leaves the Rome of your fancy—your education—nowhere. It makes Venice—Florence—Oxford—London—seem like little cities of pasteboard. I went reeling and moaning thro' the streets, in a fever of enjoyment. In the course of four or five hours I traversed almost the whole of Rome and got a glimpse of everything, the Forum, the Coliseum (Stupendissimo!) the Pantheon, the Capitol, St. Peter's, the Column of Trajan, the Castle of St. Angelo—all the Piazzas and ruins and monuments. The effect is something indescribable. For the first time I know what the picturesque is.[13]

How different this is from the slow reaction to England! James spent over a month in Rome, repeating, we may imagine, intensifying the sensations of this one day. Then he visited Naples for two weeks and proceeded leisurely to Paris and then to London. England looked less attractive, especially the people whom he observed on his return to Malvern in March.

Never from a single Englishman of them all have I heard the first word of appreciation and enjoyment of the things here that I find delightful. . . . . As for the women, I give 'em up in advance.[14]

But the country scenery, the England of

. . . . elm-scattered meadows and sheep-cropped commons and the ivy-smothered dwellings of small gentility, and high-gabled, heavy-timbered, broken-plastered farmhouses, and stiles leading to delicious meadow footpaths and lodge-gates leading to far off manors—with all these things suggestive of the opening chapters of half-remembered novels, devoured in infancy, ...[15]

was a different matter. It was the memory of that and of wonderful, intensely glowing Italy which he carried with him on his return to America in April, 1870.

Except for the letters—too few alas! have been salvaged—and possibly a lost notebook, this first trip to Europe probably meant to James a vacation for his pen. He had crossed the Atlantic to absorb all that he could of the older world and somewhere in the course of

[13] *Ibid.*, p. 24–25.
[14] *Ibid.*, p. 26.
[15] *Ibid.*, p. 28.

the trip he had rounded the corner of his youth. He tells us in the
last chapter of *Notes of a Son and Brother* that the death of Minny
Temple, early in 1870, had been felt by both him and William as the
end of their youth,[16] only to admit in the opening pages of *The
Middle Years* the impossibility of setting fairly a date for the opening
or closing of any of the volumes which make up the book of life.[17]
The student of James cannot help feeling that somewhere in the
course of this first European trip he became a man. Whether it was
the news of Minny Temple's death or, as is more likely, the European
experience which brought it about is another question not to be
definitely solved by the student any more than by James himself.
It is the result which is important, and this result is to be discerned
in his work. It is not that he began to take things *more* seriously; on
the contrary, he began to take them *less* seriously, but with no dim-
inution of interest. The change is not immediately apparent; it is
merely felt. His stories after the trip were written with less effort,
less striving. The taut tension of the early work relaxed. His few
critical notes and reviews became less shrill, more tolerant.

For two years, 1870–71, James settled down again in Cambridge,
renewing his acquaintance with Howells, enjoying the intellectual
gatherings of the place, and applying himself to creative endeavor.
Probably much was attempted or written only to be destroyed for
not a great deal was published. Each summer he took a trip, probably in quest of material—the first to Saratoga, Lake George, Burlington, and then to Newport, the second to Quebec and Niagara. As an
"occasional correspondent," he contributed reports of these jaunts to
the *Nation*. He could not refrain from judging America by Europe,
and found it lacking in tone and dignity at its resorts and watering
places. It is evident that he did not know just what to conclude
about his countrymen, and he was as hesitant in censure as in praise.
Newport, alone, a Newport often revisited where these other places
were seen for the first time, had tone, and its state of society was
somewhat near the European state. But he found it increasingly
difficult to get hold of material in America which seemed to him
worth while; nothing cried out to be expressed by a novelist who,
pen in hand, *waited* for something to call to him, and he concluded in
1871, writing to Norton of some of Howells's sketches, that America

[16] *Notes of a Son and Brother*, p. 515.
[17] *The Middle Years*, pp. 1 f.

yielded "its secrets only to a really grasping imagination,"[18] and he began to question whether he, any more than Howells, had one. "To write well and worthily of American things, one need even more than elsewhere to be a *master*. But unfortunately one is less! ....To write a series of good little tales I deem ample work for a lifetime."[19] This he wrote to Charles Norton, still in Europe. And he probably began to wonder if, had he stayed on in Europe, he could have settled down and have written there, more easily than in America. We do not know what Norton wrote in reply, but it is very likely that James's increasing restlessness in America, his smoldering desire to get back to Europe was fanned by the older American's convictions about the two so opposite civilizations. It was not the idea of James alone that Europe had something to offer which America did not. It was the general belief of the time, held preeminently by such men among James's acquaintances as Charles Eliot Norton, William Wetmore Story, James Russell Lowell, held even at that time, despite his Americanism, by William Dean Howells.[20] And it was both unfortunate and fortunate for James that the purse of his parents was open to him.

In the spring of 1872, James sailed for Europe once more with a purpose which was slightly more definite than the vague one of the trip before. For one thing, he was to write travel sketches for the *Nation* and also for the *Atlantic*. But to James himself probably that was quite incidental to the desire to get back, to see Italy again.[21] Because of the approach of summer, the visit to Italy was postponed till fall.

Meanwhile, James, accompanied by his sister and aunt, who had come to Europe with him, travelled leisurely through England and Switzerland. The Travel Sketches reveal that they visited Chester, Lichfield, North Devon, Wells, and Salisbury, with their main purpose in all these places "cathedral hunting,"[22] enjoying the "tone

---

[18] *Letters*, I, 30.

[19] *Ibid.*, p. 31.

[20] *Life and Letters of Howells*, I, 176 f, a letter written to James in 1873 speaks of Howells's longing for Italy: "At times the longing is almost intolerable with me."

[21] Lubbock unfortunately reprints but few of James's letters of this time but in his introduction he refers to one, quoting, " 'the wish—the absolute sense of need—to see Italy again' constantly increases." I, 12.

[22] *Transatlantic Sketches*, p. 34. (In every sketch James reveals his interest in cathedrals.)

of things,"[23] "morally and physically" a denser air than America's, and reminded continually of books and novels "perused in child-hood."[24]

Two months in Switzerland, however, was too long a sojourn for that country, and James wrote a sketch from there in August speaking of his "vague sense of having treated myself to an overdose of Switzerland."[25] The mountains did not attract him. He noted with interest, however, the cities of Switzerland, Geneva with its austere moral tone,[26] Berne with its gay color spots,[27] the villages with their picturesque fountains and streets, and the places made famous because of their connection with great men, but he was more than glad to board the train for Italy.

Italy! Immediately James felt refreshed. Half an hour in Turin and he had tasted every pleasure, renewed every impression of the former trip and thrilled again as intensely as before to the charm.[28] Then Milan with its cathedral, and from its roof the Lombard plain, with its "yellow, liquid, free-flowing light (as if on favored Italy the vessels of heaven were more widely opened)" was a relief after the "opaque mountains" of Switzerland.[29] The travellers spent a few days enjoying the libretto-like life at Como and a few more at Venice where "the mere use of one's eyes" was "happiness enough."[30] After a short stop in Verona, the travellers turned back into Germany for ten days.

James's adverse reaction to Germany was immediate and complete. He wrote home that the hasty and partial glimpse had been most satisfactory, clearing from his mind all uncertainty and convincing him that he could never hope "to become an unworthiest adoptive grandchild of the fatherland."[31] Germany was ugly, Munich a nightmare, Heidelberg a disappointment, and even Nuremberg not a joy forever.[32]

Soon James was in Paris alone for part of the winter of 1872 and '73. Lubbock tells us that he renewed there his acquaintance with

[23] *Ibid.*, p. 14.
[24] *Ibid.*, p. 10, 15, 21, 28, 43, etc.
[25] *Ibid.*, p. 56.
[26] *Ibid.*, pp. 58 f.
[27] *Ibid.*, pp. 67 f.
[28] *Ibid.*, p. 75.
[29] *Ibid.*, p. 81.
[30] *Ibid.*, p. 87.
[31] *Letters*, I, 33.
[32] *Transatlantic Sketches*, p. 95.

James Russell Lowell, "in afternoon walks with him between mornings of work and evenings at the Théâtre Français."[33] The one travel sketch from there deals wholly with the stage. It was, James found, a "copious source of instruction as to French ideas, manners, and philosophy,"[34] yet it was not wholly pleasing. Novel and drama alike betrayed "an incredibly superficial perception of the moral side of life,"[35] and satiated with this bad-tasting, foul-smelling intellectual food of the French theatre, James was glad, early in 1873, to turn to Rome.

For five months he revelled there. A series of sketches reveal his delight in the magic city and all it had to offer—St. Peter's, the Pincio, the Campagna and the Roman neighborhoods, the studios of his friends—something for every moment of the day, for every mood of the traveller. And at the end, trying to take account of all these things he was forced to say:

One would like, after five months in Rome, to be able to make some general statement of one's experience, one's gains. It is not easy. One has the sense of a kind of passion for the place, and of a large number of gathered impressions. Many of these have been intense, momentous, but one has trodden upon the other, and one can hardly say what has become of them. They store themselves noiselessly away, I suppose, in the dim but safe places of memory, and we live in an insistent faith that they will emerge into vivid relief if life or art should demand them. As for the *passion*, we needn't trouble ourselves about that. Sooner or later it will be sure to bring us back.[36]

Writing to Howells in June, James admitted that he had done little writing in Rome—"too many distractions and a languefying atmosphere,"—but that he had gathered and garnered many impressions for future use.[37]

James spent the summer of 1873 in Homburg, taking, we may imagine, the cure—his health was still a problem—and trying to arrange and weigh all the impressions that he had received, and incidentally add a few more about people and human nature. He wrote at least one story during the summer,[38] and quite possibly more.

---

[33] *Letters*, I, 13.
[34] *Transatlantic Sketches*, p. 98.
[35] *Ibid.*, p. 107.
[36] *Ibid.*, p. 211.
[37] *Letters*, I, 35.
[38] See New York edition of *Collected Works*, XIII, xx.

A few days in Darmstadt, and James was glad to turn his eyes south again and begin a leisurely trip through Switzerland over the St. Gothard Pass to Italy, pausing an instant on the threshold of Italy[39] to prolong the pleasure of anticipation. Within him was the cry of Hannibal: "Beyond the Alps lies Italy!"

And once more in the magic country he found that he had a "deeper impression than ever that Italy is the land for the artist"[40] with its "perfume of antiquity." A week in Siena "living at the inn and walking about the streets; these are the simple terms of my experience,"[41] and a longer sojourn in Florence in the "moist, gray, melancholy days" of autumn[42] before the tourists arrived, intensified the impression.

Late in the fall, William came from America to join Henry, and the two brothers left Florence expecting to spend the winter in Rome —after all, that was the magnet. We have to imagine the walks and the rides, the visits to churches and ruins and friends' studios, the eager comments and comparing of impressions in which the two young men indulged, each with so much to give the other in the way of intellectual companionship. Then in the midst of it all, just when they had fairly started, probably, William was stricken with malaria, and after a few anxious days they sought a healthier clime in Florence. Here they remained for the rest of the winter and spring. Henry settled down to write, beginning his novel *Roderick Hudson*, but he found time also to enjoy the art of Florence, gazing again at some of the pictures he had but glanced at before. One feels as he reads the Florentine notes written at intervals from February to April that James was coming to like Florence as well as Rome. Its atmosphere was somewhat quieter, more dignified, while its beauty was not less.

But the Florentine sojourn was not an untroubled one. For over two years James had been revelling in Europe, carefree, happy, writing when the Muse visited him, but not greatly concerned with the material problems of life. Now there loomed suddenly the question of whether he should return to America or remain in Europe, a drain, though with his parents' most willing consent, upon the family exchequer. It was all a question of what, after all, he had got out of

---

[39] *Transatlantic Sketches*, p. 240.
[40] *Ibid.*, p. 256.
[41] *Ibid.*, p. 256.
[42] *Ibid.*, p. 269.

Europe, out of Italy, and what more he could expect to get. He had wandered and observed and thought and stored away innumerable impressions, but he still felt aloof, a foreigner. In a letter to a friend in America he wrote:

The great fact for us all there (i.e. in America) is that, relish Europe as we may, we belong much more to that than to this, and stand in a much less factitious and artificial relation to it. I feel forever how Europe keeps holding one at arm's length, and condemning one to a meagre scraping of the surface. I have been nearly a year in Italy and have hardly spoken to an Italian creature save washerwomen and painters.[43]

Sometime later the decision made to return to America in the fall— he could use there the impressions stored away—he wrote to his parents:

I shall go with the full prevision that I shall not find life at home *simpatico*, but rather painfully, and, as regards literary work, obstructively the reverse, and not even with the expectation that time will make it easier; but simply on sternly practical grounds; i.e., because I can find more abundant literary occupation by being on the premises and relieve you and father of your burdensome financial interposition. But I shrink from Willy's apparent assumption that going now is to pledge myself to stay forever. I feel as if my three years in Europe (with much of them so *maladif*) were a very moderate allowance for one who gets so much out of it as I do. . . . . If at the end of a period at home I don't feel an overwhelming desire to come back, it will be so much gained. . . . . Florence, fond as I have grown of it, is worth far too little to me, socially, for me to think complacently of another winter here. . . . . If I knew any one in England I should be tempted to go there for a year, for there I could work to advantage—i.e., get hold of new books to review. But I can't face as it is, a year of British solitude. What I desire now more than anything else, and what would do me more good, is a *régal* of intelligent and suggestive society, especially male. But I don't know how or where to find it. It exists, I suppose, in Paris and London, but I can't get at it. I chiefly desire it because it would, I am sure, increase my powers of work.[44]

Europe had given him much but it had not given him companionship with men who were thinking and writing as he was. Nor did America seem to promise much more. There was Howells, to be sure, and all the older, philosophic group in Cambridge, but it was almost too staid and passive a group for a young man who

---

[43] *Letters*, I, 36.
[44] *Letters*, I, 38 f.

craved such active gatherings as the inns and taverns and coffee-houses of London had once offered to aspiring writers.

The whole spring was overcast with a gentle melancholy. A week's trip among the Tuscan cities surrounding Florence convinced James that Pisa would be "a capital place to wait for death."[45] Then Ravenna, dull, stagnant, in the sudden rush of summer, visited shortly as James was about to flee from Italy for cooler lands, made him wonder how Byron could have endured two years there.[46]

Very likely this was the melancholy which comes from exhaustion after a spurt of endeavor. The American magazines for 1874 published twenty-nine articles, reviews, and stories by James, and early the next year *Roderick Hudson* began to appear serially.[47] He had been working at a tremendous rate of speed. Indeed he was glad to pause for a moment in June at Monte Generoso and appreciate for once the sublime yet restful aspect of nature more than any people or any books.[48] He was quite another James from the one who had come to Italy six years before thrilling to art and literature and life. At last he seems to have got his fill.

The sadness increased as he went into Switzerland and Germany for the summer, for bestirring himself out of his apathy he tried to thrill again, to seek rapture in art, but northern art lacked the beauty and spirituality of the Italian, and looking at the Holbeins at Basel his heart grew heavy as he reflected "what art might have come to if it had developed exclusively in Northern hands."[49] Just before sailing for America, he took a trip through Holland and Belgium. Art, life, here were perfect prose. Italy had been poetry![50]

Landing in America in the fall of 1874, James went to Cambridge for three months but probably because he found life among his friends too distracting, he went on to New York for the winter, hoping that there he might find the *régal* of writers he desired and that there he might succeed with his critical and fictional endeavors. Away from his family and closest friends, he would at least be more independent, could apply himself with fewer outside demands upon his time to the finishing of *Roderick Hudson*. The winter of 1874 and '75 then, he spent in New York.

---

[45] *Transatlantic Sketches*, p. 324
[46] *Ibid.*, p. 337.
[47] See Phillips' *Bibliography* for the list.
[48] *Transatlantic Sketches*, pp. 344 f.
[49] *Ibid.*, p. 352.
[50] *Ibid.*, p. 385.

It is against this rapidly changing background with the varying moods which it produced in James that we must consider his work from 1870 to 1875, and it will explain in great measure its varied nature. James's first concern during these years was to live; heretofore he had seen life only through books. Now he tried to get down into it, and he succeeded to a certain extent. The greatest tragedy of James's whole existence was that he was never able to do this as fully as he wished. To the end he was more spectator than participator. But before these European years he had not even observed life directly, and even in the first of these he could see England only as the young man in *The Author of Beltraffio*, through the means of the novels he had read. The practice of writing travel sketches, however, was teaching him to look at life more directly, to use his own eyes and draw his own conclusions. Until the last year of this period, most of the stories, except three American ones, were incidental. They happened. They came to him spontaneously, growing out of what he saw and felt in other lands, Italy especially, and thus they mark an advance over the studied efforts of the earlier time. Then at the end of this period, after a spell of depression or at least of serious thought of the sort which we noted before was with James a prelude to growth, he suddenly emerged triumphant. At last he had got hold of himself, had got hold of art and, to a degree, of life. He had produced his second novel; to him, indeed, his first.

CHAPTER VIII

EVASION, AND SOME DISCOVERIES

1. *By-products of the European Trip*

James returned from Europe in the spring of 1870 with the firm intention of devoting himself to his main purpose—the writing of stories, and dared he whisper it? of novels. For a year and a half he had written nothing except his letters home.[1] On his return, then, his thought was to apply himself with new vigor. Reviewing, except for occasional sallies on his own initiative, he gave up, determined not to divide his interests. True, he wrote a few travel sketches of places in America as he roamed around in the summer of 1870 and again the next year in a more or less vain attempt to find something in America to write stories about, but this was with the intention of forcing himself to weigh American values and get them ready for his stories.[2] Fiction was at last his avowed purpose.

And though James planned that he was eventually to be the spokesman of America, an American Balzac, he discovered on his return from Europe that he had brought back in his brain the fragments of some stories, from Italy and from England, which insisted upon being put together. They concerned the adventures of American travellers over there, things he had noticed and felt; why was it not permissible to sharpen his pencil on these stories before turning to the home scene? Thus the first European sojourn had its tangible results, by-products, perhaps, it seemed then, of the real importance it had for James, but of the greatest importance in determining his future development.

These results were the neglected *Travelling Companions*, which appeared in the November and December *Atlantic Monthly* for 1870, and *At Isella*, which was published in the *Galaxy* the following

---

[1] I am concluding that the three experiments published in 1869—"Pyramus and Thisbe," a crude experiment in dialogue which appeared in the April *Galaxy*, "A Light Man," which appeared in the July *Galaxy*, and "Gabrielle de Bergerac" which appeared in the July to September *Atlantics*—were all written before the trip. We know that the last and most important one was because of Howells's reference to it. See Letters of Howells, I, 141, and also Chapter VI for treatment of it and of "A Light Man."

[2] See Chapter IX for a further consideration of the sketches.

August, and between these two the misinterpreted *Passionate Pilgrim*, which appeared in the March *Atlantic* for 1871.

These stories must be considered as incidental to the trip, growing spontaneously out of it, utilizing the materials and feelings furnished by it, with form forgotten, rather than as "concoctions," *made* stories as his previous attempts had been. And it is this very spontaneity, this lack of effort, which gives them their charm. James for the first time was writing naturally and easily. When he analyzed in these stories or spent pages over long descriptions of places in Europe, the reader feels that it was but natural here that he should do it, that, in a way, he is to be identified, with his narrator-heroes who saw and felt and analyzed too. Though placing his stories in Europe, he selected characters, except for the European ones, from his own class, his own way of thinking, people whom he could understand.

Two other points must be noted before considering the stories individually. Though James cannot be said to be following consciously any model in these stories, Mérimée had no doubt suggested to him the idea of using the travel basis for them,—of using an incident illustrative of the land visited to make the land more vivid to his traveller. The felt atmosphere is given concrete form. In Mérimée, however, the story is always the main interest and the atmosphere in *Carmen*, in *Colomba*, in *Lokis* comes out indirectly, while in James, as we shall shortly see, the incident is very slight, simply a concrete example, in *At Isella* in particular not brought in till near the end, to illustrate what has long been discussed or infused into the air by the narrator.

These three stories have their importance, however, apart from such considerations as greater ease of expression and influences of other authors. They are interesting not for what they sum up as to James's development, as all the stories hitherto have been, but for what they reveal as to the state of James's mind at this time and for what they anticipate.

2. *Italy the Land of Art and of Passion*

Two of the stories, *Travelling Companions* and *At Isella*, grew out of the visit to Italy, the most wonderful part of all Europe to James at this time. James had dreamed of Italy all his life, regretting that, as children, he and his brother had not been taken there. Now at last he had visited the country, and wonder of wonders—recall the letter from Rome—the realization had even surpassed the anticipation. In like manner, the narrator of *Travelling Companions* is seeing Italy for the first time. He has gone down into it from the north, as James had, is carried away by the massive cathedral at Milan, spends two glorious weeks among the towns of northern Italy with a volume of Stendhal in his pocket—James likewise, of course—visits Venice and is enraptured by the pictures. To give him a chance to say what he wished about Italian art, and to make a story, James brought in an American woman, travelling with her father—had he likewise met one and enjoyed the galleries with her, or merely longed to? We are not justified in carrying any biographical hypotheses beyond this point, but between Miss Evans and the narrator, we can make a picture of our young American, moved to tears by the *Last Supper* of Leonardo, by Tintoretto's *Crucifixion*, moved to ecstacy by the towns and landscape of Italy, moved to wonder, because of *La Dernière Aldini*, by the palaces of Venice. The result is a mixture of travel report and art criticism with the story incidental and not at all necessary to the interest. Italy, marvelous land!

Though not necessary, the story has its importance, however, in the light of James's later works, for here, where the young man and the young girl straying off unchaperoned miss their train after a day of ecstatic sight-seeing and are forced to stay over night in a small hotel in Padua, then to return next day before the wondering eyes and shrugging shoulders of Venice, we have the germ of all the stories that were to make up the large body treating the International Situation.[3] The man wishes to marry the girl, not because of this infraction of convention, however, for he has already proposed, but she has put him off, and now, thinking he is urging her to marry him to protect her, she refuses still more definitely. She is an American and will not be ruled by what Europeans consider the only thing: somewhat strangely her father seems to expect it too. A year later the young man meets her again and they are married; however, the important thing is not this aftermath, a sacrifice perhaps to the interest of readers who wish the happy-ever-after sort of thing, but the *contrast in point of view of two civilizations*, the independent American and the conventional European. James had glimpsed it, had felt it, had seen the folly, shallowness, and artificiality of the

---

[3] S. B. Liljegren: *American and European in the Works of Henry James*, Lund, 1920, treats the International Situation very well but does not begin with its germ in *Travelling Companions* and follow it through.

European outlook upon life in his first trip to Europe. He had not obtained it from books, and he was to see it and feel it more and more as he vacillated between the two continents till a whole series of stories dealing with it from its various angles and aspects were to come from his pen. Instead of whole-heartedly approving of Europe in *every* way, he disapproved of its false standards and found it narrow. Those readers who know only *Daisy Miller* and fail to read it noting that James wrote it sympathetically rather than critically, or in the light of these other stories which treat the situation, think that it is American standards and conventions or the *lack* of them which James is always berating. He had, rather, an international, a sort of super-national outlook; as in the question of morality *versus* passion which is to appear again in the next story, he was between the two, could see that something might be said on both sides, and inclined one way or the other simply as truth to human nature or the individual character he was portraying demanded it.

Travelling Companions gives the side of Italy which is most often seen by travellers. But there is another side, James noted, not conventional but passionate, a side of which they sometimes perhaps catch a glimpse if they have read Stendhal and know the throbbing undercurrent; but a side which it is given to few to meet directly. *At Isella* gives this side. Italy is the land now, not of art, not of convention, but of passion, the Italy discovered to James by Stendhal. Below the Alps the sun shines more brightly than in Northern climes. It quickens passion and vanity into an intenser flame, so intense that when passion and duty or adherence to convention come into conflict in one person, it is passion which quickly consumes all else and becomes the dominating force. In France, though passion ultimately triumphs, the conquest is slower, more deliberate, even painful because of an *inner* struggle and reasoning. In Italy the reaction of one being to another is immediate and instinctive and any delays or difficulties come from *outside* circumstances and not from inner debating. The Americans in *Travelling Companions*, cold and rational and perverse in their own passion, as Americans too frequently are, had been affected only by the surface of Italy, of Europe, a surface which demands things of others in the name of convention and propriety which it quite forgets itself when its own passion is awakened. The hero of *At Isella* coming slowly into Italy by foot across the St. Gothard pass, prolonging his approach that the pleasure of anticipation, the breath-taking excitement of it, may also be prolonged, *feels* Italy, even on its threshold, in a far intenser way than his predecessors. Not only does he feel it, but he meets it. James gives it to him, and to us, after many pages of description, in the form of a mysterious, agitated, beautiful woman, who reminds him at once of the "rich capacity of the historic womanhood of Italy,"[4] of Lucrezia Borgia, of Bianca Capello, the heroines of Stendhal. Had James seen such a mysterious woman as he crossed into Italy? Had he sat at a table in a café and wondered about the woman opposite? It is not unlikely, but less fortunate than the narrator of his tale he had probably been able only to wonder, to seek a reason for the agitation and the mystery, and to concoct the story which he makes his lady tell.

Hers is the case so usual in Italy, of the young girl forced against her will to marry a wealthy man, hating him more and more, finally in desperation attempting to get away to join her lover who is very ill, maybe dying, in Geneva. She is, in truth, a heroine from Stendhal, not restrained by her own reason as George Sand's heroines are, from immediately indulging her passion but from outer circumstances till at last she has rebelled and broken away. The stranger listens, moved by her beauty and "candid passion," insists that she take money from him to hire a carriage and thus hurry along without waiting for the coach, and rejoices the next morning when the innkeeper tells the pursuing husband she is not there, and he turns back.

There is no question of what is proper or what is right here. It is an unwarranted liberty to bring up the word morality in regard to the story. *At Isella* simply emphasizes again the position which we discerned James held in regard to George Eliot and the French writers. Neither regard for morality or for passion swayed him but truth to human nature. He had read Stendhal; he believed with him that passion was the dominating thing in Italians—did not their art, did not their religion also testify to it? Though they had standards which they expected others to observe, they themselves were helpless when passion had them in its power and demanded satisfaction. In *At Isella*, James sought to illustrate the Italy of romance, of passion, of life. In *Travelling Companions* he had portrayed the land of art, of cathedrals, of spiritual paintings. Were not the two necessary for a complete picture? Were they not inter-

4 *Galaxy*, Aug., 1871, p. 249.

dependent? Was not Italy then the land for the artist? No answer is yet given, but the question has arisen.

3. A Traveller in England, not A Passionate Pilgrim

It is the third of these three travel stories which offers the most interesting problem to critics and has most often led them astray. *A Passionate Pilgrim* has been taken by all of them as autobiographical and therefore documentary as to the state of James's mind in 1870.[5] What is more, it has so been taken by James himself.[6] To say that it is not, or rather, only partly so, and not in the way in which it has been taken, savors of heresy and must be proved.

The story, that of Clement Searle who returns from America to England to reclaim an estate and fortune only to find himself helpless against the staid solidity of the present owner is too well known to be repeated, but a point must be noted which critics invariably overlook—the story is told by a *friend* of Searle's, an observer, on his first visit to England, interested in recognizing it from the novels he has read, meeting Searle, listening good-naturedly to his ravings about the family estate, humoring him to the extent of going down with him to look it over, comforting him as he becomes ill from disappointment and dies, and through it all pitying him. Considered from the point of view of the narrator, the situation is vastly different from the case when it is looked at from the point of view of the passionate pilgrim, and if anyone represents James in this story, it is this narrator and not Searle as has been generally thought. The narrator, indeed, may well be James; he is young; he is alert to impressions; he is genially interested in a situation such as the plight of Searle brings up; he is James wondering what might happen in such a contingency, but he himself is *not* a case for psychologists. Searle, on the other hand, *is*—one of the reasons very likely for James's interest. He is much older; he is confirmed in his idea that he has been defrauded of his birthright, sick over it almost to madness, cranky, querulous, *not* enjoying England because he

---

[5] Though he does not mention it directly, it is from this tale that Brooks obtained not only the clew for his title but for his attitude and treatment of James as always consumed with a nostalgia for England. Miss West also misinterprets it confusing James with Searle (p. 260 of her book) and sees the influence of Hawthorne in the tone of it (p. 250 of her book). Hueffer also considers that James spoke in Searle (pp. 139 f. of his book).

[6] This is the keynote of *The Middle Years* (See Interchapter B). See also preface to Vol. XIII of *The Collected Edition*.

can think only of what he has missed. He comes nearer to anticipating what James became—though he never became despondent or really querulous—than in any way representing what James was.

It is thus necessary to distinguish carefully between the narrator and Searle, to remember that when one of them says:

The latent preparedness of the American mind for even the most delectable features of English life is a fact which I never fairly probed to its depths. The roots of it are so deeply buried in the virgin soil of our primary culture. . . . . It makes an American's enjoyment of England an emotion more fatal and sacred than his enjoyment, say, of Italy or Spain. I had seen the coffee room of the Red Lion years ago, at home—at Saragossa, Illinois,—in books, in visions, in dreams, in Dickens, in Smollett, and Boswell.[7]

and later:

There is a rare emotion, familiar to every intelligent traveller, in which the mind with a great passionate throb, asserts a magical synthesis of its impressions. You feel England: you feel Italy![8]

it is the youth speaking, gifted with insight and the power to feel, but perfectly normal and healthy; in truth, an intelligent traveller. Then when the other complains

"But haven't I been all my life long sick for England?"[9]

and again:

"I always fancied that I was made for a gentler world. . . . . I came into the world an aristocrat. . . . . I should have been born here and not there; here my vulgar idleness would have been . . . . elegant leisure."[10]

it is the defrauded heir.

The comments of the narrator, though full of enthusiasm for England as a country, are always sane. They are parallel to the comments which we noticed in James's letters, especially the last two before he returned to America, where he praised the English landscape but summed up the shortcomings of the English people.[11]

Never from a single Englishman of them all have I heard the first word of appreciation and enjoyment of the things here that I find delightful.[12]

---

[7] *Atlantic Monthly*, Mar., 1871, p. 352.
[8] *Ibid.*, p. 358.
[9] *Ibid.*, p. 356.
[10] *Ibid.*, p. 361.
[11] See Interchapter B.
[12] *Letters*, I, 26.

Much as he enjoyed England, James in 1870 had no envy of the English lot. On the contrary, strange as it may seem in view of his later trend, he frankly scorned it. The English, he felt, did not appreciate their country. They were stolid, staid, unfeeling, wrapped up in their conventions and their selfish complacency. In no way did they strive to make anything of their opportunity, and James had no desire to live among them even though it might be in an ancestral home. There is in the letters even more scorn for them than of longing on the part of an American for such things as they had and neglected. And there is the same scorn in *A Passionate Pilgrim*. The story is an adverse criticism of English life, of Richard Searle unfeeling until his birthright is threatened, then desperate and deceitful; of his sister, "fenced and protected by convention and precedent and usage; so passive and mild and docile."[13] It is *not* the passionate longing, the nostalgia of a young man for England, for James at twenty-seven did not have it.

James was simply then alert, curious, open to any impressions which might come. It may well be that as James, like his narrator, had sat over his coffee on one of the first nights of his arrival, he had heard the fragments of a conversation in a stall next his between a lawyer and his client, as he may have glimpsed in Italy a beautiful, mysterious woman. His mind seizing the clew, wondering what *might* happen if a defrauded heir should return, expanding it, enlarging it, investing it with all the romantic coloring—peacocks and family portraits and suggestions of wandering spirits—which he could imagine, produced a story. He took up the idea and played with it. He cherished it when he returned to America as an interesting case, perhaps possible, and then in a moment of expansiveness, he poured out the tale. And he did not, after he had written it, cast it aside. It was a good story, well told, though somewhat romantic. He remembered it now and then, at first, no doubt whimsically, rather proud of its artistry and even of its extravagances, later more seriously, republishing it, translating it into French, retouching its diction, till he came to think in some sort of the same fashion not of the narrator he had truthfully been but of the strange creature, Searle, whom he had built up out of his imagination. Later, feeling more and more that England *did* have something which America lacked, realizing that he, an American, could never quite achieve it, he felt himself, like Searle, deprived of a birthright which he at least would also have appreciated. Disappointed, he tried to seek refuge in the thought that he had been somehow cheated. In this respect he illustrated in his life a bit of wisdom noted by him when he read George Eliot, the underlying theory of her works—" 'our deeds determine us as much as we determine our deeds.' "[14]

The *Passionate Pilgrim* illustrates as no other story what happens when the critic approaches James from the wrong end of his development. It is the first of his stories which James chose to revive and give the dignity of a place in his Definitive Edition. It is thus invested with a glamour, an importance. Possibly it is in some ways better than the previous attempts, structurally more perfect, and more worthy to be remembered, but though the general reader may, the critic must not overlook the other attempts, and above all, he must not disregard the stories which surrounded or followed it, growing like it out of the European trips from 1870 to '75. During this time James wrote fourteen stories. All except four of these grew out of the visits to Europe. And of these ten, six, including James's first successful novel, dealt with Italy. *The Passionate Pilgrim* alone grew out of the English experience; two were to grow out of France and one out of Homburg. Which land, then, even though we were to forget the evidence of the letters and the travel sketches, must have meant most to James? Which land was his inspiration?

[14] "The Novels of George Eliot," *Atlantic Monthly*, Oct., 1866, p. 491, noticed by James in regard to *Romola* especially.

CHAPTER IX

AN HISTORIAN OF AMERICA?

1. *The American Novel*

James had returned to America, however, as we noted before, *not* to write about Europe but about his native land. And now that he had sharpened his pencil so easily and well, he turned with confidence to the main task. But though he turned with confidence, it was rather a grim sort of determination which shortly set in. To begin with, though he was to write about America, he found that he knew little about it, had little to say. His European trip had been an evasion rather than a facing of the problem.

Shortly after his return from Europe, he had taken a trip to Saratoga, Lake George, Burlington, and finally Newport. Eyes open, brain active, he had tried to get hold of material, places and people which cried out to be done, which needed an historian. He had sat upon wide hotel verandahs, the "largest" in the world at Saratoga, and had observed the women and the children.[1] But where were the men? Alas, back in the city offices condemned by the American scheme of life to toil for the money to support their wives in elegant leisure, and James had no way of getting into the offices to meet them. The few men who visited the resorts were for the most part derelicts, odd sticks, even bounders,—it could not be that they were representative of America. James wondered about possible settings for a novel, for a novel must be *placed*— witness Balzac's definite placing of his. A solid American home in Burlington, Vermont, had suggested one,[2] but he had not met the people who lived there, could only dimly imagine them, and he had turned to hunt for other places. The Newport spectacle had suggested another, where the heroine might be "infinitely realistic and yet neither a school-mistress nor an outcast,"[3] but that would have meant putting his cousins and friends in the limelight and he felt a reluctance to do this till he should have perfected his craft. America was flat after Europe. No place cried out to be done. It

[1] *Nation*, Aug. 11, 1870, pp. 87 f.
[2] *Nation*, Sept. 1, 1870, p. 136.
[3] *Nation*, Sept. 15, 1870, p. 17.

yielded "its secrets only to a really *grasping* imagination."[4] He realized in truth what he concluded as regards Howells and half suspected about himself, that his was not naturally of this sort. And yet he *must* write, not only tales, but a novel of America. The urge was there, a Cerberus more greedy than any international situation at this time and James set to work to appease it.

He wrote a novel—if a little book which, when published in book form some years later, filled but two hundred and nineteen small pages, may be called a novel. But it is certainly much more than a short story and it had behind it the ambitions of a long novel of a biographical nature. If the result was in between the two, that was not the fault of the initial plan.

James wished, Balzac fashion, to record a town, but no place offered itself. Despite this sharp handicap he determined to proceed as best he could—somewhere around Boston would do. There was another handicap too,—he had discovered no really interesting people, that is, outside his own group of friends, but he felt confident that he could invent some. He could take a man who might once have been of the group but would be carried outside it for the action—a man possibly who had been jilted in love and wanted to get outside, who wished to rearrange his life. That would offer an interesting problem. How would he do it? By finding another interest? But what should that interest be? Why not a child? A little girl who would grow up to marry him, who would thus show the other woman that he wasn't altogether undesirable. A little girl whom *he* might, in fact, bring up to marry him. That would keep him central, give the story compactness. And this might conceivably happen around Boston—or anywhere. Wasn't it human nature? Not at its best perhaps; indeed, under rather strained conditions, if not carefully handled, but with something surely of truth to man in it, and he would try to make it seem true to America.

Watch and Ward[5] so bravely undertaken, slumped beyond belief in the execution. It professed to be a realistic story of American life. It turned out to be an invented one, but not a romance. Everything about it was not observed but imagined.

Because the story had not grown out of a specific place, James was cautious about definitely locating it. He opened it presumably in Boston; he quickly transferred it to the country near this city;

[4] *Letters* of James, I, 30, (See also Interchapter B).
[5] Appeared in *Atlantic Monthly*, August to December, 1871.

he brought on some characters from St. Louis, the raw edge of civilization in America as far as James was concerned; not feeling restrained by any specific location, he sent Roger, his hero, on one occasion to Peru and Nora, his heroine, on another to Rome, and he moved the action bodily to New York for the concluding scenes. No *one* place in America is recorded for future generations, nor is America generally. For his dramatis personae, James added to his well-intentioned young gentleman and little girl, bounders, cheats, an unethical clergyman, coquettes—one a vivid Peruvian, the others pale Americans—a motley array calculated to disturb the trend of Roger's heretofore impeccable existence. Roger is deprived of a fitting social setting, of a suitable milieu, as well as of a definite geographical location. He is surrounded by people he never would have known intimately in real life while the people he would have known, James's own friends and acquaintances, are left almost entirely out through the reluctance of James to bring them in or given minor roles which they stiffly play. James tried to make Nora, born in one class and now receiving the bringing up of the other, the connecting link between the two, and divested her of any truth to life she might otherwise have had by making her the go-between. The manners of all concerned are unnatural. Everyone is awkward, ill at ease in the presence of the others. The excessive politeness of one class expresses itself in fine speeches and dribbling sentimentality; the extreme rudeness of the other in ranting and melodramatic poses. Everywhere James used the excess, himself as ill at ease as his characters, and nowhere the gentle mean.

Nor is the novel structurally any better. The story grew, we noted, not out of place, but had its genesis, George Eliot fashion, in a character or in a vague idea about one, a young man, jilted, suddenly becoming interested in a child and concluding to make her his wife. There is surely not much here for a plot, though it suggests difficulties to the skeptical, but James's task was to build one out of it, to fill in somehow the gap between beginning and end.

He began bravely. There is the conclusion of Roger's previous interest in a stiff scene where the stately Miss Morton refuses him and he vows everlasting celibacy. There is almost immediately—as soon as he returns to the hotel in fact—the beginning of his new interest. He hears a shot in the next room. He rushes in, finds a man to whom he refused money just before he left for Miss Morton's, has committed suicide. Beside him is his child, "shrieking and wringing her hands." Roger's pity is stirred by "the little forlorn, precocious, potential woman,"[6] and he decides abruptly to adopt her.

Was it the inexpugnable instinct of paternity? Was it the restless ghost of his buried hope? He thought of his angry vow of the night before to live only for himself and turn the key on his heart. . . . . But there was love and love! He could be a protector, a father, a brother. . . . . Poor little disfathered daughter,—poor little uprooted germ of womanhood! Her innocent eyes seemed to more than beseech,—to admonish almost and command.[7]

The story thus begun proceeds for a chapter rather smoothly. Roger has only to look after the education of his young charge. He gives up his business, moves to his country home, his "philosophy in this as in all things" being "to make her happy that she might be good."[8] He attempts to educate her himself; then at the advice of his cousin, Hubert, decides to send her away to school. On her return for a vacation, he realizes that his love is something other than that of father or brother, and he begins to prepare himself for his place as Nora's husband. The loosely running narrative on one hand and the introspective analysis which Roger indulges in on the other—the habit surviving from James's early stories—probably seemed to him to threaten the interest of the story. Yet he realized that the end was still a long way off as far as time was concerned and he must not get there too quickly. Accordingly he resorted to the invention of obstacles.[9] He sent Roger to South America where he had his steadfastness tempted by the Peruvian beauty with the result that Roger feels the attraction of Nora more than ever. He brought on Nora's cousin, George, a worthless scamp from St. Louis, to work upon her sympathies and Roger's wrathful jealousy. He had Roger's cousin, Hubert, amused by Roger's fantastic plan, threaten to usurp his place in Nora's affection. Roger—or isn't it still James who does it?—sends Nora to Rome under the care of the woman who formerly jilted him, now a widow, Mrs. Keith, who has become interested in his experiment, and in him. Incidentally this gave James an opportunity to expatiate on the glories of Rome, both as Nora prepares to go and in the letters she writes to Roger and

---

[6] *Atlantic Monthly*, Aug., 1871, p. 238.

[7] *Ibid.*, pp. 238–39.

[8] *Ibid.*, p. 240.

[9] Beach: *The Method of Henry James*, New Haven, 1918, p. 181f analyzes this story well as to structure and criticizes the dialogue as crude and bald.

Hubert. Roger is kept at home and a Miss Sands introduced to try her charms upon him, but to no avail. Nora is brought back, now at last "a woman turned, perfect, mature, superb!"[10] the influence of Rome. Roger has expected to make her his wife immediately, but illness intervenes, and Hubert and then George endeavor to make up for lost time. At length Roger nearly dies; Nora rushes to him and the crisis of the fever is passed successfully. Upon his recovery he proposes only to be misunderstood. Nora flees to George and to Hubert but finds that both are frauds and at length exhausted falls back into Roger's receptive arms. James had finished his American novel.

But *Watch and Ward* is not, strictly speaking, an American novel at all. It is not a slice of life. It is not a picture of a group of Americans whom James knew and respected. It is not a record of contemporary manners. It is something made up, invented, a figment of the imagination. But the result is not entertaining as the romantic stories, frankly extravagant, had been, or charming as the travel tales which had illustrated the felt atmosphere of a land. It is invention professing to be real and logical: "I shall have told my story ill if these things seem to lack logic,"[11] invention misused and abused.

Nor did the influence of any other writer, though there are suggestions of many, enter to guide James in any marked degree. We noted how he had to abjure the example of Balzac, and it is doubtful if in starting with the idea of character, James was conscious in any way of following George Eliot. He simply had to begin somewhere. Possibly the initial interest of Roger in Nora, left alone and penniless after the death of her father, had been suggested by the interest of a certain German lad, Wilhelm Meister, in the orphan he befriended on his travels. Indeed Nora's character as a child, impulsive at times, at others stubborn and blunt, stimulating Roger's perplexity, disturbing him as he wonders about the effect of heredity, parallels Mignon's nature to a certain extent. Goethe's purpose, however, was the development of Wilhelm; Mignon was simply an incident. With James, Nora is retained and made the end and not just a means.

Other fragmentary influences too are to be discerned. George Sand's influence definitely survives in the thinking of love as passion,

[10] *Atlantic Monthly*, Nov., 1871, p. 577.
[11] *Atlantic Monthly*, Dec., 1871, p. 690.

and in the discussions which are devoted to it by both the characters and the author commenting upon it. Stendhal's idea of passion he brought in briefly in a letter which Nora writes from Rome. Balzac had probably shown James how convenient cousins are for the author. Near in kinship to the principal characters they can easily be brought in and given a chance to show their baseness. The utilization of Roger's former love to help him bring up Nora savors too of French fiction which abounds in somewhat similarly inclined women. And the despised American fiction of such writers as Mrs. Rebecca Harding Davis, influenced—it must have been unconsciously—its sentimentality of expression and its crude melodrama. Beach notes the influence of Dickens upon the grotesque realism of some of the minor characters,[12] but such influence would, like that of American fiction, have been unconscious, since James was no great admirer of Dickens.[13] These many "bits" of influence with no one dominating one show that James was stumbling around trying to produce something of his own yet having nothing to work upon.

Watch and Ward was accepted by Howells for the *Atlantic* and published in five installments. The *Nation* praised the first one,[14] opposed the second,[15] and on the appearance of the final installment,[16] took James to task for not presenting people or views of life which were sufficing. James must have felt the justice of the charge. Still, seven years later, and this is most surprising, James considered this first novel good enough for him to take valuable time from much better work in order to revise and republish it in book form. Even careful verbal alterations, however, could not remedy the lack of direct observation and did not tone down the story sufficiently, and the present day reader of it, who becomes acquainted with it invariably in this edition of 1878, instead of through the pages of the *Atlantic*, finds it quite as loud and melodramatic and unpromising as the reader who seeks out the original draft.

2. *Companion Pieces*

Two experiments in dialogue and two short stories of the same period reveal that James was resolutely trying to forget Europe—

[12] Beach, p. 182.
[13] See Chapter IV.
[14] *Nation*, Aug. 3, 1871, p. 78.
[15] *Nation*, Aug. 31, 1871, p. 148.
[16] *Nation*, Nov. 30, 1871, p. 358.

that is, for story material—and to make the most of the American scene.

The two former, *Still Waters*[17] and *A Change of Heart*,[18] both subentitled "farce," were most likely written in an attempt to handle progression of action and revelation of character in dialogue, instead of in loose narrative or analysis by the author. Heretofore James had not made the most of his dialogue; it had often retarded instead of advanced the action. He had, however, as we noticed, following George Sand, often put the analysis of which he was so fond into the mouths of his characters. But when he came to leave out all narrative and analytic comment on the part of the writer, when he himself stepped out of the scene entirely, he found it necessary to resort to asides and soliloquies which are, as a result, most unnatural and grotesque. In addition, *Still Waters* fails in having too much happen in one scene, while *A Change of Heart* divides the contents of ten pages into fifteen scenes. Both dialogues were laid in America, but neither has in it anything particularly American in tone.

The two short stories, *Master Eustace*[19] and *Guest's Confession*,[20] were probably by-products of the endeavor which went into *Watch and Ward*. The former concerns itself with the bringing up of a boy, while the latter, slightly more fortunate than the vaguely located stories, probably had its genesis out of something observed on the hotel verandah at Saratoga. At least the description of L——— parallels that of the travel sketch of two years before, and its men, except for the narrator, are odd sticks and bounders.

For both of the stories James returned to the narrative framework whereby an observer or a character in the story relates the happenings. It was more convenient, James found, when he wished to bring in analysis or extra-narrative comment. Then too, this narrative framework made his stories seem more real, gave them an authenticity—they were vouched for by a person who had seen the thing happen—but this very merit led him to abuse it and bring in unnatural people and melodramatic happenings.

The first of these stories, *Master Eustace*, is even less American than *Watch and Ward*. Like *De Grey*, which it resembles in many respects, though it is not so romantic, it betrays the influence of

[17] Appeared in *Balloon Post*, Apr. 12, 1871.
[18] Appeared in *Atlantic Monthly*, Jan., 1872.
[19] Appeared in *Galaxy*, Nov., 1871.
[20] Appeared in *Atlantic Monthly*, Oct.–Nov., 1872.

George Sand. It is a story of passion. The mother had "a crude passionate theory that love, pure love is the sum and substance of maternal duty,"[21] while the son, Eustace, had an unusual affection for his dead father which, in its turn, amounted to a passion. Of love generally, Mrs. Garmyer said "It's either a passion . . . . or it's nothing. You can know it by being willing to give up every thing for it—name and fame, past and future, this world and the next."[22] Thus we are prepared for some display of the force and some tragic outcome. Much attention is given to foreshadowing this outcome. Structurally, the story is rather well built up with many hints in the shape of forebodings on the part of the narrator. For the plot itself Eustace is sent to Europe to finish his education, while Mrs. Garmyer at home meets and marries a Mr. Cope, a close friend of the family who suddenly returns from India. Eustace now comes home, enraged that his mother has thus forgotten his father, but it proves that she has in fact remembered him, that Mr. Cope is the father of Eustace. The end becomes noisily melodramatic. Eustace attempts to shoot himself but fails. His mother in the next room hears the shot and dies. And the narrator briefly tells us that the son and his father are never reconciled. George Sand could not well be adapted to American life. Structurally fair, the story fails because it is not representative or true.

Finding it difficult to apply the French theories of passionate love to America, James next tried conscience. He did not take, however, the gentle, unaggressive, yet inwardly active conscience, of George Eliot. Instead he took in Edgar Musgrove, of *Guest's Confession*, conscience of a rigid sort which concerns itself more with others than with self. As his brother, the narrator says:

He was simply the most consistent and incorruptible of egotists. He was perpetually affirming and defining and insuring himself, insisting upon a personal right or righting a personal wrong. And above all, he was a man of conscience. He asked no odds, and he gave none. He made honesty something unlovely, but he was rigidly honest. He demanded simply his dues, and he collected them to the last farthing. These things gave him a portentous solemnity.[23]

A Mr. Guest has defrauded Edgar and he demands compensation, but he is almost as much of a criminal in his rigid sense of honesty

---

[21] *Galaxy*, Nov., 1871, p. 596.
[22] *Ibid.*, p. 598.
[23] *Atlantic Monthly*, Oct., 1872, p. 389.

as Mr. Guest is in his lax sense of duty, a closer relative of some of
Balzac's heartless extortioners than of George Eliot's silently suffer-
ing characters. Slightly more true to life, however, is one character
in this story, the half-brother who relates it, and, more than James's
usual narrator, actually enters into it, falls in love with the daughter
of Mr. Guest, and at length, though not until after the death of
Edgar, effects a fairly satisfactory solution of the many difficulties
which arise. The narrator here has a real part. He is brought to
the center instead of being left on the side as a spectator. It is
through him that we see and learn of the other individuals, but he
in turn is affected by the individuals. He is not passive. He considers the whole situation backwards and forwards, meditates upon it,
and at length solves it. There is thus a faint unconscious suggestion
here of what was later to become one of James's chief aims—that
of centering everything in the consciousness of some individual.
The narrator, however, like Roger of *Watch and Ward*, is deprived
of a suitable milieu and made to appear amid the bounders and cheap
flirts of a summer hotel verandah. Even the daughter of Mr.
Guest, of higher character than her father and his associates and
quite above their baseness, is not, despite the narrator's insisting
upon it, of charm enough to make his falling in love with her seem
the plausible thing.

It is very likely that at this time another story, *Crawford's
Consistency*, which was not printed till 1876, was written.[24] It is
much like these other crude stories—it is located in America; it
employs a narrator; it is melodramatic; it has little characterization, the people being puppets of the author rather than individuals.
Then, too, the plot follows almost exactly one which James's father
suggested in a letter to the youth in 1870.[25] It concerns a man who
becomes wealthy and aspires to the hand of a fair damsel who has
been secludedly brought up and is now offered to the highest bidder.
The man wins the maid, but a wealthier man appears—in the letter
the fiancé loses his money—and the maid, acting on her mother's
instructions, retracts her vow. The man consoles himself by marrying a frowsy beauty of the town who mistreats him, but through it
all he preserves his equanimity. The story has little significance
here, but will have some in the light of a novel James was writing
in 1876. Perhaps resurrected then to appease *Scribner's* which was

[24] *Scribner's Magazine*, Aug., 1876.
[25] *Notes of a Son and Brother*, p. 96.

trying to get something from James to print, it offered a suggestion, which will be noted later, for that novel.[26] Everything, however, points to the fact that it was written in the early seventies.

These American stories, then, all reveal the same thing—that James did not know America. Or if he did know a part of it—the young men and women of his acquaintance, an artist or two, the Cambridge group—he was loath to put them upon paper in their proper setting and occupations. It would never do in the present state of his apprenticeship to try anything of that sort. He was too timid, too reticent for his own good. And so he invented situations and imported characters from other classes he did not know, probably had never spoken to but only observed, and then applied to them theories and ideas collected from his reading of French novels which would not fit American life at all, or concluded all sorts of melodramatic things about them. He *made* these stories and passed them off as real, as usual, as typical. The stories written in 1871 simply failed again in the same way that the attemptedly realistic stories of 1865 to 1868 failed. The error was repeated. But *this* time James could discern the trouble, even if he felt that he could not immediately remedy it directly.

His European stories, he suddenly realized, had made themselves; they had grown spontaneously, naturally out of his observations and experiences. Invented, imagined, of course—that was the way they had grown, but *not without some basis—that* was the important thing. He had caught the atmosphere of Italy; he had sensed the tone of England and the deplorable shortcomings of the English. America—what *was* its atmosphere? He could not answer. It might be—oh, ever so many things—but what was it really, what was the *one dominating tone of the moment*? Did it have a tone? Wasn't that perhaps just the trouble? At least, try as he had and would, he could not discover any. He had written: "To write well and worthily of American things one need even more than elsewhere to be a *master*. But unfortunately one is less!"[27] The doubt now became a fact. If he was to produce the "series of good little tales" he had dreamed of, if that was to be his lifetime, he must go where things imparted their secrets to him or allowed him to feel them and sense them fully enough to guess them, and what might illustrate them, accurately.

[26] See Chapter XV.
[27] *Letters*, I, 31.

CHAPTER X

A TRAVELLER

1. *Preparation for the Travel Sketches*

It was from the standpoint of his reviewing that we considered the early experimental fiction of Henry James. In the second phase of his development, reviewing, except for a few, probably voluntary, contributions, was abandoned for a while. Two other interests, however, supplemented the fictional endeavor, the writing of travel sketches and of art notes. Neither of these had the importance of the reviews in respect to the expression of James's ideas about fiction writing, yet each, or rather both together, for after the first stumbling experiments the two were blended, had a most important place in James's development. It was in the pursuit of observations for these travel reports and in the wandering around art museums and studios as he collected materials for his art notes, that James found, at last, material for his fiction. We cannot find the germs of all of his stories in his reports and notes, —indeed the germ is sometimes to be found in the stories of others, yet we know from the fact that James's stories are based upon a situation imagined as possible at Homburg, a painter in Florence who dreams of uniting the good points of all great madonnas in one supreme picture, an incident illustrating the conflict of a new and an old civilization in Rome, that travel and art gave James a concrete basis upon which to erect his stories.

Because of this, it is important to look again at the sketches, which were used in part for the biographical background of this section, and to consider this time not so much *where* James travelled, but *how* he travelled, how he used his eyes and his brain as well, *what* appealed to him, and also, more remote yet important, to consider how he wrote the reports, what influences were at work or not at work, to see that the same earnest desire to do well, ran through this line of James's endeavor as permeated the other.

Strictly speaking, the travel sketches began with those of American scenes written as James sought for material for his short stories and his novel in the summers of 1870 and '71. These early ones were quite incidental to his main purpose and in themselves have no value in addition to that which has already been mentioned.[1] They brought James, however, to the attention of the editors of the *Nation*, in which they were published, in a new light and they revealed to them a young man who might report well were he actually inspired and stirred by what he saw. Hence when James began to contemplate in the winter of 1871 and '72 a return to Europe, they lost no time in proposing to him that he write sketches and send them to the *Nation*.

James accepted the commission gladly and immediately began to prepare in two ways for the later execution of it. He read many travel sketches to see how others reported and reviewed several of them for the *Nation*, and, because he knew that writing of Europe and things European would require a great deal of art criticism, he began to try his hand on what the museums of Boston and New York offered, submitting these notes to Howells for the *Atlantic*. He had written in a review of Hamerton's *Contemporary French Painters* in 1868: "It is no more than just, that, before sitting down to discourse upon works of art, a writer should be required to prove his familiarity with the essential conditions of the production of such works,"[2] and these first art notes are an attempt to show that familiarity. James's early dawdling in Hunt's studio had introduced him to the technique of art, and Hamerton's book had given him an idea of how to criticize art. However, his practice notes are stiff and awkward, and, in general, apply the same principles to painting which James had evolved about fiction—the necessity of truth, of spirit, of reflection, of passionate conviction.

Even more conscientiously did James apply himself to the study of the travel sketches of other writers. Reviews of Tyndall's *Hours of Exercise in the Alps*,[3] revealing that James knew Ruskin's Alpine notes as well, of Taine's *Notes sur l'Angleterre*,[4] of Gautier's *Tableaux de Siège*,[5] revealing that James was well acquainted with Gautier's travel notes, of Hawthorne's *French and Italian Journals*,[6] appeared from November, 1871, to March, 1872. Before this, in 1868, we remember, James had reviewed Taine's *Italie* and Ho-

[1] See Chapter IX.
[2] *North American Review*, Apr., 1868, p. 718.
[3] Appeared in *Atlantic Monthly*, Nov., 1871.
[4] Appeared in *Nation*, Jan. 25, 1872.
[5] *Ibid.*
[6] Appeared in *Nation*, Mar. 14, 1872.

wells's *Italian Journals*.[7]   And during the next two years he was to criticize Gautier more thoroughly[8] and to review sketches by Laugel[9] and others by Montégut.[10] References in the reviews and the sketches themselves reveal that James was familiar with Ruskin's art notes,[11] Leslie Stephen,[12] Feydeau,[13] M. du Pays,[14] the handbooks—Bädeker and Murray[15]—and possibly, though the evidence is very slight, with Goethe's *Italienische Reise*.[16] For this task as for his stories, James proceeded studiously and conscientiously. Of all these travellers, however, but one, Gautier, as we shall presently see, was to exert any positive influence upon James's own sketches, which may be said to be a reaction against Taine's tendency to reduce facts to philosophy, on the one hand, and Hawthorne's and Howells's "intellectual irresponsibility," on the other.

2. *Observer of Art*

Thus prepared James landed in England in the spring of 1872. From May of that year till August, 1874, he sent more than a score of sketches to the *Nation* in fulfillment of the commission entrusted to him. Much as the readers of the *Nation* may have benefited by the glimpses which he gave them of lands and art beyond the sea, James himself benefited much more. Indeed, this commission was one of the most fortunate things that could have happened to James at this time. He became an active observer. Of course, he had used his eyes to a certain extent before—Balzac and George Eliot had taught him the wisdom of it—but he had not gone around with the definite purpose of making a conquest of the material world, of seeing all that there was to be seen, then of trying to record it exactly for those less fortunate than he who could not observe it directly but only through his pen.

[7] See Chapter VII.

[8] Three reviews on various works by Gautier reveal James's interest in the travel reports of the French writer; See *North American Review*, Apr., 1873, for a long article on Gautier; *North American Review*, Oct., 1874, for a review of posthumous works; *Nation*, Nov. 12, 1874, for a review of *A Winter in Russia*.

[9] Laugel's *Italie, Sicile, Bohême* reviewed in *Nation*, Feb. 27, 1873.

[10] Montégut *Souvenirs de Bourgogne*, reviewed in *Nation*, July 23, 1874.

[11] Numerous references throughout the articles.

[12] Evident in review of Tyndall's Book, *Atlantic Monthly*, Nov., 1871, p. 635.

[13] *Transatlantic Sketches*, Boston, 1875, Houghton Mifflin, 1893, p. 95.

[14] *Ibid.*, p. 393, "the excellent handbook of M. du Pays."

[15] *Ibid.*,—numerous references throughout the book.

[16] *Ibid.*, p. 219.

In each of the countries visited, one and more frequently both of two things engaged the attention of James—art and people. The former interest took two forms, interest in cathedrals and interest in paintings. Sculpture, too, at least in Italy, must have held him perhaps even more than painting but he kept that interest in reserve for his stories. One is led to suspect because of the great place which cathedrals and paintings occupy in the sketches, that the commission might have had in it some clause suggesting that he report to America on these two subjects or that he, when asked to write some sketches, made up his mind in default of any preformed theory such as Taine had, to unify his impressions by making these two forms of art his main concern. James's interest in people was a more subjective interest, closely connected with the writing of fiction, and it often intruded upon his cathedral notes and art criticism. Probably, however, he saw and studied many people of whom he never spoke in his sketches, but reserved along with the sculpture, for his stories.

The first four sketches deal with England, and here the main pleasure was that of cathedral hunting, so much easier, James thought, than picture hunting because there are fewer great cathedrals and the "mass and presence of each specimen is great, so that, as they rise in the mind in individual majesty, they dwarf all common impressions."[17] In his tour of the towns of southern England, James's walks invariably led him to the cathedrals and he carefully enumerated the peculiar architectural interests of each— the "long-drawn aisle" and great choir window at Lichfield,[18] the Norman towers of Exeter,[19] the "elaborate elegance" of the façade and the "even, sober, mouse-colored gray tone" of Wells,[20] the lonely columns and empty windows of the relics at Glastonbury,[21] the blond character of Salisbury.[22] As he progressed, he gradually became more proficient and easy in his remarks, but in all he caught the subdued tones of Anglicanism.

The churches of Italy drew from James more eager response. In Italy, however, his interest was divided between the two forms in which the religious nature expressed itself below the Alps—

[17] *Transatlantic Sketches*, p. 34.
[18] *Ibid.*, pp. 23 and 24.
[19] *Ibid.*, p. 35.
[20] *Ibid.*, pp. 45 and 46.
[21] *Ibid.*, p. 52.
[22] *Ibid.*, p. 53.

architecture and painting. As in England, his walks invariably led him to the churches, but once in the churches, he often sought out as of greatest interest the frescos and paintings, and then emerging, he hunted up palaces and galleries where other religious paintings were to be seen. Early in his trip Milan Cathedral (which had already served James as the meeting place of the American tourists in *Travelling Companions*), not as beautiful as many other churches but "grandly curious, superbly rich," raised in him the question as to what the main point in architecture really is, beauty or mass, for more than any other it represents "difficulties annulled, resources combined, labor, courage, and patience. And there are people who tell us that art has nothing to do with morality!"[23] But the "prime treasure" of Milan was the "beautiful tragical Leonardo," and James, as he stood before it, could only re-echo Gautier's praise of it:

I doubt whether our children will find in the most majestic and most luckless of frescos much more than the shadow of a shadow. . . . . The picture needs not another scar or stain, now, to be the saddest work of art in the world; and battered, defaced, ruined as it is, it remains one of the greatest. . . . . Every painter ought once in his life to stand before the Cenacolo and decipher its moral. Pour everything you mentally possess into your picture lest perchance your "prepared surface" should play you a trick![24]

Art in Italy, whether the art which built massive cathedrals or painted beautiful frescos had its moral, its lesson for those who would be artists. Pour all you have into your work. And it is this lesson which we shall soon hear again in James's stories.

In Venice, James quite ignored the architecture of St. Marks and the other churches—perhaps he felt that Gautier and Ruskin had said all there was to be said of them and despaired of doing it as well—and passed on to discuss the paintings of the galleries and churches. Here, perhaps again handicapped by what Gautier had done so thoroughly in regard to Titian and Veronese, as well as lesser painters, James centered his attention upon Tintoret, to

---

[23] *Ibid.*, p. 78 (James described Milan Cathedral again in 1874, see pp. 340f.)

[24] *Ibid.*, pp. 81 f. Compare with Gautier's paragraph, *Italia*, Paris, 1855, p. 79: "La première impression que fait cette fresque merveilleuse tient du rêve: toute trace d'art a disparu; elle semble flotter à la surface du mûr, qui l'absorbe comme une vapeur légère. C'est l'ombre d'une peinture, le spectre d'un chef-d'oeuvre qui revient. L'effet est peut-être plus solennel et plus religieux que si le tableau même était vivant: le corps a disparu, mais l'âme survit tout entière."

him greater than all the others, and endeavored to bring out the real strength of this painter which he seems to have felt Gautier had missed.

His reputation rests chiefly on a more superficial sort of merit—his energy, his unsurpassed productivity, his being, as Théophile Gautier says, *le roi des fougueux*. These qualities are immense, but the great source of his impressiveness is that his indefatigable hand never drew a line that was not, as one may say, a moral line. No painter ever had such breadth and such depth; and even Titian, beside him, has often seemed to me but a great decorative artist. . . . . . Titian was, assuredly, a mighty poet, but Tintoret—Tintoret was almost a prophet.[25]

James saw what the Frenchman had overlooked—a moral and spiritual note in Tintoret. And he felt that this artist alone of the great Venetians had it, differing here from Ruskin who discerned it even in Veronese.[26]

Criticism of paintings James suspended in Rome, preferring there to talk about the churches, which were "the churchiest churches in Europe—the fullest of gathered details and clustering association."[27]   There was the beautiful church of Santa Maria Maggiore where one could sit for half an hour at the base of one of the marble columns of the beautiful nave and enjoy a perfect feast of fancy.[28]   And there was St. Peter's so large that one could use it for a promenade on rainy days, but also possessing a simple beauty which the massive structure in Milan had quite lacked.

It seemed to me from the first the hugest thing conceivable—a real exaltation of one's idea of space; so that one's entrance, even from the great empty square, glaring beneath the deep blue sky or cool in the far-cast shadow of the immense façade, seems not so much a going in somewhere as a going out. I should confidently recommend a first glimpse of the interior to a man of pleasure in quest of new sensations, as one of the strongest the world affords. There are days when the vast nave looks vaster than at others, and the gorgeous baldachino a longer journey beyond the far-spreading tessellated plain of the pavement, when the light has a quality

[25] *Ibid.*, p. 91. It is interesting to note that James slightly misquotes Gautier who said of Tintoret, *Italia*, p. 295: "Tintoret est *le roi des violents*. Il a une *fougue* de composition," etc. James evidently confused the place of the two French words meaning violent. In Gautier's work, Titian and Veronese receive much more attention than Tintoret.

[26] *Ibid.*, p. 91. James speaks here his scorn of Ruskin in his phrase "whose eloquence, in dealing with the great Venetians, sometimes outruns his discretion."

[27] *Ibid.*, p. 126.

[28] *Ibid.*, p. 125.

which lets things look their largest, and the scattered figures mark happily the scale of certain details. Then you have only to stroll and stroll, and gaze and gaze, and watch the baldachino lift its bronze architecture, like a temple, within a temple, and feel yourself, at the bottom of the abysmal shaft of the dome, dwindle to a crawling dot.[29]

And again:

The supreme beauty of the church is its magnificently sustained simplicity. It seems—as it is—a realization of the happiest mood of a colossal imagination.[30]

Yet the effect of the whole church to a "traveller not especially pledged to be devout" was a message of contentment rather than of aspiration, and the mind could expand there "immensely, but on its own level."[31] It was the most satisfying expression of Catholicism that James discovered, for Catholicism generally somewhat perplexed him and yet it fascinated him too.

In the sketches dealing with Florence, written in the fall of 1873 and the winter of 1874, James wandered again from the beautiful churches to the paintings, and here, free from any French forerunner, he indulged more extensively than before in criticism of painters. He followed, however, the more or less loosely enumerative method—discussing one picture, or one artist, after another—which Gautier had used in regard to the Academy at Venice. Like Ruskin, he was quick to discover a moral note in an artist, but unlike Ruskin, he did not consider this the main thing nor imagine it existed where it was absent. He took each artist for what he was worth—one for morality, perhaps, another for beauty of conception or composition, and so on. That he had relaxed somewhat his demands upon art and had thus developed is apparent when he says:

We do, in fact, as we grow older, unstring the critical bow a little and strike a truce with invidious comparisons. We work off the juvenile impulse to heated partisanship. . . . . We perceive a certain solidarity in all cultivated effort, and are conscious of a growing urbanity in our judgments. . . . . We have, in short, less of a quarrel with the masters we don't delight in, and less of an impulse to renew the oath of eternal friendship with those in whom, in more zealous days, we fancied we discovered peculiar meanings. The meanings no longer seem quite so peculiar. Since then we have dis-

[29] *Ibid.*, p. 130f.
[30] *Ibid.*, p. 131.
[31] *Ibid.*, p. 132.

covered a few in the depths of our own genius which are not sensibly less valuable.[32]

Accordingly his praise of Tintoret to the disparagement of Titian and Veronese in Venice was forgotten, and Titian's "portentous image of the emperor Charles" and his still greater portrait of the "formidable young man in black"[33] and then a *Baptism of Christ* by Veronese called forth James's praise. Of the last he said:

I doubt whether painting, as such, can go further. It is simply that here at last the art stands complete. The early Tuscans, as well as Leonardo, as Raphael, as Michael, saw the great spectacle in beautiful, sharp-edged elements and parts. The great Venetians felt its indissoluble unity and perceived that form and color and earth and air were equal members of every possible subject; and beneath their magical touch the hard outlines melted together and the blank intervals bloomed with meaning. In this beautiful Paul Veronese everything is part of the charm—the atmosphere as well as the figures, the look of radiant morning in the white-streaked sky as well as the beautiful human limbs, the cloth of Venetian purple about the loins of the Christ as well as the eloquent humility of his attitude.[34]

Yet the Madonnas of Filippo Lippi, of Botticelli, of Andrea del Sarto, and the marvelously beautiful *Madonna of the Chair* of Raphael were all wonderful in their way too. The notes speaking of them were written in the spring of 1874, but previous sojourns in Florence had made these Madonnas, so numerous yet so varied, each with its peculiar strong point, the most interesting thing in the city to James, and from a contemplation of them had already come one of the germs of a short story which we shall consider in the next chapter.[35] Returning to Florence, James had studied them again, finding in them much food for thought and often food for edification.

Other religious pictures, notably Fra Angelico's *Crucifixion*, Ghirlandaio's *Last Supper*, and Botticelli's *Coronation of the Virgin* attracted James in varying ways. The *Crucifixion*, masterly rendering of the "single, concentrated, spiritual emotion" of Pity was almost too serious a sermon, but it caused him to wonder how Fra Angelico, "immured in his quiet convent, away from the streets

and the studios," had learned enough of life and of art to become
a "genuine, finished, perfectly professional painter."[36] Ghirlandaio,
less intensely religious and spiritual in his *Last Supper*, but no less
reverent, James could better understand; he was more satisfying
to a modern young man.[37] Botticelli detained and perplexed and
fascinated him, because alone among painters of religious subjects
he possessed invention and the adventurous fancy which went
"a-Maying, not on wanton errands of his own, but on those of
some mystic superstition which trembles forever in his heart."[38]

In all these notes upon Italian art there is no thesis, no guiding
principle.   James visited the churches and walked through the
galleries observing and remarking sometimes one thing, sometimes another, a student of art open to impressions. A thesis of a
sort, however, evolved from all that he had learned in Italy, was
shortly to appear as James went north and considered the art
which had developed in Germany and Holland and Belgium. As
represented by Holbein it was "a very admirable art in its own way
—firm, compact, and comfortable, sure alike of its ends and means,"[39]
but

The heart grows heavy as one reflects what art might have come to if
it had developed exclusively in northern hands. The Italian painters of
the great schools certainly often enough fall short of beauty—miss it,
overlook it, wander erringly to one side of it; but its name, at least, is
always on their lips and its image always at their hearts. The early Germans do not seem to have suspected that such a thing existed, and the
painter's mission, in their eyes, is simply to appropriate, ready-made, the
infinite variations of grotesqueness which they regard as the necessary
environment of the human lot.[40]

And again later:

Early or late, German art rarely seems to me a happy adventure.[41]

In Holland, James noted the "undiluted accuracy," the truth to
life and nature of the painters, but the great artists, Rembrandt,
Potter, Ruysdael, and Gerard Dow gave him no impressions at
all.[42] Their art was true, but that was all. Belgium offered him

[36] *Translantic Sketches*, pp. 296f.
[37] *Ibid.*, pp. 297f.
[38] *Ibid.*, pp. 299f.
[39] *Ibid.*, p. 351.
[40] *Ibid.*, p. 352
[41] *Ibid.*, p. 376.
[42] *Ibid.*, p. 388.

Rubens, but though Montégut had considered Rubens a thinker, James found that he "absolutely did *not* think."[43] Even the superb *Descent from the Cross* was "painting by improvisation and not by reflection."[44]

What were the ingredients of art then? Two, at least, were beauty and thought. The artist must seek the beautiful. The artist must also reflect. It is not enough that he be boldly realistic, that he copy life faithfully and exactly. He must interpret life—see the beauty of it though this beauty may be hidden ever so deeply beneath the surface; realize the meaning of it and give this meaning to mankind. The holy pictures of the Italian artists had done this. The realistic paintings of the northern artists had not done it. Life interpreted was of more worth and value than life exposed. James had wondered about it before. He was sure of it now. Italian art had entered his consciousness to answer again for James the question raised in him by Goethe. It made him desire, too, to find the beautiful.

3. *An Observer of People*

Of still more direct and immediate importance as far as James himself was concerned during his two years in Europe, was the opportunity afforded him to study people. On his previous trip he had seen some around whom stories had quite naturally grown, travellers or inhabitants of the lands visited who had suggested many things to him. Consequently, on this trip he had come with the purpose of finding material playing no small part. Most of this material, however, he stored away in his brain for use in his stories, allowing only a small part of it to trickle into his sketches yet everywhere in these sketches his interest in people is apparent.

He liked the English countryside because "the English landscape is always a 'landscape with figures',"[45] while in Switzerland he cared not a whit for the mountains. "I relish a human flavor in my pleasures, and I fancy that it is a more equal intercourse between man and man than between man and mountain."[46] He was not Ruskin, content to stand upon an isolated peak before daybreak and follow through the atmospheric changes wrought by the

[43] *Ibid.*, p. 395.
[44] *Ibid.*, p. 396.
[45] *Ibid.*, p. 15.
[46] *Ibid.*, p. 56.

day, finding not an equal intercourse but one which lifted him up to higher things. Art might do this for James, but nature could not, and he accordingly preferred the paths which led to villages or, even more, a good interior with the suggestions of people who had once lived there—the "social atmosphere" of places. It was still better again to find these places inhabited by living, breathing individuals whom one could watch.

However, James was often delightfully inconsistent in his reactions. It was probably due to his mood. Tourists in Switzerland at times fretted him, especially the "terrible German element" and the crowds on the Sheideck pass.[47] Later he confessed that he was glad to see the tourists there; it was "a 'show country'" anyway.[48] In Rome he often sought relief from the "swarming democracy" of his fellow tourists in the calm quiet of St. Peter's[49] and breathed a grateful sigh when the exodus of foreigners occurred in May and one could see and enjoy the few good Italians who were left.[50] In Homburg, however, he quite relished the opportunity which the gathering of many nationalities there gave him to compare and contrast them. Indeed, here, free from artistic diversions, he found he could advance his study of human nature as it expressed itself in different nations. There were his own countrymen:

Superficially, no people carry more signs and tokens of what they are than Americans. I recognize them, as they advance, by the whole length of the promenade. The signs, however, are all of the negative kind, and seem to assure you, first of all, that the individual belongs to a country in which the social atmosphere, like the material, is extremely thin. American women, for the most part, fill out the ideal mould with wonderful Paris dresses; but their dresses do little toward completing them, characterizing them, shelving and labelling them socially.[51]

Contrasted with these American women were the English:

The usual English lady, marching heavily about under the weight of her ingenious bad taste, has indescribably more of the air of what one may call a social factor—the air of social responsibility, of having a part to play and a battle to fight. Sometimes, when the battle has been hard, the lady's face is very grim and unlovely, and I prefer the listless, rustling personality of my countrywomen; at others, when the cause has been graceful and the

[47] *Ibid.*, p. 62.
[48] *Ibid.*, p. 231.
[49] *Ibid.*, p. 132.
[50] *Ibid.*, p 181.
[51] *Ibid.*, p. 359.

victory easy, she has a robust amenity which is one of the most agreeable things in the world.[52]

And there were the Germans and the French:

The smokers and drinkers are the social element at the Kursaal—the dominant tone is the German tone. . . . . I have learned no especial German secrets, I have penetrated into the bosom of no German families; but somehow I have received—I constantly receive—a weighty impression of Germany. . . . . . The French are a light, pleasure-loving people; ten years of the Boulevards brings no essential amendment to the phrase. The Germans are heavy and fair-haired, deep drinkers and strong thinkers; a fortnight at Homburg doesn't reverse the formula.[53]

Indeed, there was something solid, substantial about the Germans which the French and Italians lacked and which aroused in the American traveller an envy of "the powerful German temperament and the comprehensive German brain."[54]

Individuals, however, interested James more than crowds. He was always on the lookout, hoping that some one person would attract and hold his attention. Probably many did, and a few strayed into the sketches while others were kept for his stories. There was a young priest discovered at his devotions in a tiny, tawdry church in Rome, quite oblivious of the Carnival which raged outside. James was immediately interested and could he have answered the questions which arose in him, he undoubtedly would have made the incident into a story.

In the whole deserted place, he alone knelt there for religion, and, as I sat respectfully by, it seemed to me that I could hear in the perfect silence the far-away uproar of the maskers. It was my late impression of these frivolous people, I suppose, joined with the extraordinary gravity of the young priest's face—his pious fatigue, his droning prayer, and his isolation—which gave me just then and there a supreme vision of the religious passion—its privations and resignations and exhaustions, and its terribly small share of amusement. He was young and strong and evidently of not too refined a fibre to enjoy the Carnival; but planted there with his face pale with fasting and his knees stiff with praying, he seemed so stern a satire on it and on the crazy thousands who were preferring it to *his* way, that I half expected to see some heavenly portent out of a monastic legend come down and confirm his choice. But, I confess, though I am not enamored of the Carnival myself, that his seemed a grim preference, and this for-

[52] *Ibid.*, p. 360.
[53] *Ibid.*, pp. 360 f.
[54] *Ibid.*, p. 363.

swearing of the world a terrible game—a gaining one only if your zeal
never falters; a hard fight when it does![55]

And during that same Carnival, loud, noisy, disappointing, there
was among the revellers one "capering clown" who again raised
questions in James which he could not answer.

One clever performer especially pleased me, and I should have been glad
to catch a glimpse of the natural man. I had a fancy that he was taking a
prodigious intellectual holiday, and that his gayety was in inverse ratio to
his daily mood. He was dressed like a needy scholar, in an ancient evening
coat, with a rusty black hat and gloves fantastically patched, and he carried
a little volume carefully under his arm. His humors were in excellent taste,
his whole manner the perfection of genteel comedy. . . . . Many of his
sallies I lost; those I caught were excellent. His trick was often to begin
by taking some one urbanely and caressingly by the chin and compli-
menting him on the *intelligenza della sua fisionomia*. I kept near him as
long as I could; for he seemed to me an artist, cherishing a disinterested
passion for the grotesque. But I should have liked to have seen him the
next morning, or when he unmasked that night, over his hard-earned supper,
in a smoky trattoria![56]

And there was a shepherd on the Campagna who was actually
to be used shortly in a story, who was even perhaps in a way the
germ of the story as he suggested "old world meanings to new world
eyes."

By one of those happy chances which keep observation, in Italy, always
in her best humor, a shepherd had thrown himself down under one of the
trees in the very attitude of Meliboeus. He had been washing his feet, I
suppose, in the neighboring brook, and had found it pleasant afterwards
to roll his short breeches well up on his thighs. Lying thus in the shade,
on his elbow, with his naked legs stretched out on the turf, and his soft
peaked hat over his long hair crushed back like the veritable bonnet of
Arcady, he was exactly the figure of the background of this happy valley.
The poor fellow, lying there in rustic weariness and ignorance, little fancied that he was a symbol of old-world meanings to new world eyes.[57]

And there were many others, a young American painter in Venice,
"painting, forsooth, the interior of St. Marks!"—how James envied him for a moment[58]—a beautiful child at Torcello,[59] another

[55] *Ibid.*, pp. 119 f.
[56] *Ibid.*, pp. 133 f.
[57] *Ibid.*, pp. 153 f. (See next chapter—"Adina".)
[58] *Ibid.*, p. 86.
[59] *Ibid.*, p. 88.

"artistic infant" having difficulties as he ate ice cream in Siena,[60] a "perfect mountain of a woman" in Berne who was brought forth on to the piers each morning and left till night—a kind of "patroness of Berne,"[61] "a rigid Abigail" from England proceeding grimly into Italy to join her lady;[62] there was frequently a monk here or a nun there, and James often stopped to contemplate them. He might sometime need one of these very people for his stories. The most interesting, however, as we said before, he probably did not record in his sketches but stowed away in his memory or kept revolving in his mind till stories developed around them.

4. *Characteristics of the Sketches*

As an observer, then, of art, of people, James wandered through Europe. And many of his observations he recorded exactly as he saw them and sent them back to America to the editors of the *Nation* and occasionally also to Howells for the *Atlantic*. They were so well received that on his return to America James assembled them and published them as a book entitled *Transatlantic Sketches*.[63] Though they were not originally composed with this purpose in mind, they do not suffer any too obvious lack of unity. James's own personality, his enthusiasm, his response to life, and his interest in the way the artistic consciousness dealt with life unifies them. He felt life and art even more intensely, pondered them more seriously than Gautier—certainly more than Howells and Hawthorne—though he did not always express himself in as glowing terms as the French writer. The temperament of James, and thus his expression, was often restrained by the very force of his feelings and thought; that of Gautier was fed and nourished.

Yet Gautier had influenced James. We have already noticed how Gautier's cricitism of paintings had been before James in Milan and Venice and how his method of discussing art had somewhat influenced James in Florence. Gautier had also shown James that the observations of a traveller were better when given each for what it was worth with no attempt to theorize or philosophize too deeply about them, least of all to bend them to fit a thesis as Taine had. In addition to this, Gautier had undoubtedly affected James's

---

[60] *Ibid.*, p. 260.
[61] *Ibid.*, p. 234.
[62] *Ibid.*, p. 252.
[63] Published by James R. Osgood & Co., Boston, 1875.

style of writing, his expression. James had praised Gautier's "light, descriptive prose," calling him "the poet of the look of things."[64] in his first review dealing with the French writer. In his second, he had praised it again, more specifically and in detail. Gautier, he felt, "made one of the heaviest kinds of writing one of the lightest."[65] He was an "inimitable model."

> The author's manner is so light and true, so really creative, his fancy so alert, his taste so happy, his humour so genial that he makes illusion almost as contagious as laughter; the image, the object, the scene, stand arrested by his phrase with the wholesome glow of truth overtaken. . . . . He loved words for themselves—for their look, their aroma, their colour, their fantastic intimations.[66]

It was this aspect of Gautier—his lightness, his truth, his happy taste, his genial humor, and his affection for words—that James assiduously followed. He tried to express his thought in the most felicitous way. He realized that words are to the writer what colors and pigments are to the artist of the brush, and he set himself to the task of getting words which would express himself truly and beautifully. Not immediately did he become stylistically as perfect as Gautier of course, but whatever of lightness, of color, of flavor James's prose came gradually to have in the travel sketches was due to the influence of Gautier. His first sketches of England are somewhat stiff but gradually he fell into the happier expression of his model. Had James not read Gautier, we may be sure, because of his early realistic stories, that he would have analyzed Europe and things European in a ponderous way and would have expressed himself still more ponderously and didactically. Under the influence of Gautier, James set out to forge for himself a perfect style.

One other author must be mentioned—not for the fact that he did influence James but rather because he did not. This author was Goethe, but not the Goethe of *Wilhelm Meister*,—rather the Goethe of the *Italienische Reise*. Once James referred to him vaguely in speaking of the Piazza at Assisi: "Goethe, I believe, found it much more interesting than the mighty, medieval church, and Goethe, as a cicerone, doubtless could have persuaded you that it was so, but in the humble society of Murray we shall most

[64] *Nation*, Jan. 25, 1872, p. 61.
[65] *North American Review*, Apr., 1873, p. 313.
[66] *Ibid.*, pp. 313 f.

of us find deeper meanings in the church."[67]   The sketch in which
this reference occurs was written in the winter of 1873 and '74
after James had been joined by his brother William, and it may
well be that Henry's vague idea of what Goethe had said was due
to William who had read the *Italienische Reise* long before.[68]   If
Henry James had been acquainted with Goethe's book, references
to the German writer would undoubtedly have appeared on many
of the pages dealing with Rome, for to both James and Goethe
Rome meant much the same tremendous thing. Rather than to the
sketches written on James's second visit, it is necessary to return
for a moment to the letter written on the occasion of the first:

Here I am then in the Eternal City. . . . From midday to dusk I have
been roaming the streets. Que vous en dirai-je? At last—for the first
time—I live! It beats everything: it leaves the Rome of your fancy—your
education—nowhere. It makes Venice—Florence—Oxford—London seem
like little cities of pasteboard. I went reeling and moaning thro' the streets,
in a fever of enjoyment. In the course of four or five hours I traversed almost the whole of Rome. . . . .[69]

From this, now turn to Goethe's first impressions.

Ja, ich bin endlich in dieser Hauptstadt der Welt angelangt![70]

and again:

Nun bin ich sieben Tage hier, und nach und nach tritt in meiner Seele der
allgemeine Begriff dieser Stadt hervor. Wir gehen fleissig hin und wider;
ich mache mir die Plane des alten und neuen Roms bekannt, betrachte
die Ruinen, die Gebäude, besuche ein und die andere Villa; die grössten
Merkwürdigkeiten werden ganz langsam behandelt, ich thue nur die Augen
auf, und seh' und geh' und komme wieder; denn mann kann sich nur in
Rom auf Rom vorbereiten.[71]

Rome was to each the most wonderful experience that had yet
happened to him. Each looked upon it as the climax of his life up
to that time, and each time as James went back during the next
decade the wonderful experience of the first visit seemed to repeat
itself. When he was away from Rome, he dreamed always of returning. Goethe, after the first thrill of excitement, settled down to
study Rome and Italy, to attempt to explain them as the product

[67] *Transatlantic Sketches*, p. 219.
[68] See *Letters of William James*, Boston, 1920, I, 91.
[69] *Letters of Henry James*, I, 24.
[70] Goethe: *Italienische Reise*, Works, Vol. 22, Stuttgart, 1895, p. 114.
[71] *Ibid.*, p. 119.

of forces. James, of course, did not do this, but had he read Goethe's *Italienische Reise* instead of Taine's more arbitrary *Voyage en Italie*, he might have become a philosopher with a flexible theory more than an observer. I am not sure, however, that his purpose or ours would have been better served by that. As it was, James as well as Goethe brought away from Rome ideas and principles, though often they were but half formed in James's case, which were as von Klenze says of Goethe,[72] to guide their intellectual and moral life ever after. James brought away also ideas and theories which were to guide his artistic life, and as a still more material benefit, he brought a place to locate *Roderick Hudson*.

[72] von Klenze: *The Interpretation of Italy*, Chicago, 1907, p. 84.

CHAPTER XI

TWO CIVILIZATIONS

The trip to Europe in 1869 had had its tangible results—three short stories, by-products of the trip itself. Now the longer European sojourn from 1872 to the late summer of 1874 was likewise to have its results—more stories, but not by-products this time. They were main products, for James, realizing the happy success of the stories which had grown spontaneously out of the earlier visit, had come to Europe this time not for a vacation and rest but for the purpose of writing, of getting material which he could make into stories. The writing of the travel reports and notes was secondary to his main purpose. But, though secondary, it had its importance which we noted in the preceding chapter. The observations which James made as he wandered about gathering materials for the notes which he was under commission to the *Nation* to write, offer *one* of the clues to James's future development. He became an active observer, instead of remaining a more or less passive one.

Travel, however, offers not the only clue. There was something else. And it was the same something which along with the absorbing of impressions had from his earliest years been James's chief delight—reading. And now, more frankly than ever before, James allowed Balzac, Mérimée, Musset, to give him not just suggestions for method or manner of writing but·the germs of his stories. He saw possibilities which these authors had not developed or made the most of—other ways of treating similar situations, or the reverse situation—and proceeded to develop a story on his own initiative. It cannot be said that he plagiarized. He simply caught the suggestion from the stories of others, combined it with his own observations, developed it by means of the imagination which he had trained in his early romantic attempts, nourished it by the atmosphere of Europe, and produced a story of his own. We have noted before how James liked to treat one subject from several sides. Now, in taking hints from other authors, in reversing their situations, he was merely doing what he had already done as regards his own stories. Gradually as he became more proficient, as, too, things he observed insisted upon being written about, he began not with a borrowed hint but with these observations—the contrast of two civilizations—and worked up a situation to illustrate it. Thus reading and travel—travel, it must be remembered, in which the two main interests were art and people—worked together in James and caused him to produce seven short stories and a novel.

1. *Stories Growing Out of the Interest in Art and Books*

The first four of these stories were directly influenced by James's reading and his interest in art. In *The Madonna of the Future*[1] and *The Sweetheart of M. Briseux*[2] paintings and painters appear and the influence of Balzac is to be discerned; in *The Last of the Valerii*[3] an antique statue and the interest of people in relics of the past, an interest which appears again in *Adina*,[4] form the story with the guiding influence that of Mérimée.

The Madonna of the Future caught its germs from or was influenced by Balzac's *Le Chef d'Oeuvre Inconnu* and also Musset's *Lorenzaccio*, facts which have been quite ignored by former critics of James. Balzac's story of the artist who believed he knew the secret of how to paint living and breathing people but was disillusioned after ten years of work on his master piece by the careless remark of a young man that there was "rien sur sa toile" was reversed by James. His story is of a man who spends years studying the madonnas of the museums of Florence, planning to paint the picture of a woman which will unite all the best points of all the great madonnas in one supreme masterpiece, but he is also disillusioned by a thoughtless young man who this time reveals to him that his intended model has grown old and leads the artist to see that he himself is old. "Old—old! . . . . If she is old, what am I? If her beauty has faded, where—where is my strength? Has life been a dream? Have I worshipped too long?—have I loved too well?"[5] In both cases the charm is broken and the artist dies of grief.

Balzac's story was laid in Paris. The finished picture was to have been not a madonna, but a beautiful living woman, with all the earthly charms of woman. James located his story in Florence. The masterpiece was to be a madonna, instinct with spiritual mean-

---

[1] Appeared in *Atlantic Monthly*, Mar., 1873.
[2] Appeared in *Galaxy*, June, 1873.
[3] Appeared in *Atlantic Monthly*, Jan., 1874.
[4] Appeared in *Scribner's Monthly*, May and June, 1874.
[5] "Madonna of the Future," *Atlantic Monthly*, 1873, p. 289.

ings. Perhaps the many wonderful madonnas of all schools and periods in the galleries and churches of Florence, perhaps James's attempt to pick out the best one, his finding that there was no best but something good in one, another something in another, had suggested to him the story of an artist who would try to paint a supreme one, and this in turn had suggested Balzac's story as a model. Indeed, we cannot finally tell whether it was Balzac or the museums of Florence which gave James the first clue and he is silent on the subject in the preface to the volume of the Collected Edition which contains the story, but both Balzac and the museums worked together in the result. The problem is further complicated by the fact that Musset's *Lorenzaccio*, translated by James in his youth and perhaps reread at this time,[6] may indeed have suggested Florence as a setting. At least one minor person and one brief scene in it suggested the name of the artist Theobald, and was responsible in two short speeches for the character which the artist in James's story was to have:

Tebaldeo speaks: "Mes ouvrages ont peu de mérite; je sais mieux aimer les arts que je ne sais les exercer. Ma jeunesse tout entière s'est passée dans les églises. Il me semble que je ne puis admirer ailleurs Raphael et notre divin Buonaretti. Je demeure alors durant des journées devant leurs ouvrages, dans un extase sans égale."[7]

And again:

"Je passe les journées à l'atelier. Le dimanche je vais à l'Annonciade ou à Sainte-Marie; les moines trouvent que j'ai de la voix, ils me mettre une robe blanche et une calotte rouge, et je fais ma partie dans les choeurs, quelquefois un petit solo; ce sont les seules occasions où je vais en public. Le soir, je vais chez ma maîtresse, et quand la nuit est belle, je la passe sur son balcon. Personne ne me connaît, et je ne connais personne."[8]

The entire life of James's Theobald is spent in much the same manner, his time divided among the churches, his studio, and the abode of his mistress.

James's story thus has much in common with Balzac's story and with a part of Musset's drama. He had no intention of hiding the fact, but frankly had one of his characters remind the reader that Theobald's painting may prove to be simply like that of the painter " 'in that tale of Balzac's—a mere mass of incoherent scratches and

---

[6] See Interchapter A.
[7] Musset: *Oeuvres Completes*, Paris, 1888, IV, 53.
[8] *Ibid.*, p. 60.

daubs, a jumble of dead paint.' "[9]   Another tells Theobald that he reminds him of "that charming speech of the Florentine painter in Alfred de Musset's Lorenzaccio" and quotes the second of the speeches given above.[10]   For this reason one is inclined to believe that the Madonnas of Florence furnished the first suggestion to James and that he then recalled Balzac and Musset to help him work up his story.

The result, however, surpasses both the story of the painter which is but hinted at in Musset's drama, and Balzac's story which it closely parallels in some parts of its plot development. It emerged from James's hands a masterpiece on its own account. He threw himself into the writing of it, put his own ideas and feelings about art and Italy and an American in Italy into it, and gave it a fire and passion which is not in Balzac's well developed little story. Balzac's story is structurally well worked out. James's story is that and more—it is passionately felt. And the narrator who tells the story—or more strictly the narrator who *first* told the story, for James complicated his device of using a narrator, H., who appears in the story by the addition of a narrator who retells the story H. has told him—was James himself, the James of the travel reports and art notes. He began: "It relates to my youth and to Italy: two fine things!"[11]   As soon as he had arrived in Florence, even though it was late at night, he had set out for a stroll around the city. As he gazed at Michael Angelo's David and Cellini's Perseus, he had been joined by Theobald, a figure invented not simply to work out the plot, but to express one side of a question which the art of Italy and the culture of the continent brought up in the mind of a young American traveller. Theobald, like the narrator, like James, had to confess to an American origin. Theobald lamented it, expressing the difficulties which beset an American who wished to succeed:

"We are the disinherited of art! . . . . We are condemned to be superficial! We are excluded from the magic circle. The soil of American perception is a poor little barren, artificial deposit. Yes! We are wedded to imperfection. An American, to excel, has just ten times as much to learn as a European. We lack the deeper sense. We have neither taste nor tact nor force!"[12]

[9] *Atlantic Monthly*, Mar., 1873, p. 285.
[10] *Ibid.*, p. 285.
[11] *Atlantic Monthly*, Mar., 1876, p. 276.
[12] *Ibid.*, p. 278.

That was, indeed, one side of the situation, but there was another side. James gave it in the answer which his narrator had ready for the querulous artist.

"But do you know my own thought? Nothing is so idle as to talk about our want of a nutritive soil, of opportunity, of inspiration, and all the rest of it. The worthy part is to do something fine! There's no law in our glorious Constitution against that. Invent, create, achieve! No matter if you've to study fifty times as much as one of these! What else are you an artist for? Be you our Moses . . . . and lead us out of the house of bondage!"[13]

That was the other side. The two characters represent the two sides which James felt in himself, and the story is devoted to showing the futility of Theobald's side which talked and lamented but did not act. *The Madonna of the Future* reminds us of *The Passionate Pilgrim* in giving thus the reactions of Americans to an older civilization, but here, as in the former case, the critic must carefully notice where the emphasis falls. This is perhaps more difficult in the second story for Theobald does represent more directly some of James's own ideas than Searle did. James had written to Norton, we remember, "to write well and worthily of American things one need even more than elsewhere to be a *master*,"[14] but it was not the agonized cry of an author who despaired. It was the voice of one who was seeing the difficulties and planning to evade them. *The Madonna of the Future* was now James's answer to himself, his squarely facing his own problem. What though an American *had* ten times or fifty times as much to learn, need that deter him if he had the will? No! And it was James's will, his determination to succeed, which made this story the best thing he had yet done. The story has form; it has feeling; figurative, imaginative though it is, it rings true; it is an allegory of life.

James's next story, unfortunately, was not so good. Again he depended upon Balzac's *Le Chef d'Oeuvre Inconnu* but with greater differences. *The Sweetheart of M. Briseux* is the story of a masterpiece which *was* painted, while the woman who posed for it was forgotten. A traveller tells how he has sought in the musty musée of a small French town the picture of a fair young lady in a yellow shawl. Another person, a little white-haired woman, quite obviously an old maid, has come to gaze at it too. Suddenly the man perceives her likeness to the lady of the portrait, despite the difference in

---

[13] *Ibid.*, p. 278.
[14] *Letters of Henry James*, I, 31.

years, and she reveals to him the story of the painting of the masterpiece, the first of the works of M. Briseux to bring to him fame.
Twenty years before, she had accompanied a young American
painter and his mother to Europe while he studied. They had become engaged, but she had refused to marry him before he should
have proved his ability. He, poor chap, lacked it as well as the will
to apply himself. She had offered herself as a model—surely his
beloved would inspire him if anything was to—and he had tried
to paint her. One day a poor young artist had come into the studio,
had seen the model and the crude, half-finished painting and seizing
the brush while Harold was out of the room, had in a few touches
proved what he could do with such a model. She had consented to
pose for him, though it had meant the breaking of her engagement,
and he had produced the Lady in the Yellow Shawl. After that
his way had been easy. As for her: "I had served his purpose and
had already passed into the dusky limbo of unhonored victims, the
experience—intellectual and other—of genius,"[15] forgotten except
for the immortality conferred upon her by the famous painting.

The situation is slightly suggestive of what might have happened
had the artist in *Le Chef d'Oeuvre Inconnu* been able to paint the
portrait of Gillette after the young painter had loaned her to him.
The situation is changed, however; here the young girl offers herself and is unforgiven by her fiancé; in Balzac's story, the fiancé
offers her and she refuses to return to him when she sees how he has
disillusioned the artist. In this case, Balzac's story is the more
effective.

The contrast of the two artists with its moral for a would-be one
is similar to the question raised in *The Madonna of the Future.*
The Sweetheart of M. Briseux, however, is inferior to *The Madonna
of the Future* in several respects. It is not as well proportioned; it
throws into emphasis the character of the little old woman while the
more interesting characters of the two artists are seen only vaguely
through this mild and gentle person; and it lacks the feeling, the
passionate conviction about art which made its predecessor
great.

Balzac had served James's purpose, and in the next story, *The
Last of the Valerii,* he took his hint from Mérimée. Long years before,
under the influence of La Farge, James had read *La Venus d'Ille,*

[15] *Galaxy*, June, 1873, p. 778.

had been so enthralled by it, that he had translated it and sent it off to a New York weekly periodical which cruelly had neither acknowledged nor printed it;[16] but James had remembered the story as he had remembered Musset's play and now that he was in Europe where he was everywhere reminded of a pagan past, he recalled the story once more and very likely reread it. Mérimée's story seemed even more real, more possible in Italy than it had when he first read it. One felt the pagan past there, almost an active influence. Every bronze, every marble statue of antiquity seemed almost alive to James, seemed a person from the past who disturbed in its sleep underneath the earth of centuries might, now that it had been disinterred, exert some baleful influence upon persons of today. Of course, Mérimée's story *was* untrue; a statue could not claim a man as its own and smother him in its nuptial bed embrace, but wasn't it conceivable that a man might fall in love with the beauty of a statue, so much more enigmatic, perplexing because of its silence than a human being, and have his peace of mind quite disturbed? Might not the worship of art which was beautiful lead to something of that sort? Wasn't that really what had happened to his painter in Florence? Italian art, so lovely, so beautiful, threatened to disturb James's own peace of mind. What effect might it not have upon a man who was not a rational American, but a "sturdy young Latin," a superstitious pagan rather than a good Catholic, a man born in Italy with the blood of the pagan centuries in his veins? The germ took root and developed. How could it fail to with the atmosphere of Italy fostering it?

James retained the situation of lover, sweetheart who becomes his wife, and statue of Mérimée's story, but he worked it over and improved it in many ways. He gave the girl an active part in the story making her the one who first becomes interested in statues and who in the end solves the situation she has unwittingly caused. In Mérimée's story she is left as the helpless, innocent victim, along with the young man not quite so innocent, of the statue his father had discovered. And James made her an American girl, thrilled to be marrying into an ancient Italian family, but sincere, genuinely in love with her count, though she is determined, too, to dig up the old statues which rumor has it are buried under the soil of the ancestral domain. Aided by her godfather who tells the story,

[16] *Notes of a Son and Brother*, pp. 93f. See Interchapter A.

James made of Martha a most attractive and true portrait. The count, last of his line, he carefully sketched, too, in an endeavor to explain the survival of pagan instincts in him. He recalled Hawthorne's Donatello and tried to make his count more probable.

At first the count opposes the whim of his wife to excavate for hidden treasures.

"Let them lie, the poor disinherited gods, the Minerva, the Apollo, the Ceres, you are so sure of finding . . . . and don't break their rest. What do you want of them? We can't worship them. Would you put them on pedestals to stare and mock at them? If you can't believe in them, don't disturb them. Peace be with them! . . . . Yes, by Bacchus, I am superstitious! . . . . Too much so, perhaps! But I'm an old Italian, and you must take me as you find me. There have been things seen and done here which leave strange influences behind! . . . . Don't dig up any more, or I won't answer for my wits!"[17]

but the girl, true to American girls, has her way, and not a bronze Venus but a marble Juno is discovered. Immediately the count becomes excited, pours out a libation, secretly carries away the hand which has been broken from the statue, changes his former devoted attitude toward his wife to one of inattention, almost of indifference, becomes sombre and thoughtful but confesses he is "prodigiously happy," and reverting to the past, becomes a pagan in every sense of the word. The wife at first is dazed and then realizes gradually that the count's love for her has been transferred to the goddess. She endures passively until she finds a roughly extemporized altar before the statue and the evidence of a sacrifice. Then her grief turns to active indignation, and she orders the statue buried again. Its baleful spell is broken, and the count, relieved, returns to his wife—yet the hand of the Juno he keeps in a cabinet of curios.

As in the case of the first story patterned after Balzac, in this one modeled after Mérimée, James actually improved upon his model. He made his story more compact—in Mérimée's the figure of the father intrudes and the two young people move more as puppets of the author's plan than as independent beings. He made it less improbable and fantastic; it has in fact a germ of truth and warning in it. Like *The Madonna of the Future* it is an allegory, more true than untrue. He sketched his characters carefully. The young girl is as realistic, first in her enthusiasms, then in her qualms

[17] *Atlantic Monthly*, Jan., 1874, p. 73.

and fears, as any figure James had yet produced, while the count himself is not wholly improbable. *The Last of the Valerii* is again a masterpiece, unfortunately excluded from the Collected Edition for some reason, but surely not for that suspected by Beach for fear of plagiarism.[18] The story is James's, not Mérimée's. He had studied the French writer to such an advantage that he could defeat him on his own ground.

Shortly after writing *The Last of the Valerii* James tried the same thing he had in regard to the story written under the influence of Balzac. He wrote another story, even less like Mérimée's, and more his own, but, as in the first case, the initial impulse was dead, the heat and fervor generated as James had realized he was actually equalling the master had cooled. *Adina* was not based on any tale of Mérimée's, not even *La Venus d'Ille*; it was based, however, upon James's own story, *The Last of the Valerii*. It took the idea of pagan past as contrasted with civilized present and reversed the situation of the story. Again it was laid in Italy; again it took for its hero an Italian representing the past, but this time James used the poor peasant whom he had observed upon the Campagna and who had been to him "the symbol of old-world meanings to new-world eyes" as he had reclined "in rustic weariness and ignorance."[19] Again James used an American girl for his heroine. Adina Waddington, however, is much less satisfying, less substantial than her predecessor, and she is the one who gives way to the past, who becomes pagan, rather than winning the past over to herself. The statue of Juno was the point of contention in *The Last of the Valerii*; a golden topaz with the image of Tiberius upon it causes the complications in *Adina*. The young Italian, Angelo, "something better than a mere peasant," but carefree, happy, pagan, is playing with it when an American, Sam Scrope, perceives him and offers him a small sum for it. Not realizing its worth, Angelo parts with it. Scrope has it polished, rejoices that he has come into possession of the finest intaglio in the world, has no qualms whatever as to the

<hr />

[18] Beach: *The Method of Henry James*, p. 189. Beach fails to consider that "The Madonna of the Future," which James did include, even more than "The Last of the Valerii," was based in part on the story of another author. That James did not fear the charge of plagiarism is shown by the fact that later he translated both stories into French for publication in the *Revue des Deux Mondes*, where they appeared as "La Madone de l'Avenir," Apr. 1, 1876, and "Le Dernier des Valerius," Nov. 15, 1875.

[19] *Transatlantic Sketches*, p. 154; see chapter X.

small price he paid for it because, had he offered more, the young man would have suspected its value and Scrope never could have purchased it. But Angelo has liked his toy and suddenly does realize its value. Meanwhile Scrope becomes engaged to the American girl, Adina Waddington, who is touring the continent with her mother. Adina shudders at the bold intaglio and hopes Scrope came by it honestly. Angelo observes Adina with Scrope and seeks to destroy Scrope's peace of mind by winning the attention of Adina. She is fascinated by the romance of having a poor Italian lover dog her footsteps and spend the night in the garden of the hotel under her window, and finally she disappears with Angelo. Scrope flings the fatal intaglio into the Tiber. Like the Juno it must be returned to its rest.

The story is related by a narrator, a friend of Scrope's, who does what he can to make it seem true. The plot is one which should have been worked out in terms of character and James needed to call to his assistance the example of more authors than just Mérimée. James's characters are not well-rounded; they have no depth, and seem but one-sided puppets in the author's hands, manufactured to bring out the difference, as James sensed it, between the pagan and the civilized, and each side is distorted so that one seems fantastic, the other grotesque.

These four stories, even the first two where the influence was predominantly Balzacian, bear witness to the influence of Mérimée upon the technique of Henry James, an influence which has already been felt and observed in a slight measure but which, until now, is not to be discerned as an active force. It was due to Mérimée's example, we have already surmised, that James used the device of a narrator, a minor participant in the action, to make his stories seem more real and utilized an incident to bring out concretely the atmosphere of a land visited by a traveller. This is what he had done in the early European stories; it is what he has just done again in their sequels where he is more successful because, following Mérimée's example more closely than before, he made the incident the main thing, let it by itself bring out the atmosphere, making any discussion of this atmosphere an integral part of the story.

A review of *Dernières Nouvelles* published in February 1874,[20] the month after *The Last of the Valerii* was published, gives further

---

[20] Appeared in *Nation*, Feb. 12, 1874.

and even more specific evidence in James's own words of the great
influence Mérimée had had upon him, counteracting by his "extraordinary conciseness" James's tendency to analyze and to follow
the expansive effusiveness, the copiously gushing narrative of
George Sand whom he had highly praised six years before and still
thought much of. Since the last tales of Mérimée were not his best
in James's opinion, he began the review with an estimate of the
French writer's "limited but singularly perfect talent," based on
a consideration of all of his stories.

Victor Hugo would have been none the worse poet for a little of Mérimée's
conscious sobriety, and Madame Sand would have been none the less
readable for occasionally emulating his extraordinary conciseness . . . . the
shortest way to describe Mérimée would perhaps be to say that he is the
absolute reverse of Madame Sand. He is unlike her in the *quantity* of his
genius as well as the quality. . . . Such as they are . . . . we confess that
Mérimée's chiselled and polished little fictions, and, indeed, the whole
manner and system of the author, have always had a great fascination for
us. He is, perhaps, the most striking modern example of zealous artistic
conciseness—of the literary artist who works in detail, by the line, by the
word. There have been poets who scanned their rhythm as narrowly as
Mérimée, but we doubt whether there has ever been a prose writer. His
effort was to compress as large an amount of dramatic substance as possible into a very narrow compass, and the result is that, though his stories
are few and short, one may read them again and again, and perceive with
each reading a greater force of meaning. Some of the earlier ones are most
masterly in this pregnant brevity; the story seems to say its last word, as
the reader lays it down, with a kind of magical after-resonance. We have
often thought a selection might be made from these tales, and presented
to young narrators as a sort of manual of their trade, a guide for the
avoidance of prolixity.[21]

The example of Mérimée was for James's tales in 1873 what the
example of Gautier was for his travel reports. Both artists en-
joined upon him the necessity of working "in detail, by the line,
by the word," as well as by the whole, compressing "as large an
amount of dramatic substance as possible into a very narrow
compass."

This was the side of Mérimée which had most affected James's
practice in his own stories, but he could recognize and admire
another side also.

[21] *Ibid* p 111

With his brutal subjects and his cynical style, Mérimée is doubtless thoroughly disagreeable to such readers as are not fascinated by his artistic skill. To tell a terrible little story without flinching—without expressing a grain of reprobation for the clever rascal who escapes under cover of the scuffle in which his innocent rival has his brains blown out, or a grain of compassion for the poor guilty lady whose husband or father, brought upon the scene by the crack of pistols, condemns her to convent-cell for life; not to be sentimental, not to be moral, not to be rhetorical, but to have simply a sort of gentlemanly, epicurean relish for the bitterness of the general human lot, and to distill it into little polished silver cups—this was Mérimée's conscious effort, and this was his rare success.[22]

James's temperament was less epicurean than Mérimée's, especially where the "bitterness of the general human lot" was concerned; he chose less brutal subjects; he was rarely cynical; his imagination as in *The Last of the Valerii* did better when held to the possible— for it *was* possible that a beautiful statue might disturb the peace of mind of a highly imaginative being—but he had the same love of artistry of form, of perfection of detail, a desire to distill his stories into "little polished silver cups," though he had not until now been able to write stories which revealed it. Nowhere again is the evidence of the effect of Mérimée upon the sensitive artistic consciousness of James as apparent as in these four stories written in 1873, or possibly in 1872,[23] but we may be sure that all his life as James strove for compactness, for artistry, for perfection of form in his short stories and novels, he was frequently recalling the example of the French writer.

There was, however, still another concern than artistry for an earnest young writer. There was again, life.

2. *Stories Growing Out of Life*

James was greatly encouraged by the success he had had redoing Balzac and Mérimée. He knew that two of the stories were excellent, and Howells wrote to him from America, praising them, especially *The Madonna*, speaking freely of "the undissenting voice of acclaim" with which it had been hailed,[24] and eagerly demanding more. But James, emboldened by his personal success, the confident feeling of power that had been born in him, turned a deaf ear upon

[22] *Ibid.*, p. 111.

[23] The stories were often kept back some time by such editors as Howells before publication and we have no way of dating exactly the writing of these four.

[24] *Life and Letters of Wm. Dean Howells*, I, 175, letter dated Mar. 10, 1873.

Howells—of course he was gratified by the praise, but he had other things in mind—and set to work to make stories no longer out of borrowed hints but out of life. He might recall other authors now and then perhaps, but he would not consciously remember or depend upon them. People and situations in which people found themselves, rather than statues and paintings, spoke to him and demanded to be spoken of. In his first European stories his own feelings had sought an outlet. In the stories which he had just written, he had let American girls with their dreams of romance play a part. Now his countrymen wandering about Europe or settled there began to stand out against this background in such a way and with such a meaning that he, in turn, began to see stories emanating not from the background but from the characters themselves. In America no people had stood out and asked for a historian. That had been the trouble. Americans in Europe, however, did need one if only to show how they differed from the Europeans. He had sensed this in *Travelling Companions*. It was inevitable that a longer sojourn in Europe should bring it still more emphatically before him.

When in the summer of 1873, James settled in Homburg temporarily quite away from the spell of Italy and of art, he felt under the spell of people. It was here that he wrote *Mme. de Mauves*,[25] according to his own confession,[26] though whether from germs gathered here or in France the preceding winter we have no way of knowing, and it was here certainly that *Eugene Pickering*[27] had its conception, though in this case we have no knowledge of whether James wrote it here or not. But Homburg, we noted in the preceding chapter, was interesting, endurable because of the "comings and goings of a multifarious European crowd"[28] allowing James to compare the "national idiosyncracies" of Germans, French, English, and Americans, and to philosophize about them. It was, perhaps, the philosophizing even more than the observations which produced the stories. The observations furnished the hints; thought and cogitation which savored of psychology developed them, and

[25] Appeared in *Galaxy*, Feb. and Mar., 1874. Spelled "Madame de Mauves" when reprinted in 1875. ("Adina" appeared after this but it was so closely connected with "The Last of the Valerii" that it was considered with that. There is no way of telling which was written first.)
[26] See preface to Vol. XIII of the Collected Edition.
[27] Appeared in *Atlantic Monthly*, Oct. and Nov., 1874.
[28] *Transatlantic Sketches*, p. 359.

the stories must accordingly be considered from this angle more than from the angle of technical construction.

Mme. de Mauves, as one of the minor characters writes to the young American, Longmore, who is to become its hero, is

".... the miserable story of an American girl, born to be neither a slave nor a toy marrying a profligate Frenchman, who believes that a woman *must* be one or the other. The silliest American woman is too good for the best foreigner, and the poorest of us have moral needs a Frenchman can't appreciate. She was romantic and wilful, and thought Americans were vulgar .... M. de Mauves cared, of course, for nothing but her money, which he's spending royally on his *mêmes plaisirs.*"[29]

And she urges him to

"prove to Mme. de Mauves that an American friend may mingle admiration and respect better than a French husband."[30]

The story is the illustration of how Longmore does this. James thus tells us in the beginning what the outcome will be—satisfying morally if not emotionally—but despite this he keeps our interest, due chiefly to the care with which he touched off his characters.

James made the initial situation seem possible and real by explaining that Euphemia Cleve, an American girl, had been educated in a French convent among the daughters of old families, and largely by means of "ultramontane works of fiction" which had given her the idea that birth was the only guaranty of an ideal delicacy of feeling and thus of happiness. The marriage with the debt-ridden but titled brother of one of her school mates had followed, and at the time the story opens, perhaps half a dozen years later, she has been disillusioned and has settled back, resigning herself to her lot, trying simply to live with her sorrow. But Longmore comes from America, sees her, pities her, longs to make her smile, and the profligate French husband, annoyed at the stiffness of his wife, at her evident scorn of his immoral life, hopes viciously and then fully expects that she will find her affections hopelessly involved with Longmore to the end that her own actions will justify his. But M. de Mauves fails to reckon with the fact that both Euphemia and Longmore are Americans, in whom conscience and reason and dignity are stronger than passion. They meet the situation bravely; they discuss it—a bit too sententiously to be wholly

[29] *Galaxy*, Feb., 1874, p. 218.
[30] *Ibid.*, p. 218.

true to life—and they part. James's desire to finish the affair completely led him to explain briefly the dénouement: M. de Mauves's
interest in his wife has been reawakened by the enigma of her
conduct but she remains obdurately superior and scornful, and he in
despair, blows out his brains. Longmore hears of this but "still
lingers at home." "The truth is, that in the midst of all the ardent
tenderness of his memory of Mme. de Mauves, he has become
conscious of a singular feeling, for which Awe would be hardly
too strong a name."[31]

Mme. de Mauves is a story of character, of certain aspects of
human nature. It had probably grown up around some American
woman, married to a Frenchman, whom James had suspected of
trying to live with a sorrow. From this his imagination had built up a
story based upon his knowledge of American and French tempera-
ments. To make it seem probable, he had returned to his former
bête noire and had indulged in careful analysis of character. At
the end, conscious that perhaps he had been overscrupulous, he
confessed with Longmore that he was forced to regard Euphemia
with a kind of "awe." Thus he forestalled the charge that he had
been untrue when he had intended to be true.

James's basic principles, however, were true to human nature,
at least to the American side of it. His analysis of character brings
them out, and, it should be mentioned in passing, is not over-
indulged in or abused when kept in his own hands and not put
into the mouths of his characters. James's error appears in what
he made his characters say and do. Unlike Dickens, he knew man
but not men. Longmore, the practical young man from America,
who

. . . . could fairly claim that in a sentimental way he asked very little
of life—he made modest demands upon passion . . . . like many spirits of
the same stock he had a lurking principle of asceticism to whose authority
he had ever paid an unquestioning respect.[32]

and Euphemia, reaping now the returns of her early dreams and
sentimentality, who says:

"I believe . . . . that I have nothing on earth but a conscience . . . . nothing
but a dogged, clinging, inexpugnable conscience. Does that prove me to
be indeed of your faith and race, and have you one for which you can say

[31] *Galaxy*, Mar., 1874, p. 374.
[32] *Ibid.*, p. 363.

as much? I don't say it in vanity, for I believe that if my conscience will prevent me from doing anything very base, it will effectually prevent me from doing anything very fine."[33]

are true to American nature. Euphemia's fine speech, however, reveals James's error at the same time it reveals his insight. What woman would analyze herself so carefully to a man? And what man would answer:

"I'm delighted to hear it, ... We are made for each other. It's very certain I too shall never do anything fine. And yet I have fancied that in my case this inexpugnable organ you so eloquently describe might be blinded and gagged awhile, in a fine cause, if not turned out of doors."[34]

Euphemia's conscience would admit of no capitulation; Longmore's might "in a fine cause," but not otherwise.

Their final meeting offers another instance of James's violation of the principle of vraisemblance. If Euphemia simply refused to see Longmore when he makes his last call upon her instead of seeing him and offering him a chance "to do gallantly what it seemed unworthy of both of them that he should do meanly,"[35] we could understand her much better. James, however, was too interested in what she could be made to say grandly and transferred what might, indeed, have been her thoughts when she was by herself to actual conversation. Euphemia might have planned in her boudoir to meet Longmore with certain reasons but she should not have been able to carry out the speeches when the meeting came. Their parting should have resulted from things which were felt and sensed rather than said.

Even though it was not for the hint which James gives in the maiden name of Euphemia—that of Cleve—the reader would be led to note the similarity between this heroine and that rare creature of French literature, the Princesse de Cléves. There is no exterior evidence in any reviews or notes that James had read Madame de la Fayette's book, but the nature of the two fine heroines is similar— it should be mentioned that the American one seems more true to her nationality and temperament than the excellent French one does to hers—and the mistake which James made in having his people think out loud and do grand things may be traced to the

[33] *Ibid.*, p. 358.
[34] *Ibid.*, p. 358.
[35] *Ibid.*, p. 369.

example of the French novel, forerunner of so many psychological novels.

All this has concerned us with the American characters in the story, and it is not for an American critic who has far less first hand knowledge of French character than James himself had opportunity of gathering, to judge finally of that side. However, an American feels that a reply should be made to Mlle. Garnier, who assails this tale and other early stories of James as not doing justice to the French.[36] M. de Mauves and his sister, Madame Clairin, are not attractive people, but they are very like some of the unsavory French men and unscrupulous French women whom one meets in Balzac, in Feuillet, in Feydeau, and it was upon such characters, no doubt, that James based them. He wished to illustrate the difference between morality and immorality and its relation to human nature which he had noted earlier as he discussed the question of morality *versus* passion. What more natural, than that when he himself wished to show the evil side, he should follow the lead of the French moderns whom he had exhorted to turn to paths of virtue. Certainly if extent of treatment, frequency of appearance of the situation in literature, was any indication of its truth, these writers who had so many similarly minded brethren were to be listened to though one might shudder also at their frankness. In writing of the Parisian stage, James said "Novel and drama alike betray an incredibly superficial perception of the moral side of life. It is not that adultery is their only theme, but that the treatment of it is so singularly vicious and arid."[37] Thus far James had not stopped in France long enough to study all sides of French character, but he had seen enough of it to support the opinion that French writers were not far from wrong, though he loathed their vicious treatment and carefully avoided it in his own handling of immoral husbands and sisters-in-law.

Mme. de Mauves has challenged our attention from quite a different standpoint from the stories of this period hitherto considered, and a word remains to be said comparing it with them. James's first concern in *The Madonna of the Future* and *The Last of the Valerii* and their sequels was to make a story; the contrast

[36] Marie-Reine Garnier: *Henry James et la France*, Paris, 1927. Chapître II, in particular, questions James's knowledge of French characters and French institutions.
[37] *Transatlantic Sketches*, p. 107.

of two civilizations entered but as secondary to story element. His first concern in *Madame de Mauves* was to depict the characters and the conflict between two nationalities where the basic principles of human nature in each are totally different. Story interest gave way to philosophical. James took one bold step; he conquered the temptation to use a narrator who would vouch for the truth of the story, his practice in all of the other stories written in '73 and '74, and related it directly, usually looking at Euphemia, however, through the eyes of Longmore. As he dispensed with the useful narrator, he gave his attention to the developing of his characters, noting all the barely perceptible changes in their feelings, prolonging the action by slow, careful, thorough exposition of the successive phrases and bringing each to a head in dialogue. The story has little action, yet it is a long story as far as pages are concerned, much longer than its forerunners. It is, however, not monotonous; it does not drag, for the reader is interested in the insight into human nature revealed by James and amused perhaps a trifle at the magnificent speeches. He realizes that, though James strides a bit too widely here, this, more than *The Madonna of the Future* and *The Last of the Valerii*, promises something different, something individual which may sometime come as a contribution to literature from the author.

Mme. de Mauves had its companion piece too, *Eugene Pickering*,[38] in consideration of which the comments regarding James's knowledge of human nature as well as those about his acquaintance with men, their speech and their actions, must be slightly modified.

While James was being visited by the muse Euphemia, as he tells us, in a "dampish, dusky, unsunned room" in Homburg,[39] he occasionally took time from his writing to stroll about the Kursaals and wonder what might have happened there in those days not so very far distant before the gambling rooms had been closed. What might have happened to an American there? In *DeGrey*, in *Master Eustace* he had felt it necessary to send his young men abroad to complete their education, he had hinted at escapades which serves this purpose, but he had forced the reader to wait till the return of the youth to America before involving him in a story. Now James conceived what might very likely have happened over the gambling tables, what might have been the influence which

[38] Appeared in *Atlantic Monthly*, Oct. and Nov., 1874.
[39] See preface to Vol. XIII of Collected Edition, p. xx.

educated the lad. Nor was it difficult to with the many "irregular characters" who still loafed about the place, seeming to "wear away the dull remainder of existence in a kind of melancholy, ghostly hovering around the deserted Kursaals."[40]   What more natural than that one of them as she existed some years before, a "faded, crumpled, vaporous beauty, ... something in the way of a Bettina, a Rahel,"[41] who wrote novels "in the George Sand manner but really out-Heroding Herod,"[42] should have got hold of the lad and made use of him to serve her purpose for awhile, then have carelessly tossed him aside? He would, of course, this American youth, have taken it all most seriously. His being "educated" by it would have depended, in fact, upon his taking it seriously.

In some respects the story which results from these reflections is true to life; in others it is not and it is both in quite the reverse aspect of *Mme. de Mauves.* Though James probably summoned Bettina von Arnim, Rahel Varnhagan, and George Sand to his aid in constructing the character of the female adventuress, he must actually have known, have talked with and observed carefully a young lad like Eugene Pickering, for he draws him very well, topping off his descriptions with little marks which betray a close observer of life. The boy is quite natural and wholly delightful; he acts and talks in a natural way. The manner in which he is first presented to the reader by the narrator—for James reverted to the use of such an individual again—is especially felicitous. Awkward, gauche, nervously excited, he is, it is all too apparent, having his first glimpse of life and not wholly understanding it, and as he stares in "ingenuous, unconscious absorption" at the playing, the "faded, crumpled, vaporous beauty" beckons him to come to her.

He stared a moment, rather blankly, unable to suppose that the invitation was addressed to him; then, as it was immediately repeated, with a good deal of intensity, he blushed to the roots of his hair, wavered awkwardly, and at last made his way to the lady's chair. By the time he reached it he was crimson and wiping his forehead with his pocket-handkerchief. She tilted back, looked up at him with the same smile, laid two fingers on his sleeve, and said something, interrogatively, to which he replied by a shake of the head. She was asking him, evidently, if he had ever played, and he was saying no. . . . She drew from her pocket a double napoleon,

[40] *Transatlantic Sketches*, p. 355.
[41] *Atlantic Monthly*, Oct., 1874, p. 398.
[42] *Atlantic Monthly*, Nov., 1874, p. 514.

put it into his hand, and bade him place it on a number of his own choosing. He was evidently filled with a sort of delightful trouble; he enjoyed the adventure, but he shrank from the hazard . . . . Suddenly in desperation, he reached over and laid the piece upon the table.[43]

The number wins, of course, and he looks round the tables "with a gleeful, conscious laugh."

Thus auspiciously begun the story presently takes time off from the action to explain Eugene's antecedents, and it is here that James began to err. Eugene, he felt, must be made not just an ordinary American but one who had been unusually carefully brought up, unusually protected, a "regular garden plant." Then his enthrallment by the doubtful charms of the frowsy female would be all the more intense, but it is, if anything, the less readily to be believed because of this careful education. A boy less narrowly brought up, with his past less fully explained by James might have been made quite such a delightful puppet as Eugene becomes in the hands of his Bettina.

This woman, Madame Blumenthal, with antecedents as dubious as Eugene's are certain, amuses herself for a time with him. His friend, the narrator, ascertaining some of the facts of her past, appeals to her to spare the youth and attempts to warn him with the result that each becomes more interested in the other. The fact that Eugene is due shortly at Smyrna to marry a young girl whom he has never seen—the French custom of parentally arranged unions brought somewhat strangely into American life—and that he has a letter in his pocket from there which he refuses to open, makes the boy only the more rash. At last he tosses wisdom to the winds and disappears with the German frau. But, of course, he reappears shortly, sadder and wiser, grateful, however, for the experience. "It's worth it all, almost . . . . to have been wound up for an hour to that celestial pitch."[44] Reminded of the letter, he opens it only to find that Miss Vernor of Smyrna has also rebelled at the nuptial arrangement of their fathers and expects to be released. This decides him; he realizes she is worth winning and goes to Smyrna to try to win her. Miss Vernor and her letter, however, are both unimportant parts of the story. They are only mechanical devices which might have been omitted altogether though they help to complicate

[43] *Atlantic Monthly*, Oct., 1874, p. 398.
[44] *Atlantic Monthly*, Nov., 1874, p. 522]

the situation a bit and furnish an interesting ending for Eugene after his disillusionment.

The conversation in this story is much better than that in *Mme. de Mauves*. The speeches are not studied but natural. Eugene sometimes talks in a "big" way, but it is consistent with his character, consistent with the situation that he should, and he is sometimes silent or briefly curt, a perplexing enigma to his friend who wishes he would talk it out with him. In this respect, Eugene is true to life, proving that in some cases James had studied men to advantage. Altogether, however, this story is less noteworthy than its predecessor; it contrasts two civilizations but takes more superficial differences for its theme, and it accordingly does not reveal as serious and as discerning a philosopher in its author.

3. *The Odd Stick*

These six stories, carefully written little tales, two of them at least masterpieces, two others running them a close second and promising greater things to come, had one strange bedfellow, a story deserting Europe, laid in America, *Professor Fargo*.[45] It need not delay us long. It is the fantastic tale of a magician who deals in higher mathematics and spiritualism, and his assistant, Colonel Gifford, an old man who has been unfortunate in life, and reduced to poverty, must now serve the Professor in his questionable practices. They are assisted by Gifford's deaf and dumb daughter who reminds James of Mignon, but hardly the reader. The father reminds him of Don Quixote, but again not the reader. They are too poorly drawn for that. The story consists of the fact that while the colonel occupies his spare moments with a scientific experiment, believing he is on the way to a great discovery, the professor makes love to the daughter and disappears with her. The characters are unnatural, not even parallel to the figures of literature James thought of as he wrote the story. Nor has the result any artistic merit. It is simply one of the "queer cases" in James's stories which we are to meet now and then and wonder not only why he wrote it, but how he could have done it. It is quite probable that it was written not at the same time as its companions in publication, but when James was experimenting with the American scene between the two trips to Europe and was resurrected in 1874 when the magazines were beginning to beg for his stories. Surely its effect must

[45] Appeared in *Galaxy*, Aug., 1874.

have been to prove to James that he had better leave America, leave freaks and odd sticks, alone.

What he *could* do, what he *might* do, as well as what he should not attempt, was certainly by now, 1874, apparent to Henry James. He could write delightful little tales of Europe, of its art, of its spell. He could write short stories about Americans in Europe. Could he now write a novel—not directly of America—but of materials such as he had used in his sketches and short stories?

CHAPTER XII

A REVIEWER AGAIN

1. *The Minor Reviews*

Before we look at James's answer to the question raised at the end of the last chapter, it is necessary to pause a moment and consider the reviews with which he was occasionally supplementing his original writing in 1873 and '74. Though he had abandoned this practice when he had felt that it might be hampering his own writing of stories, he had not intended to give it up entirely. Reviewing paid well, and when he came across new books by writers who were outstanding in one way or another, he found it was no effort and no handicap to write a short notice. Sometimes he was even stimulated into writing a long critical article which helped him reassemble in close quarters his own fluctuating ideas about fiction, and he was, under the influence of one author, to draw up a fresh platform and prepare to make a fresh start in the fictional endeavor.

In 1873, six reviews and in 1874, fourteen, appeared in the American magazines which were interested in James as a critic. Of these, nine were directly called forth by fiction, while five of the others touched upon novelists indirectly.

These critical notes are interesting from three standpoints. Some of them, which have already been noted, throw light on the work produced in this phase of James's development. Others show that certain currents were surviving from the first phase of his growth. Still others reveal the entrance of new ideas or the further development of earlier ones into more exact and abiding principles, and point toward the third phase. Sometimes the same review does all three of these things.

Of the reviews which throw light on the work of the second phase, those upon Gautier and Mérimée have already been considered in part.[1] What remains to be noted is not so much how these two authors affected him as how they did not. With both it was the temperament of the author which was displeasing to James. He had admired and even imitated Mérimée's "chiselled and polished lit-

[1] See Chapters X and XI.

tle fictions," he had learned a lesson in form and artistry from them, and he had, in an effort to be just, praised Mérimée's objectiveness in the review which he had accorded *Dernières Nouvelles.* Yet even this review, if it is read carefully, shows that James did not wholly relish the objectiveness of Mérimée, artistic though it was. He was so objective that he seemed to be coldblooded, cynical. This is brought out more clearly in the first paragraph of a review which was written when *Lettres à Une Inconnue* appeared but which was not published till it was included in the volume entitled *French Poets and Novelists* in 1878.[2] Again James noted a young story-teller should study Mérimée, but he added a word of indirect warning:

"The moral element in his tales is such as was to be expected in works remarkable for their pregnant concision and for a firmness of contour suggesting hammered metal. In a single word they are not sympathetic. . . . . Where sentiment never appears, one gradually concludes that it does not exist; and we had mentally qualified this frigid artist as a natural cynic."[3]

The letters confirmed this opinion. Mérimée as he had revealed himself there continued to interest James with his "most distinct and curious individuality" but did not command his admiration. He was out of tune with life.

Gautier had entered James's life from 1872 as an active influence but he had had effect upon the travel reports rather than upon the stories. That James was well acquainted with Gautier's fiction and thought highly of all of it, except *Mademoiselle Maupin,* is brought out in a long review, which can be more properly styled a critical article, which appeared in 1873.[4] He praised especially *Le Capitaine Fracasse*; it was "a model of the picturesque," "a triumph of the picaresque," "a masterpiece of good humour." "It ranks, in our opinion, with the greatest works of the imagination produced in our day."[5] James greatly enjoyed it, but he had no wish to imitate it. Gautier's "pagan bonhomie" was as objectionable as Mérimée's "epicurean relish for the bitterness of the general human lot." The human interest in *Le Capitaine Fracasse,* as in all of Gautier's stories, was inferior to the picturesque.[6] The novel was filled with admirable details which revealed, as the travel sketches had, that

[2] This article bears the date 1874 in the volume of essays.
[3] *French Poets and Novelists,* p. 308.
[4] *North American Review,* Apr., 1873.
[5] *Ibid.,* pp. 324f for these references.
[6] *Ibid.,* p. 321.

Gautier's "observation was penetrating and his descriptive instinct was unerring,"[7] but when all was said, "we remember the perusal of most good novels as an intellectual pleasure . . . . an affair of the mind. The hours spent over the 'Capitaine Fracasse' seem to have been an affair of the senses, of personal experience, of observation and contact, as illusory as those of a peculiarly arid dream."[8] And the same was true of Gautier's short tales, picturesque, imaginative, many of them true in their way, but this was not the way which James desired to follow.

A similar attitude is met in a review, attacking Paton's *Life of Henry Beyle*[9] where James took the occasion to state briefly his idea of Stendhal. The *Chartreuse de Parme*, similar in its sensuous and picturesque elements to Gautier's masterpiece, James claimed, was to be "numbered among the dozen finest novels that we possess,"[10] and Stendhal's method, that of collecting anecdotes or facts from the records of old families and making them into stories, he pronounced excellent,[11] but it was one which was, unfortunately, rarely at the disposal of novelists. But of Stendhal generally, the author whose conception of passion had influenced *At Isella*, James wrote in 1874: "Among writers called immoral, there is no doubt that he best deserves the charge: the others, beside him, are spotlessly innocent."[12] He had "the love of the beautiful per se" but did not apply it to the best purpose. He was immoral.

That James reacted in this way to Mérimée and Gautier and Stendhal was largely due to the survival from his earlier phase of certain influences, and this is to be discerned still more clearly in other reviews.

Most important was the influence of George Eliot. We must recall for a moment the course of James's former interest in her. He had praised the English authoress in 1866 with gusto and then with modification. He had been sure that she was great in *her* way, but he had not been sure that it was *the* way. She had then produced a few good novels, but he had felt that there was not a masterpiece among them. Reviewing her poem, *The Spanish Gipsy*, in 1868, he had revealed that he thought her much greater as a novelist than as

[7] *Ibid.*, p. 312.
[8] *Ibid.*, p. 324.
[9] Appeared in *Nation*, Sept. 17, 1874.
[10] *Ibid.*, p. 188.
[11] *Ibid.*, p. 188.
[12] *Ibid.*, p 189.

a poet; he had admired her intellect and her sober reflection; and reviewing French authors he had urged upon them some of the things for which George Eliot stood, her point of view, her morality, as more desirable in literature than their lack of it. This same note played now behind the criticism of the stories of Mérimée, Gautier, and Stendhal, and behind that accorded to Sandeau's *Jean de Thommeray*[13] and Flaubert's *La Tentation de Saint Antoine*,[14] which James in a brief review pronounced "tremendously pictorial," but picturesque in an artificial and coldblooded way. It was a refrain running underneath, often more felt than expressed, yet apparent in such a statement as, "M. Flaubert and his contemporaries have pushed so far the education of the senses and the cultivation of the grotesque in literature and the arts that it has left them morally stranded and helpless."[15] As James turned to consider the state of fiction at that time in France, he bore in mind the strength of George Eliot. Gradually with the publication of other works by George Eliot there was dawning in James a recognition of her as a really great novelist. *Middlemarch* had been published in 1871–72. Unfortunately James did not review it, but he referred to it shortly as "making us demand even finer things of her than we did before."[16] Consequently he was disappointed when, instead of another novel, another book of poems, *Jubal and Other Poems*, came from her pen. He reviewed this,[17] and revealed that he thought her poems were "interesting failures," proof of a genius that had temporarily taken the wrong road. At the end of the review, he regretted the sadness of the moral note in George Eliot; it seemed to be that of skepticism rather than of faith, yet he admired her nevertheless. She had, at least, a moral note. He waxed most indignant when the *Spectator* mistook Hardy's *Far from the Madding Crowd* as by George Eliot under an assumed name.[18] Hardy was "imitative" in his pictures of dingy pothouses and manners, not original and clever, and to compare the two, much less to mistake them as one and the same was a sacrilege.

Another influence was surviving—to the critic, the influence back of that of George Eliot though James himself did not recognize it

[13] Appeared in *Nation*, Feb. 5, 1874.
[14] Appeared in *Nation*, June 4, 1874.
[15] *Ibid.*, p. 366.
[16] *North American Review*, Oct., 1874, p. 485. (Phillips errs when he includes this review in the work published in 1875, *Bibliography*, p. 117.)
[17] *Ibid.*
[18] Appeared in *Nation*, Dec. 24, 1874.

as such. He thought better of Goethe, however, than he had in his raw youth when he had violently assailed the philosopher as no novelist at all. James gave no review to any work by Goethe but he referred to him in the review of a novel by Cherbuliez and he considered him as a dramatist in a review called forth by a French translation of *Faust* which had a preface by Dumas fils. In reviewing *Meta Holdenis*,[19] James ran rapidly through all of the novels by Cherbuliez, praising them, especially *Comte Kostia* very highly. The Swiss author had Goethe's seriousness—"M. Cherbuliez has read Goethe to good purpose, and his first two novels were the work of a man who took things seriously."[20] Isn't this proof that Goethe should be read seriously, that James considered now that he had read him seriously and, he hoped, to good purpose? The attack made by Dumas fils in the preface to the translation of *Faust* James understood as that of a Gallic mind upon a German.[21] Each had a different standard of morality. Each had a different standard in writing; the books of Goethe lacked form but stimulated thought; those of most French writers, especially Dumas fils himself, had perfection of form but lacked reflection. "How, indeed, was M. Dumas to endure Goethe for an hour?"[22] To Goethe generally James paid a tribute: "Goethe certainly had an immense respect for reality, and no man was ever a greater collector and conservator, as one may say, of facts."[23] This was from the youth who had objected to Wilhelm and his female friends because he had not been told how they were dressed, how they looked. There were now, in James's opinion, it is evident, other kinds of facts to be collected and used by the novelist. Thus, though we deplored that James had not read the *Italienische Reise*, we can see that he was more of an admirer of Goethe than before. However, James failed to see, or at least to note in his reviews, if he did see, the influence of *Wilhelm Meister* upon the two main novels of Gautier. Possibly it was because Goethe meant to him thought, while Gautier, who must have modeled, in part, at least, his hero's connection with the theatrical troupe in *Le Capitaine Fracasse* upon Goethe's novel and who had brought into *Mademoiselle Maupin* Shakespearian criticism as Goethe had in his novel,

---

[19] Appeared in *North American Review*, Oct., 1873.
[20] *Ibid.*, p. 462.
[21] Review in *Nation*, Oct. 30, 1873.
[22] *Ibid.*, p. 294.
[23] *Ibid.*, p. 294.

meant to James beauty of expression but no thought at all, no knowledge of man or woman but the epidermis.[24]

In speaking of the influence of Mérimée upon the short stories of
James in the preceding chapters, we noted that his example had
tended to counteract in James the influence of George Sand which
was so evident at the end of the first phase. But that he still admired
her copious fluency, perhaps even envied it, is evidenced in several
reviews. He spoke of one author whom we shall consider in detail presently, as lacking that "faculty of rapid, passionate, almost reckless improvisation,—that of Walter Scott, of Dickens, of
George Sand. This is an immense charm in a story-teller; on the
whole, to our sense, the greatest,"[25] but he had discovered that this
great charm had to be a natural one and that he himself did not
possess it, and with this discovery was coming the interest which
was leading him to scrutinize and study authors who were great in
quite opposite ways. However, the regard for George Sand was to
remain with James in lessening degrees for some time longer.

James's attitude toward the books that he read is best brought
out in a review which he wrote upon Hugo's *Ninety-three*.

There comes a time, in most lives, when points of difference with friends
and foes and authors dwindle, and points of contact expand. We have a
vision of the vanity of remonstrance and of the idleness of criticism. We
cease to look for what we know people cannot give us—as we have declared
a dozen times—and begin to look for what they can. To find this last and
enjoy it undisturbedly is one of the most agreeable of intellectual sensations.[26]

The remark is not especially significant in regard to Hugo for James
had to stretch his standards to discover a grain of goodness in Hugo's
picturesqueness, but it is emphatically ·significant in respect to
James's frame of mind in 1874. The statement parallels another
which we have already observed him making in Florence in regard
to painting,[27] very likely at this same time. The two taken together
indicate that James had come to a place where he perceived "a certain solidarity in all conscious effort" and was "conscious of a growing

[24] See *North American Review*, Apr., 1873, p. 321. James, however, did note the
influence of Scarron upon Gautier.

[25] See review of Turgénieff's *Frühlingsfluthen* and *Ein König Lear des Dorfes*,
North American Review, Apr., 1874, p. 326.

[26] *Nation*, Apr. 9, 1874, p. 238.

[27] See Chapter X.

urbanity" in his judgment, "a sort of the man of the world disposition to take the joke for what it is worth, as it passes."[28] The impetuous, arbitrary attitude of youth had gone; in its place had come that of a sympathetic, gently forbearing man. He was now to consider books for what they were worth, to become interested in them if they contained promising elements but not to be disturbed if they lacked certain things of which he approved—he ceased to look for what authors could not give him and began to look for what they could. And when he found that an author could give him something, he allowed nothing to deter him from studying the author and learning his lesson.

2. Turgénieff

There was one novelist in Europe at that time who more than any other was constituted to serve as a guide for Henry James. There was Ivan Turgénieff. James was not to meet him personally till late in 1875 when, craving intimate acquaintance with the Russian, he was deliberately to seek him out in Paris,[29] but during 1873 and 1874 the influence of Turgénieff was, through his novels, entering James's blood like a tonic serum. It was causing him to reassemble his generally grasped ideas upon fiction and to strengthen them with the addition of new elements bearing upon the technical treatment of them, and to narrow them down to more specific principles. It was giving him ideas about characters and plot which he was shortly to try out in novels of his own. All this is apparent in a critical article, called forth by the German translation of two of the Russian's novels, but which surveyed and studied the whole field of his endeavor.[30] The article was published in April 1874. As a manifesto of James's own ideas, it is highly important. Turgénieff belonged, James noted, "to the limited class of very careful writers. It is to be admitted at the outset that he is a zealous genius, rather than an abundant one. His line is narrow observation."[31]

---

[28] *Transatlantic Sketches*, p. 290. The notes are dated broadly February–April, 1874.

[29] Hueffer errs when he conjectures that James may have met Turgénieff in 1873 in Hamburg; see p. 133 of Hueffer's book, and Interchapter C and Chapter XIV of this thesis for the facts.

[30] Review of *Frühlingsfluthen* and *Ein König Lear des Dorfes*, *North American Review*, Apr., 1874. In this first essay upon Turgénieff, James spelled his name Iwan Turgéniew. Later he used the more frequent Turgénieff.

[31] *North American Review*, Apr., 1874, p. 326.

In this way he differed from Scott and Dickens and George Sand, lacking the great charm of rapid, passionate improvisation, but James, we noted, had found that he too lacked that natural charm and he rejoiced to find an author who, lacking it, had something to atone for the deficiency.

Turgénieff, he found, had studied life carefully, thoroughly, the inner aspects as well as the outer, and it was life which he gave us in his novels. "If his manner is that of a searching realist, his temper is that of a devoutly attentive observer, and the result of this temper is to make him take a view of the great spectacle of human life more general, more impartial, more unreservedly intelligent, than that of any novelist we know."[32] He was better than Balzac because less of a showman. He cared for more things in life than any novelist save George Eliot.

Every class of society, every type of character, every degree of fortune, every phase of manners, passes through his hands; his imagination claims its property equally, in town and country, among rich and poor, among wise people and idiots, *dilettanti* and peasants, the tragic and the joyous, the probable and the grotesque. He had an eye for all our passions, and a deeply sympathetic sense of the wonderful complexity of our souls.[33]

Turgénieff had then that knowledge of human nature which James had emphasized ever since he read *Wilhelm Meister*. Not only did James consider this greatness of the Russian novelist generally but he began to study it *technically*, trying to discern Turgénieff's ways and means that he might follow them. He wished to get some pointers for his own novels, and he made some important discoveries. "He is a story teller who has taken notes. . . . . His tales are a magazine of small facts, of anecdotes, of descriptive traits, taken, as the phrase is, sur le vif."[34] Turgénieff seemed to James to have proceeded notebook in hand as he collected facts for his stories just as a traveller proceeded in the collecting of them for reports and travel sketches. "He has a passion for distinctness, for bringing his characterization to a point, for giving you an example of his meaning."[35] He made his descriptions clear and emphatic by the use of examples; they were concrete rather than general. "His figures are

[32] *Ibid.*, p. 330; when reprinted in *French Poets and Novelists*, 1878, "devoutly" was changed to "earnestly."

[33] *Ibid.*, p. 330.

[34] *Ibid.*, p. 326f, "sur le vif" was changed to "from life" when reprinted in 1878.

[35] *Ibid.*, p. 327.

all portraits; they have each something special, something peculiar, something that none of their neighbors have and that rescues them from the limbo of the gracefully general."[36] And in the light of these discoveries, James studied Turgénieff and his great skill in portraiture, for one of Turgénieff's lessons for James was the reducing of human nature to portraits.

Turgénieff's skill was greatest in his portraits of women— Hélène and Lisa, Katia and Tatiana, even Gemma. Was there anywhere in fiction a group of young girls "more radiant with maidenly charm?" "If there are no heroines we see more distinctly, there are none we love more ardently."[37] For over all the portraits of these heroines played a gentleness, a humanity which was similar to that James had noted in George Eliot. Turgénieff's portraits of women were quite free from the irony which sometimes unfortunately entered those of his men. Turgénieff must have known many fine women, women of a nature more dignified, more restrained more complex than the often carelessly passionate French type. His fair Muscovites had a "spontaneity, an independence quite akin to the English ideal of maiden loveliness"[38] and a purity, a restricting conscience quite akin to the New England temperament—"a hint of Puritan angularity."[39] It was chiefly because Turgénieff's heroines had the same basic qualities as American girls that James turned to study them. The interplay of passion and the restraint exercised by conscience was a problem which an American novelist must meet and who better than Turgénieff could be studied for such a purpose? George Eliot stifled passion. Turgénieff let it play, witness Hélène and Lisa and all the others, but he also brought it into sharp conflict with conscience, and out of the two produced a situation which had intensity, and it was this situation which made the story. Character and plot were interdependent.

There was another point, another lesson, which James noted in Turgénieff which was still more important than his knowledge of life and the technical use he made of it. There was the moral use.

Turgénieff had, James believed, "a passion for shifting his point of view" but his object was "constantly the same—that of finding an incident, a person, a situation, *morally* interesting."[40] His guiding

[36] *Ibid.*, p. 327.
[37] *Ibid.*, p. 329.
[38] *Ibid.*, p. 337.
[39] *Ibid.*, p. 340.
[40] *Ibid.*, p. 331.

principle in the choice of characters and situations seemed to be that they should be "morally interesting." Morality, then, which to James had been for some time a matter to be treated objectively, free from the fetters of the author's point of view, could be regulated, he found, by the subject one chose. The author was free to select any subject he wished, but it was better from all standpoints for him to *wish* to take "morally interesting" subjects.

But what made a subject morally interesting? Turgénieff answered the question for James in almost every one of his stories. Failure. At least that was one thing which did it. Adversity tried and tested a man and proved his true worth, and he was much more interesting to the reader and perhaps a stronger lesson if he failed, if he found himself gradually overcome by life, than if he succeeded, found himself gradually overcoming life. Dmitri Rudin was more interesting as a character than Wilhelm Meister.

James discovered from Turgénieff's stories that there were two kinds of failure which were especially adapted to treatment by the novelist. One was the failure which came from within, a flaw in character as in the Aristotelian sense of tragedy, such as Turgénieff portrayed in Dmitri.

Dmitri Rudin is a moral failure, like many of the author's heroes—one of those fatally complex natures who cost their friends so many pleasures and pains; who might, and yet, evidently, might not, do great things; natures strong in impulse, in talk, in responsive emotion, but weak in will, in action, in the power to feel and do singly.[41]

And it was exactly this kind of nature, one which filled every detail of the description just given, that James was to give us shortly as we shall see, in his second novel, which he was probably thinking of even as he penned these lines.

The other kind of failure came from without—adversity which overwhelmed a noble nature to such an extent that the nature became ennobled by it. Such a situation Turgénieff had used in his *Nest of Noblemen* with its wonderful heroine, Lisa, and her lover Lavretzsky, torn cruelly apart just as their love became clear to them by having their duty become more clear. The moral interest of the triangle was greater to Turgénieff than the sentimental one: "A pair of lovers accepting adversity seem to him more eloquent than a pair of lovers grasping at happiness."[42] And it was this situa-

[41] *Ibid.*, p. 335.
[42] *Ibid.*, p. 339.

tion which James had treated in *Mme. de Mauves*—probably Tur-génieff had influenced it—and was to treat a second time in his third novel, and often again thereafter.

James's attitude toward morality was not changed by Turgénieff for both novelists had the same point of view as to right and wrong and believed in the necessity of regulating it by truth, but James's treat-ment of morality, the way it was to appear in his books, was affected. He began consciously to search for subjects which were "morally interesting" and until he could discover some of his own, he often bore in mind the kind of subjects treated by Turgénieff.

There was one shortcoming, nevertheless, which James detected in Turgénieff, and to him it was a big one. Bringing his article to a conclusion after a careful appraisal of each of the outstanding novels of Turgénieff's as well as of many of the short stories, James said: "The great question about a poet or a novelist is, How does he feel about life? What in the last analysis, is his philosophy?"[43] And Tur-génieff, he found took life hard, terribly hard. "The foremost impres-sion of M. Turgéniew's reader is that he is morbidly serious, that he takes life terribly hard. We move in an atmosphere of unrelieved sadness."[44] He was a pessimist, disappointed in the land he loved. When his melancholy was spontaneous, it was powerful, because perhaps after all there was some reason for it, but at times, as if from habit, it seemed to James to become wanton, and then James dis-liked it for irony accompanied it. Life *is* a battle, James realized, but a writer should face it squarely and not make it appear even worse than it is. If possible, idealism should be brought to the relief of realism. "We value most the 'realists' who have an ideal of deli-cacy, and the elegiasts who have an ideal of joy."[45] Turgénieff then was not James's ideal story-teller. The ultimate novelist must be "altogether purged of sarcasm." Is there not in this again a note from George Eliot? Like Turgénieff she was sad, but unlike him, she was never ironic—her sadness caused a tenderness. Turgénieff was tender of his heroines, but not always of his men—nor of life.

One must note that it was from the standpoint of his own fiction writing that James looked at Turgénieff and that, accordingly, he did not interpret the Russian novelist absolutely correctly. He dis-sected Turgénieff; he took him apart. Because he was seeking the

[43] *Ibid.*, p. 350.
[44] *Ibid.*, p. 350.
[45] *Ibid.*, p. 355.

ways and means of writing novels, he did not see that Turgénieff was a great whole, that his use of failure grew out of his point of view about life, that that came from his Russian temperament, and that he had no conscious intention or thought of searching for persons or incidents or situations which were "morally interesting" but only of portraying his own countrymen who happened to be "morally interesting" to one American reader at least. As criticism then, James's essay on Turgénieff falls short. Yet this intensive study of the novels of Turgénieff and these conclusions which James drew—inaccurate as they are in regard to the Russian novelist—were to help James more than had he understood Turgénieff, for he formulated principles which he could use in his own novels. And James's primary purpose, it must be remembered, was to make himself into a great novelist. Criticism was but a means.

CHAPTER XIII
RODERICK HUDSON

1. *James's Second Novel*

The long circuitous approach which we have made to James's second novel will, I hope, help us to understand it and the influences which made it what it is instead of another failure like his first. James himself had made a circuitous approach. Ten years had passed since James had first openly dedicated himself to fiction. And it may almost be said that ten years had gone into the making of *Roderick Hudson*, for from the first James had had his mind made up to be a novelist. Once before he had tried and failed. He had not been ready. Since that time he had applied himself still more directly to preparation for this novel. Of course many things which had happened during those ten years were now forgotten by James, but he had learned by his mistakes as much as by his successes. His fictional education had been a sifting and sorting of many elements and fewer had been retained than had been cast aside. In *Roderick Hudson* we can see what he salvaged. James's own process over ten years had simply been in varying degrees a repetition of what Roderick's is in three months in Rome.

"What becomes of all our emotions, our impressions . . . . all the material of thought that life pours into us at such a rate during such a memorable three months as these? There are twenty moments a week—a day, for that matter, some days—that seem supreme, twenty impressions that seem ultimate, that appear to form an intellectual era. But others come treading on their heels and sweeping them along, and they all melt like water into water and settle the question of precedence among themselves. The curious thing is that the more the mind takes in, the more it has space for, and that all one's ideas are like the Irish people at home who live in different corners of a room and take boarders."[1]

Looked at as a purely physical performance, *Roderick Hudson*, was as James wrote later in the preface to the Collected Edition, "begun in Florence in the spring of 1874, designed from the first for serial publication in *The Atlantic Monthly*, where it opened in January 1875 and persisted through the year."[2] Begun in Florence,

[1] *Atlantic Monthly*, Mar., 1875, p. 298.
[2] Collected Edition, I, v.

it was continued during the summer in Germany, the fall in Cambridge, and the winter in New York. It was not even finished when it began to appear in monthly fragments. James later confessed that he had "liked" the writing of it but must have "fallen short of any facility or confidence" since it had taken him so long to complete it, yet this he said in the light of his later endeavors and the critic who approaches it from his early ones, finds in it a youthful assurity of stride as well as exuberance. It is much more confident in tone than anything he had yet done. It is almost triumphant.

A synopsis must precede a discussion of its contents for in many ways the story speaks for itself.

Rowland Mallet is a young man with a fortune which enables him to do as he pleases, and in his pleasures Europe looms large. Just before sailing for a sojourn there, he visits a cousin in Northampton and meets Roderick Hudson, a young man who is submitting himself to the reading of law while he dreams of becoming a sculptor. Rowland has long considered himself a patron of the arts in a general way, and now he sees a chance to become one more specifically and actively. He offers to take Roderick to Rome and give him his opportunity. Roderick accepts with glee, and the opposition of his mother is finally overcome. Even as his plans are made to take Roderick to Europe, Rowland begins to regret them for he meets Mary Garland, Roderick's cousin, and feels an interest in her which he believes might lead to marriage. But his word is given to Roderick, and, it soon develops, to Mary too, for Roderick overflowing with good humor has believed himself to be in love with Mary and they have become engaged.

The story, thus begun, skips over three months rapidly, Rowland introducing Roderick to Europe in much the same way James proceeded on his visits to the continent—England, Paris, Milan, Venice, Florence, and then Rome! Here a stop is made and Roderick begins to absorb impressions which he presently puts to good purpose in producing a magnificent Adam, following it with an Eve. Rowland gives a dinner in celebration asking among others, Gloriani, who, disillusioned, devotes his art to modeling ugly things, and Sam Singleton, who by dint of hard work is slowly making his way as a painter. Roderick, flushed with the feeling of success, outlines his artistic future.

"I care only for perfect beauty. There it is, if you want to know it! That is as good a profession of faith as another. In future, so far as my things are not positively beautiful, you may set them down as failures. For me, it's either that or nothing . . . . I mean to go in for big things; that's my notion of my art. I mean to do things that will be simple and vast and infinite. You'll see if they won't be infinite! . . . . I mean to produce a Juno that will make you tremble, a Venus that will make you swoon."[3]

Gloriani scoffs and predicts his failure:

"You can't keep it up!" . . . . "passion burns out, inspiration runs to seed. Some fine day every artist finds himself sitting face to face with his lump of clay, with his empty canvas, with his sheet of blank paper, waiting in vain for the revelation to be made, for the Muse to descend. He must learn to do without the Muse!"[4]

But whether Gloriani's words have any effect or whether Roderick is simply exhausted from the strenuous winter of impression-gathering and work or whether he is in truth destined to carry out the prediction, he finds his Muse is fickle, and on Rowland's advice he leaves for a summer of rest in Germany. When he rejoins his friend in the fall, it proves to have been a summer of dissipation,— on the one hand a Eugene Pickering experience, on the other, gambling debts— and Roderick has come out of it not affected for the better. He listlessly resumes his days at the studio, working by fits and starts, asking Rowland:

"Is this of necessity what a fellow must come to . . . . this damnable uncertainty when he goes to bed at night as to whether he is going to wake up in a working humor, or in a swearing humor? Have we only a season, over before we know it, in which we can call our faculties our own?"[5]

But almost as he speaks, the door opens and Christina Light, her mother, her poodle, and the Cavaliere Giacosa, having heard of Roderick's fame, enter. The dazzling beauty of Christina quite overwhelms Roderick. Here is a Muse of flesh and blood and he begs to be allowed to do her bust. Mrs. Light is nothing loath provided she may have it when it is finished, and the sittings are arranged. Rowland looks on helpless, feeling that only harm is to come of this.

The bust is soon completed, but Roderick's visits to the Casa Light continue, much to the annoyance of all except the divine Christina. He is something to amuse her while she is waiting on the marriage market for the Duke or Prince with a long enough ancestry and a full enough purse to satisfy her mother. Rowland appeals to her to spare Roderick, telling her of Roderick's engagement to Mary, but this only makes Christina more interested.

Roderick neglects his work, seems no longer to care greatly whether he is to succeed or fail, and delivers himself of many an ominous harangue upon genius to Rowland, who finds it impossible to reason with his friend.

Matters proceed in this course for some time, both Mrs. Light and the cavaliere urging Rowland to help them and he at length appeals again to Christina, this time on behalf of Roderick's genius. She seems to have an immense concern for what Rowland thinks of her, and after listening to him, annoying him not a little by her attitude, writes him: "I have done it. Begin and respect me!"

But she has done it dramatically and Roderick is quite as distraught as ever, especially when he hears of her engagement to Prince Casamassima. Rowland perceives now that Roderick is actually on "the descensus Averni" and is tempted to smooth the way.

He felt, in a word, like a man who has been cruelly defrauded and who wishes to have his revenge. Life owed him, he thought, a compensation, and he should be restless and resentful until he found it. . . . . In his melancholy meditations the idea of something better than all this, something that might softly, richly interpose, something that might reconcile him to the future, something that might make one's tenure of life strong and zealous instead of harsh and uneven—the idea of concrete compensation, in a word—shaped itself sooner or later into the image of Mary Garland.[6]

But because of Mary he is led to appeal once more to Roderick asking him to send for his mother and Mary to see if perchance they cannot help him.

They arrive and the final catastrophe is delayed. Roderick actually gets hold of himself enough to model his mother's head while Rowland escorts Mary through Rome, interested in the reactions of the New England girl whose life has been limited up to this time by West Nazareth and Northampton. Mary is hesitant, apprehensive, but gradually comes to feel the charm of Rome.

But when the head of Mrs. Hudson is finished, Roderick loses hold of himself again and tells Rowland that his love for Mary is dead. For *her* sake again, Rowland pleads with him, urging him to leave Rome, but he refuses to until after the date set for Christina's marriage.

[6] *Atlantic Monthly*, Aug., 1875, pp. 136 f.

And it happens that Christina presently enters the scene once more. Quite uninvited she strays into a party given by Madame Grandoni for Mary and Mrs. Hudson. She introduces herself to Mary, and the two girls stand in sharp dramatic contrast.

Several days later Rowland is summoned to the Casa Light. On his way he stops at Mrs. Hudson's hotel and finds her disturbed over a mysterious letter from her son saying they are not to see him for a week. Rowland hunts him up and finds him reclining in sensuous enjoyment of the news that Christina has refused the prince. He berates him sharply, and goes on his mission to the Lights. The cavaliere urges him to persuade Christina to recall the Prince or they will have to take unpleasant means to force her. From the cavaliere's interest, Rowland sees suddenly that he must be Christina Light's father. Speaking to her, however, he finds he cannot urge her to go against her better reason and marry Casamassima, for she shows him that the meeting with Mary Garland had caused an ideal to be born in her and that she cannot bring herself to marry without love. But she says also that she will no longer bother Roderick; she has never cared for him as a lover or husband but wishes he were her brother. Rowland admires her and hopes that her parents will let her off. But the sword of Damocles is brought down, and the next day comes the report that Christina is married to the Prince.

There follows a terrible scene where Roderick reveals to his mother and Mary that he is mentally bankrupt as well as financially and that he has ceased to care for anything. Rowland is ready to retire but all three appeal to him to see them through, hoping Roderick can yet be rescued from himself. For Mary's sake he escorts them to a villa in Florence and then to an inn in the Alps, but Roderick slowly and steadily continues to disintegrate. Gradually Mary comes to understand him and Rowland begins to hope that some day he can make up to her for Roderick's lack. Roderick cries out against the perfidy of Christina blaming her for all that has happened to him. Then one day Christina and her Prince suddenly wander into the scene, Christina more beautiful, more dangerous than ever, for, forced to marry the Prince, she now intends to "cultivate rapture." Roderick beholds her, all his resentment going, all his desire returning.

A day or two later he seeks to borrow money from Rowland in order to follow Christina. Failing, he goes to Mary who gives him all she has. He tells this gloatingly to Rowland who calls him a "transcendent egotist" caring for nobody but himself. Rowland amazes Roderick when he reveals his own love for Mary. Roderick confesses he has been "hideous" and leaves for a climb in the mountains. A thunderstorm comes on; Roderick does not return, and his body is found at the bottom of a steep, rocky slope.

2. *Criticism of Roderick Hudson.*

It must be at once apparent that *Roderick Hudson* grew largely out of James's experience, out of his sojourns in Rome, out of his hopes about art, yet it must also be apparent that other things entered too—Why did James make his hero a sculptor? Why did he have him fail? Why did he provide him with a companion? Why did he emphasize the love element instead of the art? The preface written in 1906 does not directly answer these questions. It is good critically, but most unsatisfactory as to the actual construction of the book, and an explanation must be sought in James's previous work.

In noting the books which James reviewed during the second phase of his development there was one we overlooked because it was neither travel sketch nor novel. This was the *Correspondence de Henri Regnault* reviewed in the *Nation* for January 2, 1873, and it was from this book, from this painter, that James undoubtedly secured the first clew for *Roderick Hudson*. True, James made his hero a sculptor, and he changed the outcome. Rome was more fitted, he believed, to stand as the muse of sculptors than of painters—Florence might have served that purpose—but he wished to "do" Rome and Regnault's early experiences there as he delayed work gathering, absorbing impressions seemed to him an experience which might be that of a sculptor as well. It had, indeed, been that of a novelist. The review reveals that James was tremendously interested in Regnault:

In spite of its brevity, there is something singularly complete in Regnault's career, and we may almost expect that, as time goes on, it will become poetized and etherealized, and assume a sort of legendary hue. . . . . He made the utmost of his life while it lasted, for though at moments he bitterly accuses himself of recklessness and waste of time, yet he *lived* incessantly in a way altogether foreign to characters of a less generous temper—with an intensity of perception and enjoyment, and a rapidity of development, which make a kind of breathless effort of the perusal of his letters.[7]

[7] *Nation*, Jan. 2, 1873, p. 13.

As first conceived, *Roderick Hudson*, no doubt, was to be a sort of legend woven around the French painter's seeming procrastination, brilliant rise, and sudden, tragic end.

The germ came from Regnault. It was fed and nourished by James's own experience. Each return to Rome brought out increasingly its charm, so exhilarating to one of the artistic temper yet so demoralizing as far as production was concerned. When James came to write his novel, he was able to place his story definitely and solidly in Rome, though he failed, as he noted later, in regard to the early scene in Northampton.[8] St. Peter's, the Coliseum, the Vatican, the villas and the gardens and the Roman neighborhoods, done with Balzacian thoroughness, give it a substantial foundation to stand upon and an atmosphere to pervade it. The whole book breathes the magic air of Rome so wonderful in its achievement that it seemed veritably to mock the mean struggles of the present even while it nursed them. James hurried Roderick from Northampton to Rome for the development of his talent. But when he got Roderick there, he made the charm of Rome—and of other things—more fatal than beneficent and reversed the career of Regnault. Roderick starts off in a flare of success and fizzles out.

Now this may have been due in part to the fact that James found Rome too distracting as far as work was concerned, but it was due more to the fact that James had been reading the novels of Turgénieff. The Russian had recently taught him that the most interesting characters for fiction writers were not moral successes like Wilhelm Meister but moral failures, and James patterned Roderick's character upon that of Dmitri Rudin as he had summed it up in the article on Turgénieff:

Dmitri Rudin is a moral failure, like many of the author's heroes—one of those fatally complex natures who cost their friends so many pleasures and pains; who might, and yet, evidently, might not, do great things; natures strong in impulse, in talk, in responsive emotion, but weak in will, in action, in the power to feel and do singly.[9]

Everything that Roderick does, every word that he speaks illustrates one or more of the traits enumerated above. The description is so faithfully carried out in the novel that Roderick even more than

---

[8] *Collected Edition*, I, x f. Though James lamented his failure to "do" Northampton, he did not note his success in "doing" Rome.

[9] *North American Review*, Apr., 1874, p. 335.

Dmitri illustrates the type which is still more pointedly condensed in the story to:

The great and characteristic point with him was the perfect absoluteness of his own emotions and experience. He never saw himself as part of a whole; only as the clear-cut, sharp-edged, isolated individual, rejoicing or raging, as the case might be, but needing in any case absolutely to affirm himself.[10]

All this is, of course, fatal. Because he thinks only of himself, the character brings disaster onto himself. Heroes of this type, James saw, gave the author more opportunity than heroes who succeeded or heroes whom death cut off early in their career, for there was something pictorial, dramatic, in a man who because of some incompleteness in his nature, dragged himself down.

Yet Roderick, it must be admitted, is not sole agent of his downfall. His failure does not, like Dmitri's, wholly come from within. His collapse is assisted by his passion for Christina and her ill treatment of him. Like Lucien de Rubempré, Balzac's supreme example of a moral failure, he is pushed down, or at least his fall is hastened, by a woman whose emotions are quite as exclusive as his own. He sees in her the Muse which may make his art thrive. She sees in him an amusing plaything for a few weary months till a husband is found for her. James evidently felt unable to depict a nature which went to pieces wholly by itself. He brought in Christina and the passion she engendered to assist him, and then he felt it necessary to emphasize this passion—the influence of George Sand—and unfortunately made Christina, as he noted in the preface, "well-nigh sole agent" of Roderick's downfall, thrusting too determinant a function upon her.[11]

Regnault, Turgénieff, Balzac, George Sand, George Eliot, too, in the sympathetic understanding which James had of Roderick, entered into the conception of the novel. James's own experience in Rome entered also. And James's experiments with fiction entered the execution, so that the novel, when it was completed, had in it something distinctly new in the field of fiction and distinctly Jamesian.

The most important thing in the story does not concern Roderick but is in the part Rowland plays. In the preface James wrote that, despite the title which the novel bears, the "center of interest

[10] *Atlantic Monthly*, Nov., 1875, p. 559.
[11] *Collected Edition*, I, xiv.

throughout 'Roderick' is in Rowland Mallet's consciousness, and the drama is the very drama of that consciousness," that the subject is not Roderick's adventure but Rowland's "view and experience of him."[12] This is, indeed, what happens in the story. Rowland is the first of those characters through whose consciousness the situation and the action are revealed, which were to be James's contribution to the novel. However, the whole thing was in the beginning not quite as intentional as James's later words indicate. In the preface, James did not explain why he used Mallet in this way, or how he had happened to stumble into this original manner of relating a story, but to the critic who has considered James's short stories and read the review of Wilhelm Meister, a reason should be apparent.

Rowland Mallet's place is the direct outgrowth of the use of a narrator, furthered by James's interest in the thoughts of his characters.[13] In almost all of his stories up to this point, we have noted James employing a narrator as a technical device to make his story seem true—a person vouched for it. He had found, also, and this is most important in considering the evolution of his method, that it gave the story a unity of point of view, and thus made it stronger, more compact, to have one person see and tell all. Seeking unity in a long novel, a unity which he had failed to get in *Watch and Ward*, he determined to make use of Rowland as he had at times made use of Longmore in *Mme. de Mauves*.[14] Rowland is literally the narrator taken into the story, treated objectively, spoken about rather than speaking, and everything which happens is seen as Rowland sees it, is seen *through* Rowland. There is not a scene recorded in the book, no meeting of the lovers, unless James could arrange in some way to have Rowland present, albeit sometimes an unwilling eavesdropper, but an eavesdropper and a recorder nevertheless. Then between the scenes, Rowland thinks, and the story is given continuity. It is as though James had written the novel using Rowland as the narrator and then had rewritten it to avoid the excessive use of the first person. The result was so successful that James frequently used it in his longer stories and novels for it gave the same value of reality and of truth and unity of point of view which a narrator did and got away

---

[12] *Ibid.*, p. xvii.

[13] So far as I know, no critic has noticed this reason, though practically all, of course, have noticed the result, directed thereto by the preface.

[14] James also employed Mrs. Draper for this purpose in *Mme. de Mauves* when circumstances interfered with his using Longmore.

from the unattractive use of the first person in a long story.   In
addition, it enabled James to treat the mind of one of his characters,
to go, as he liked, beneath the surface and see the drama, far more
exciting than any outer actions, which took place there.

The relation of Rowland to the story is to be noted from still
another standpoint which James quite neglected in the preface—he
had by 1906 passed so far beyond it—but which again we can understand because of some of the earlier stories. Because Roderick is seen
through Mallet, the story may almost be said to have two heroes.
Is not the real situation, however, somewhat like that which we have
often seen before in James's stories, that we have in Roderick one side
and in Rowland another side of a complete man, of, if you wish,
James's own nature?   In Roderick is the artistic temperament
without the power to realize itself in production; in Rowland is the
power, the will to do, coupled with financial means and regard for
others, but without the inborn ability.   The clew to Rowland's
character is given early:

"Do you know I sometimes think I am a man of genius, half finished?
The genius has been left out, the faculty of expression is wanting; but the
need for expression remains, and I spend my days groping for the latch
of a closed door."[15]

and to Roderick's somewhat later:

"The poor fellow is incomplete, and it really is not his own fault; Nature
has given him his faculty out of hand and bidden him be hanged with it![16]

Man is a dual nature, and it is this duality which is pictured here,
though the two sides are treated separately. To be successful, both
sides must come to some sort of an inner agreement, both sides must
cooperate; the dreamer must also be the doer, and vice versa.
Roderick dies twice, his genius and then his body. Rowland is destined to live on, patronizing the arts, calling upon Mary Garland,
and waiting patiently for what will never be.

Thus the story has its warning and like *The Madonna of the Future* may be called an allegory of life. Behind it is the wisdom of a
philosopher, a young man who had studied himself, had seen the
two sides balanced in himself, but had decided that the most interesting figures for novels were those where one side or the other was
dominant.

[15] *Atlantic Monthly*, Jan., 1875, p. 4.
[16] *Atlantic Monthly*, Aug., 1875, p. 130.

This decision was an important one, but it had its danger and James did not wholly escape it. In fact he courted it. One must admit that James's characters, all of them, are lifelike, but they are so in a narrow way, rather than in a broad. In his zest for distinctness, James allowed himself to be over-ridden by the idea of a dominant trait. This resulted, or course, in clearcut features, but the edges are too sharp.

This is most noticeable in regard to Roderick and Rowland. Since each represents one side of the artistic temperament and illustrates traits which James found in his own nature, he had only to put himself upon paper, and he succeeded in making them lifelike in speech and action and thought. But in trying to keep them distinct and to make their distinctness apparent to the reader, he over-stressed impetuosity in Roderick and moderation in Rowland. Because of his method, James could get at Roderick only through Rowland's thoughts about him or through Roderick's conversation, and this led him to make the latter somewhat too staccato. As for Rowland, James had him keep calmly on, occasionally disturbed by the shortcomings of his friend but preferring to meditate and philosophize about him rather than to have it out. Not infrequently the reader wishes to prod Rowland, to urge him to wake up and do something, but he is in every sense of the word inactive when it comes to the vital things of life but good in arranging small things. If anything, then, he is too true to the nature with which James endowed him.[17]

Singleton and Gloriani, though minor characters, have an importance because each represents another side of the artistic temperament, and though they enter rarely, they give the picture fullness. Singleton, as the young artist who makes his industry atone for the

[17] How consciously James tried to distinguish between the two men can be discerned if one compares the *Atlantic* version with the one in book form which immediately followed its serial run. (Published by James R. Osgood and Company, Boston, 1876, copyright, 1875.) In the former, both men usually speak in the contracted form of subject and verb; in the latter, Rowland seldom does while Roderick does when excited, and uses the full form of subject and verb when determined. James also made a few other changes in single words and punctuation which further differentiate the two. All these changes he retained, or changed again, in the 1879 edition (Published by Macmillan and Company, London) where he extended the practice of careful revision to the portions of straight narrative and to the conversation of Rowland and Mary. *Roderick Hudson* was thus revised twice before 1880, a fact which has been ignored by critics; Mr. Havens notes the second revision but not the earlier one (P. M. L. A., June, 1925).

scantiness of his inborn ability, is especially well done, while Gloriani, disillusioned, hardened by the treatment the world gives an artist who starts with ideals, is effectively and sympathetically touched off. Here, too, the idea that one trait must stand out, governed James, but it is less objectionable, because the characters do not play leading parts.

With his women characters, James succeeded less than with his men, and this he noted in the preface confessing he had been too much concerned with the antithesis offered by the two most important women, Mary "plain," Christina "colored."[18] Poor Mary fares the worse. She is so plain that she fails to attract the reader's interest and sympathy, as James doubtless intended she should, and causes him to wonder why she was given an important part in the book. We do not wholly understand Roderick's falling in love with her nor Rowland's increasing interest. Both, however, might have been made plausible and probable had she been brought to the front more in the opening chapters and made to speak the mind she undoubtedly has. But that would have threatened her plainness. James could not run this risk for his desire for distinctness was already handicapped by the method he was using. He could look at Mary only through Rowland. Though James allowed Rowland to think about Mary, he gave him little opportunity to see her till her arrival in Rome.[19] Then with her perplexities growing because of Rome and Roderick, both not understandable to her, she is seen at a disadvantage by the reader who becomes impatient for the dazzling, brilliant Christina to appear once more. And Christina, James realized, offered so many possibilities to the novelist and was so little "done" in this book that he had to take up her half-finished portrait and complete it in *The Princess Casamassima* ten years later. Christina, too, suffers from method; because we see her through Rowland, we do not realize how desperately she has cared for his opinion, how she has tried to impress him, till Roderick reveals it to him in the end, and then we see that possibly there has been a tragedy for Christina as well as for Roderick.

The faults in *Roderick Hudson* are largely due to overzealousness, and James is not to be berated too sharply when there is so much of

[18] *Collected Edition*, I, xix.
[19] In the 1879 edition, James rewrote much of the conversation of Mary with Rowland in the latter part of the book, making it more subtle, in an attempt to show her charm and wit.

merit. A method which is a new thing in the field of fiction, is in use, the natural outgrowth of the stories in which James used a narrator, and of his interest in the minds of his characters. It has its shortcomings, but practice is going to enable James to detect and avoid them, and it has, decidedly, its advantages. As yet there are no finished portraits, but there are pointings in that direction, and some are presently to appear. Dramatic situations, action and dialogue as the illustration of character, are much in evidence. And the conception of the novel as an art, well made, its parts cohesive, suggestions anticipating outcome, interest heightening to a climax and falling in a denouement is apparent.

James could at last consider himself a novelist!

INTERCHAPTER C
THE BACKGROUND, 1875–1881

At the beginning of 1875, Henry James was in New York, fever-ishly finishing *Roderick Hudson* which was just beginning to appear in the *Atlantic Monthly*, getting a selection of his stories,[1] which had already appeared in the magazines, and another of his travel sketches,[2] ready to come out in book form, and writing numerous reviews and notes for the *Nation*. One of the reasons why James had left Cambridge for New York was, no doubt, that he might be near the publishing offices of this weekly and thus get books to review regularly. It is not unlikely that he signed a contract with the editors whereby he was to write a review a week—few weeks were missed though sometimes James substituted "notes" on art or the theatres for reviews. He evidently stayed on in New York until well into the spring and maybe into the summer, which possibly was passed at New Brighton.[3] There are unfortunately almost no facts avail-able about this year in America, which was in many ways a turning point in James's career. Whether much of it was spent in Cambridge is doubtful.[4]

But something happened in America—perhaps he found life here, as he had feared, was not "simpatico"; perhaps after *Roderick Hudson* and his tales, he concluded his forte might be treating Americans in foreign lands. Anyway, late in the fall, he was hurrying back to Europe with commissions for letters on Paris for the *Tribune* and for reviews and notes for the *Nation* in his satchel, letters of introduction in his pocket, and vague ideas about another novel in his brain. Howells wrote dolefully to a friend: "Harry James is gone abroad again not to return, I fancy, even for visits."[5] And shortly the

---

[1] *A Passionate Pilgrim*, Boston, 1875, contains also "The Last of the Valerii," "Eugene Pickering," "The Madonna of the Future," "The Romance of Certain Old Clothes," "Madame de Mauves."

[2] *Transatlantic Sketches*, Boston, 1875.

[3] See a vague reference in *A Small Boy and Others*, p. 26.

[4] Lubbock errs (*Letters*, I, p. 41) when he speaks of the year 1874–75 as hav-ing been spent in Cambridge. He ignores James's preface to *Roderick Hudson* and the art and theatre notes published in the *Nation* which reveal that the winter and probably the spring at least were spent in New York.

[5] *Life and Letters of Wm. D. Howells*, I, 215; the letter is dated Dec. 18, 1875.

letters to the *Tribune* began, eking out the few personal ones salvaged by Lubbock.

James stopped a few days in London[6] and then went to Paris. It is evident from the first of his letters to the *Tribune* that he went there in a tentative mood but found himself fairly well satisified:

But no American, certainly, since Americans were, has come to Paris but once, and it is when he returns, hungrily, inevitably, fatally, that his sense of Parisian things becomes supremely acute. . . . . Our friend comes back with a standard, with an ideal, and it is now his pleasure to see whether the city of his predilections will keep her promises. It is safe to say that, as a general thing, she does, and that at those points where she is really strong, she wears well . . . . one inevitably comes to think that the problem of existence is solved more comfortably here than elsewhere. . . . . So far as a man lives in his senses and his tastes, he certainly lives as well here as he can imagine doing; and so far as he lives by the short run, as it were, rather than the long, he is equally well off.[7]

He began immediately to form as many points of contact with the city and French life as possible. He went to the art exhibits.[8] He went to Versailles to consider the functioning of the government in the critical political period.[9] He went regularly to the opera and to the theatre, finding here a slight disappointment and wondering if the best days of French drama were over.[10] Gradually too he made the acquaintance of different members of the literary group— most important of all Turgénieff, who was, we can infer because of the article of 1874 and later ones, the main reason why James had come to Paris. Turgénieff introduced him to Flaubert and took him to some of Flaubert's Sundays where he met Edmond de Goncourt, Zola, Daudet, Montégut, Gustave Doré, and Maupassant. Turgénieff also asked him to musical Thursdays and rather dingy Sundays *en famille* at Madame Viardot's and Madame de Blocqueville's.[11] But the spring was not entirely happy. To be sure James wrote to Howells the last of May:

I am turning into an old, and very contented, Parisian: I feel as if I had struck roots into the Parisian soil, and were likely to let them grow tangled and tenacious there. . . . . Of pure Parisianism I see absolutely

[6] See Note in the *Nation*, Dec. 16, 1875.
[7] *New York Tribune*, Dec. 11, 1875, p. 3; the letter is dated Nov. 22.
[8] See *New York Tribunes* for Dec. 25, 1875; Feb. 19, 1876; May 13, 1876.
[9] See *New York Tribune* for Jan. 8, 1876 (many letters touch upon politics).
[10] See *New York Tribunes* for Dec. 11, 1875; Jan. 29, 1876.
[11] See *Letters*, I, under dates of Apr. 11, 1876 and May 28, 1876.

nothing. The great merit of the place is that one can arrange one's life here exactly as one pleases—that there are facilities for every kind of habit and taste, and that everything is accepted and understood. Paris itself meanwhile is a sort of painted background which keeps shifting and changing and which is always there, to be looked at when you please, and to be most easily and comfortably ignored when you don't.[12]

Yet as to one of the reasons why he had come, he added:

I have seen almost nothing of the literary fraternity, and there are fifty reasons why I should not become intimate with them. I don't like their wares and they don't like any others; and besides they are not *accueillants*.[13]

There is a note of disappointment in the confession. James excepted for praise, however, Turgénieff, who was, after all, an outsider like himself, and Flaubert, whom one did have to recognize was an artist though one disliked the wares of his followers. To understand James's reaction, however, it is necessary to wait until we come to the critical work for at this point the latter, more than the letters explains his aloofness.[14]

Turgénieff left Paris presently for the summer months, Flaubert also, and perhaps this and the increasing dullness of a town where everyone who could left, and everything stopped in the summer had something to do with the fact that presently James himself found the city unendurable and sought relief in a tour to the coast—Rouen, Havre, and Etretat. From the latter place late in July came the abrupt explosion in a letter to William:

I have done with 'em (the French) forever, and am turning English all over. I desire only to feed on English life and the contact of English minds —I wish greatly I knew some. Easy and smooth-flowing as life is in Paris, I would throw it over tomorrow for an even very small chance to plant myself for a while in England. If I had but a single good friend in London, I would go thither. I have got nothing important out of Paris nor am likely to.[15]

Etretat was pleasant and cheap, however, and he remained there for several weeks probably debating with himself what his next big move should be. He had not settled it when he turned to the south of France in the middle of August to join the Childes near Orléans. Here he found the country life with its chateaux and curés and peas-

---

[12] *Letters*, I, 48; the letter is dated May 28, 1876.
[13] *Ibid.*, p. 49.
[14] See Chapter XIV.
[15] *Letters*, I, 51; the letter is dated Etretat, July 29, 1876.

ants quite equal to a George Sand novel[16] and for a time he forgot his displeasure. Then he took a short trip to Biarritz where by driving across the border to San Sebastian, he got a taste of Spain, bull fights and all.

The fall of 1876 was passed in Paris, but it is unfortunately a blank as far as details are concerned—another crucial period unlighted by sketches or letters.

By the middle of the winter, James was settled in London. Lubbock conjectures that it was William who urged him to try the one city which, apprehensive of loneliness, he had left untried.[17] But James's fear proved unfounded, and, introduced widely by friends as well as by his budding fame as a novelist and writer of stories, he found himself very popular. His letters home abound with the names of well-known people—Sunday evenings at Huxley's intellectually more pleasant than those at Madame Viardot's or Flaubert's had been, breakfasts and dinners with Lord Houghton, whose guests once, and perhaps again, included John Morley, Gladstone, Tennyson, and Dr. Schliemann.[18]

During the spring and summer of 1877 he took many short excursions turning them to financial profit in charming sketches. He was alert to every phase of life—the Oxford-Cambridge boat race, derby day at Epsom, Commemoration week at Oxford. He looked up every castle and interesting house which he found listed in guide books or heard people mention. Places that had been lived in spoke of an interesting past and seemed to breathe stories. Friends, probably realizing his interest, invited him to their charming country homes for weekends, and he went eager as a child on a quest for buried treasure. Two weeks in Warwickshire introduced him, he felt, into the core and center of the English world, and he learned "a great many English secrets" about how the upper classes spent their time in the country.[19]   When in London between trips, he walked the streets, hunted up, Murray in hand, the many interesting places within a twenty mile radius of the metropolis passing a "series of suburban afternoons" in Hyde Park, Windsor Castle, Eton College, Hampton Court, Richmond Park, and other places.[20]   Yet he was still of two minds about London. In one of his sketches he wrote:

[16] See "From Normandy to the Pyrenees," *Galaxy*, Jan. 1877, p. 104.
[17] *Letters*, I, 42.
[18] *Letters*, I, pp. 52f.; the letter is dated March 29, 1877, to William.
[19] See "In Warwickshire," *Galaxy*, Nov., 1877, pp. 225 f.
[20] See "Suburbs of London," *Galaxy*, Dec., 1877, pp. 778 f.

. . . . one's liking for London—a stranger's liking at least—is at the best an anomalous and illogical sentiment, of which he may feel it hardly less difficult to give a categorical account at one time than at another. I am far from meaning by this that there are not in this mighty metropolis a thousand sources of interest, entertainment, and delight: what I mean is, that for one reason and another, with all its social resources, the place lies heavy on the foreign consciousness. It seems grim and dusky, fierce and unbeautiful. And yet the foreign consciousness accepts it at last with a kind of grudging satisfaction, and finds something warm and comfortable.[21]

London was slenderly provided with innocent diversions, compared with other European cities, and he did not approve of the aristocratic constitution of English society which kept the upper classes too refined to seek pleasures outside their homes and the poor too miserable to afford it. But in a letter to a friend in America he wrote:

I feel now more at home in London than anywhere else in the world— so much so that I am afraid my sense of peculiarities, my appreciation of people and things, as *London* people and things is losing its edge. I have taken a great fancy to the place; I won't say to the people and things; and yet these must have a part in it. It makes a very interesting residence at any rate: not the ideal and absolutely interesting—but the relative and comparative one.[22]

And this feeling was to persist, despite the fact that in the fall James ran over to the continent to visit Paris and irresistible Italy for a few months.

Paris in the fall of 1877 had never seemed "better humoured," and he realized that he must be "infected with the baleful spirit" of the cosmopolite.[23] Adding and subtracting points about English and French nature, he felt that *after* America he liked England best. He took a side trip to Rheims and Laon to see the cathedrals, and after the fall elections in Paris, he turned south with breathless expectancy to Italy. But Turin, Genoa, Spezia were not old Italy, James realized with a pang of regret; they were fast becoming modernized.[24] Florence, however, had never been more lovely than in that brilliant week in yellow October, and he began to feel that not being a part of life there was somehow to miss an exquisite chance.[25] He made the most of his short stay, paying his respects

---

[21] "London in Midsummer," *Lippincott's Magazine*, Nov., 1877, p. 605.
[22] *Letters*, I, 54; the letter is dated Aug. 7, 1877.
[23] "Paris Revisited," *Galaxy*, Jan., 1878, pp. 5 f.
[24] "Italy Revisited," *Atlantic Monthly*, Apr., 1878, pp. 438 f.
[25] "Recent Florence," *Atlantic Monthly*, May, 1878, pp. 586 f.

again to the galleries and spending much time in the garden of a villa which overlooked the city and breathing its air. Sighing deeply he left for Rome, that other magic city, where he lingered for seven wonderful weeks. It was the old story—Rome too fascinating for work. After he had broken away from the fatal charm, he wrote in a letter:

Italy was still more her irresistible ineffable old self than ever, and getting away from Rome was really no joke. In spite of the "changes"—and they are very perceptible—the old enchantment of Rome, taking its own good time, steals over you and possesses you, till it comes really almost to a nuisance and an importunity. That is, it keeps you from working, from staying indoors, etc. To do those things in sufficient measure, one must live in an ugly country; and that is why, instead of lingering in that golden climate, I am going back to poor, smutty, dusky, Philistine London.[26]

London then was the place for work, and after another stop in Paris, James was back in the Philistine city by Christmas time, and he probably settled down to work upon a fourth novel. By May he wrote home:

I have submitted myself without reserve to that Londonizing process of which the effect is to convince you that, having lived here, you may, if need be, abjure civilization and bury yourself in the country, but may not, in pursuit of civilization, live in any smaller town.[27]

He considered himself "still an outsider," but just beginning to get *into* things, not least among them Sundays at George Eliot's.

The Leweses were very urbane and friendly, and I think that I shall have the right *dorénavant* to consider myself a Sunday *habitué.*[28]

The summer of 1878 in London was rather dull but he found himself liking it, and September brought a first visit to Edinburgh, which he enthusiastically acclaimed as "the most romantic and picturesque capital" in Europe.[29]   Then there was a visit with the Clarks, English people of leisure who, like many others, went to Scotland each fall for the hunting. Through them he received initiation into the gay life of the lesser nobility as they went for sports or balls or picnics to estates near by.[30]

[26] *Letters*, I, 57; the letter is dated Paris, Dec. 15, 1877.
[27] *Ibid.*, p. 59; the letter is dated London, May 1, 1878.
[28] *Ibid.*, p. 61; the letter is dated London, May 1, 1878.
[29] "In Scotland, I," *Nation*, Oct. 10, 1878, p. 225.
[30] See "In Scotland, II," *Nation*, Oct. 24, 1878, pp. 254 f., and *Letters*, I, 62 f.

On his return to London James entered again into the life of the place, in the course of the winter dining out "107 times,"[31] and frequently leaving the city for weekends or longer periods in the country, he came to conclude:

Of all the great things that the English have invented and made a part of the glory of the national character, the most perfect, the most characteristic, the one they have mastered most completely in all its details, so that it has become a compendious illustration of their social genius and their manners, is the well-appointed, well-administered, well-filled country-house.[32]

Christmas he spent at one of these places in the north. Another time, curious about watering places, he went to Hastings and put up at a hotel. Shortly after the New Year he probably went to Italy: there is nothing in his letters or sketches to denote this, but the preface to *The Portrait of a Lady* says that this novel was begun during the months spent in Florence during the spring of 1879.[33] The sketches show that he was back in England in time to spend Easter among the anemones and primroses in Monmouthshire on the edge of Wales.[34] On his way back to London, he visited the Isle of Wight, Portsmouth, Chichester, Cambridge, and Newmarket. It is most evident that he was studying England and the English, and in the summer he wrote to a friend:

I am so fond of London that I can afford to abuse it—and London is on the whole such a fine thing that it can afford to be abused! It has all sorts of superior qualities, but it has also, and English life, generally and the English character have, a certain number of great, plump, flourishing uglinesses and drearinesses which offer themselves irresistibly to criticism and irony.[35]

He was definitely in London and adjusted to it. In the fall of 1879, Lubbock tells us he went again to Paris for three months, and in the spring of 1880 to Florence and Naples for a few months,[36] but by this time James had stopped writing travel sketches and there are no letters which tell us his reaction. These frequent vacations from London, however, silently tell a story—in the fact that he went, and again in the fact that he returned, feeling upon each return a

[31] *Letters,* I, 69.
[32] "The New Year in England," *Nation,* Jan. 23, 1879, p. 66.
[33] Preface, *Collected Edition,* III, v.
[34] "English Vignettes," *Lippincott's,* Apr., 1879, p. 407.
[35] *Letters,* I, 69.
[36] *Ibid.,* p. 43.

little more solidly placed in London than before. By the fall of 1880 he wrote to Charles Eliot Norton:

I am at least now a thoroughly naturalized Londoner—a cockney "convaincu." I am attached to London in spite of the long list of reasons why I should not be; I think it on the whole the best point of view in the world. There are times when the fog, the smoke, the universal uncleanness, the combined unwieldiness and flatness of much of the social life—these and many other matters—overwhelm the spirit and fill it with a yearning for other climes; but nevertheless one reverts, one sticks, one abides, one even cherishes! Considering that I lose patience with the English about fifteen times a day and vow that I renounce them forever, I get on with them beautifully and love them well. . . . . Taking them altogether, they are more complete than other folk, more largely nourished, deeper, denser, stronger. I think it takes more to make an Englishman, on the whole, than to make anyone else—and I say this with a consciousness of all that often seems to me to have been left out of their composition. But the question is interminable, and idle in the bargain. I am passing a quiet autumn.[37]

The Londonizing process was completed.

Again the background is complex, and one wonders how, doing all this running around, James found time to write the many reviews, notes, sketches, stories, and novels which are listed in Phillips. The reason, however, is that James's business in life was by 1875 settled, even though his location was not. He knew definitely what he could do. He was no longer an apprentice or dabbler in literature He was a novelist, able to call himself without shame a novelist. His reviews and notes were accepted by the *Nation*. His critical articles and sketches and short stories were taken without question by the *Galaxy*, *Scribner's*, and *Lippincott's*, while his novels were grabbed, if one may use a word which seems to express Howells's eager action more than any other, by this friend for the *Atlantic*. In Paris, the *Revue des Deux Mondes* requested James to translate some of his short stories into French. In England, Leslie Stephen gladly printed some of his stories in the *Cornhill Magazine*, while *Macmillan's Magazine* obtained the right in England to publish *The Portrait of a Lady*. Editors and companies in both England and America began to publish collections of his stories, of his critical articles, and his novels. And in Germany his stories were translated and published. From 1875 to 1881 was the most strenuous period of James's entire development, yet it was, too, the easiest and the happiest.

[37] *Letters*, I, 74.

CHAPTER XIV

A QUESTION OF TEMPERAMENT

1. *The Reviewer in 1875*

Between the second and third phases of Henry James's early development, there was no break, no interruption of work, like that we noted between the first and second. James had, by the end of 1874, got hold of himself, and he was ready to proceed with an ease and an assurance and a resulting productivity which immediately startle the critic who has been following his slow development up to this time. All of a sudden James came to a realization of his powers. Perhaps the return to America and appreciative friends had something to do with it. Perhaps the beginning of *Roderick Hudson* in the place of honor in the *Atlantic* had more. He found himself acclaimed by his countrymen with all the feasting that usually attends the return of a prodigal. His work was eagerly sought. He began to write with a new gusto and vigor, willing to neglect fiction for a time while he turned his powers to quick financial returns in writing reviews and, much more important, critical articles.

The many reviews, however, are surprisingly unimportant in James's development, both as a critic and a novelist. By 1868 James had proved that he could write a few pertinent paragraphs on any book which was handed to him, and the reviews which he began to dash off regularly again for the *Nation* in 1875, except for a greater ease and facility of expression and a less dogmatic and intolerant attitude, the result of the conclusions reached in Europe the previous spring,[1] add little to our knowledge of James as a reviewer, and but two, both on the same book, give any light on him as a novelist. Considered collectively, the only interest which they have for the student of James is in their great number and their wide range, a range which included history, sociology, travels, biography, letters, memoirs, poetry, drama, criticism, and fiction. Books of travel were most frequently reviewed, among them Latouche's *Travels in Portugal*,[2] the inferior English translation of

[1] See Chapter XII.
[2] *Nation*, Oct. 21, 1875.

Gautier's *Constantinople*,[3] Baxley's *Spain*,[4] Wilson's observations on Tibet,[5] and Southworth's on Africa.[6] These no longer show James as a student of travel reports as the reviews of the early seventies did. He had learned, now he judged, tolerantly however, or merely expressed his interest in the lands visited. The reviews of letters and memoirs—Lady Duff Gordon's,[7] Livingstone's,[8] and others—show his interest in such books as documents of human nature, but there is no evidence in the reviews or the books themselves, or in James's subsequent fiction, that he found anything which he used later. Possibly the generally low calibre of the novels given to him to review—Cherbuliez's *Miss Rovel*,[9] Frances Elliot's *The Italians*[10] and inferior novels by Miss Alcott,[11] Ouida,[12] Miss Thackeray,[13] and Mrs. Oliphant[14]—account for his indifference in treating them. Howells's *A Foregone Conclusion*, however, stimulated him to review it for the *North American Review* as well as for the *Nation*,[15] and here he found something to praise and to remember. He admired especially his friend's portrayal of the American girl in Florida Vervain and her forerunner, Kitty, of *A Chance Acquaintance*.

They have been American women in the scientific sense of the term, and the author, intensely American in the character of his talent, is probably never so spontaneous, so much himself, as when he represents the delicate, nervous, emancipated young woman begotten of our institutions and our climate, and equipped with a lovely face and an irritable moral consciousness.[16]

The praise is just but there is a hint of envy for James realized that Howells with three novels to his credit had, though he had started

[3] *Nation*, July 15, 1875.
[4] *Nation*, May 20, 1875.
[5] *Nation*, Nov. 11, 1875.
[6] *Nation*, Dec. 2, 1875.
[7] *Nation*, June 17, 1875.
[8] *Nation*, Mar. 11, 1875.
[9] *Nation*, June 3, 1875.
[10] *Nation*, Aug. 12, 1875.
[11] *Nation*, Oct. 14, 1875.
[12] *Nation*, July 1, 1875.
[13] *Nation*, Sept. 23, 1875.
[14] *Nation*, Sept. 23, 1875 (in the same review).
[15] *Nation*, Jan. 7, 1875; *North American Review*, Jan., 1875.
[16] *Nation*, Jan. 7, 1875, p. 12.

later, "arrived" before him, and he approached his own fiction writing with a new determination which was not, however, to bear fruit for some time.

The reviews of books of criticism—among others Stopford Brooke's *Theology in the English Poets*,[17] Swinburne's *Essays*,[18] and Sainte-Beuve's *Premiers Lundis*,[19] and *English Portraits*[20]— are unsatisfactory because in the case of the first two, James was not especially interested in the subjects or the point of view of the critics, and in the case of Sainte-Beuve, he was given inferior works of the critic to review. Still these last two have an importance, for in the review of *Premiers Lundis*, James expressed admiration for Sainte-Beuve's endeavor in his last years to revise his old articles and regretted that death had interfered before the completion of the task. In 1875, James was already thinking of revision as the duty of a writer who wished his work to survive, and if we turn to the collection of James's early stories which was shortly to appear as a volume entitled *A Passionate Pilgrim and Other Tales*,[21] and search carefully, we can detect him beginning the practice.[22] In the review of *English Portraits*, James wandered from the book to speak of Sainte-Beuve generally, and here there are a few sentences which are significant in view of James's own critical interests:

The great critic had as much of what is called human nature as of erudition, and the proof of his genius was the fashion in which he made them go hand-in-hand. He was a man of books, and yet in perception, in divination, in sympathy, in taste, he was consummately a man of the world! .... These are his general characteristics, and the portrait would be only more interesting in going down into detail. . . . . Then would appear his patience, his religious exactitude, his marvellous memory, his exquisite fancy—all the

[17] *Nation*, Jan. 21, 1875.

[18] *Nation*, July 29, 1875.

[19] *Nation*, Feb. 18, 1875.

[20] *Nation*, Apr. 15, 1875.

[21] Published by James R. Osgood and Co., Boston, 1875. Contents: "A Passionate Pilgrim," "The Last of the Valerii," "Eugene Pickering," "The Madonna of the Future," "The Romance of Certain Old Clothes," "Madame de Mauves."

[22] The changes made at this time were slight, usually of a single word here and there in the interest of greater felicity of expression or of meaning, and are nothing more than any conscientious author might make when assembling magazine stories for reprinting in book form.

[23] *Nation*, Apr. 15, 1875, p. 262. James was puzzled by Sainte-Beuve's neglect of Balzac.

accomplishments and virtues and graces of the literary passion. On the other hand, we should touch in a dozen different directions his limitations and his defects. . . . . They would be limitations of temper, of morality, of generosity, and they would also now and then be limitations of taste. . . . . Sainte-Beuve's faults of taste were those of omission, not of commission.[23]

Here James expressed his critical ideals—contact with the world and all that went with it, hand-in-hand with erudition, contact with books. In addition, it was well to have what Sainte-Beuve often lacked—generosity, morality, and taste.

Of James's reviews written in 1875 as a whole, and of many of his later ones, it must be concluded that they were simply by-products, made up of material and energy which would otherwise have lain fallow, for the sake of financial return. They are not even as important as the occasional reviews of the two previous years where James had been free to review books or not as he chose. But there was no profiteering on the part of James, for there is every evidence that, unlike the busy reviewer of our day, James read the books assigned to him and gave his honest verdict. This done, however, he promptly forgot, except in the case of Howells and of Sainte-Beuve, all that he had observed and written, for in 1875 he had more important concerns than book reviewing.

2. *The Critic*

One of these other interests, and indeed the only one assiduously pursued for some time, was the beginning of a series of critical articles on French authors, mainly novelists, for the *Galaxy*. While the *Nation* recognized him as a reviewer, the *Galaxy* recognized him as a critic, and James saw a great difference in the two and felt that he had a great opportunity. He turned to do in the articles, tentatively at first and then boldly, what he had not been able to do in the reviews—to reveal that he really *was* a critic, on the scale of Sainte-Beuve with knowledge of the world and book-learning, and also, and this is most important in the case of James, with generosity and morality and taste. The articles, accordingly, reveal not a mind groping out after ideas, pondering them, tentatively trying them, in time assimilating or discarding them as the early reviews did, but a mind which was in possession of ideas, using them as principles and standards by which to judge others. In those upon novelists it is evident that James's ideas upon fiction were by 1875 definitely adjusted into the unwritten formula reached as the result of the conclusions and experiences of the past ten years, whereby truth was the essential thing—truth grasped by observation and thought and regulating morality and art, but itself regulated by a certain taste which kept it from objectionable ground. It was a compound of realism and idealism, and while it tried to be generous, it was adamant when its taste was offended.

Despite the fact that the articles apply rather than evolve theories and greatly in addition to their interest as criticism, the *Galaxy* articles, two in particular, give the student a most important light on James's early development. After the first two, which were called forth by recently published volumes of letters and memoirs and are little more than carefully extended reviews,[24] James did the most daring and ambitious thing he had yet done. He wrote a long and detailed article criticizing Balzac.[25] And then he turned to the so-called "sons" of Balzac—Bernard, Flaubert, and the Goncourts.[26] Armed with his standards, for which in some respects Balzac himself had been responsible, James summoned the French realists to the stand, investigated their cases, and passed judgment. He wrote the two articles before he went to France;[27] they show how he studied the ground and knew what he was going into, and they explain in advance why he was to find the Paris group of realists obnoxious. And it is these two articles, together with a few notes and reviews and two other critical articles which James wrote after he went to Paris, which must concern us for the rest of this chapter. The important thing in the third phase of James's early development is not how he developed in the sense of broaden-

[24] "The Letters of Madam de Sabran," appeared in the October *Galaxy*, "The Two Ampères," in the November. Both give résumés of the lives of the writers as revealed in their letters and journals, but refrain from passing judgment. James evidently felt that a critic should not criticize writings which were not intended for publication, but he says a few things on the wisdom of those who collect and edit them.

[25] "Honoré de Balzac," *Galaxy*, Dec., 1875.

[26] "The Minor French Novelists," *Galaxy*, Feb., 1876.

[27] Though both were published after James was located in France, conditions of publishing are such that they must have been written and in the office of the *Galaxy* before James sailed in November. Even if the second was written after his arrival in Paris, it must have been written before he met Flaubert. Unfortunately I cannot find the date of the first meeting, but it seems unlikely that it occurred before the last of December (*Letters of William James*, Boston, 1920, Vol. I, p. 182), and quite probable that it did not occur till much later. Both articles are to be taken as expressing James's ideas *before* he met the realists, ideas which contact served only to strengthen.

ing, but how he narrowed, how he entrenched himself more firmly in the position which he had taken, with a Russian novelist on one side, and an English on the other, asking for truth to life, but against the French brand of it. It will become apparent from the articles and such few notes and reviews as can be brought in to illustrate his stand, that this stand was largely a question of temperament, moral rather than artistic, that its roots were deeply imbedded in James's nature, and that it was inevitable that he should, at the end of a year, have found himself glad to withdraw from the distasteful literary atmosphere of Paris for the healthier one of London.

3. James and Balzac in 1875

The article on Balzac appeared in December, 1875. It is the first complete account to come from the pen of James, of the French novelist under whose banner he had started to write reviews and stories eleven years before. One recalls his early praise of Balzac as the greatest of story tellers, the historian of his age, and one approaches the article expecting to find a continuation of this tone. One finds instead, that, though praise is there, it is limited and qualified and restricted, so much so that the tone generally is one of censorship and disapproval. It is at once apparent that Balzac no longer stood to James as the novelist par excellence for young writers to follow. What has happened? one asks, and then realizes that, although in his second phase, James tried more or less successfully to follow the example of Balzac in his stories, he was strangely silent about the French novelist in his reviews. His own ill luck in trying to be an historian of America and his acquaintance with novelists who were but secondarily historians of time and place and primarily historians of life at large, writers who did not attempt to be all embracing but were selective in regard to their material, had perhaps made him skeptical. The article of 1875 proves the point. Yet it is not wholly negative. James tried to be generous, and he thought of the writing of the article itself as a tribute, for Sainte-Beuve and French critics generally had overlooked or but inadequately treated[28] this writer, who was, whether one praised him without stint or not, a force, and a force to be reckoned with in fiction. He recognized Balzac's strength. He recognized his limitations. The article is a curious but interesting blend-

[28] James began his article with a brief account of previous criticism of Balzac.

ing of praise and disapproval which may be summed up as a *regret* that Balzac, given his industry and his ability, had not also been given another thing which would have made him respect these more and employ them to the best end.[29]

James recognized Balzac's great attempt:

To be colossally and exhaustively complete—complete not only in the generals but in the particulars—to touch upon every salient point, to illuminate every typical feature, to reproduce every sentiment, every idea, every person, every place, every object that has played a part, however minute, however obscure, in the life of the French people—nothing less than this was his programme.[30]

and he admired coldly the way in which Balzac proceeded to carry out his program.

He was conscious of the necessary talent and he deemed it possible to acquire the necessary knowledge. This knowledge was almost encyclopedic, and yet, after the vividness of his imagination, Balzac's strongest side is his grasp of actual facts. . . . . He made his *cadres*, as the French say; he laid out his field in a number of broad divisions; he subdivided these, and then he filled up his moulds, pressing the contents down and packing it tight.[31]

But the attempt was more interesting to James than the achievement, for, as he scrutinized this, he became suspicious. Everything was in the Comèdie Humaine, but he felt that it was not always there in just the right way, not always presented in just the right light. Balzac's task had been too large. He had proceeded in the only way in which one could proceed in such a matter, by means of observation and imagination, but James was inclined to believe that Balzac did not always play fair in the way he used the two. He saw that as a basis for the "vast mosaic pavement," Balzac had formed an intimate knowledge of Paris; then, having obtained

[29] Faguet: *Balzac*, Paris, 1913, speaks (p. 128) of the inequality in Balzac's work,—"Et en un mot il manquait de goût." James reviewed Faguet's book when it appeared (See *Notes on Novelists*, New York, 1914, pp. 143 f.) and praised it highly. In essential points upon Balzac, James and Faguet agree.

[30] *Galaxy*, Dec., 1876, p. 819. For the quotations from the articles I have used the magazines, since James revised the articles when he assembled them for *French Poets and Novelists*, 1878. This revision, though there are evidences of it in each essay, was not extensive; it was confined to single words and phrases. In very few places where, probably, there were misprints in the magazine, did it affect the original meaning except to make it more exact. I have indicated in my footnotes the most important of the revisions in the passages quoted.

[31] *Ibid.*

his place, that he had begun to collect his figures using boarding houses and the streets for his observations.[32] James commended the practice if one did not abuse it, but he suspected that Balzac had used his imagination to reach into the lives of many people whom he saw only in passing and here he had erred for he was "profoundly and essentially roturier" and could not enter into the life of the salons with grace and understanding. Balzac had also been "conscious that he needed a philosophy—a system of opinions" and here again he had equipped himself, getting all sorts of ideas so that he would be able to deliver himself on every subject. As a result, he was "so vast and various that you find all kinds of contradictory things in him,"[33] both good and bad, and each one so strongly expressed that James found it difficult to criticise him, for as soon as he objected to one thing, another quite the opposite appeared and made him wonder if his first judgment had been fair.

Accordingly James proceeded carefully, measuring Balzac by the principles he had obtained from other authors rather than by Balzac's own standards. Not knowing Balzac's age except through his novels, James could only doubt whether he had been true to all phases of it or not, and he did not press the point except for questionings here and there. But his implication is that it is better not to do an age wholly if it means bringing in everything Balzac brought in. Never once did he call Balzac "historian," as he had so loudly acclaimed him in 1867 accepting then, without question, Balzac's own presumptuous term.[34] In 1875, James spoke of him as a "realistic romancer" and there is a great difference between the two terms.[35]

James was less hesitant when he came to speak of Balzac's attitude toward morality. He felt that here there was more of a negative nature than of an affirmative. Both virtue and vice appeared in Balzac's novels but Balzac was stronger in treating vice.[36]

---

[32] *Ibid.*, pp. 816 f.

[33] *Ibid.*, p. 821. ("Vast" was changed to "large" in 1878.)

[34] See Chapter VI.

[35] In 1902 in writing of Balzac's *Deux Mariées*, James used "historian" again, admiringly applied.

[36] In writing of Balzac's morality, Brunetière (*Honoré de Balzac*, London, 1906) admits that Balzac's scoundrels stand out more prominently than his good people (p. 205) but says that Balzac's novels are to be considered "neither 'moral' nor 'immoral' but simply what they are and what they had to be, inasmuch as they are a 'representation' of the life of his time." (p. 224)

What he represents best is extremely simple virtue, and vice, simple or complex, as you please. In superior virtue, intellectual virtue he fails; when his superior people begin to reason they are lost—they become prigs and hypocrites, or worse.[37]

Consequently James concluded that Balzac was morally and intellectually superficial.

The moral, the intellectual atmosphere of his genius is extraordinarily gross and turbid; it is no wonder that the flower of truth does not bloom in it, nor any natural flower whatever. The difference in this respect between Balzac and the other great novelists is most striking. When we approach Thackeray and George Eliot, George Sand and Turgénieff, it is into the conscience and the mind that we enter, and we think of them primarily as great consciences and great minds. When we approach Balzac, we seem to enter into a great temperament—a prodigious nature. He strikes us half the time as an extraordinary *physical* phenomenon. His robust imagination seems a sort of physical faculty, and impresses us more with its sensible mass and quantity than with its lightness and firmness. . . . . He had no natural fancy of morality, and this I cannot help thinking a serious fault in a novelist.[38]

Ranked beside George Eliot and Turgénieff, even beside George Sand, Balzac lacked that "natural sense of morality" which James had long believed was essential in a novelist. Sometimes Balzac seemed to possess it—in the portraits of Eugénie Grandet, Madame Claës, Popinot, Madame Montsauf, but these people with their virtue steady and untempted seemed to be happy accidents, while the rule in Balzac's novels was the representation of active, unscrupulous vice. His strong characters were always self-centered characters. They thought only of themselves—of power, of position, of riches. They wished "to get on in this world, to succeed, to live greatly in all one's senses, to have plenty of things!"[39] His novels depicted powerful struggles toward these ends. Often, indeed, failure came rapidly and inevitably, for the people overshot their aim, but "in place of a moral judgment of conduct," Balzac gave "an aesthetic judgment,"[40] sacrificing morality not to truth but to

[37] *Galaxy*, Dec., 1875, p. 822.
[38] *Ibid.*, p. 823 f. ("firmness," probably a misprint in the *Galaxy*, was changed to "fineness"; "fancy" to "sense" when the essay was republished in *French Poets and Novelists*, 1878. There were other minor changes, such as "most" to "extremely"; "them" to "these writers"; "thinking" to "but feel," and "I" to "we.")
[39] *Ibid.*, p. 824.
[40] *Ibid.*, p. 825.

art, striving to be dramatically effective and not infrequently succeeding. James probably had in mind such cases as the disaster which overtakes Lucien de Rubempré or César de Birotteau. The latter is one of the least objectionable of the misers, but Balzac played up the dramatic and pictorial possibilities of his failure, far more interested in these than in the moral or spiritual as Turgénieff would have been.

In discussing Balzac's lack of morality, James implied even more than he said. It is evident that he suspected Balzac of belittling art. Art was a high thing. As such it should be respected and allowed to serve only in the noblest of causes. But Balzac was a "prodigious nature" rather than a great mind or soul, and he degraded art. James brought directly into play in judging Balzac the lessons he had learned from George Eliot and Turgénieff and indirectly all that he had absorbed in the galleries of Italy.

James, however, found one thing to praise in Balzac—his ability to describe, to picture his settings and his characters. In this he was great. With Balzac "The place in which an event occurred was in his view of equal moment with the event itself; it was part of the action; it was not a thing to take or leave, or to be vaguely and gracefully indicated; it imposed itself; it had a rôle to fill; it needed to be made as definite as anything else."[41] Could one ever forget the "dark and chill abode in which poor Eugénie Grandet blooms and fades," or the "beautiful old house at Douai, half Flemish, half Spanish, in which the delusions of Balthazar Claës bring his family to ruin," or the "magnificent account of the 'pension bourgeoise des deux sexes et autres,' kept by Madame Vauquer, née de Conflans"?[42] Balzac explained events on the basis of setting. That was wise, James felt, when environment played a part in life, but it did not always, and sometimes in Balzac's hands setting became more important than event. Then Balzac seemed to describe simply for the love of evoking places and quite forgot that he was a novelist supposedly engaged in telling a story.[43]

Greater than Balzac's description of places and not as open to the fault which arose from over emphasis, were his portraits of people. Here James considered him supreme, greater even than Turgénieff, his nearest rival.

[41] *Ibid.*, p. 825 ("rôle to fill" changed to "part to play," 1878).
[42] *Ibid.*, p. 826.
[43] Faguet notes the same thing, *Balzac*, p. 60—"très souvent Balzac décrit pour décrire."

This latter (portraiture of people) is Balzac's strongest gift, and it is so strong that it easily distances all competition. . . . . If Balzac had a rival, the most dangerous rival would be Turgénieff. . . . . With Turgénieff as with Balzac the whole person springs into being at once; the character is never left shivering for its fleshy envelope, its face, its figure, its gestures, its tone, its costume, its name, its bundle of antecedents. But behind Balzac's figures we feel a certain heroic pressure that drives them home to our credence—a contagious force of illusion on the author's own part. The imagination that produced them is working at a greater heat; they seem to proceed from a sort of creative infinite, and they help each other to be believed in. It is pictorially a vaster, sturdier, more systematic style of portraiture than Turgénieff's. . . . . And it is not only that his figures are so definite, but that they are so plausible, so real, so characteristic, so recognizable. The fertility of his imagination in this respect was something marvellous.[44]

Yet in what follows of praise of specific portraits, one feels that James preferred the portraits of Turgénieff, because they were generally of more pleasing people, handled more kindly and with a different emphasis. For Balzac's emphasis, he found, was "inordinately" upon the sexual quality while the conscience was "inordinately sacrificed."[45] Balzac relished the "personal, physical quality" of his women—"their attributes, their picturesqueness, the sense that they give him of playing always, sooner or later, into the hands of man."[46] James's praise was limited by a resumption of the objections he had raised about Balzac's morality and his truth. He recognized that Balzac occasionally pictured virtue but saw that it was often of a queer sort, and the few portraits of good women, such as Madame Bridau, Madame Grandet, Mademoiselle Cormon, Madame Séchard, were altogether too rare.[47] Here, too, because Balzac hated the bourgeoisie, he inclined toward scorn and irony in painting it. His admiration and his sympathy he reserved for his courtesans, the long array of unscrupulous females upon which he depended as his chief bid for fame. James refused to praise this series, considering it "fit only to have a line drawn through it as a laborious and extravagant failure."[48] He also thought that

[44] *Galaxy*, Dec., 1875, p. 827 ("vaster" was changed to "larger," 1878).
[45] *Ibid.*, p. 832.
[46] *Ibid.*, p. 833.
[47] Taine takes a similar view in Section IV, entitled "Le Monde de Balzac" of his essay on Balzac, *Nouveaux essais de critique et d'histoire.*
[48] *Galaxy*, Dec., 1875, p. 834.

"Balzac's young gentilhommes, as possible historical figures" were completely out of the question.[49] The whole thing was the attempt of a presumptuous plebian to portray the aristocracy, and the figures, like their creator, were *poseurs*.

Balzac, James seems to have felt, did not understand, except in a few cases, the qualities which made people best fit to serve as heroes or heroines of novels. Turgénieff did. After reading Turgénieff James had concluded, we must remember, that the novelist should search for characters who were "morally interesting." Balzac seemed to seek those who were morally displeasing.

Through the whole essay plays James's disapproval of Balzac's point of view, his lack of morality, but at the end realizing that he had said more about Balzac's faults than about his merits and remembering that the man was great, James tried to balance the two sides in a concluding paragraph.

. . . . the greatest thing in Balzac cannot be exhibited by specimens. It is Balzac himself—it is the whole attempt—it is the method. This last is his unsurpassed, his incomparable merit. That huge, all-compassing, all-desiring, all-devouring love of reality which was the source of so many of his fallacies and stains, of so much dead weight in his work, was also the foundation of his extraordinary power. . . . . He is an enormous tissue of contradictions. He is at once one of the most corrupt of writers and one of the most naif; the most mechanical and pedantic, and the fullest of *bonhomie* and natural impulse. He is one of the finest of artists and one of the coarsest. Viewed in one way, his novels are ponderous, shapeless, overloaded; his touch is graceless, violent, barbaric. Viewed in another, his tales have more colour, more composition, more grasp of the reader's attention than any others. . . . . One may say briefly, that in so far as his method was an impulse, it was successful, and that in so far as it was a theory, it was a failure. But both in instinct and in theory he had the aid of an immense force of conviction. . . . . M. Taine says of him very happily that, after Shakespeare, he is our great magazine of documents on human nature. When Shakespeare is suggested I feel rather his differences from Shakespeare—feel how Shakespeare's characters stand out in the open air of the universe, while Balzac's are enclosed in a peculiar artificial atmosphere, musty in quality and limited in amount, which persuades itself with a sublime sincerity that it is a very sufficient infinite. . . . . He has against him that he lacks that slight but needful thing—charm. But one's last word about him is that he had incomparable power.[50]

[49] *Ibid.*, p. 835.
[50] *Ibid.*, pp. 835 f.

Balzac, then, was great, powerful, but he might have been without much effort, nay, with only the possession of taste, much greater. He was a "physical phenomenon," "a prodigious nature" rather than " a great mind." He had power but no restraint, no spirituality.

The effect that Balzac was having upon James in 1875 can easily be discerned and understood, if this critical article is compared with the one which he wrote upon Turgénieff, a year and a half before. Behind the latter was seen a young writer who was studying another writer, his good points and his weak points, his method and his manner, with a view to learning something from them which he himself could use. In his early phase, James had approached Balzac in that way. But in 1875 he judged him. He treated him objectively. He had assimilated his lesson; he knew that it was well to describe persons and places vividly, that it was well to be historical if one could be fairly and truly so. These things he would not forget, but now he found nothing more to study. Instead he found a warning. Respect your talent. Make it serve a high purpose. He had passed beyond the place where Balzac could help him.

4. Followers of Balzac: Bernard, Flaubert, the Goncourts

To make sure that he was not making an error in thus repudiating Balzac, James turned to consider in his fourth *Galaxy* article, the authors who, in one way or another, *had* followed Balzac.

In the article, which he entitled *Minor French Novelists*, James turned first to consider Bernard because Sainte-Beuve had acclaimed him as the first of Balzac's pupils. James disagreed—protégé of Balzac but not pupil. Bernard had "the lightness, the ease, the gayety, the urbanity, the good taste, the good spirits, the discretion . . . . of the cultivated French character at its best."[51] He was the "last of the light writers in whom these gifts are fresh and free."[52] Balzac was the first of the heavy. Neither had any natural sense of morality—"no moral emotion, no preferences, no instinct, no moral imagination in a word,"[53] but in Bernard's novels this deficiency weighed far less than in Balzac's, because Bernard's tone was light. He took things easily; he made no pretensions.

[51] *Galaxy*, Feb., 1876, p. 220.
[52] *Ibid.*, p. 220.
[53] *Ibid.*, p. 223.

It is to be inferred that in 1875, James enjoyed reading Bernard, whom he admitted was shallow and second-rate, more than he did Balzac. He almost envied his gayety and lightness.

Bernard was dead, and the French world, following Balzac, had now gone in for heaviness. James looked at the state of French fiction from 1850 to 1875, selected the most characteristic from the formidable array of realists, and endeavored to sum up for his own satisfaction more than for the readers of the *Galaxy* the tendency of the times.

The most characteristic work in this line, in France, of the last five-and-twenty years, is the realistic, descriptive novel which sprang out of Balzac, began in its effort at intensity of illusion where Balzac left off and which, whether or no it has surpassed him, has at least exceeded him. Everything in France proceeds by "schools," and there is no artist so bungling that he will not find another to call him "dear master." Gustave Flaubert is of the school of Balzac; the brothers de Goncourt and Emile Zola are of the school of Flaubert. This last writer is altogether the most characteristic and powerful representative of what has lately been most original in the evolution of the French imagination, and he has for ourselves the further merit that he must always be strange and curious.[54]

Flaubert, the Goncourts, Zola, son and grandsons of le père—he must study them. Yet in the article James confined himself to the first two; Zola "the most characteristic and powerful representative" of the latest development was so "strange" and "curious" that he did not attempt him, and the last sentence of the quotation, though it appears harmless, is charged with disapproval and irony.

Flaubert, James saw, was the connecting link between Balzac and the younger school, a kind of literary dictator who took the principles of the master, discarded all but what he considered the most important, reemphasized these, and doled them out to his school. He was more of a middleman than a producer for he himself had written little and that little was of an uneven sort. Only once, in *Madame Bovary*, had Flaubert achieved success, James felt, yet all of his works bore the "marks of most careful preparation," and "to a discriminating taste"[55] he had written nothing which did not repay attention, whether or not one could follow him.

He at least had a theory for the writing of fiction, and this James stated and explained as follows:

[54] *Ibid.*, p. 224 ("left off" was changed to "stopped," 1878).
[55] *Ibid.*, pp. 224 f.

M. Flaubert's theory as a novelist, briefly expressed, is to begin on the outside. Human life, he says, is before all things, a spectacle, a thing to be looked at, seen, apprehended, enjoyed with the eyes. What our eyes show us is all that we are sure of; so with this we will, at any rate, begin. As this is infinitely curious and entertaining, if we know how to look at it, and as such looking consumes a great deal of time and space, it is very possible that with this also we may end. We admit nevertheless that there is something else, beneath and behind, that belongs to the realm of vagueness and uncertainty, and into this we must occasionally dip. It crops up sometimes irrepressibly and of course we don't positively count it out. On the whole, we will leave it to take care of itself, and let it come off as it may. If we propose to represent the pictorial side of life, of course we must do it thoroughly well—we must be complete. There must be no botching, no bungling, no scamping; it must be a very serious matter. We will "render" things—anything, everything, from a chimney pot to the shoulders of a duchess—as painters render them. We believe there is a certain particular phrase, better than any other, for everything in the world, and the thoroughly accomplished writer ends by finding it. We care only for what *is*—we know nothing about what ought to be. Human life is interesting, because we are in it and of it; all kinds of curious things are taking place in it (we don't analyze the curious—for artists it is an ultimate fact); we select as many of them as possible. Some of the most curious are the most disagreeable, but the chance for "rendering" in the disagreeable is as great as anywhere else (some people think even greater), and moreover the disagreeable is extremely characteristic. The real is the most satisfactory thing in the world, and if once we fairly get into it, nothing shall frighten us back.[56]

Now this it will immediately be seen is quite contrary to James's theory of the novel. His idea was to begin with the undercurrents of life, the things which not the eye but the thought revealed to the novelist. He did not wholly disregard the pictorial side, but he considered it secondary, and he often left it, as Flaubert left the reflective side, to take care of itself. Thus Flaubert and James began at opposite ends. James shunned the curious and the disagreeable, thought they were not necessarily characteristic of life, and sought the wholesome, if possible what partook of the spiritual. He dealt with the inner man; Flaubert with the outer. As for "rendering," James believed it was a good plan if not made the main thing.

[56] *Ibid.*, pp. 225 f. The second sentence was changed in 1878 to "Human life, we may imagine his saying, is before all things a spectacle, an occupation and entertainment for the eyes"; "get into it" was changed to "advance in this direction"; "don't" was expanded to "do not."

After understanding human nature, one should carefully interpret it in the best words in order to be effective, but words were a means, not an end. He admired Flaubert's careful search for the "particular phrase," but he regretted that he had not used it for a better purpose.

Only once had Flaubert applied his theory with brilliant success, and this made James still more skeptical of it. If once, why not again? In *Madame Bovary* realism had said its last word and its best word, for, as if by accident, this novel was not only a great pictorial success but an even greater moral one. The life of poor, depraved Emma was presented so objectively and yet so vividly that it carried in itself a moral lesson. There was no need for Flaubert to suggest any remedy. The facts are so horrible and

. . . . the accumulation of detail is so immense, the vividness of portraiture of people, of places, of times and hours is so poignant and convincing, that one is dragged into the very current and tissue of the story; the reader seems to have lived in it all, more than in any novel we can recall. At the end the intensity of illusion becomes horrible; overwhelmed with disgust and pity, the reader closes the book.[57]

Practically, then, in this, if unintentionally, Flaubert had been a potent moralist—"Every out-and-out realist who provokes serious meditation may claim that he is a moralist."[58] Had Balzac in his pictures of courtesans and fine ladies produced serious meditation instead of dubiety and scorn, James's verdict of him might have been different. There is no admiration, no envy, however, in James's recognition of what Flaubert had done. Serious reflection might be produced by the depiction of virtue quite as much as by the painting of vice. The more direct way of uplifting the mind, of encouraging it by positive example, was better than the indirect one of repelling it. An Englishman or an American could never write the story of an Emma Bovary. Flaubert had little for an alien temperament.

And Flaubert himself had never approached *Madame Bovary*. Its successor, *L'Education Sentimentale*, which employed the same method with less spontaneity, James pronounced "elaborately massive and dreary."[59] As James was interested primarily in Flaubert

---

[57] *Ibid.*, pp. 227 f.

[58] *Ibid.*, p. 225. This is the reading of the sentence as it appeared in *French Poets and Novelists*, 1878, where "serious" supplants "curious," probably an error in the *Galaxy*.

[59] *Ibid.*, p. 229.

as a realist, he paid little attention to his romantic novels.[60] He recognized briefly the high degree of "historical imagination" displayed in the unpleasant *Salammbô*,[61] censored its successor as a mere shadow,[62] and indicated that he thought Flaubert's energy, his erudition, his imagination, his invention, had, in all that he had written, been strangely misapplied. There was a waste of talent, an abuse of art. Even before James went to France, he could see all around Flaubert intellectually.

When James turned to censure the Goncourts who represented a further narrowing of the influence of Balzac, he felt still more that application and artistry had been misdirected.[63] He characterized them as the most Parisian thing he knew.

Their culture, their imagination, their inspiration, are all Parisian; a culture sensibly limited but very exquisite of its kind; an imagination in the highest degree ingenious, and, as the French say, *raffiné*—fed upon made dishes. Their inspiration is altogether artistic and they are artists of the most consistent kind. Their writing novels strikes me as having been a very deliberate matter. . . . . They inevitably went into "realism," but realism for them has been altogether a question of taste—a studio question as it were. They also find the disagreeable particularly characteristic.[64]

One who has followed James's observations upon Balzac and Flaubert realizes that this objective statement of the character and aims of the Goncourts is really heavy with disapproval. James chose his words with care. Their culture was "exquisite," their imagination "ingenious," "raffiné"; their inspiration "artistic" to be sure, but deliberately so. They were not born artists. They had made themselves, and they had, unfortunately, gone into "realism" because that was the thing of the hour in France. They had got up their subjects, however, not from life but in the studio.

James praised with a hint of irony the quality of the art which they used to develop their subjects. "A novel, for them is a suc-

---

[60] In an essay written to serve as the preface to an edition of *Madam Bovary*, 1902, and reprinted in *Notes on Novelists*, 1914, James considered the interrelation of the romantic and realistic elements in Flaubert.

[61] *Galaxy*, Feb., 1876, p. 229.

[62] James had reviewed this in the *Nation*, June 4, 1874. See Chapter XII.

[63] This last third of the article was omitted when *French Poets and Novelists* was printed. Evidently in 1878, James did not consider the Goncourts worth recognizing.

[64] *Galaxy*, Feb., 1876, p. 230.

cession of minute paintings on ivory, strung together like pearls on a necklace."[65]   But women who were careless of their virtue and profligate men, James implied, were hardly suitable subjects for miniatures. There was a strange confusion of fitness. *Germinie Lacerteux, Manette Solomon, Soeur Philomène*, were exquisite art but unsavory matter. Only *Renée Mauperin* was in any way agreeable, and Renée herself was too modern and too knowing. Did the Goncourts know nothing at all of the existence of a spiritual principle? Evidently not.

In conclusion, James pronounced the judgment of disapproval which was felt behind the objective beginning:

They are even more characteristic (of the school of Flaubert) than some stronger writers; for they are not men of genius; they are the product of the atmosphere that surrounds them; their great talent is in great part the result of sympathy, and contact, and emulation. They represent the analysis of sensation raised to its highest power, and that is apparently the most original thing that the younger French imaginative literature has achieved. But from them as from Gustave Flaubert the attentive reader receives an indefinable impression of perverted ingenuity and wasted power. The sense of the picturesque has somehow killed the spiritual sense; the moral side of the work is dry and thin.[66]

"Perverted ingenuity and wasted power," then, impressed James as the outstanding traits of Flaubert and the Goncourts who were the most characteristic writers in France in 1875. They had artistic ideals but they lacked spiritual ones. Thus they did not use their artistry in the best cause. Like the women whom they painted, they prostituted their virtue.

5. *The French Year*

But James went to Paris? Yes. However, he went not blindly, as many critics infer,[67] but with his eyes open, knowing in advance what he was going into, on his guard, hoping as any writer of thirty-

---

[65] *Ibid.*, p. 231.

[66] *Ibid.*, p. 232.

[67] Brooks: *The Pilgrimage of Henry James*, Chapter III, misunderstands the state of mind in which James approached Paris and reads much into the scene which cannot be found in James's observations. Hueffer: *Henry James*, Chapter III, makes no attempt to establish the chronology of James's essays later published as *French Poets and Novelists*, but considers them in a lump and fails to see how they explain his actions. Roberts: *Henry James's Criticism*, Chapter II, misunderstands the temper in which James went to Paris.

two might hope, to meet older novelists, even though he realized full well that he would not agree with their point of view about morality and their ideas about subjects for fiction, trusting that it would not be too disagreeable, yet wholly prepared to keep his ground. And he went, not because of Flaubert and Zola and the Goncourts, but because of a stranger in their midst, Ivan Turgénieff. Turgénieff was there; Turgénieff had settled in Paris except for occasional visits to Russia; Turgénieff might be as dominating a force as Flaubert; Turgénieff should be able to deflect the current in literary discussions to subjects of a moral and spiritual nature. But though James went to Paris because of Turgénieff and though he met him, became friends with him, obtained new ideas and impetus from him, as we shall shortly see, Turgénieff was one matter and the followers of Flaubert another, and James's literary experiences in Paris broke sharply into two parts. There were the meetings of the realists in Flaubert's smoke-filled salon at the top of a house in the Faubourg Sainte-Honoré, and there were the "talks à deux" in dusky cafés with Turgénieff.

To understand James's reaction to the former, the critic must depend almost wholly upon the frame of mind in which James approached the group. There is but one thing in the reviews intermittently sent to the *Nation* in 1876—the closing paragraph of a review of Baudelaire's *Les Fleurs du Mal*[68]—which reveals any light on the matter, and almost as little, as far as literary importance goes, in a series of letters on different phases of French life which James wrote for the *New York Tribune*.

In the review, after criticizing Baudelaire adversely, James took the occasion to express his reaction to the exponents of "art for art."

To deny the relevancy of subject matter and the importance of the moral quality of a work of art, strikes us as, in two words, ineffably puerile. We do not know what the great moralists would say about the matter—they would probably treat it very good-humouredly; but that is not the question. There is very little doubt what the great artists would say. These geniuses feel that the whole thinking man is one, and that to count out the moral element in one's appreciation of an artistic total is exactly as sane as it would be (if the total is a poem) to eliminate all the words in three syllables, or to consider only such portions of it as were written by candlelight. The crudity of sentiment of the advocates of "art for art" is often a striking example of the fact that a great deal of what is called culture may

[68] *Nation*, Apr. 27, 1876.

fail to dissipate a well-seated provincialism of spirit. They talk of morality as Miss Edgeworth's infantine heroes and heroines talk of "physic"— they allude to its being put into and kept out of a work of art, put in and kept out of one's appreciation of the same, as if it were a coloured fluid kept in a big-labelled bottle in some mysterious intellectual closet. It is in reality simply a part of the essential richness of inspiration—it has nothing to do with the artistic process and it has everything to do with the artistic effect. The more a work of art feels it at its source, the richer it is; the less it feels it, the poorer it is.[69]

The diatribe loses nothing by being appended to the review of a book of verses. If anything it gains, showing that James felt the need to express himself upon the question of "art for art" so urgently that he seized the slight excuse offered by Baudelaire's poems. He mentioned no names, but it is not difficult to supply some. Flaubert was the leader of the advocates of "art for art." Flaubert's rooms, where Edmond de Goncourt, Zola, and the young aspirants to fiction, Daudet and Maupassant, gathered, reeked with discussions of the matter. Turgénieff attended the meetings, but though he showed reserve and an aloofness, he was on the whole, tolerant and not enough of a partisan or a pleader to uphold the things which he recognized in his novels.[70] Flaubert's group ruled the day, too little, too narrow to see what great artists recognized—the inter-relation of art and morality. They talked of morality as of a kind of medicine to be used sparingly.

In the letters to the *Tribune*, James resorted to literary topics only when items of the day ran thin. One letter written after James had been seven weeks in Paris reveals his "private elation" that he was an American and not confined by any arbitrary principles or personal motives to any one school.

You ask a writer whose production you admire some question about another writer, for whose works you have also a relish. "Oh, he is of the School of This or That; he is of the queue of So and So," he answers, "We think nothing of him; you mustn't talk of him here; for us he doesn't exist." And you turn away, meditative, and perhaps with a little private elation at being yourself an American able to enjoy both Mr. A. and Mr. X., who enjoy each other so little.[71]

[69] *Ibid.*, p. 281. When reprinted in *French Poets and Novelists*, 1878, "ineffably puerile" was changed to "very childish"; "these geniuses" to "people of that temper."
[70] See James's article on Turgénieff, *Atlantic Monthly*, Jan., 1884, and the *Journal des Goncourts*, tome cinquième.
[71] *New York Tribune*, Feb. 5, 1876; the letter is dated Jan. 18.

Another letter written in April shows that he found one member and probably others of the school of Flaubert not entirely pleasing. James praised the "cleverness" of Zola's *Eugène Rougon*, but objected to its brutal indecency, saying of the author

Emile Zola, a pupil of Gustave Flaubert's, is, as a novelist, the most thorough-going of the little band of out-and-out realists. Unfortunately the real for him, means exclusively the unclean, and he utters his crudities with an air of bravado, which makes them doubly intolerable.[72]

The statement is brief, yet it is charged with meaning. One must remember that this was the spring when France, indeed, was finding Zola too outspoken and presently stopped the serial publication of *L'Assommoir*, driving Zola to defend himself noisily and start on even more extreme realism. Is it any wonder that the young man from America was repelled? But one must not overlook the "unfortunately." It was a matter of regret to James that these writers did not employ their "cleverness" to a better purpose. They, like Balzac, might have been so much greater than they were. What we surmised as regards the Goncourts was true of all the French writers who congregated at Flaubert's—"perverted ingenuity."[73]

James's letters to his family and friends, all too few of which are available, speak most emphatically of his state of mind at various times, but they do not explain it. They simply indicate, as we noted in the interchapter, that in April he was on fairly close terms of acquaintance with Turgénieff and Flaubert, liking both personally

---

[72] *New York Tribune*, May 13, 1876; the letter is dated Apr. 22.

[73] Further insight into James's reactions to Zola may be gained from an article which he wrote almost thirty years later, but it cannot be taken too literally. James then wrote in part: " 'Well, I on my side,' I remember Zola's saying, 'am engaged on a book, a study of the *moeurs* of the people, for which I am making a collection of all the 'bad words,' the *gros mots*, of the language, those with which the vocabulary of the people, those with which their familiar talk bristles.' I was struck with the tone in which he made the announcement—without bravado and without apology, as an interesting idea which had come to him, and that he was working, really to arrive at character and particular truth, with all his conscience; just as I was struck with the unqualified interest that his plan excited." ("Emile Zola," *Notes on Novelists*, p. 40, originally appeared, *Atlantic Monthly*, Aug., 1903.) The reference here is to the shortly-to-be condemned *L'Assommoir*. Note that in this paragraph written in 1903, James said Zola spoke "without bravado." Compare it with the brief remark made on the spot, very likely in reference to the very occasion when Zola made the announcement. This shows the necessity of approaching James in a parallel way.

but seeing all around the latter intellectually;[74] that in May, he was turning into a contented Parisian, but, though he went to Flaubert's Sundays and liked him, he had really seen little of the literary fraternity and did not care to;[75] that in July he was done with the French forever and would escape to England in a moment if he had a friend there.[76] Between these conclusions the critic must insert the reasons.[77]

But is this difficult? Are not all of them already suggested in the two *Galaxy* articles and confirmed in the review on Baudelaire and the two letters in the *Tribune?* Out-and-out realism was objectionable, and artistry, while in itself a most desirable thing, was not to be enjoyed when cultivated assiduously and made to serve in an unclean cause. One does not need to seek the reason as Brooks does in the treatment which the French writers, Flaubert especially, accorded James.[78] Though the writers generally did not go out of their way to welcome him, Flaubert at least, so James's letters indicate,[79] was always most kind when he called. As for James's being hurt at thirty-two, as Brooks believes, by some rebuff— if indeed there was any—such a conclusion fails to understand the James who listened, bored and sarcastic, while the French writers discussed Daudet's *Jack* and ignored George Eliot's *Daniel Deronda*[80] and who was himself often privately elated at being an American and not of the school of Mr. A. or Mr. X. The most likely conjecture

[74] *Letters*, I, 46.

[75] *Letters*, I, 48 f.

[76] *Letters*, I, 51.

[77] There is nothing in books treating Flaubert, Goncourt, Zola, Daudet, and Maupassant which gives any light on their relation to James. Sometimes critics have used James's essays and letters to furnish facts for books on the realists, but they have evidently found nothing in the works of the realists which bears upon James, nor have I. Goncourt mentions in his journal under the date of March 5, 1876, a gathering at Flaubert's where "un petit jeune homme inconnu" was present. (*Journal des Goncourts*, Paris 1891, p. 267.) This may have been James. If so, the remark shows just how little Goncourt had noticed James.

[78] Brooks: *The Pilgrimage of Henry James*, pp. 57 f. Brooks bases his induction largely upon a doubtful letter written by Flaubert which Hueffer claims to have seen (Hueffer: *Henry James*, p. 55) wherein Flaubert voiced his offense at a young American who had criticized Mérimée's style. There is no proof, except Hueffer's inference, that the young American was Henry James.

[79] It is important to note that James liked Flaubert *personally*, and went to pay his respects to him on the last Sunday before Flaubert left the city for the summer. Brooks and Hueffer claim James "hated" Flaubert. James was above petty personal feelings.

[80] *Letters*, I, 42. Lubbock refers to a letter which he does not print.

is that James went occasionally to Flaubert's, usually accompanied by Turgénieff, and listened to the discussions, taking little or no active part in them, feeling aloof and secretly rejoicing in it. Flaubert he liked personally, but he felt that he saw around him intellectually, and his attitude was one of private condescension, surprized that Flaubert should hold such strong artistic principles but should apply them so ill. He found, too, that the voices at Flaubert's were those of his followers— Goncourt, Zola, Maupassant, Daudet— that these voices dominated. Remember what he wrote: "I have seen almost nothing of the literary fraternity and there are fifty reasons why I should not become intimate with them. I don't like their wares; and they don't like any others; and besides they are not *accueillants*."[81] Perhaps they did not like him, but neither did he like them.[82]

6. *Turgénieff*

But this side of the French year which brought James into contact with Flaubert and his followers is but the negative side of the story, and there is an affirmative. As we noted before, James really did not go to France because of the out-and-out realists but because of Turgénieff. And Turgénieff when he was not childishly playing charades at Madame Viardot's was more kind and helpful than James had dared expect. He was "adorable."

The few, yet glowing references to Turgénieff in James's letters and a review of *Terres Vierges* in 1877 in which James named Turgénieff as one of two living novelists whose works he then considered a literary event,[83] justify the critic in turning in this case to a later article, of a biographical even more than of a critical nature, written

<hr />

[81] *Letters*, I, 48.

[82] James's later articles on Flaubert, Maupassant, Daudet, and Zola (see especially "Gustave Flaubert," *Macmillan's Magazine*, Mar., 1893; "Guy de Maupassant," *Fortnightly Review*, Mar., 1888; "Alphonse Daudet," *Century*, Aug., 1883; "Emile Zola," *Atlantic Monthly*, Aug., 1903) are more tolerant than they would have been had he written them during his French year. Ten years, even less in the case of Daudet, were to bring a relaxation of stand even as ten years had once before brought a reversal of judgment. Time was to prove that Zola had the power to make himself noticed even outside of France, that Maupassant was a skilled artist, that Daudet had within him the stuff from which masterpieces are made. But even in these later articles there is often on the lips of James the statement that he would not write that way if he could (see especially the article on Daudet). He came to recognize the ability of the French writers as later works made it apparent but he continued to recoil from their outspoken realism.

[83] *Nation*, Apr. 26, 1877.

in 1883 at the time of Turgénieff's death,[84] to see what the friend-ship meant for James. In Turgénieff's case, time was to prove that the personal qualities which James had enthusiastically surmised about the Russian in 1874[85] were even finer, that Turgénieff was kinder, broader, greater in every way than he had believed it pos-sible for any man to be.

James apparently used his early article as a means of introducing himself to Turgénieff, but this, he hastens to inform the reader had no effect upon Turgénieff, who was quite beyond being impressed by what others said of him, and the critic can understand why Tur-génieff ignored the article. Yet he welcomed the young man warmly:

I shall never forget the impression he made upon me at that first interview. I found him adorable; I could scarcely believe that he would prove—that any man could prove—on nearer acquaintance as delightful as that. Nearer acquaintance only confirmed my hope, and he remained the most approach-able, the most practicable, the least precarious man of genius it has ever been my fortune to meet. He was so simple, so natural, so modest, so destitute of personal pretension, and of what is called the consciousness of powers, that one almost doubted at moments whether he were a man of genius, after all.[86]

Notice the adjectives; Turgénieff was "the most approachable, the most practicable, the least precarious man of genius" he had ever met; he was "simple," "natural," "modest," "destitute of personal pretension"—everything which Goncourt and Zola, even Flaubert, were not. And in the gatherings at Flaubert's it was Turgénieff, to whom James listened, perceiving admiringly the way Turgénieff kept apart morally and spiritually even while he sympathized with the artistic principles of the group.[87] To these realists, "the only duty of a novel was to be well written." It might deal with any subject in the world. To Turgénieff as to James, art was important, but life was more so. And life had its fine, its noble side quite as much as its vile, nay more than its vile; it had its depths as well as its surfaces, and it was the business of the nov-elist to see this noble side and these depths. If he could reveal them in a well-written novel, so much the better; but life came first,

---

[84] "Ivan Turgénieff," *Atlantic Monthly*, Jan., 1884.
[85] See Chapter XII.
[86] *Atlantic Monthly*, Jan., 1884, p. 43 ("precarious" was changed to "unsafe" when the essay was reprinted in *Partial Portraits*, 1888).
[87] *Ibid.*, p. 46.

art second, and if the two conflicted, it was the second which had to be sacrificed.

More than the Sundays at Flaubert's then, James appreciated the "talks à deux" in Turgénieff's little green sitting room at Madame Viardot's or his library at Bourgival, or over long noonday breakfasts in dusky cafés where the discussion was often prolonged to late afternoon.[88] "For myself, at least, at such times, there was something extraordinarily vivifying and stimulating in his talk, and I always left him in a state of 'intimate' excitement, with a feeling that all sorts of valuable things had been suggested to me."[89] Such dejeuners as these, or dinners where Turgénieff brought Russian friends, meant more to James than had he been asked to those exclusive dinners of the *société des cinq* of which Edmond de Goncourt made so much in his journal.[90]

In the course of these talks, Turgénieff revealed his theories of fiction to the young man from America and explained how his concern for life regulated his art. He had been censured—probably by Flaubert's group,—for want of architecture and his novels were not read in France, but this did not bother him. He had his theories and his standards and he kept to them. James had loosely grasped these in his previous article when he noted Turgénieff's skill in portraiture and choice of subjects, and now as a consequence of the talks he was able to state them conclusively and compactly:

The germ of a story, with him, was never an affair of plot—that was the last thing he thought of; it was the representation of certain persons. The first form in which a tale appeared to him was as the figure of one individual, or a combination of individuals, whom he wished to see in action, being sure that such people must do something very special and interesting. They stood before him definite, vivid, and he wished to know, and to show as much as possible of their nature. . . . . He had their *dossier*. . . . . With this material in his hand he was able to proceed; the story all lay in the question, What shall I make them do? He always made them do things that showed them completely; but, as he said, the defect of his manner and the reproach that was made him was his want of "architecture"—in other

<hr />

[88] Yarmolinsky in his book, *Turgenev, the Man, his Art, and His Age*, New York, 1926, runs over the facts of the acquaintance of James and Turgénieff as they are to be discovered in James's letters and essays. His interest, of course, is Turgénieff, and he does not discuss the influence of the older man upon the younger.

[89] *Atlantic Monthly*, Jan., 1884, p. 51.

[90] The five were Flaubert, Turgénieff, Zola, Daudet, and Goncourt. See also Daudet's article on Turgénieff in *Trente Ans en Paris*.

words, of composition. . . . . The thing consists of the motions of a group of selected creatures, which are not the result of a preconceived action, but a consequence of the qualities of the actors.[91]

Turgénieff thus gave James something to think about in writing his stories. James had frequently begun with an individual or a group of individuals, but he saw that perhaps he had not been sure enough of the *dossier* of each when he started to write, and that he had not always made them do things which showed their character *completely*. He had long held that action should be consistent with character, should grow out of it, but the *degree* of consistency, the· fact that action should be deliberately chosen in order to bring out character fully, thoroughly, so that in the end the character had been "done," he had not grasped. This rule he now added to his own rules for development and tried out, as we shall shortly see, even too thoroughly in a novel he was engaged upon while in Paris, and then regulated, as he continued to practice it, till it came to be one of the guiding principles of his method. The year, then, was not without profit. He found, however, that Turgénieff had to leave Paris for long intervals, to retire to Bourgival, or return to Russia, in order to write. And when James had learned Turgénieff's lesson, he also left.

7. *George Eliot Again*

Another thing was confirming James in the stand he had taken. This was a sustaining influence from across the channel, the monthly appearance of a chapter or two of *Daniel Deronda*. A note in the *Nation* when it first began to appear tells us that he was glad to have it come in installments: "George Eliot's writing is so full, so charged with reflection and intellectual experience, that there surely is no arrogance in her giving us a month to think it over and digest any given portion of it."[92] The opening chapter seemed a narrow wedge, but promising, and he waited excitedly for its successors, writing home for the opinions of the family about it. He longed to discuss it with some one, but the French group was quite oblivious of its existence.

[91] *Atlantic Monthly*, Jan., 1884, pp. 51 f. In the preface to *The Portrait of a Lady*, *Collected Edition*, Vol. III, James refers again to Turgénieff's method of procedure, but speaks more as if Turgénieff had merely confirmed him in ideas which he had already had. His indebtedness is thus more apparent in the article.

[92] *Nation*, Feb. 24, 1876, p. 131.

When the novel was finished, he wrote a long article upon it using the interesting critical device of a conversation among three people to give him license to approach it from all angles and to analyze it and George Eliot's ability completely.[93] Of the three people, Theodora expresses unqualified praise, Pulcheria great disgust, while Constantius, who admits he reviews books and has written one novel, reconciles the two sides and gives George Eliot her just due. It is thus the verdict of Constantius—James, of course, in disguise—which must chiefly occupy us, and it shows that in 1876 James was studying George Eliot, as well as Turgénieff, and indirectly explains once again why he could not endure the realists of Paris.

Constantius admits to Pulcheria that *Daniel Deronda* has its weak points—it is the "weakest" of George Eliot's novels, far below *Middlemarch*. Yet he assures Theodora that he has read it with great interest and enjoyment, delighting in its "intellectual brilliancy" and its "deep, rich English tone in which so many notes seem melted together."[94] He agrees with Theodora that George Eliot has observed life and rendered it truly—look at Gwendolen and Grandcourt; but he admits to Pulcheria that she has invented some of her characters—Daniel, yes, and the whole Jewish element. She can do English portraits successfully but not Jewish. Constantius feels that George Eliot seized and portrayed the character of Gwendolen very forcibly:

"Gwendolen's whole history is superbly told. And see how the girl is known, inside out, how thoroughly she is felt and understood! It is the most *intelligent* thing in all George Eliot's writing, and that is saying much. It is so deep, so true, so complete, it holds such a wealth of psychological detail, it is more than masterly."[95]

Constantius envies George Eliot's knowledge and insight. He sees that Gwendolen is both a type and an individual and that George Eliot chose very carefully the events which bring out Gwendolen's pathetic story. (Here he applies the principles Turgénieff had taught James.) Constantius notes that, though Daniel was poorly executed, the conception of Daniel and the situation in which he finds himself is excellent.

[93] Appeared in *Atlantic Monthly*, Dec., 1876.
[94] *Ibid.*, p. 686.
[95] *Ibid.*, p. 692 ("superbly" was changed to "vividly" when the essay was reprinted in *Partial Portraits*, 1888).

"I quite agree with you as to Deronda's going in for the Jews and turning out a Jew himself being a fine subject, and this quite apart from the fact whether such a thing as a Jewish revival is at all a possibility. . . . . The subject is a noble one. The idea of depicting a nature able to feel and worthy to feel the sort of inspiration that takes possession of Deronda, of depicting it sympathetically, minutely, and intimately—such an idea has great elevation."[96]

And James, who spoke in Constantius, made a mental note to remember how well Gwendolen was known and the situation in which Deronda found himself, for future use.[97]

Pulcheria, eager to belittle George Eliot, suggests that Turgénieff has handled a similar idea in *On the Eve* much more vividly. Whereupon Constantius states the difference between Turgénieff and George Eliot:

"One is a poet, the other is a philosopher. One cares for the aspect of things and the other cares for the reason of things. George Eliot, in embarking with Deronda, took aboard, as it were, a far heavier cargo than Turgénieff with his Insaroff. . . . . George Eliot wished to show the possible picturesqueness—the romance, as it were—of a high moral tone."[98]

But Constantius makes no attempt to say which author is the greater. This must indicate that James himself was undecided as to the one he preferred. Both were thinkers, both had insight into human nature, the quality which long before James had demanded of the novelist; but George Eliot brought her beliefs into the foreground of her novels, while Turgénieff carefully kept his in the background. George Eliot was primarily interested in her theories and ideas, the reason of things; Turgénieff was most interested in his characters, the aspect of things. It was a difference in emphasis and much was to be said for both sides.

Constantius admits, however, that philosopher though she was, George Eliot's novels lack the bigness of the greatest works of literature, and this he attributes to the age in which she lived. It forced her to criticize narrowly rather than to show the results of her reflections broadly and this was unfortunate.

". . . . there seems to me to be two very distinct elements in George Eliot—

[96] *Ibid.*, p. 687.

[97] For the use of the thoughts inspired by Gwendolen, see Chapter XIX; for the use of a situation similar to Deronda's, see *The Princess Casamassima*, where Hyacinth, unwitting son of the nobility, goes in for socialism.

[98] *Atlantic Monthly*, Dec., 1876, p. 688.

a spontaneous one and an artificial one. There is what she is by inspiration and what she is because it is expected of her. . . . .

"She strikes me as a person who certainly has naturally a taste for general considerations, but who has fallen upon an age and a circle which have compelled her to give them an exaggerated attention. She does not strike me as naturally a critic, less still as naturally a skeptic; her spontaneous part is to observe life and to feel it, to feel it with admirable depth. Contemplation, sympathy, and faith—something like that, I should say, would have been her natural scale. . . . . But she has chosen to go into criticism, and to the critics she addresses her works. I mean the critics of the universe. Instead of feeling life itself, it is 'views' upon life that she tries to feel." [99]

Instead of by life itself then, as Turgénieff was, George Eliot in her later novels seemed to be dominated by "views" upon life. Her work was now of the study; it was no longer the spontaneous overflow which proceeded from reflective observations along the countryside, in pothouses and homes, as her earlier novels had been. But though she was now of the study, she had stepped into it from contact with the world and retained many of the good effects of that. She treated her people with an immense kindliness. Sometimes she depicted them as caught in ironic situations, but her touch was always sympathetic. And she did, Constantius concludes, give life in her novels, a "vast amount of it." *Daniel Deronda* was lacking in art, but " 'In life without art you can find your account; but art without life is a poor affair.' " [100]

This last sentence, which does not belittle art but merely places it second, is the most significant single statement to come from the pen of James during 1876. It announces his stand, the culmination of years of pondering, of backing and filling. By himself James had advanced to it while George Eliot and Turgénieff had confirmed him in it. The sentence, too, especially the last clause, expresses his reaction to the realists of France. They had put art first. And yet, James yearned for a reconciliation of life and art. [101]

George Eliot was the other novelist whom James named with Turgénieff when he reviewed *Terres Vierges* in 1877 and wrote: "There are only two living novelists, the appearance of whose new productions constitutes anything that can be called a literary

[99] *Ibid.*, p. 690.
[100] *Atlantic Monthly*, Dec., 1876, p. 694.
[101] That he himself was to achieve a reconciliation, see Chapter XIX.

event."[102]   Allied to George Eliot and Turgénieff, then, was Henry James. English, Russian, American—the three had, broadly speaking, the same point of view about morality, the same regard and respect for life, the same reserve in treating it. The English writer had for a long time been confirming the way James looked at life; the Russian more˙recently had affected the way he treated life in his novels. George Eliot had influenced his attitude, made him philosophic and psychologic yet kept him kindly and sympathetic; Turgénieff had influenced his method and his practice. These two influences were now to continue more strongly than ever. The effect of George Eliot is for a time still to be more felt than seen by the critic, while the ideas given to James by Turgénieff were, it will be presently apparent, immediately put into practice.

[102] *Nation*, Apr. 26, 1877, p. 252.

CHAPTER XV

THE AMERICAN: ROMANCE OR TRUTH

1. *Benvolio*

While he was still in America, James amused himself by dashing off a whimsical little story telling about a young poet, Benvolio.[1] He was a kind of fairy prince, possessing in his poetic imagination a magic ring. Like princes and poets, he was a rather restless individual, in fact "a tissue of absolute contradictions."[2] "It was as if the souls of two very different men had been thrown together in the same mold and they had agreed . . . . to run the machine in alternation."[3] Existence was beginning to bore him, and he began to try to "get entangled" with human life. He had a friend—perhaps she was a little more than a friend—the Countess, a fascinating young widow of the George Sand type, "who was made to charm, to play a part, to exert a sway."[4] But she needed "a complement, an alternative, what the French call a *repoussoir*,"[5] and this he found in Scholastica, a grotesquely wise, soberly demure, young woman. Between the two he dallied. He felt the need of both; one stimulated his imagination; the other stirred his intelligence. But neither was content with half his allegiance. Both tried to enslave him, the Countess at length resorting to vile trickery and defeating herself when she sent Scholastica away, thus killing the contrast. Benvolio turned against her in fury for it was, he said, only the contrast which he cared for. At length, however, he followed Scholastica, but, James tells us sadly, his poetry became most dull.

It is not difficult to see that Benvolio represents Henry James, not a poet, but a story teller who dallied between Romance and Realism, who courted sometimes one, sometimes the other, but was most happy when he was by himself, dreaming of the charms of each and effecting a reconciliation of them. In the story, Scholastica seems to have won the victory. Yet did she? Benvolio's poetry

[1] Appeared in the *Galaxy*, Aug., 1875.
[2] *Ibid.*, p. 209.
[3] *Ibid.*, p. 210.
[4] *Ibid.*, p. 212.
[5] *Ibid.*, p. 214.

suffered. The story, thus, had a moral, not so much for the reader, as for James's self. He felt himself inclining towards Scholastica, surfeited by the dazzling beauty of the Countess, disturbed by her lack of scruples, yet he warned himself not to break with her entirely.

Benvolio may well serve as a prologue to the third phase of James's fiction.

I. *The American.*

With *Roderick Hudson*, James had become definitely a novelist and his dominating desire was to follow up the advantage gained by that novel. He tells us in the preface to its successor that, as he had been seated some years before in an American horse car, an idea had come to him:

. . . . the situation in another country and an aristocratic society of some robust but insidiously beguiled and betrayed, some cruelly wronged, compatriot: the point being in especial that he should suffer at the hands of persons pretending to represent the highest possible civilization and to be of an order in every way superior to his own. What would he "do" in that predicament, how would he right himself, or how failing a remedy, would he conduct himself under his wrong? . . . He would behave in the most interesting manner—it would all depend upon that: stricken, smarting, sore, he would arrive at his just vindication and then would fail of all triumphantly and all vulgarly enjoying it.[6]

The situation must be noted. It reveals James's regard for America, his desire in 1876 to present his country in the best possible light.

The terms of the solution did not come to him in America, but once in France, "the who? the what? the where? the when? the why? the how?" inevitably came and the story *The American*, published from June 1876 to May 1877 by Howells in the *Atlantic*, was written, beginning to appear serially even before James finished it.

Christopher Newman, *the* American, is "a powerful specimen of an American" endowed in the first pages with all the characteristics of the general type as James envisaged it in 1876. Everything is promising, though it is evident that he is a "practical man," a man of business. He is quite different from any of the Americans who have appeared up to this time in James's books—a man who has made himself and who consequently believes in himself and in his power to do anything he wishes. After amassing a fortune, he has

[6] *Complete Works*, II, vi.

come to France as a first step in enjoying it. He runs across Tristram, a former acquaintance who now lives in Paris. And in the hands of Mrs. Tristram the plot begins.

Newman confesses to her that he has made enough money " 'to rest awhile, to forget the confounded thing, to look about me, to see the world, to have a good time, to improve my mind, and, if the fancy takes me, to marry a wife.' "[7] In the latter quest she undertakes to help him. She has a friend of convent days, Claire de Cintré, once cruelly forced to marry an old count but now a widow, who answers in bearing, dignity, goodness, and loveliness all Newman's requirements when he says " 'My wife must be a magnificent woman.' "[8] Claire belongs to the remnants of the old nobility, a caste which is adverse to outsiders, but Mrs. Tristram sees in this fact an added interest while Newman sees no obstacle, for has not he always been able in America to get anything he pleased? Thus if it is his fancy to marry Claire, he can.

He meets her, finds her charming, and decides to look into the matter. But from the first time he attempts to call and is told by a superior sort of person, who later proves to be her elder brother, that she is not in, he realizes he may have to do with a formidable adversary, perhaps a treacherous one.

The summer with Claire's absence from town intervenes; and Newman makes the most of the time to see Europe in a leisurely, strolling sort of way. In the fall he returns to France, takes up his abode in a splendid apartment, and applies himself to winning Claire. On his next call, he is received by the lady and meets her younger brother, Valentin. A fast friendship immediately develops between Valentin, supreme representative of a French *gentilhomme*, whose only part in life is to amuse himself, and Newman. It is not long before Newman tells Valentin of his desire to wed Claire. Valentin is amazed, and then because he admires Newman so much, and sees he is deadly in earnest, he promises to do what he can, but he warns Newman that he will find them a strange family.

The next day Newman approaches Madame de Cintré, telling her in one of the longest speeches of his life what kind of man he is and all that he can do for her—all that deep admiration can give and immense wealth can buy. She listens, but says she has decided

---

[7] *Atlantic Monthly*, June, 1876, p. 659.
[8] *Ibid.*, p. 668.

never to marry again. Newman repeats his protestations, restates his promises, and she finally consents to continue to see him if he will not speak of the subject for six months. The case has to be referred to Claire's mother, the Marquise de Bellegarde, and to her elder brother, Urbain, the Marquis. They disapprove highly; but the money consideration is such that they cannot afford to object flatly, and they promise to let Newman try to win Claire if he can. It seems to Newman a victory; six months will be ample time to prove to Claire and to her people his worth.

At the end of six months, indeed, Newman has conducted his courtship so discreetly that Claire finds she cannot refuse the love and happiness he promises her, though she is disturbed that he does not care for her family nor they for him. Newman's happiness, however, knows no bounds. The time for discretion is past, and true to American type, he telegraphs his good fortune to friends in America, then relates to the Bellegardes the congratulations which come in return, and announces his intentions of giving a great celebration for them and his Paris friends in his rooms. The Marquise is scandalized, but Newman's happiness is so intense that he cannot feel the chill of her disapproval. She explains that he must not give a party, but, since one seems to him necessary she will give one, introducing him to *her* friends, and Newman slightly disappointed at not playing the host himself, is forced to accept her plan.

It is this ball which proves Newman's undoing. By the time it comes off, his good nature has reappeared, and with an air of happiness he brazenly roams through the salons of the old house in the Rue de l'Université, where all the old families are assembled, and accepts his good fortune too noisily for the dignified Marquise. She is the more disturbed in that a distant cousin, a Lord Deepmere from England, both wealthy and titled, has appeared and she realizes that the ball might better have been in honor of him. But Claire confesses to Newman at the end of the evening that she is very happy, and he parts from her with a feeling of immense well-being.

Meanwhile a subplot which has been appearing at intervals through the story now becomes entangled with the main plot. Newman has become acquainted with a Mlle. Nioche, a copyist in the Louvre, ordering some pictures from her and taking French lessons from her father. He has introduced Valentin to the girl and

Valentin has tried to disillusion him about her character. But Valentin has become even more interested in her, from a purely speculative view, than Newman, and quite disturbs his friend by his interest. On the evening after the ball, Valentin, much to Newman's disgust, gets involved in a quarrel with a man over Noemie which brings about a challenge to a duel, and despite Newman's attempt to interfere, he goes gaily to Switzerland to settle the affair.

Newman, his heart heavy with this, goes to call on Claire and finds her about to leave for the country. Confused at his coming before she has escaped, she tells him that their engagement must be broken, that she cannot marry him. Newman is staggered, begs and beseeches her to reconsider. She refers him to her mother and her brother who sit stonily by, and they tell him the marriage is impossible, improper. He charges them with treachery, but they deny it. They gave him his chance to win Claire's acceptance; now they have used their authority to force her to withdraw it.

Newman determines to follow Claire to Fleurières, but before he can leave, a telegram calls him to the deathbed of Valentin. There is, of course, no alternative, and he hurries to Valentin finding him dying painfully yet with something of his usual gay spirits, from the wound received in the duel. Valentin perceives Newman's sadness and knows there is another cause than his own condition. He guesses the real cause, and at length Newman tells him all, and Valentin, chagrined, apologizes for his family. Then, wishing to aid his friend, he whispers as he dies that Newman ask Mrs. Bread, a servant, for a family secret which he can use to force the Marquise to give in.

Newman goes to Fleurières for Valentin's funeral, and as soon as he feels it is proper, calls upon Claire. She persists in her refusal, at length, however, bursting into sobs and giving Newman to understand that it is beyond her power to do other than to obey her mother. Then she tells him she is going into a Carmelite convent. This is too much for the American, and he begs her, implores her not to do this, even though she must give him up, but to no avail. The convent offers a refuge to her.

Still hoping that something may be gained—revenge if not Claire—Newman seeks out Mrs. Bread, and learns that the Marquise hastened the death of her husband in order that she might marry Claire to the Comte de Cintré. Mrs. Bread gives Newman a paper which the late Marquis wrote on his deathbed charging his wife with his death. Newman feels that he has the Marquise and her son in his power, and forthwith calls on them, threatening to tell of the crime. They are agitated, but imply that the Marquis was insane and tell Newman they had far rather Claire should become a nun than marry him. And Claire on her side, has acted quickly, going immediately to the convent and refusing to see any one. Nothing seems left for Newman but his revenge, but suddenly all thought of such an action seems repulsive to him and quite as low and mean as the base actions of the Bellegardes, and he leaves Paris to travel. Later he returns, determined to settle there forever, walks up the street where the convent is located, gazes longingly at the walls, and then realizing that it is futile to nurse his sorrow, that everything at last is over, burns his paper and returns to America.

3. Criticism of The American.

The American, it will immediately be seen, did not, like Roderick Hudson, grow out of James's personal experience. It is not at all autobiographic. The hero is not an artist, not a young man born of well-to-do and cultured parents, but a self-made business man who has earned his living since childhood and who owes most of his wealth to the manufacture of wash tubs. He is more typically an American than Roderick or Mallet or James himself. The heroine and her family are people who lived in 1875 in those houses on the Rue de l'Université which were closed to outsiders. The fact that Newman gets in is due to his frank effrontery. James himself had never entered, had only perhaps glimpsed such a person as Claire or her brothers, as he passed by. But, he had his idea—that of the "robust but insidiously beguiled and betrayed," the "cruelly wronged compatriot," who should suffer "at the hands of persons pretending to represent the highest civilization," and yet emerge superior to these people, and when the Rue de l'Université suggested the place where this might happen, he plunged into his story.

Though James tells us in the preface that the idea had come to him in America long before he wrote the novel, he does not mention what was most likely the germ of the idea. Behind it all was a previous short story of his own, crude, unreal, probably written, as we surmised before, in the early seventies at a suggestion from his

father and disinterred when he was in America to appease *Scribner's*.[9]
Crawford's Consistency deals sketchily with a similar situation and
idea—a young man is jilted by a young girl at her mother's command;
other sad things happen, but through it all he preserves his equanimity and thus shows his superiority. The story is laid in America
and fails to ring true. James probably realized this and saw that,
for the first part to be convincing, the man must be pitted against
a civilization which should really seem to be externally at least,
superior to his own, and decided to re-use the situation when the
details—the specific who? what? where? when? why? and how?—
should come. In Paris, they appeared. It was not just Paris and
its streets, however, which supplied them. Direct observation played
only a minor part, while the major influence was that of another
visitor within the walls—Turgénieff. Then, too, imagination thrust
itself in, and well nigh spoiled the whole thing.

Turgénieff had already suggested what became part of "the
what?" and "the why?" before James met him, for he had shown
him as early as 1874 that two lovers accepting adversity were morally more eloquent than when they grasped at happiness.[10] The
lady then must suffer as well as the man. They must be equal
victims. In the details of working out this two-sided situation,
James borrowed directly from Turgénieff. Claire, like Lisa of *A
Nest of Noblemen*, enters a convent when it becomes impossible for
her to marry her lover—the cause is of course different—and the
lover is irresistibly drawn to the sacred spot for a mute farewell.

Turgénieff had also brought to James's attention certain desirable things about "the who?" which further acquaintance emphasized and modified. A review of *Terres Vierges*[11] published just as
The American was completing its run in the *Atlantic*, expresses
principles which had been present in James's mind for some time
and especially while he was working on his novel. With a change of
names, this review might in fact be adapted to James's novel—not
that these two books are alike but that the things which James noted

[9] See Chapter IX. "Crawford's Consistency" is the first of James's stories to
appear in *Scribner's* (August, 1876) but a letter from Howells to James (*Life in
Letters*, I, 181) shows Howells's anxiety lest *Scribner's* obtain anything of James's
as early as 1873. Evidently there was cause for alarm, and James at length yielded,
sending his inferior things to this rival of the *Atlantic*.

[10] See Chapter XII.

[11] Appeared in *Nation*, Apr. 26, 1877.

generally of Turgénieff are the things which a critic must note of James.

Ivan Turgénieff's heroes are never heroes in the literal sense of the word, rather quite the reverse; their function is to be conspicuous as failures, interesting but impotent persons who are losers at the game of life. . . .Their interest, in his hands, comes in a great measure from the fact that they are exquisitely conscious of their short-comings, thanks to the fine and subtle intelligence, that "subjective" tendency, with which he represents all Russians who are not positive fools and grotesques as being endowed. His central figure is usually a person in a false position, generally not of his own making, which according to the peculiar perversity of fate, is only aggravated by his effort to right himself.[12]

Now this, especially the last sentence, fits Newman's case—he is in a false position, not of his own making, which is aggravated by his attempts to right himself. It fits Newman's case even more than it does Roderick's, who was, indeed, a failure, somewhat conscious of his shortcomings, if we are to consider his railings against the fickleness of talent as sincere, but who made little effort to right himself. Newman is thus an advance over Roderick who was a moral failure, while Newman, though he fails to secure what he desires, is morally a success. Lavretsky rather than Rudin was his prototype. It should be noted, however, that James's treatment of failure is not colored by pessimism as Turgénieff's is. James was serious, but not pessimistic, and he had a certain idealism,[13] which is to be discerned in the way in which he made Newman conscious not so much of his shortcomings as of his superiority to the people who work against him, and thus compensated in his own mind for his loss.

In the "talks à deux" Turgénieff suggested part of "the how?" —not all of it, for the method of presentation of the story was James's own, a modification, as we shall see later, of the method used in *Roderick Hudson*. But method of presentation apart, Turgénieff told James that it was a wise plan to make one's hero do things which would show him completely.[14] James took this as so literally important that he resorted to inventing extreme complications— the murder story and the opportunity for revenge that it offers— to afford Newman a supreme chance to show and to feel how very

[12] *Ibid.*, p. 252.
[13] For James's criticism of Turgénieff's lack of this quality, see Chapter XII.
[14] See Chapter XIV.

superior he is. The depiction of Newman's state of mind at the end is excellent, but whether it wholly justifies the means which bring it about is open to question. One almost wishes that James had followed Turgénieff's example rather than his rule—that he had stopped his story with the parting of the lovers, as Turgénieff did in *A Nest of Noblemen*, adding but a short resumé of subsequent actions. Newman's character has already been shown clearly, truly, effectively, quite completely enough without the final proof of his greatness. Another author than Turgénieff, however, was at work upon James, as we shall shortly see, and the temptation to bring in romance, deceiving one's self in the belief that one was doing it in the cause of complete character portrayal, was too great to be refused.

But Turgénieff it was, and Balzac, too, who made James careful of all of his portraits in this novel. Not only Newman, but Claire and Valentin, Mlle. Nioche and her father, and many of the lesser characters exist as individuals. Newman is especially well done; he is an individual as well as a type. Though he is dominated by his Americanism, this is a composite trait, and Newman's character is broader, fuller, more complex than that of Roderick or of Rowland. Next to Newman, Claire had to be presented roundly and thoroughly, and since James's method prevented him from getting directly into her mind, he depended upon his other characters, as well as upon her speech and action, to help him out. She is anticipated as Newman outlines his desires in a wife; she is described as Mrs. Tristram replies to him, and then she is presented to the reader when Newman first meets her and again many times thereafter, always "a consummate woman, nobly planned," and by means of repetition, her character at length is "done."[15]

One of the most pleasing characters in the novel is Valentin, the French *gentilhomme* whose nature is so different from that of the American. That he and Mlle. Nioche and the wife of Urbain de Bellegarde are true to French types we can take the word of M. Bentzon.

---

[15] James regretted in his preface that he omitted the delicate clew to Claire's conduct, but if her obedience to her mother seems unnatural to an American mind, one has only to turn to a travel sketch giving James's reflections during the summer of 1876—See "A French Watering Place," *New York Tribune*, Aug. 12, 1876. Here James noted the world of hidden meaning in the way in which a French girl says "Ma mère."

Nous ne nous étonnons pas de trouver Newman si vivant, si réel; ce qui nous émerveille, c'est la verité du caractère de Valentin de Bellegarde, l'un des derniers types du gentilhomme français galant, expansif, spirituel, dont toutes les vertus se bornent au sentiment un peu vague, mais exalté néanmoins, de l'honneur, qui, à la grande surprise de Newman, parle sans cesse des femmes, convient de ses bonnes fortunes et n'a rien trouvé à faire en ce siécle, où les gens de sa sorte n'ont plus de place, que de se battre pour le saint-père, quitte à se faire tuer ensuite, tout sceptique qu'il sort, pour les beaux yeux d'une fille perdue.—C'est encore la jeune marquise de Bellegarde. . . . . c'est surtout Mlle. Nioche, ce joli monstre intéressant par son ambition et sa rouerie natives, qui *fait de la peinture* au Louvre en attendant l'occasion favorable et immanquable de se lancer dans les hautes régions du demi-monde.[16]

This tribute from an experienced French critic in 1883 should make writers who come later in a world which has greatly changed[17]— even Newman would act differently today—hesitate before questioning the truth of James's French characters.

There are two French characters in the novel, however, whose truth James himself came to doubt—the Marquise, who was born English, and her elder son.[18] This part of the "the who?" which is also the keynote of "the what?", came from James's imagination— unless, indeed, one can say that it came from his determination, aided and abetted by his imagination. James had his idea—that Newman should be misused by people who seemed superior to him, but that he should show his superiority by refusing to take revenge— and he was so obsessed by it that he invented the terms which should help him carry it out. At the time, he did not realize that he was going too far, for the exterior of the houses of the Rue de l'Université suggested austerity and hostility. He was, however, quite as guilty as Balzac, of using his imagination to get inside. And his imagination, we must remember, had long been fed upon George Sand's novels, and was during 1876 being fed again as James reread her novels preparatory to writing a critical article which her death, in May, seemed to call for.[19] She had suggested that mothers were often proud and domineering, that men might be haughty and cold

---

[16] *Revue des Deux Mondes*, May 1, 1883, pp. 126 f.

[17] Garnier: *Henry James et la France*, Paris, 1927 considers that James had little understanding of French nature when he wrote this novel.

[18] See preface to Vol. II of the *Collected Edition*.

[19] See the next chapter.

and villainous, that one might, in fact, make one's characters what one chose to. James, with little, if any, thought about truth, went ahead with his plot, and made the Marquise and Urbain act as his idea seemed to demand. As he noted later in the preface he made a mistake; they would really have jumped at Newman and his millions, dissembling their greed behind proud hesitancy. Unless Lord Deepmere's title and wealth had been made more real and available, they would never have retreated. What he had produced was not life, but "arch romance."

However, the Marquise and Urbain seem true in the early part of the book—so well have they there been drawn—and the critic would have to hesitate and resort to the facts of history before calling the novel basically untrue, were it not for the preface, and were it not also that, before the end of the book, romance of another sort, vulgar romance, enters.[20] James might have cut the string which tied the balloon of experience to the earth without the reader's discerning it, had not George Sand, like the Countess in *Benvolio*, forced her attentions upon him and led him, unwittingly, to go too far. When he was searching for a supreme test for Newman's character, she saw her chance, and whispered of a chateau in the country, falling to ruin, gloomy, dismal, and then of the murder which had been committed there by the Marquise, the knowledge of which might be Newman's to use or not to use. James, believing he was simply doing what Turgénieff advocated—bringing out his hero completely—seized the situation and the grewsome incident and made the most of it. From then on, the characters of the Marquise and Urbain become glaringly improbable.

The American thus is a hybrid of Turgénieff and George Sand. Therein lies its anomaly, its defects, but also for the critic, its interest. It shows James trying to be real, trying to be true, yet all unwittingly led astray by the influence of a woman and an imagination which, when unbridled, was apt to wander too far and too wide. Vivid as its romantic parts are, and important as they are in the plot, the balance, however, tends to the side of Turgénieff and it is there supported by another influence, pervasive rather than apparent in any outspoken way. In the sympathy and understanding

---

[20] Strange to note, James says nothing in the preface about the matter of vulgar romance which is much more glaring a slip than the error in the characters of the Marquise and Urbain.

with which James handled Newman and Claire and Valentin, and in his high moral tone, there is a touch of George Eliot—Scholastica who was patiently biding her time.

The American, however, is not just a compound of things which other authors gave to James. Part of "the how?" was James's own. He looked at the story from the point of view of Newman, in fact through the consciousness of Newman—"the interest of everything is all that it is *his* vision, *his* conception, *his* interpretation."[21] This was at times difficult, for Newman is not as wise, does not see or understand as readily as his predecessor, Mallet, and it was, of course, part of the plan that he should not. At times, then, James stepped into the story himself to call the reader's attention to a raised eyebrow, a significant gesture which quite escapes Newman. This is not objectionable, and *The American* marks a distinct step ahead in the method which James was evolving. In *Roderick Hudson* the main character is seen only through the eyes of another, and the reader gets at his thoughts only through his conversation with Mallet; sometimes, too, Mallet seems to be as much of a main character as Roderick and the interest is divided. In *The American* the reader is brought into direct communion with Newman's thoughts and feelings. He hears him talk, but he sees him thinking, and he knows what he is thinking about. As the story progresses, Newman talks less and thinks more, but the reader does not lose by this. He is with him all the time. At the end he thoroughly understands Newman. He knows, too, that Newman, by himself, is the main character, that the story is his affair and not by any possibility that of a friend, and his sense of form is gratified. *The American*, then, has something of promise.

[21] *Collected Edition*, Vol. ii, p. xxi.

CHAPTER XVI

THE PARTING OF THE WAYS

1. *James and George Sand.*

The student of James is not surprised at the intrusion of romance into *The American*, for James had long been an admirer of George Sand. Indeed, he had admired her much longer than he had Turgénieff. During 1876, too, if we look again at the letters which he wrote to the *New York Tribune*, we shall see that the name of "the greatest *improvisatrice*" in literature was mentioned far more frequently than that of any other writer. Her death early in the summer had something to do with it, calling from him first a brief word and then a whole letter of regret. It was "a great loss to literature,"[1] and he turned to reread some of her earlier novels, confessing, however, that he did not find them "as easy reading" as he once had, but saying of her entire output, "they are a very extraordinary and splendid series, and certainly one of the great literary achievements of the time."[2] He continued to read her novels, perhaps in part as a reaction from the disturbing realism of Flaubert's rooms, and more as a preparation for writing an article for the *Galaxy* which her death seemed to call for. Yet the more he reread—or tried to—the less desire he had to write the article.[3] Still, when he took a trip to the seaside and then to the south of France, rocks and sea, and then chateaux and peasantry reminded him of her novels, and it was really inevitable that something from her should have got into *The American*. George Sand was his countess. Yet even as he felt her charms, he realized her restrictions—she was an *improvisatrice*, working by means of her imagination and her fancy rather than by observation and thought and high ideals of morality. She had no scruples about art or about life, and he did. It was probably not long before James saw that she had had a bad effect upon *The American* and he turned against her and against romanticism even as he had turned against extreme realism. The year 1876 was in many ways a turning point.

[1] *New York Tribune*, July 1, 1876, p. 3 (dated June 9).
[2] *New York Tribune*, July 22, 1876, p. 3 (dated June 28).
[3] See *Letters*, I, 51.

In regard to romanticism, this is more evident from what happened afterwards than from the year itself. Afterwards there was
occasionally a romantic story, which was vastly inferior to the other
work,[4] and sometimes the intrusion of romance into a story which
was based upon observation and thought.[5] Afterwards, too, in 1877
and again in 1879, there was critical work which shows James definitely bidding farewell to his Countess. He promised to think of
her sometimes, but he vowed he would not give her all of his attention. With the increasing attraction which George Eliot and
Turgénieff had for James, it was inevitable that the active influence of romanticism should stop.

The important critical articles published in 1877 were two—one
upon Alfred de Musset, and another, the dreaded homage to the
dead, upon George Sand, which turned out to be not a homage at all.[6]

The article upon Musset appeared the month before the one
upon George Sand and was probably a by-product of that, called
forth by a life of Musset which James had very probably read while
looking for material for his other essay. After studying the relations
of the two lovers, however, he decided that the intimate affairs of
authors' lives were not the business of critics of their works, and he
turned to what was. He noted that the period of Musset's best
work had followed the rupture with George Sand, and that though
his work was still romantic, it was finely so, much more finely so
than that of the false George. This was because Musset's imagination was of such a high order, his taste and touch so delicate and

---

[4] "Theodolinde," *Lippincott's*, May, 1878, another version of the-man-in-love-
with-a-statue situation of "The Last of the Valerii;" "Longstaff's Marriage,"
Scribner's, Aug., 1878, George Sand adapted unsuccessfully again to Americans;
"The Diary of a Man of Fifty," *Harper's*, July, 1879, with a George Sand heroine,
are predominantly romantic. "The Ghostly Rental," published *Scribner's*, Sept.,
1876, but probably written sometime before, betrays the influence of Poe and
Hoffman. All of these are outside the main stream of development as it had by
now defined itself.

[5] See Chapter XVII. (It also appeared sometimes in the stories written after
1881.)

[6] "Alfred de Musset" appeared in the *Galaxy*, June, 1877; "George Sand," in
the *Galaxy*, July, 1877. Two other critical articles had preceded these in the
Galaxy, "The Letters of Honoré de Balzac," Feb., 1877, and "The Théâtre Français," Apr., 1877. Neither is important in James's development. The former con-
fines itself to the facts of Balzac's life as revealed in his letters; James found that
they only confirmed his opinion of Balzac's grossness and lack of charm. The
latter is concerned with the actors and actresses of the French stage. All four
articles were reprinted in *French Poets and Novelists*, 1878.

exquisite, and his regard for his art so noble. If one had all these high attributes, romanticism was worthy, and James gave Musset almost unrestricted praise saying much for what he was and but very little for what he was not.

He spoke of Musset's want of finish in his poetry, only to say that his exquisite feeling and ineffable grace between them quite made up for the lack.[7] He touched only lightly upon the matter of truth—"it is not fair to say of anything represented by Musset that it is caught in the act" and added immediately, "Just the beauty and charm of it is that it is not the exact reality but a something seen by the imagination—a tinge of the ideal, a touch of poetry."[8] He singled out for mention, of the poems, the *Nuit de Mai*, the *Nuit d'Août*, the *Nuit d'Octobre*, the *Lettre à Lamartine*, the *Stances à la Malibran*; of the plays, *On ne badine pas avec d'amour* and *Lorenzaccio*, which we remember James had once translated, and also used in a short story;[9] of the nouvelles, *Emmeline* and *Frédéric et Bernedette*.[10] Yet, and this is the important thing, all of the praise bestowed by James upon Musset is surprisingly objective. It is quite the most objective criticism which has come from James's pen, and it shows that while he praised he did not envy, for he realized that his temperament, his ability, and Musset's were at opposite poles. Musset did fine things in the name of the imagination; he did ignoble ones. Thought rather than imagination must be his guiding principle.

The article upon George Sand, however, is not objective. It is condemnatory. It is not a homage at all. To be sure, James gave an account of her life and wrote an appreciation of her ability, but he threw the emphasis not upon what she did, but upon what she lacked and did not do. He praised only to qualify. In this way the article is similar to the one upon Balzac, a regret expressed, a judgment passed, a repudiation of the things of which he did not approve. And it is colored with even a touch of exasperation that he had ever listened to the whisperings of the Countess.

Her power and her deficiency were related. Her great strength was her "unequalled faculty of improvisation; her great weak-

---

[7] *Galaxy*, June, 1877, p. 799.
[8] *Ibid.*, p. 802.
[9] See Chapter XI.
[10] *Galaxy*, June, 1877, p. 797.

ness was her "peculiar want of veracity."[11]   She simply did not care whether things were true or not; she never allowed facts to make her uncomfortable.[12]   One could not trust her.   She appeared to be a philosopher with all of her lengthy, yet easy and fluent analysis, but she "philosophized upon a great many things which she did not understand . . . . she never took herself too much *au serieux*."[13] Though she was not always her own dupe, perhaps never, the reader might not be so fortunate; he might, indeed, be carried away by the fluency of her style, the charm and spell which she cast over him. That was the danger if one read her only once, but if one returned to her, one might then discover, as James did, that the charm was not sufficient.

James must have felt that in some ways he had been tricked. Even the point where George Sand had formerly seemed to him greater than George Eliot, he now questioned.   It was George Sand's merit that she portrayed passion and gave the reader ideas upon the affairs of the heart:

Miss Austen and Sir Walter Scott, Dickens and Thackeray, Hawthorne and George Eliot, have all represented young people in love with each other; but no one of them has, to the best of my recollection, described anything that can be called a passion—put it into motion before us, and shown us its various paces.   To say this is to say at the same time that these writers have spared us much that we consider disagreeable, and that George Sand has not spared us; but it is to say furthermore that few persons would resort to English prose fiction for any information concerning the ardent forces of the heart—for any ideas upon them.   It is George Sand's merit that she has given us ideas upon them—that she has enlarged the novel-reader's conception of them and proved herself in all that relates to them an authority.[14]

But James was dubious as to the extent to which such revelations should go.   He felt that there was too much of such "amatory disquisitions" in George Sand's novels.

There is to my taste a great deal too much of it; the total effect is displeasing. The author illuminates and glorifies the divine passion but she does some-

---

[11] *Galaxy*, July, 1877, p. 47.

[12] *Ibid.*, p. 48.

[13] *Ibid.*, pp. 52 f.

[14] *Ibid.*, p. 55 ("disagreeable" was changed to "objectionable," when the essay was printed in *French Poets and Novelists*, 1878).

thing which may be best expressed by saying that she cheapens it. She handles it too much; she lets it too little alone. Above all things she is too positive, too explicit; too business-like; she takes too technical a view of it.[15]

He much preferred the discretion exercised by the English mind. Discretion was unknown to George Sand; she had in its place "a sort of benevolent, an almost conscientious disposition to sit down . . . . and 'talk over' the whole matter,"[16] whether the reader cared to or not. Her early novels were in this respect somewhat less objectionable than her later, for as she proceeded, she became more argumentative and began to play with her topic intellectually. James liked *Valentine*, but *Lucrézia Floriani* and its successors had, he felt, a falsity of tone.

George Sand's morality was also to be questioned. "She never accepts a weakness as a weakness; she always dresses it out as a virtue,"[17] making it appear moral when it was not. She was, then, doubly dangerous. He himself had been taken in once; he had held up George Sand, along with George Eliot and Turgénieff, to Balzac for her morality,[18] but now he saw on rereading her that she really had no moral taste. In *Jacques*, in *Léone Léoni*, in *Mademioselle Merquem*, the people did the queerest things and pretended to be moral. He saw that they were not.

Once he had praised George Sand's style; he had envied it and had wished to catch its fluency.[19] He still was willing to praise it, but since the discussions in Flaubert's room style, though still desirable, seemed to him secondary to form, and this George Sand's novels lacked. As a result, though it was easy to read her books for the first time, reperusal was difficult.

It has been said that what makes a book a classic is its style. We should modify this, and instead of style say *form*. Mme. Sand's novels have plenty of style, but they have no form. Balzac's have not a shred of style, but they have a great deal of form. Posterity doubtless will make a selection from each list, but the few volumes of Balzac it preserves will remain with it much longer, I suspect, than those which it borrows from his great contemporary.[20]

[15] *Ibid.*, p. 56.
[16] Ibid., p. 56.
[17] Ibid., p. 60.
[18] See Chapter XIV.
[19] See Chapter VI.
[20] *Galaxy*, July, 1877, p. 59.

Ten years before James had predicted that posterity would read both Balzac and George Sand welcoming the latter as a refreshing breath after Balzac.[21] Now he considered Balzac was the more valuable, a prophecy which has been proved by time.

But George Sand's great defect which James could not get away from was her untruthfulness and he returned at the end of his article and explained again what he meant, trying, however, to give her what praise he could:

In saying that George Sand lacks truth the critic more particularly means that she lacks exactitude—lacks the method of truth. Of a certain general truthfulness she is full to overflowing; we feel that to her mind nothing human is alien. I should say of her not that she *knew* human nature, but that she felt it. At all events she loved it and enjoyed it. She was contemplative; but she was not, in the deepest sense, observant. She was a very high order of sentimentalist but she was not a moralist. She perceived a thousand things, but she rarely in strictness, judged; so that although her books have a great deal of wisdom, they have not what is called weight. . . . M. Taine calls her an idealist; I should say, somewhat more narrowly, that she was an optimist. An optimist "lined," as the French say, with a romancer, is not the making of a moralist. George Sand's optimism, her idealism, are very beautiful, and the source of that impression of largeness, luminosity, and liberality which she makes upon us. But I suspect that something even better in a novelist is that tender appreciation of actuality which makes even the application of a single coat of rose-colour seem an act of violence.[22]

Thus James bade farewell to the author who had once been his benefactress. She had shown him the desirability of passion in a story; she had helped him develop ease in narration; she had taught him how to handle analysis naturally. He had thoroughly assimilated what he had learned from her—the good things at least— and he was now proceeding with little thought of his debt. George Sand had not survived reperusal. She, like Balzac, was now shoved onto the top shelf. The mean was somewhere between the two—Turgénieff and George Eliot.

2. *The Life of Hawthorne.*

At the risk of violating slightly the chronology of James's development, it is necessary to turn to his *Life of Hawthorne*, published in 1879,[23] to see that this stand of his upon romanticism was

[21] See Chapter VI.
[22] *Galaxy*, July, 1877, p. 61.
[23] Published in London and New York, 1879.

not directed at one author whom he had come to distrust, but was maintained, though in a politely modified form, even in the face of an author whom he felt was great and constituted his country's chief bid for recognition in the field of literature.

Morley, the editor of the English Men of Letters series, had asked James to do a biography of Hawthorne. James realized that in this respect he could do little but restate the facts of his country-man's life as they were apparent in his notebooks and in the life already written by Lathrop. However, he felt that he could inter-pret Hawthorne, and he accepted the commission and wrote what is more important as a critical study then as a biographical sketch. Fired with patriotism to America as well as to fiction and with his critical conscience more alert than it had ever been, James attempted to state Hawthorne's contribution, though it had been a sacrifice on the altar of romanticism, as strongly yet as fairly as possible. He gave due honor where honor was due and admired Hawthorne as "the most beautiful and eminent representative of a literature .... the most valuable example of the American genius."[24]   The tribute is generous, surprisingly so. Yet it is also fair. Coming as it did from the pen of James, it is unusually objective. Yet in a few brief statements which recur regularly, the careful searcher may de-tect James's preference for realism, and since we are studying James and not Hawthorne, it is these side remarks which are first of all important. Yet it is important, too, to see how James managed to turn even these disapproving side remarks into objective praise.

James realized that America had furnished a shallow soil for "the flower of art," and he regretted that Hawthorne had ignored in his notebooks and short stories the Salem of his own time so com-pletely, that he had not commemorated some of the types of his native place.[25] Certainly he was an American, a product of the moral and religious soil of New England, and his stories were American in a narrow way, permeated through and through with Puritanism, but the problems of sin and conscience he conceived and expressed fancifully, allegorically, rather than realistically and exactly. Per-haps, James admitted, there was an advantage in this. It was Hawthorne's great charm.

This is the real charm of Hawthorne's writing—this purity and naturalness of fancy. For the rest, it is interesting to see how it borrowed a particular

[24] *Hawthorne,* New York, 1879, p. 2.
[25] Ibid., p. 45.

colour from the other faculties that lay near it—how the imagination, in this capital son of the old Puritans, reflected the hue of the more purely moral part, of the dusky over-shadowed conscience. The conscience, by no fault of its own, in every genuine offshoot of that sombre lineage, lay under the shadow of the sense of *sin*. . . . . There were all sorts of possible ways of dealing with it. . . . . Hawthorne's way was the best; for he contrived by an exquisite process, best known to himself, to transmute this heavy moral burden into the very substance of the imagination, to make it evaporate in the light and charming fumes of artistic production. But Hawthorne, of course, was exceptionally fortunate; he had his genius to help him.[26]

In the last remark, it is evident that James realized his own limitations; to very few was it given to write as Hawthorne did, converting truth and morality into the "very stuff of the imagination" so that they gained, instead of lost, thereby.

But Hawthorne's imagination unfortunately was not always pure and rich. Sometimes it degenerated into fancy and this lesser faculty James greatly distrusted. It caused Hawthorne to use conceits and allegories. In his metaphysical moods he was nothing if not allegorical, and here James made a side remark which in view of some of his own work, must be quoted:

. . . . allegory, to my sense, is quite one of the lighter exercises of the imagination. . . . . I frankly confess that I have, as a general thing, but little enjoyment of it, and that it has never seemed to me to be as it were, a first-rate literary form . . . . it is apt to spoil two good things—a story and a moral, a meaning and a form.[27]

Yet James had used allegory himself, and was, though he was now declaring himself against romanticism, to use allegory again in a way peculiar to himself.[28] With James, however, allegory, especially as he used it later, was never over prominent as with Hawthorne. It was often hidden deeply.

Though Hawthorne had not preserved the Salem of his time, James recognized that he had "as regards the two earlier centuries of New England life, that faculty which is called now-a-days the historic consciousness,"[29] and that in a few tales, really too few, he had caught and preserved some of the New England past. Yet he la-

[26] Ibid., pp. 56 f.
[27] Ibid., pp. 61 f.
[28] Particularly in the short stories of the nineties which deal with authors and authorship.
[29] Ibid., p. 66.

mented that Hawthorne's desire for the picturesque had led him to seek the unusual, while his fancy had converted the facts into legends. Thus the tales were not truly historical. "Hawthorne, to say it again, was not in the least a realist—he was not to my mind enough of one."[30]

Of Hawthorne's major works, James thought *The Scarlet Letter* was the best having the mark of his best things, "an indefinable purity and lightness of conception" in spite of its sombre tone.[31] He praised Hawthorne for being interested in the consequences that followed Hester's and Arthur's ill-advised love affair rather than the affair itself. But he saw two faults—"a want of reality and an abuse of the fanciful element, of a certain superficial symbolism."[32] The first fault he noted in regard to the part played by the characters:

The people strike me not as characters, but as representatives, very picturesquely arranged, of a single state of mind; and the interest of the story lies, not in them, but in the situation, which is insistently kept before us, with little progression, though with a great deal . . . . of a certain stable variation; and to which they, out of their reality, contribute little that helps it to live and move.[33]

Of the abuse of the fanciful element, James said: "In *The Scarlet Letter* there is a great deal of symbolism; there is, I think, too much. It is overdone at times and becomes mechanical; it ceases to be impressive, and grazes triviality."[34] He felt this especially in regard to the mystic *A* which the minister found upon his breast. It might have been mentioned once, but not several times. And then the *A* appeared in the sky. James felt there was danger of the sublime becoming the ridiculous.[35] At the end of his account of this novel James caught himself up, guilty of having expatiated on its defects, and undid his censure by saying that these defects were really "of the slenderest and most venial kind,"[36] but surface flaws, that *The Scarlet Letter* had style and depth and charm. "One can often return to it; it supports familiarity, and has the inexhaustible charm and mystery of great works of art."[37]

[30] Ibid., p. 65.
[31] Ibid., p. 108.
[32] Ibid., p. 110.
[33] Ibid., pp. 110 f.
[34] Ibid., p. 113.
[35] Ibid., p. 115.
[36] Ibid., p. 116.
[37] Ibid., p. 116.

As James progressed in his study, his refrain—he is not a realist —became more frequent. Yet James remembered increasingly that he was a critic, and he realized that he should not take Hawthorne to task for what he was not and had no intention of being when he was so delightfully something else. Accordingly when he came to *The House of the Seven Gables*, he praised it for being only vaguely true. That was, indeed, its charm.

The House of the Seven Gables has however, more literal actuality than the others, and if it were not too fanciful an account of it, I should say that it renders, to an initiated reader, the impression of a summer afternoon in an elm-shadowed New England town. It leaves upon the mind a vague correspondence to some such reminiscence. . . . . The comparison is to the honour of the New England town which gains more than it bestows. The shadows of the elms, in *The House of the Seven Gables* are exceptionally dense and cool; the summer afternoon is peculiarly still and beautiful; the atmosphere has a delicious warmth, and the long daylight seems to pause and rest. But the mild provincial character is there, the mixture of shabbiness and freshness, the paucity of ingredients. The end of an old race—this is the situation that Hawthorne has depicted, and he has been admirably inspired in the choice of the figures in whom he seeks to interest us. They are all figures rather than characters—they are all pictures rather than persons. But if their reality is light and vague, it is sufficient, and it is in harmony with the low relief and dimness of outline of the objects that surrounded them. They are all types, to the author's mind, of something general, of something that is bound up with the history, at large, of families and individuals, and each of them is the center of a cluster of those ingenious and meditative musings, rather melancholy, as a general thing, than joyous, which melt into the current and texture of the story and give it a kind of moral richness.[38]

Thus James arranged it with his conscience, critical as well as fictional, to give Hawthorne his due. One notes, however, that James evinced no envy of his predecessor in the field of American fiction, that he had no desire to go and do likewise. The attitude and tone of the book are the same in greater degree as those of the critical article on Musset.

The *Life of Hawthorne*, not only gives James's stand upon romanticism; it marks still more the peak of his early critical development. It must be repeated again that the essay is largely objective, and it is only because we have been studying James's development and

[38] Ibid., pp. 120 f.

know that he was deserting romanticism,[39] that we can gather the hidden significance of the refrain. Otherwise we would not be able to tell where James stood. Consider the final paragraph:

He was a beautiful, natural, original genius, and his life has been singularly exempt from worldly preoccupations and vulgar efforts. . . . . His work will remain; it is too original and exquisite to pass away; among men of imagination he will always have his niche. No one has had just that vision of life, and no one has had a literary form that more successfully expressed his vision. He was not a moralist, and he was not simply a poet. The moralists are weightier, denser, richer in a sense; the poets are more purely inconclusive and irresponsible. He combined in a singular degree the spontaneity of the imagination with a haunting care for moral problems. Man's conscience was his theme, but he saw it in the light of a creative fancy which added, out of its own substance, an interest, and, I may almost say, an importance.[40]

In its objectivity, in its sincerity, in its successful attempt to be just, in its carefully drawn distinctions, in its even tone, this—and it is typical of the whole essay—is much purer criticism than anything which has yet come from the pen of James.

During the last five years a great change had taken place in James's criticism. The essay on Turgénieff in 1874 was largely personal in its motive. James was then primarily interested in studying Turgénieff from the standpoint of his own endeavors in fiction. Since 1875, he had been more genuinely critical, passing judgment rather than searching for ways and means. But he had sometimes been personal in his judgment. The essay on Balzac was often colored by his impatience. The one on George Sand, though it followed a tolerant and appreciative one on Musset, was at times condescending, at others vehemently condemnatory. James's morality and taste had interfered with his generosity. These three qualities which James had mentioned in 1875 as highly desirable in a critic, lamenting then that Sainte-Beuve did not have them, he had found were really incompatible. In *The Life of Hawthorne*, he did not try to apply them, but he substituted another quality, larger, broader, in a way embracing all three, for them, a quality which he was even then learning from Sainte-Beuve himself—the quality of

[39] James was to return to romanticism occasionally, yet with a difference, for in such things as his ghost stories, his interest was in the psychological effect of imagination upon his characters rather than in any romantic aspect of his plots.

[40] Ibid., pp. 176 f.

justness.[41] He looked at the writer from the writer's standpoint, not from his own. When a brief aside inadvertently crept in, he followed it, as if conscience-stricken, with a long explanatory appreciation of the quality he had seemed to censure, shifting his point of view from his wishes to Hawthorne's intentions. When, as in the case of the degeneration of Hawthorne's imagination into fancy, in *The Scarlet Letter*, James continued to criticize Hawthorne negatively for a few pages, he did it in respect to the way in which Hawthorne by overzealousness, fell short of his ideal, not of James's.

James was now truly a critic of the quality of Sainte-Beuve, whom he had doubtless been studying and was the following January to criticize more fully and understandingly than four years before, saying in part: "the critic, in his conception, was not the narrow law-giver, or the rigid censor that he is often assumed to be; he was the student, the inquirer, the observer, the interpreter, the active, indefatigable commentator, whose constant aim was to arrive at the justness of characterization."[42] A critic of this sort James had now become. From reviewer who wished to reform American literature and to himself learn how to write, he had risen to the ranks of a critic who was a student, an observer, an interpreter, an active, indefatigable commentator, governed by the constant aim of arriving at the "justness of characterization." His own taste, his own morality had not slackened in the demands which they made upon himself, but they were relaxed when he came to criticize others.

This change which is certainly to be lauded from the standpoint of James, causes the student of James one regret. From now on the path of criticism and the path of fictional endeavor were to be widely separated. Often, indeed, they were to go in different directions. No longer, accordingly, will the criticism, except for an essay called *The Art of Fiction*,[43] and that which James bestowed upon himself in his prefaces, give the student ideas which he may safely take to judge and measure James's own fiction. Critic and novelist were now to be two persons. For some time they had been drifting apart. James the Critic emerged with the *Life of Hawthorne* in 1879. Meanwhile James the Novelist was slowly but surely coming into his own.

[41] See an essay on Sainte-Beuve's *Letters*, *North American Review*, Jan., 1880.
[42] Ibid., p. 56.
[43] Published in *Longman's Magazine*, Sept., 1884.

CHAPTER XVII

AMERICA AND EUROPE

1. *England—Adjustment.*

Toward the end of 1876, James went to England. It would be effective if one could immediately add—because of George Eliot. But one cannot. He had already met her, one remembers, and he was to renew his acquaintance with her, in time feeling free to drop in to her Sundays.[1] Much as he enjoyed her novels, he was probably a bit in awe of her personally, and it is doubtful if he discussed with her any of the problems of fiction. Indeed, she showed a tendency to "*aborder* only the highest themes,"[2] philosophy, probably, rather than fiction. No, he did not go to England to talk with George Eliot or to discuss with any one the problems of fiction. Such things were not discussed in England as in France. And there were no schools. Each author was on his own, and that was what James now wanted. He wished to be free to do anything that he pleased and as he pleased.

In the last year he had done a great deal of thinking and he had definitely settled in his mind certain things, the objectionable elements of realism, those of romanticism no less, and he wished now to work out a middle road between the two. It was something that he had got to do by himself and that he could best do by practice and experiment, but he did not wish to plunge into it too quickly, and except for one story which will be considered shortly, James took practically all of 1877 as a vacation from fictional endeavors.

He kept his pen busy in other ways, writing a few reviews and somewhat more important beginning a series of travel sketches which reveal that he was adopting the means he had employed some years before in respect to the continent, in order now to become acquainted with England and things English. These sketches are even more delightful than James's earlier ones. They are more mature. Their tone is more even. Then, too, they are more individual; James forgot all about the way Gautier wrote except for the

[1] See Interchapter C.
[2] *Letters*, I, 61 (dated May 1, 1878).

ease and charm of style which he had already assimilated, and he wrote these sketches independently of any direct influences.

One realizes, however, more than before that it was a novelist who was writing the sketches for he was interested almost solely in things which had pictorial qualities and would serve as settings for his novels, and in people. In his early sketches of England he had been primarily interested in cathedrals; now he turned to manor houses, castles, rectories, places that had been lived in and had social connections. He studied them in themselves, describing them carefully, and then he imagined—we can see it between the lines—what had happened to the inhabitants or who they were and what they had done, but he kept these imaginings to himself. He was still more interested in the people who were now living in the charming homes where he was asked to visit and from which he was taken to call in other equally charming ones. Everyone seemed to have leisure, to be living not strenuously, but fully and completely. There was that walk of a rainy Sunday afternoon across the quiet fields to a magnificent house, where his friend had left their cards and turned away, James dolefully disappointed, only to be summoned back and ushered into a drawing-room where two charming ladies sat, and they had talked about "town," and tea had been served.[3] There were those rosy-cheeked, healthy maidens, "'nice girls' as they say in England," who played tennis so agilely and gracefully[4]. Sometimes he might need English homes and English maidens for his stories, so he set about to study them for he was not yet sure that he quite understood them. That boy and girl across the room, talking in such a desultory manner—were they flirting?[5] He did not exactly know.

When James was in London, he continued his observations. There were the streets of the city and the parks and the river boats on the Thames which one took when one went to Greenwich for dinner.[6] Always there were people. There were the crowds on the morning of the Oxford-Cambridge race,[7] and the crowds on Derby Day, a bit over hilarious, a degree too intoxicated,[8] but interesting

[3] "Abbeys and Castles," *Lippincott's*, Oct., 1877, p. 436.

[4] "In Warwickshire," *Galaxy*, Nov., 1877, p. 672.

[5] Ibid., p. 674.

[6] See "London at Midsummer," *Lippincott's*, Nov., 1877, and "The Suburbs of London," *Galaxy*, Dec., 1877.

[7] See *Nation*, Apr. 12, 1877.

[8] See "Three Excursions," *Galaxy*, Sept., 1877.

for the insight which they gave him into another phase of English life.

As one reads these sketches, one is led to believe that if James had not come to England directly because of George Eliot, he might indeed have come because of her novels which he had noted were so full of the "deep, rich English tone in which so many notes seem blended together."[9] He had discerned in them that England was a country which had a tone, made up, perhaps, of many elements, but deep, rich, pervading. He had seen from them that England must abound in materials for the novelist, and he had come to find them. For many years he was to continue his study, but the results of it, for the most part, he was not going to use in his fiction till 1879 and after. We shall later observe him just beginning to use some of his materials, but since our study ends with 1881, we shall miss the greater use which he made of them. Consequently it would be beside the point to consider them, delightful as they are in themselves, in more detail now.

2. *Americans in Europe and Europeans in America.*

James was not dependent upon England, however, to supply him with materials for his fiction. He had brought some materials and ideas and intentions with him, and after the novelty of being in England again had worn off, and he had collected himself, he sat down to experiment with his chosen craft. It had now definitely defined itself as that of the novelist instead of the scribbler of short tales, but he wrote tales and nouvelles for practice occasionally when brief treatment seemed to him better adapted to the subject or germ.

From a day or two of the summer of 1876, spent at Havre, where one evening and again in the early dawn James had watched the steamers coming and going across the Atlantic,[10] he had brought to London the germs of *Four Meetings*.[11] Whether he had seen a model for Miss Caroline Spenser waiting dispiritedly near the wharves and had wondered about her is not to be determined. He does not comment upon the story in any way in the preface to the volume which contains it in the Collected Edition. But it is quite likely that James had wondered what the effect would be upon a person to get to

---

[9] See Chapter XIV.
[10] See "Summer in France," *New York Tribune*, Aug. 12, 1876.
[11] Appeared in *Scribner's*, Nov., 1877.

Havre and then to turn around almost immediately, as the boats did, for America. He took his germ, secured his victim out of the limbo of his memories of New England spinsters, decided to give her thirteen hours in Europe, realized he must explain what she was before and what she became afterwards to make the account complete, and trusted the whole affair to a narrator whom he permitted to see Miss Spenser four times.

The first time had been in New England. The narrator had gone there to pay a visit before he returned to Europe. At a party, he had met Miss Spenser, a drab, quiet teacher of music, who, however, had kindled into life at the mention of Europe, questioned him eagerly about it, and betrayed her "passion" to see Italy, to see the picturesque. To this end, she had admitted she was scrimping and saving. Three years later at Havre, going to meet his brother, he had suddenly come across Miss Spenser. She had come to Europe! And now she was waiting for her cousin who studied art in Paris and would show her around. The next afternoon the narrator, in some apprehension about the faith of the art student, had hunted up Miss Spenser and learned that she had given her cousin all her money and was about to return to America! Her disappointment had been softened by the fact that her cousin needed the money because he had married a Countess, and that she herself might return some day to visit them. Five years later, again in New England, the narrator had sought a fourth meeting. He had found Miss Spenser in her shabby little home, now bitter and sharp, no longer wishing to go to Europe. The cousin in Paris had died; his wife, a fake countess, had come to live with her, and it was most evident from the behavior of this "countess" that Miss Spenser was seeing Europe!

The story is a masterpiece of graphic concision, for the four meetings, retold by the self-effacing narrator, are quite sufficient to present the life history of poor Miss Spenser. It is related objectively and at the same time sympathetically and is to be cited as a case where the employment of a narrator achieves the effect sought after as no other method would have. All that is omitted, the years of toil, of struggle, of hope, and then of disappointment, are more vivid to the reader in their effect upon the character of Miss Spenser than had they been dwelt upon by an ever-present author. It shows in this respect, perhaps, that the discussions of form and artistry held in Flaubert's rooms had had some effect upon the alien visitor, but *Four Meetings* is more strictly original in idea, conception, and execution than most of James's previous stories. He did not consciously borrow from anyone.

Four Meetings was the only story published in 1877, but together with *The American* it gave James a suggestion for his next novel, *The Europeans*,[12] which came out in the *Atlantic* in 1878. Not all Americans had the opportunity of going to Europe. Why not send some Europeans, as he had sent the fake countess, to America and let the Americans see Europe by proxy? Newman's situation might be reversed. How would Bostonians accept Europeans? James, of course, had observed Boston and Cambridge outdoing themselves for Dickens, a celebrity from England, but he proposed for this sketch not to take a well-known person of reputable character, but people of the free and easy mode of living of the continent. Confront the Puritans with such, and what would happen? He was faced with the problem as to why such people would come to America—revolutions not having then forced the nobility of foreign lands to seek refuge across the seas— and he was faced also with the matter of getting them into close connection with American life. His idea was good, but it had its drawbacks. So desirous was he to do it, however, that be brought his imagination into play and resorted to romanticism, trying to reconcile it to realism, to help him begin. He made his Baroness Munster and her brother Felix American in their ancestry and cousins of his New England family, but he explained that both had been born abroad, bred in the European tradition, and that the sister had come by her title by virtue of her morganatic marriage with a prince who now wished to have the bond dissolved. Thus the European point of view and the glamour of nobility was secured while the coming to America was made possible, if not wholly plausible.

The next problem was what they would *do* in America, but strangely this did not bother James greatly—simply hunt up their cousins, look at the cousins, and let these cousins look at them. And this is about all there is to it. There is, to be sure, much marrying and giving in marriage in the two hundred and seventy pages of the book, and there is a romance which comes to naught, but the plot or plots or, better still, minor happenings, are of no consequence, and

[12] Appeared in *Atlantic Monthly*, July-Oct., 1878.

the only thing that matters is the view that Europe has of New England and New England takes of Europe. The book is really exposition parading as narrative rather than a well-developed story. Even so, it has its interest, for though the criticism gets under way by means of somewhat dubious antecedents, it presents when it begins, a picture of part of the American scene in the mid-nineteenth century.

Europe's verdict is that Americans lead a gentle, tranquil, simple, serious life, that they are sad.

"No, they are not gay. . . . . They are sober; they are even severe. They are of a pensive cast; they take things hard. I think there is something the matter with them; they have some melancholy memory or some depressing expectation. It's not the epicurean temperament. My uncle, Mr. Wentworth, is a tremendously high-toned old fellow; he looks as if he were undergoing martyrdom, not by fire, but by freezing. But we shall cheer them up; we shall do them good. They will take a good deal of stirring up, but they are wonderfully kind and gentle."[13]

Felix tells this to Eugenia when he returns after his first call upon his cousins, and this note is often struck. It appears most delightfully perhaps in a conversation between Felix and his interesting cousin Gertrude, the one who most wishes to see life but feels guiltily that such a desire must be wrong. The whole conversation is excellent but too long to be given in full. At the end Felix has nearly convinced Gertrude that she should try to "enjoy" life.

"What ought one to do?" she continued. "To give parties, to go to the theatre, to read novels, to keep late hours?"
"I don't think it's what one does or one doesn't do that promotes enjoyment," her companion answered. "It's the general way of looking at life".
"They look at it as a discipline—that's what they do here. I have often been told that."
"Well, that's very good. But there is another way," added Felix, smiling: "to look at it as an opportunity."[14]

But America has its views of the visitors. It does not express them verbally, but it looks askance at the Baroness who gazes at one so intensely, who has a surprising way of doing just as she pleases who tells fibs with an amazing alacrity, who takes it upon herself to educate the young man of the family, George Sand fashion. No

[13] *Atlantic Monthly*, July, 1878, p. 67.
[14] Ibid., Aug., 1878, p. 167.

one can quite decide when she is lying—with the facility of a Balzacian *femme du monde*—and when she is not. Mr. Wentworth feels
ill at ease in her presence. His son, after a short encounter, veers
away. Even Gertrude does not care for her. Then there is Felix,
happy, unconcerned, carefree. America cannot understand his
habits of elegant vagabondage, or the way he looks at life. America
is apprehensive of allowing its well-loved but slightly perverse
daughter to marry him, and Gertrude has to rebel to secure her
desire. If America is censured, ironized a bit, it is gently,lovingly
done, while the reproof cast upon Europe is without shading, and
America stands out by contrast.

But we must remember that it is only a part of America—the
Boston scene—and a still smaller part of Europe—an unscrupulous
baroness and her bohemian brother, who for the sake of convenience
had been given American ancestors—that James took for his exposition. From his abode just off Piccadilly in London, James dared put
into his book some of the people among whom he had lived—his
own friends and acquaintances—and there is a reality, even though it
is somewhat stiffly handled, about these people who lived in the country, seven miles from the heart of Boston. In Mr. Wentworth,
James gives us a portrait of a type which has already disappeared
from America—the cultured, refined New England gentleman of
moderate wealth and Puritanical views who welcomed his foreign
relatives as an "extension of duty." In Clifford, his son who was
expelled from Harvard for imbibing a little too freely—a minor
form of sowing one's oats, James seemed to think, which would not
be repeated; in Charlotte, the elder sister who ran the household
and wished because of her own love for Mr. Brand, the Unitarian
minister, to see him achieve realization of his love for her sister; in
Robert Acton, who, alone, had travelled, even into China, and had
increased a fortune already large when it came to him; in, finally, the
delightful heroine, Gertrude, who, with her desires and her repressions, is "done" more fully and completely than any of the rest,
James achieved figures which will perhaps be remembered as time
goes on as representatives of the mid-nineteenth century in Boston.
Gertrude, especially, one of the first of the modern maids, should be
known to her descendants who have by now far outdistanced their
ancestress.

Boston is there also as a background. Its horse cars and ceme-

teries, the broad lawns and spreading elms, the spacious rooms of
the homes on its outskirts, even the church bells breaking through
the Sabbath stillness are there. These things which are now no more
are preserved in *The Europeans.*

It makes one regret that James did not desire to "do" America
strongly enough to devote himself wholeheartedly to it. He had often
tried, of course, and failed, but here he succeeded, at least as far as
the expositional character of his novel is concerned. *The Europeans*
was written in London. From a distance, James could secure a per-
spective which helped him see the outstanding features of the Boston scene. William, in America, however, did not like it. He called
it "thin" and "empty."[15] Thin and empty it is as a story, Henry
admitted that; but deep enough and kindly enough as a picture of
New England, and one is exasperated that William interfered and
perhaps turned Henry from other attempts of a similar sort which
might in time have embodied true stories as well as true pictures.

Before William objected, however, James had already written
another story which in the first of its two parts was an attempt to
"do" another aspect of America—*The International Episode.*[16]
James realized that in *The Europeans* he had given only the Boston
attitude to foreigners and he knew that the New York attitude was
somewhat different. He turned now to give this, using two Englishmen, a lord with an old and legitimate title, and his friend as the
visitors. When the scene was transferred to New York, the problem
as to why they should come and how they would get "in" was immediately simplified. James easily got them to America on the pretext of some railroad investments, but once in New York, he made
them quite willing to hand the business over to an American mag-
nate, who, in turn, hands them over to his wife at Newport, saying:
" 'It's a matter of national pride with me that all Englishmen should
have a good time . . . . . So please to consider yourself my property;
and if anyone should try to appropriate you, please to say, Hands
off; too late for the market.' "[17] They are somewhat amazed and
amused at the situation, but seize it as a novelty. In Newport, Lord
Lambeth finds Bessie Alden, the sister of his hostess, interesting
with her abrupt and frank queries about English customs, and is
on the verge of falling in love when he is recalled home.

[15] *Letters*, I, 65.
[16] Appeared in the *Cornhill Magazine*, Dec., 1878 and Jan., 1879.
[17] *Cornhill Magazine*, Dec., 1878, p. 692.

To this first part, James added a sequel, a tables-turned sort of thing, where Bessie and Mrs. Westgate, leaving Mr. Westgate still in his office, go to London. Bessie wishes to let Lord Lambeth know of their arrival, but Mrs. Westgate who has been here before and knows it is almost impossible for Americans to get into British society, warns her that this would never do. They must wait. In time they meet Lord Lambeth accidentally, and he renews the acquaintance, charmed again with Bessie's frankness and independence.—" 'She's not afraid, and she says things out, and she thinks herself as good as anyone. She is the only girl I have ever seen that was not dying to marry me.' "[18] Somewhat alarmed, his mother, the Duchess of Bayswater, and his sister, Lady Pimlico, hurry to call upon Mrs. Westgate and Bessie and make it plain that the marriage of Bessie with Lord Lambeth is impossible. Bessie secretly thinks otherwise; she knows she can have the English lord if she desires, but when shortly he does propose, she prefers to turn him down— an act which Mrs Westgate interprets as just revenge.

In writing *An International Episode* James changed the direct, expository criticism of point of view which was so pronounced an element in *The Europeans* to indirect. He handled his criticism more subtly, trying by the adoption of an ironic manner of speaking to imply that all was not perfect in the two social worlds, and by means of action to show it. The Americans ran after the English. The English ran away from the Americans. Mr. Westgate's early speech gives one attitude; the frigidly courteous call of the titled ladies gives the other, while the plot illustrates it, with Bessie's independence in blandly refusing a title after it has been offered, a pretty stroke contrived to put Americans on the upper side.

More important than this indirect method of criticism, however, is the discovery to be made about James's interests, afforded by contrasting the two parts of the story. In the first part, the action drags, nothing comes of anything, and more interesting than action is James's description of American scenes of the seventies. The glitter of New York hostelries, the luxury and size of the boats one took to go to Newport, the immense hotels there, and then the large cottages with their wide verandahs and sumptuous furnishings are described in detail. This is all very interesting, but it is not story and has no connection with the story. James is quite as guilty here as Balzac

---

[18] *Cornhill* Jan., 1879, p. 84

of describing for the love of it, or perhaps, for a less excusable reason, to fill up space.

When James transferred his scene to England in the second part, he sensed a more taut situation, the opportunity which it offered to play off character still more effectively than in America. Things might come to a head in England. His interest in both story and character immediately increased, and he shifted his attention from the treatment of scenes to the treatment of persons, in particular to that of Bessie Alden. In America Bessie is mildly curious about England, about Lord Lambeth's family and position; he answers a bit amused and jocosely evasive. In England suddenly she comes to a realization of existing conditions, feels the frigidity of the English toward Americans, contrasts that with her own feelings, begins to make inductions, faces things frankly, and at length decides that she wants more out of life than a dull, prosaic, cautious Englishman. The second part is, thus, as far as story elements —character and plot—are concerned, much superior to the first. This is most significant. In Europe Americans stood out and offered possibilities to the novelist much more than in America. Life quickened into drama.

3. Debut of the American Girl.

James's real interest was, indeed, not Europe come to America, but America gone to Europe. It is to be observed still more in the brilliant success of a story which preceded An International Episode by a few months—Daisy Miller, the American girl in printer's ink who, upon her appearance in Cornhill's[19] and then when pirated in Boston, took Europe and America by storm, making more of an effect upon the two continents than any American girl in flesh. James not only exposed her character, unfortunately as often misunderstood by readers as by the people who surrounded her, but related a dramatic tale about her. He made her into a real story, a tragic one, and did not leave her, as he had Gertrude, on the way to seeing life, or as he did Bessie, adjusting herself to it. But, had Daisy remained in America, had she never gone to Europe, she would not have been noticed, and there would have been no story to tell.

The story is too well known to require any retelling of the plot, and it has been too often criticized to need any but some comments which will undo the false interpretation often put upon it and show its place in James's development. Many readers come away from

[19] Appeared in the Cornhill Magazine, June-July, 1878.

the story with the attitude of Mrs. Costello that Daisy is a disgrace to America, an unscrupulous, unrefined, uncultured, vulgar flirt, or with that of Winterbourne before he is enlightened by Giovanelli, that she is an intensely interesting person but unfortunately not of the right sort. They have failed to read to the end; they have failed to note the words put unfortunately for Daisy in the mouth of the disreputable Giovanelli, who alone understands her: " 'She was the most beautiful young lady I ever saw, and the most amiable.' And then he added in a moment, 'And she was the most innocent,' "[20] or the words Winterbourne, who at length does believe him, says to Mrs. Costello, telling her he has done Daisy an injustice for " 'She would have appreciated one's esteem.' "[21]

Daisy's great tragedy is not wholly of her own making; it is in large part the result of all the stiff-backed Americans who formed an exclusive colony in Rome, and who, more narrow than the Romans themselves, resented the intrusion of any but the elect. The story is not an adverse criticism of Daisy, but a sympathetic portrayal of this American girl and an adverse censoring of this Europeanized American group. And members of this colony it was, no doubt, who later convinced James that Daisy was not true to life.[22] She had grown out of the casual remark of one of these people[23] but when she appeared in a story, they objected, mistakenly thinking to themselves probably that James had done an injury to American girls, but telling him when he insisted upon his kind intention and the fundamental purity which he had brought out, that, in that case, he had poetized her. They trembled lest he do more of this sort of thing.[24]

But true, or not, and I prefer to agree with Howells and consider her true, Daisy is an admirable creation. In his moment of insight into her character, James saw what more superficial observers always overlook, the fact that there were depths there, unsounded,

[20] *Cornhill Magazine*, July, 1878, p. 67.

[21] Ibid., p. 67.

[22] See preface to Vol. XVIII of the *Collected Edition*, p. VII.

[23] Ibid., p. v.

[24] These inductions are based upon the preface of James and the remarks of Howells as to the reception afforded the story. See *Century*, Nov., 1882, p. 25, and *North American Review*, Jan., 1903, p. 126. The story of Daisy Miller was to be converted into a comedy and privately printed in 1882, then published in *The Atlantic Monthly*, Apr.-June, 1883. It is, as might be expected, much less effective in that form.

unappreciated, which, had they been given encouragement, would have made her an entirely different girl. He understood human nature. Daisy is not far different fundamentally from Christina Light, from Bessie Alden. Her misfortune, like Christina's, is in her mother and her surroundings. Had she been given guidance of the right sort, even just a word as Bessie is by Mrs. Westgate, had she been given esteem, she would have responded, and America would have seen cause to be proud of her. But America in 1878 was of a different opinion. First *Lippincott's* refused to publish the story; then-when it did appear in *Cornhill's* "indulgently accepted" by Leslie Stephen, less scrupulous American publishers proceeded to "pirate" it, and the whole country rose in wrath against Daisy's creator. They failed to understand the story.

This was due in some part perhaps to the method used. Daisy is presented through Winterbourne, the young American student who has lived long enough among foreigners to understand them and to forget the girls of his native land. He is not the narrator, but it is his eye and his consciousness that James used as a means of portraying Daisy. He is interested in her; he is intrigued by her; he is often perplexed by this "inscrutable combination of audacity and inno-cence,"[25] and it is because of this that Daisy has been misunderstood. James's method was in his way. As in *Roderick Hudson*, the main character is dependent upon another character. In the end, of course, Winterbourne attempts to give Daisy her due praise, but before this he has often been disturbed and has condemned to himself her actions. The reader remembers these things and overlooks the eulogy for he does not quite see why there should be a eulogy. The glass through which James looked was too opaque.

The main thing to be noted, however, in respect to the last three stories and their place in James's development is the prominent position given in each to an American girl. In *Roderick Hudson*, James had neglected Mary Garland and Christina Light; in *The American*, except for Mrs. Tristram, a minor character, he had avoided American women; but in *The Europeans*, *An International Episode*, and *Daisy Miller*, James placed the American girl in the lime light and directed his attention at his heroine. As a result, Gertrude, Bessie, Daisy are "done." It is noteworthy that in each case, James felt himself to be dealing with a complex character, a being of desires and repressions, of curiosity and frankness, of auda-

---

[25] *Cornhill Magazine*, July, 1878, p. 51.

city and innocence. Such, he saw, American girls were. That was their interest. They were many-sided, with depths as well as surfaces. They were independent toward their families, toward their suitors, toward everyone, as French and English girls were not.[26] They wanted to realize their own individuality. They wanted to live. They offered then a great possibility to the novelist. These three stories of 1878 were experiments with the portraits of American girls. Unfortunately Gertrude, who is the most interesting person in *The Europeans*, suffers because James did not consider her sufficient to carry the weight of the story by herself and brought in too many subordinate figures, who in no way approach her but clutter up the background. Bessie does not come into her own till the last part of *An International Episode*. But Daisy, even though she is looked at through Winterbourne, is the whole of her story. She is the focal point throughout. Her mother, her impossible brother, her cavalier, are necessary appendages, and she stands out from among them against the background of Europe. In America she would have had no story but that of a marriage without high lights or low lights, and the settling down into an easy maturity, for without the waving of a magic wand, she would have had no European cousins nor English lords come to visit her. It was necessary for her to go to Europe to meet the perplexities of life.

The question arises—Why did James suddenly evince this interest in his heroines? Was it due to Turgénieff and his fair Muscovites who had seemed to him like New England girls in so many ways? In part. But it was due more directly to another influence, an American one. Recall again the two reviews of Howells's *A Foregone Conclusion*[27] which James had written on his return from Europe in 1874. He had praised his friend's novel, remember, highly and with a hint of envy. He had praised especially the portrait of Florida Vervain, and he had recalled that of Kitty in *A Chance Acquaintance*. In these two heroines, "delicate, nervous, emancipated young women, begotten of our institutions and our climate, and equipped with an irritable moral consciousness,"[28] James had believed that Howells had "outlined his field."[29] Moreover, it had seemed to him that Howells, to use a vulgarism, had "hit" it. He

---

[26] See especially two travel sketches: "A French Watering Place," *New York Tribune*, Aug. 26, 1876, and "In Warwickshire," *Galaxy*, Nov., 1877.

[27] See Chapter XIV (The reviews were published in January 1875).

[28] *Nation*, Jan. 7, 1875, p. 12.

[29] *North American Review*, Jan., 1875, p. 212.

had found the subject which it was most important for American fiction to note and do justice to and preserve—the American girl. He had discovered her possibilities for the novelist. He had studied her, understood her complexities, and portrayed them. As he read Howells's novel in 1874, James had undoubtedly resolved to devote himself to the same cause, but he had delayed treating her till he should have time to study her, so that he could really "do" her and not, as in some of his own early stories, but suggest her charm. It was Howells, then, who started James in active pursuit of the American girl, and who, in Florida Vervain, suggested that she became, as James had half surmised, most interesting when she left her native land for Europe. Perhaps, indeed, this was one reason why he himself had returned to Europe—to study her there.

CHAPTER XVIII
THE PRACTITIONER

1. *In the Interest of Word and Phrase.*

As James's fame increased by means of his critical articles, short stories, and novels, he found that publishers were quite as avid to republish some of his former productions as to get hold of new material. There was an increasing demand, especially in England, for books by the young author who had recently stepped into the international limelight. But desirous of the pecuniary return as he probably was, James yet did not feel like risking his reputation by giving the publishers free hand to reprint his earlier things as they pleased. It had become apparent that some of these were to live, and as he glanced at them, noting a crudity here, another there, he suddenly realised that he did not wish them to survive in an imperfect state when it was in his power to better them. Consequently he turned in the midst of new work to the revision of old and carried on the practice which he had tentatively begun in 1875[1] and was henceforth increasingly to indulge in, of tampering with and changing work which he had once thought good enough to appear under his own name.

But this early revision, interesting to the student of James's style and important in any consideration of the evolution of that, needs concern the student of his fictional development but briefly, for it is unapparent unless the original and rewritten texts are carefully collated, and played no part in the evolution of his fictional method, though in one respect shortly to be mentioned, it reveals additional insight into the main direction of James's interests in the late seventies. *Watch and Ward* was originally so loud and melodramatic that James evidently found it impossible to put it into an altogether satisfactory form, and finally he sent it to the publishers in America altered throughout though not often improved.[2] He was more particular in preparing *French Poets and Novelists*, a collection of his critical articles, for a London company;[3] though he

---

[1] See Chapter XIV.
[2] Published by James R. Osgood and Co., Boston, 1878.
[3] Published by Macmillan and Co., London, 1878.

did not change his original verdict or meaning in passing his critical judgments, except in a few places where there probably were misprints before, he often substituted felicitous synonyms, increasing a congruity which was already marked in the magazine versions. He was still more careful when he turned to prepare *Roderick Hudson* for its first London appearance.[4] Already, in 1875, he had revamped it in places—chiefly the dialogue between Roderick and Rowland where he differentiated the sharply opposed types—for Osgood to publish in Boston.[5] But this he did not now consider sufficient. Accordingly he went over the entire novel, often reworking the portions of straight narrative, as well as the dialogue, with his guiding principles felicity, smoothness, and clarity. More interesting is the fact that James now redid in the latter part of the novel the conversation of Mary and Rowland, apparently endeavoring to make Mary less plain, trying consciously to bring out her gentle wit and charm. The talk of Christina he changed but little, for his concern was the slightly angular but exquisitely sensitive daughter of New England who was seeing Europe for the first time. This interest in Mary, however, is simply one indication of the trend of James's intentions at this time, and would not stand out with any special significance were it not for the positive testimony of other things.

2. *The American Girl: Variations of the Type.*

Much elated over the furore caused by *Daisy Miller*, James had evidently decided to study the American girl, that charming, complex creature, more thoroughly, and to work toward a longer treatment of her. He knew that he had at last got hold of something which American fiction had long neglected or but half treated, and full of confidence he turned to study his young countrywomen. A glance around, even in Europe, revealed to him many variations of the type—daughters of the newly rich, daughters of the poor, some who came to Europe for clothes, others who came for culture, and still others who came for no particular reason, but were alert, eager, inquisitive, ready for anything that might happen. The problem grew complex. There were many American girls, and they were not all Daisy Millers. Some were less attractive, some were more, but all these intensely alive individuals were most interesting and offered seemingly a great opportunity to the novelist. He wished to "do"

---

[4] Published by Macmillan and Co., London, 1879.
[5] Published in 1876, copyrighted 1875.

one who would be exceptionally attractive, who would still all the adverse criticism which Daisy had unfortunately aroused, and already in the winter of 1878 and '79, he had this individual vividly in mind,[6] but what he wished to do for her would, he realized, take time and thought and care, and he turned to experiment on some lesser persons.

He wrote two short stories, *The Pension Beaurepas* and *A Bundle of Letters*, and two novels, *Confidence* and *Washington Square*. These are to be considered as practice pieces, not only in treating the American girl, but even more important, in experimenting with method—*how* he should portray her. These two things mark the fiction published in 1879[7] and the second novel which appeared in 1880. Only this last is in any way outstanding, but all are important in what they were to lead to.

As short stories, little can be said for either *The Pension Beaurepas*[8] or *A Bundle of Letters*.[9] They are frankly studies. The young man who relates what he sees at the pension Beaurepas confesses in the first paragraph that he is a novelist and has come to the pension to study human nature because Balzac and Stendhal found boarding houses convenient for purposes of observation. The narrator is James in disguise, and perhaps the account which follows is really, in parts at least, what James himself had seen and heard. The narrator, in order to make his study extensive and thorough, not only observes and talks with the two American girls who are also at the pension but discusses them at length with Madame Beaurepas, who from her vantage point has studied human nature for forty years, with M. Pigeonneau, whose heart flutters at the rustle of petticoats, and with the parents of the girls, cautious, cultured Mrs. Church, and financially embarrassed Mr. Ruck. Thus an all round view is obtained. There is a suggestion of plot in this story for Aurora Church who has been brought up in Europe as a *jeune fille* but is, she endeavors to convince the narrator, *not* a *jeune fille*, envies Sophie Ruck, who may wander when and where and as she will, and endea-

---

[6] See Chapter XIX.

[7] One story "The Diary of a Man of Fifty," which appeared in *Harper's Magazine* and *Macmillan's*, July, 1879, will not be considered because it does not belong to the main line of James's development. It has some slight interest, however, as a possible indirect reference to James's state of mind in abjuring residence in Florence.

[8] Appeared in *Atlantic Monthly*, Apr., 1879.

[9] Appeared in *The Parisian*, Dec., 1879.

vors unavailingly to get out of her mother's control. To this end, she hints to the narrator that she will welcome him as her deliverer. He ignores the hint, and Aurora is dragged away to another pension by her mother.

In *A Bundle of Letters*, a boarding house again serves as setting, and this time James utilized all of his characters as narrators. That is, he intercepted their mail as it left the house, and published it uncensored and uncommmented upon. Thus the characters reveal themselves and each other as they write in a gossipy way about their fellow inmates. Again an all round view is obtained. There is no plot, but there is decidedly a situation for all of the six correspondents—Miss Miranda Hope from Bangor, Maine, Miss Violet Ray from New York city, Miss Evelyn Vane from England, Lewis Leverett from Boston, Dr. Staub from Germany, and M. Verdier, a native of Paris—look more or less askance at each other. The attention is centered upon the two American girls—the English girl is used only for contrast—but nothing happens in the way of real complications.

If *The Pension Beaurepas* and *A Bundle of Letters* have little value as stories, they are interesting as studies, for in them James portrayed with insight and understanding three kinds of American girls, three variations of the type as it existed in the seventies. He was on a small scale historian of his time. There is preserved for future generations the American girl who was educated in Europe, brought there early in her life by a widowed mother who had much "culture" but little money and spent her life running from one cheap pension to another, endeavoring to keep her daughter innocent and unspotted in hopes to marry her some day to a wealthy man. This poor girl, the victim of her mother, is represented by Aurora who knows only too well what an anomaly she is.

"I have to pretend to be a *jeune fille*, I am not a jeune fille; no American girl can be a *jeune fille*; an American girl is an intelligent, responsible creature. I have to pretend to be very innocent but I am not very innocent. . . . To do very simply things that are not at all simple,—that is the American girl."[10]

James, it is obvious, was sorry for her, blaming not the girl but her mother for her condition.

Then there is the American girl who first went to Europe alone and unchaperoned, the pioneer, seeking to know "life" and to ob-

[10] *Atlantic Monthly*, Apr., 1879, p. 479.

tain "culture" but thoroughly loyal to her country. Such is Miranda Hope, slightly silly in her letters about the nice young man back home, but perfectly capable of taking care of herself even though she goes to museums for rendezvous and takes French lessons from a Frenchman who might presume too much were it not that her very openness quite takes away his desire.

Then, third,. there is the American girl of the seventies whose father had made money which she proceeded to spend, spoiled, assertive, who ruled her parents and refused to listen to caution or prudence. Both Miss Ruck and Miss Ray represent this species, but neither is as completely "done" as Aurora or Miranda, nor are they endowed with the beauty and charm of Daisy, to whom, in some ways, they are related.

As none of these girls is involved in any complication, no depth of character is revealed. It is evident, however, that Miranda would rise adequate to the occasion should one occur, and that Violet and Sophie would assert themselves, though ruthlessly and unpleasantly, if anything crossed their plans. Aurora is the weakest and least able of all, but she, it must be remembered, has long been away from America and is neither an American girl nor a *jeune fille*. None of these girls, however, would do for the supreme presentation of the type which James had in mind and this is why he used them so lightly in these short, quickly written studies.[11] He practiced with these, and it is important again to note the all-round view that he endeavored to get of each of them, using narrative devices in each story which enabled him to approach the girls from many angles.

3. Confidence.

In *Confidence*, which began to appear serially in August and ran for six months,[12] James turned to experiment with the American girl and with method on a larger scale. He wrote a novel. He involved the girl in a story. He not only involved her, but he gave her a part to play, and thus proved, so he would have the reader believe, not only her charm but her capability. And because frequently people misjudged the American girl, did not see her values, he felt free to use as his means of approach to her the eyes and mind of a stupid man, who nearly loses his chance of happiness because of his blindness.

[11] In the preface to Volume XIV of the *Collected Edition*, James wrote that "*A Bundle of Letters* was written in a single long session."
[12] Appeared in *Scribner's Monthly*, Aug., 1879. to Jan., 1880.

The plot revolves around the many involutions of the state of mind of Bernard Longueville regarding Angela Vivian, an American girl who, for the sake of economy, lives abroad with her mother. He is called into consultation by a wealthy scientific friend of his, Gordon Wright, who is thinking of marrying Miss Vivian, and discovers in her a girl whom he has met somewhat unconventionally, though not improperly, in Sienna a short time before. He is perplexed by her; at first she ignores him; then, having discovered that Wright has asked Longueville to "size her up," she talks vivaciously and acts erratically, and Longueville concludes she must be a coquette. He tells Wright and Wright goes away. Two years later Wright informs Longueville that he has married Blanche Evers, a frivolous, flighty piece of femininity who had been with the Vivians at Baden-Baden. Longueville fails to understand this step of his hitherto cautious friend, especially when he visits Wright and notes his wife's arrant flirting with Captain Lovelock, a hang-over also from the Baden-Baden days. Feeling too that Blanche may have designs upon himself, Longueville hurries to California and then shortly to Europe. He is, it is apparent, restless, rather unhappy, but with no reason as yet apparent. At Blanquais-les-Galets, however, he comes across Angela again and suddenly discovers that he is in love with her. Restrained by false scruples about his previous relation to her and fearful of the harm he may have done her in dissuading his friend, he dallies till suddenly he realizes that her modest love for him has been from the beginning the clew to her erratic actions. He proposes, explains his previous base act, and is accepted, for Angela assures him that Wright, despite his advice, had proposed, and that she had turned him down. Longueville is relieved and very happy. Except that not much has happened and Angela has not yet shown her ability, the book might well end here. Wright, however, unexpectedly appears, charges Longueville with treason, says he is about to divorce Blanche, and insists that Angela is to marry him. This clever lady perceives that Wright really loves Blanche, and that Blanche loves him, but is flirting in a miscalculated attempt to make him jealous and thus win his affection. Angela then proceeds by seeming to agree to all that Wright demands, to open his eyes so that he willingly goes back to Blanche, and the end comes out satisfactorily for all concerned.

Confidence is a weak novel. This is due partly to the method James used, or rather misused, and partly to the fact that he seems to have been trying to write a light comedy of intrigue, with many minor misunderstandings and involved situations, with many scenes and rapid changes, with much dialogue and little straight narrative. Its lightness, however, is only illusion, an attempt to be clever which fails. James went out of his way here. Seeking a clew, the student can find two possibilities. In 1878, James was studying French drama, looking forward to the time when he could try his hand at writing plays.[13] It may be, then, that the brilliant repartee of Augier's and of Sardou's characters had some effect upon the way James handled his dialogue in this novel, causing him to try to make it sprightly and pointed. But the narrative portions are uneven too, and an even closer influence was doubtless exerted by the novels of Howells, who touched serious things lightly and gently. James, slightly envious, tried to do the same thing, but he did not achieve the right effect. It was more in his nature to proceed slowly, thoughtfully, analytically.

As much at fault as the attempted lightness, however, is James's arbitrary use of his method and the strange choice which he made for his perceiving consciousness. Undoubtedly his main interest was the enigmatic Angela, but he presented her through Longueville, using the latter's mind as the glass through which he viewed everything. But the glass is discolored and out of focus. Longueville at first is but mildly interested in Angela and like Winterbourne, draws conclusions which later prove to be wrong. James often reported the conversation of Longueville with Angela in an attempt to bring her out, but he was under the necessity when giving her side of it in the first half of the book, of misleading Longueville, and even more than in *Daisy Miller*, the reader receives an impression which remains though Longueville comes to believe in Angela enough to marry her. In the middle of the book James often left Angela out of the scene for many chapters while he took Longueville on his travels. When he gave her a more active part at the end of the book, the reader is forced to go with Longueville to England and learn of how she is manipulating things in Paris by means of her letters to him. Thus James employed his method, faithful to the principles of it and mechanically observing the restrictions it imposed. But only once,

---

[13] *Letters*, I, 60. Henry writes to William, May 1, 1878, " . . . . it has long been my most earnest and definite intention to commence at play-writing as soon as I can. . . . . My inspection of the French theatres will fructify. I have thoroughly mastered Dumas, Augier, and Sardou."

when Longueville analyzes his somewhat abrupt realization of his love for Angela, did James take advantage of the method and write a few pages that are supremely indicative of his ability. Had James dared, however, to use Angela as his glass, he might have succeeded, for if we are to believe the implications, Angela's mind from the first is far more full of Longueville than his is of her, and Angela is clever enough to understand the situation—does she not discern that Wright has meanly asked his friend to "size" her up; does she not succeed in giving him a false impression; does she not finally make everything come out satisfactorily?

4. *Washington Square*.

It is very likely that James was keenly aware of the decidedly manufactured and artificial quality of *Confidence*, and that he wrote his next novel in a determination to get back to the essentials of story-telling.[14] At any rate *Washington Square*[15] is quite as simple and straightforward as *Confidence* is complex and involved. James reduced the elements of character and plot to a minimum that he might give his attention to treatment. He selected a heroine with one outstanding and dominating characteristic—her goodness; he reduced her career to two facts—that her suitor trifles with her affection and that her father breaks its spring; and he located the story in America.

The opening chapters of the story sum up briefly the early life and character of Catherine and explain her father's attitude toward her. Dr. Sloper, we are told, has always regarded his daughter with disappointment and irony, taking out upon her all of his bitterness over losing his son and his wife early in his life. Catherine has always been a good girl, but she is neither handsome nor brilliant, and her goodness has served only as an irritant to her father who might have excused her sex, had she inherited her mother's beauty or his own wit.

When the main action of the story begins, Catherine is about twenty with no prospects except that of inheriting a fortune some day. This is enough, however, for Morris Townsend who presently

[14] Though James seems to have thought well of *Confidence* in a letter to Miss Norton (*Letters*, I, 71) and ill of *Washington Square* in a letter to Howells (*Letters*, I, 73) his attitude was probably due in each case to the persons to whom he was writing.

[15] Appeared in *Cornhill Magazine*, June to November, 1880 (with illustrations by du Maurier) and *Harper's Magazine*, July to December, 1880.

appears and begins to pay court to the surprised girl. She finds herself dissimulating and trying to cover her happiness that someone should come to call upon her, and her father begins to taunt her. Dr. Sloper suspects the mercenary motives of the young man who has no obvious business, and making inquiries, finds his suspicions are justified. He makes up his mind that he will never allow Catherine to marry Morris, but sees for himself some amusement at the expense of his daughter. When she dutifully tells him that Morris has proposed and she has accepted, he bluntly refuses his consent, saying that if she marries against his wishes, she will forfeit her inheritance. The threat makes little impression, but her father's disapproval and unkind words cut Catherine deeply. Presently he forbids Morris the house, and she begins to find that there is "a great excitement in trying to be a good daughter,"[16] all the more so because her Aunt Penniman, sister of the doctor who keeps house for him, urges the girl to elope. Catherine will not wholly disobey her father, but she corresponds with Morris and meets him in secret. Her father continues to taunt her, and at length she tells Morris she will marry him whenever he is ready. But of course, he will not be ready until Dr. Sloper relents about the inheritance.

The affair is at a deadlock, and Dr. Sloper sees it may last indefinitely. He becomes weary of it all and exasperated at Catherine's stubbornness. He decides to take her to Europe in hopes Morris will withdraw. She goes obediently but of course reluctantly. Because she has left her suitor in America and her father continues to abuse her, the year abroad has no effect upon Catherine except to strengthen her love for Morris and to lessen her regard for her father. When she returns to New York, she finds her erstwhile suitor disturbed that she has not won her father to their side, but she says: "'Nothing is changed—nothing but my feeling about father . . . . .I have been as good as I could, but he doesn't care. Now I don't care either. I don't know whether I have grown bad; perhaps I have. But I don't care for that. I've come home to be married—that's all I know.'"[17] Morris, however, hedges. He says that he cannot bear to have her give up her luxury for his poverty, and at length she discerns why he has been interested in her. She gives way in private to a terrible outburst of grief, then stolidly composes herself, and calmly tells her father, when next he chides her, that she has broken the engagement.

[16] *Harper's Magazine*, Sept., 1880, p. 598.
[17] Ibid., Nov., 1880, p. 909.

As far as Catherine is concerned, her life is over. Nothing which happens now can have any effect upon her. James wished to prove this beyond any shadow of a doubt, and so he added a few chapters detailing subsequent events and showing her passivity. Her father tormented by the fear that she may later marry Morris, tries, as he is dying, to extract a vow from her that she will never marry him. She refuses to give him any satisfaction, and he adds a codicil to his will reducing greatly his bequest to her. The girl is past feeling this now, and she is still fairly well off because of what her mother left her. In time, Morris reappears. Abetted by Aunt Penniman, he again proposes thinking that a little is better than nothing, but Catherine looks at him, sees how his one concern has been to make himself comfortable, and refuses him.

After *Confidence, Washington Square* stands out as a masterpiece. Simple it is, to be sure, but that is its charm. James did not fly in the face of the possible here, but did all that he truly and artistically could with his meagre materials. But James did not proceed without guidance, and it is the nature of this guidance that is most interesting to the student of his development. In composing and writing *Washington Square*, James thought of a novel which fifteen years before in his second review he had held up to story-tellers— Balzac's *Eugénie Grandet*.[18] It is evident that despite James's repudiation of Balzac in 1875, Balzac had taught James some things which he now felt it well to recall, and he set to work on a similar story in an endeavor to get back to some of the essentials of story-telling. But there are points of difference as well as those of likeness, and James is not just an imitator for he adapts and even improves upon the materials and treatment of his predecessor.

In looking at the two novels, the things that one notices first are that basically the characters of Catherine and Eugénie are alike, and that their stories, broadly considered, are the same. Both girls are fundamentally good; both are somewhat plain physically, but not unattractive to people who place the radiance which comes from nobility of soul above mere prettiness; both have reached their twenties (Eugénie is twenty-three) without knowing the meaning of love except as it is a feeling for parents. When love comes to them, however, Catherine is affected differently from Eugénie. Catherine remains primarily a creature of conscience, more disturbed by the

[18] See Chapter II.

fact that she cannot decide just where her duty lies than by her love. Eugénie becomes tremulous with her passion; she even makes advances, and she pours her gold into her cousin's hands with no thought of duty and even a grim sort of happiness that she is thus braving her father's ire. James's heroine is not a copy; she is the American counterpart, and James played up the element of conscience believing it to be the dominating factor with his countrywomen.

As for the stories of the two heroines, each is the account of what a cruel father and a false suitor between them can do to a sensitive nature. James brought father, suitor, and daughter into closer relationship than Balzac did. He made the fortune-seeking Morris really interested—Charles is but partly—and the father an abettor of the match even while he disapproves of it. Thus James focalized his interests and made the story more compact, gaining an advantage artistically which will shortly be pointed out.

From the standpoint of James's development, however, not the characters nor the story, but the treatment is of most importance, and here James followed Balzac closely. He abjured all use of a narrator or an interpreter or a perceiving consciousness in favor of straightforward narrative such as Balzac used. He told the story as he saw it and not as one of his characters did. If James had simply used the same method that Balzac did—this common narrative form—we would not be justified in saying that he followed Balzac, but when *Washington Square* and *Eugénie Grandet* are placed side by side, and when James's early review is recalled, it is evident that he had Balzac's novel before him as a model even as he had advised Miss Prescott to use it.[19] For James opened his novel with an account of setting and antecedent action; he carefully explained everything which would help the reader to understand the relation of father and daughter and thus the ensuing action, before he began the main story; and then at the end he detailed quickly but completely subsequent events. *Eugénie Grandet* begins and ends the same way; the story is in between. In the review of so many years before, James had upheld this method of procedure at the beginning of a novel as one of the fundamentals of good narrative, so that when once started, the story might move. He had also commented upon the skill with which Balzac sketched his setting, and with the same

[19] See Chapter II.

kind of skill, and in addition, a gentleness born of reminiscence, he depicted Washington Square, apologizing for doing it so thoroughly because "it was here, at any rate, that my heroine spent many years of her life.[20] Then with Balzac's psychological objectivity he described his different people, analyzing them carefully and making them stand out by telling little anecdotes about them. All this he put at the beginning; he set the stage and enumerated his personnel.

As James developed his story, he drew away from Balzac and gave his concern to the things which had long interested him—how to look at and bring out not only the story but the minds of his characters, how to get under the surface, and then how to make his main interest stand out and his novel artistically effective. The use of the direct approach at once allowed him to look where he pleased and to see all he pleased. He could look at Catherine; he could enter her mind and see it perplexed and distraught, then grimly determined, and finally resigned, but he did not have to stay there. He could enter the mind of her father and see him mean and cruel, then justly baffled and irritated and made more revengeful by all that his search for amusement causes. He could see the duplicity in the actions of the romantic Aunt Penniman and the mercenary motives of Morris and reveal the true state of affairs to the reader while Catherine remains unsuspecting. The use of one of his characters as a glass would have kept him from seeing all this, and no one of the characters is fitted to serve as such—Catherine is too blindly trustful; the others too self-centered.

But in order to secure unity, James focussed his attention upon Catherine. He looked at the machinations and actions of the others as they bore upon Catherine, as they were directed at her, and not at all as they involved the instigators themselves, except, as in the case of the doctor when this was necessary to explain their future actions toward her. Everything points at Catherine. Unity, compactness, intensity result to a degree which is unknown in Balzac's novel where the interest frequently strays to Grandet and his money bags and business affairs. Artistically, then, *Washington Square* is very strong.

Yet James made one error of which Balzac was never guilty. James named his novel after place, thus implying that he was

[20] *Harpers' Magazine*, July, 1880, p. 209.

"doing" Washington Square. Adequately done as a background, it is most inadequately done in itself. Only one episode of its "social history" is told, and the story of Catherine Sloper, though it might very likely have happened, should not have been branded as outstandingly typical of this place which in the mid-nineteenth century stood for so much in New York social life. It might well be one novel of several,—would that James had written the others—which, taken together Balzac fashion, might have been called after the Square or even Scenes from New York Life, but by itself it should never have been given such a pretentious title. Call this novel after its heroine, however, as Balzac called the parts of his larger units, and the difficulty disappears for the emphasis is shifted. The novel then is a masterpiece with a suitable title, small, compact, but quite ample to serve the character who inspired it.

Are we to conclude from *Washington Square* that James was returning to the fold of Balzac? Not necessarily, for James had never objected to the side of Balzac which influenced *Washington Square*. The novel thus cannot be considered an apology for the repudiation of 1875, though it may be called a pretty gesture of friendliness. In the article upon Balzac, it must be remembered, James had searched for what was most typical and had weighed Balzac accordingly. Though he had mentioned Eugénie as outstanding among Balzac's virtuous characters and her abode as unforgettably pictured, though he had praised in general Balzac's ability to describe people and places and his narrative ease, he had thrown the burden of his criticism upon the things of which he disapproved—the predominance of the vulgar and the immoral, the lack of taste—and he undoubtedly still felt a repugnance for that side of Balzac. Because *Washington Square* was a novel and not a critical article, James was free to follow only the things in Balzac of which he approved. Then he went a step farther, as we have noted, and improved upon his model in some respects, thus showing that he had control of his craft. In his next novel we shall note how he was to improve still more, especially upon points where he now followed Balzac. We shall note, also, his greater ease and power as he proceeded—not under Balzac but along by the side of Turgénieff and George Eliot.

Henry James was ready to do a big thing.

CHAPTER XIX

THE PORTRAIT OF A LADY

The beginning of the 80's marked the end of James's early fictional development. There was the little masterpiece which we have just considered, *Washington Square*. There was also a large masterpiece, *The Portrait of a Lady*,[1] which, the preface written in 1907 states,[2] was started as early as the spring of 1879, designed from the first for serial publication in the *Atlantic Monthly* and *Macmillan's* where it began to appear in the fall of 1880. The commencement of its composition and appearance thus overlapped the ending of the writing and publication of *Washington Square*, but *The Portrait of a Lady* shows much more conclusively the ability of Henry James. It proves that he could do things on a large scale, deal with big effects, was a great humanist and a great artist as well. It is most interesting, too, for though it shows the imprint of Turgénieff and George Eliot upon James, it reveals also his individuality and independence. What we are to observe in this novel is not James slavishly working under the direction of the Russian or the English novelist, but James, having assimilated the lessons of both, treating a subject similar to one of George Eliot's with the skill which came from combining the best principles of each, supplementing them with his own theories, and emerging a novelist who was not only in possession of the secrets of his craft, but could do with them what he wished. *The Portrait of a Lady* shows that the days of hesitation and stumbling experiment were definitely ended.[3]

1. *Synopsis of the Novel.*

The story of Isabel Archer opens around a tea table on the wide spreading lawn of an old English countryhouse. Three men are having their tea and talking idly. Two of the men, Mr. Touchett and

[1] Appeared in *Macmillan's Magazine*, Oct., 1880 to Nov., 1881, and in *The Atlantic Monthly*, Nov., 1880 to Dec., 1881.

[2] *Collected Edition*, III, v.

[3] They were to begin again, of course, in respect to the drama, and James's attempts to become a dramatist, and he was to continue to experiment in the use of his method in his stories, but his experimentation there was to be strong and confident; he knew how far he could go, what his method was and was not suited for.

and his son Ralph, are invalids; the elder is confined to a wheel chair, while the younger strolls about rather insecurely. They are obviously Americans—Americans, however, who have lived for a long time in England and have acquired the appearance of ease and leisure and comparative luxury which James had found in his visits to country homes was the outstanding mark of the English.[4] The third man, Lord Warburton, comes naturally by this same appearance; he has the "air of a happy temperament fertilized by a higher civilization" and in addition is "remarkably well made."[5] The tea is served, the shadows lengthen, and the three begin to speculate upon an American girl, the niece of Mrs. Touchett, who is expected to arrive at Gardencourt. And into this setting and this group, Isabel presently comes, confidently yet charmingly, and her story is ready to begin.

But why has she come, and what is she to do? Mrs. Touchett, James shortly explains, had discovered her niece in an old home in Albany, had sensed her poverty and approved of her independent bearing, and in an excess of charity, had proposed to show her the world. And Isabel who had "a great desire for knowledge," "an immense curiosity about life and was constantly staring and wondering," and "whose deepest enjoyment was to feel the continuity between the movements of her own heart and the agitations of the world,"[6] had seen in the offer of her aunt a chance to *live*, a chance to escape from mere existence, which, it seemed, would be her lot if she remained in America and married Caspar Goodwood.

Though she is brought first to Gardencourt at a time when Mr. Touchett is failing rapidly, she finds that, even in this quiet place, life is far more exciting than in America. There is her cousin, more or less inactive physically, but interested in her, amused by her, curious about her. There is her uncle, kind and sympathetic. There is also the English lord who brings his sisters, the two Misses Molyneux, to call, who asks Isabel to his estate, and who presently proposes. And Isabel—can it be she who has craved for romance doing this?—refuses him, gently and kindly, telling him that she does not wish to marry. He is urgent, and she amazes him and even herself a little bit when she says " 'I can't escape my fate . . . . I can't escape unhappiness. . . . In marrying you, I shall be trying to,' "

---

[4] See Interchapter C and Chapter XVII.
[5] *Atlantic Monthly*, Nov., 1880, p. 587.
[6] Ibid., Nov., 1880, p. 603.

explaining that to marry him would be to separate herself " 'from life, from the usual chances and dangers, from what most people know and suffer.' "[7] Then Caspar follows her to Europe, and she, irritated at his persistence, commands him to leave her alone for two years.

Ralph learns of Isabel's refusal of wealth and title. His cousin becomes still more interesting to him. He realizes that he may have " 'the entertainment of seeing what a young lady does who won't marry Lord Warburton,' "[8] and he tells Isabel that he depends upon her to give him a "magnificent example" of the unexpected. He sees that the world interests her and that she wants to throw herself into it, but he realizes that she may find her hands tied by her poverty and that he will be defrauded of the spectacle. When Mr. Touchett, near death, suggests that his son forget his ill health and his relation to Isabel and marry her, Ralph demurs, feeling that he, much less than Lord Warburton, could satisfy Isabel's imagination. But he prevails upon his father to remake his will, leaving the greater part of his own share to Isabel.

While Mr. Touchett is ill, Madame Merle, a friend of Mrs. Touchett's, arrives for a visit, and she and Isabel are inevitably thrown together. Madame Merle brings with her a breath of the world, of cosmopolitanism, of experience, and Isabel is immediately entranced and feels that in some way Madame Merle is to affect her life. Ralph confesses his dislike and distrust of Madame Merle, but Isabel scoffs at him and walks and talks with this woman of the world, hoping that some day she may acquire the poise and charm of "a great lady." Madame Merle, on her side, is interested in Isabel. She listens to her high hopes about life and Europe, but urges her to return to America, and cites as a warning all the unattached Americans who are idly crawling over Europe and, in particular, one Gilbert Osmond, a friend of hers who lives in Florence. This man, she tells Isabel, is exceedingly clever but ambitionless and has "no career, no name, no position, no fortune, no past, no future, no anything."[9] Isabel listens to this and much more, is unconvinced, but longs for a little money to make her way easier.

Then—Mr. Touchett dies and Isabel is rich. The miracle has happened. At first she is sobered by it and feels in no hurry to take

[7] Ibid., Jan., 1881, p. 24.
[8] Ibid., Feb., 1881, p. 184.
[9] Ibid., Mar., 1881, p. 341.

advantage of the power it bestows, but presently she sets forth with Mrs. Touchett to see Europe.

When they reach Florence, Madame Merle turns up, approves of Isabel's good fortune, and takes her to call on Osmond. It now appears that Madame Merle has an immense interest in Osmond and a desire to help him, for she mentions to the cynical dilettante Isabel's wealth and intelligence, and suggests marriage. Osmond is pleased enough with Isabel's appearance to bestir himself, and he plays his part well enlisting her admiration and her sympathy, and stimulating her curiosity. His daughter, Pansy, a *jeune fille*, product of the convents and thus perfect in manners and obedience, also interests Isabel. These are unusual people, this man with his villa on the hill top, his poverty, yet his manner of a gentleman, and his daughter, and she finds herself presently listening to a declaration of love from the father. She is deeply affected; her imagination has been approaching this but suddenly it stops, and she vaguely puts him off till she has seen more of the world. Meanwhile Ralph has been watching, much amused but quite as sure that Osmond will be put in his place as Osmond is of his success.

The ensuing months are passed over rapidly, for they have no bearing upon the story beyond the fact that Madame Merle, as well as Mrs. Touchett, accompanies Isabel on her travels, and, it may be surmised, sees that Isabel does not forget Osmond. At any rate, she accepts him on her return to Florence.

The main course of the action is resumed as Isabel is waiting somewhat painfully but dutifully to explain her act to Caspar Goodwood, to whom she has given, without meaning to, all too much encouragement. The explanation over—it is not very satisfactory, for Caspar is persistent—Isabel draws a sigh of relief, but finds herself facing the curt disapproval of Mrs. Touchett who denounces Madame Merle. Then Ralph, upon whom Isabel has depended, says nothing, simply ignores the matter for a long time. Poor Ralph, however, cannot speak; he feels shocked and humiliated and he casts about for a way to save his cousin. Desperately at length he tells her that Osmond is too "small" a man for her and betrays his own interest—" 'I had sort of a vision of your future. . . .I amused myself with planning a kind of destiny for you. There was to be nothing of this sort in it. You were not to come down so easily, so soon.' "[10] Isabel is hurt and resentful and vows he will never again know what she is thinking or whether she is happy. Though the world seems against her, Osmond proves a charming lover and Isabel feels quite satisfied.

There is now a break of three years in the story, and when it is resumed, we learn at first indirectly how things have gone with Isabel. Ned Rosier, a poor young man with a taste for bibelots and a love for Pansy, asks Madame Merle how he had best proceed to win the favor of Osmond. Madame Merle is discouraging and he suggests approaching Isabel whom he has long known.

"'I think Mrs. Osmond would favor me.'

"'Very likely—if her husband does not.' . . . .

"'Does she take the opposite line from him?'

"'In everything. They think very differently.' "[11]

Isabel—can it be that she is unhappy? She appears presently, a charming and gracious hostess in the house which she and her husband have taken in Rome, and one wonders what she is hiding beneath her radiant exterior.

Her story now becomes closely involved with her stepdaughter's future. Pansy's marriage is a matter of great concern to Osmond who has high hopes for his daughter, and Isabel can give no encouragement to Rosier though she knows Pansy cares for him.

In the midst of this affair, Ralph and Lord Warburton arrive in Rome. Ralph, it appears, has seen little of Isabel since her marriage. He is very frail and has come south in an effort to stave off death a little longer and to find out if Isabel is happy. Isabel is kind to him, but she refuses to betray herself or Osmond. But Ralph's presence in Rome, even though Osmond objects to the attention which Isabel gives him, does not create the confusion which Lord Warburton's does. His interest in Isabel is still high, and it presently extends to Pansy. Osmond is elated; this is the kind of match which he desires for Pansy. Madame Merle apparently approves also, and Isabel finds her suspicion slightly stirred by this and by something she sees one day in her drawingroom—her husband and Madame Merle standing in intimate silence. She stifles this, in a great desire to please Osmond and determines to forward, if she can, the match. When Osmond bluntly tells her, however, that he depends upon her to do this very thing, a certain repugnance sets in, and she sits long

[10] Ibid., June, 1881, p. 819.

[11] Ibid., July, 1881, p. 61.

and late one night viewing the situation and her life during the three years since her marriage.

She sees sadly what a failure it has been, how mistrust has become its keynote:

.... a gulf had opened between them, over which they looked at each other with eyes that were on either side a declaration of the deception suffered. It was a strange opposition, of the like of which she had never dreamed, an opposition in which the vital principle of the one was a thing of contempt to the other. It was not her fault—she had practised no deception; she had only admired and believed. She had taken all the first steps in the purest confidence, and then she had suddenly found the infinite vista of a multiplied life to be a dark, narrow alley, with a dead wall at the end.[12]

She feels Osmond's hatred, a hatred born when he discovered that she had ideas of her own which he could not change.

He had thought at first he could change her, and she had done her best to be what he would like. But she was, after all, herself—she couldn't help that; and now there was no use pretending, playing a part, for he knew her, and he had made up his mind.[13]

She sees how everything from the beginning has led to this gulf, and she wonders, with a shudder, what will come next, what ought she to do. Though Osmond hates her, she does not hate him for she is conscious every once in a while of a passionate wish to please him, as now in the matter of Pansy's marriage. She will help him here, though she knows that she herself is the one really beloved by Lord Warburton. She cannot, however, give up her talks with Ralph, much as they displease Gilbert, for Ralph is dying and must be kept from guessing what a failure her life is. But even as her mind is made up in these several regards, she remembers a vision—"that of her husband and of Madame Merle grouped unconsciously and familiarly."[14]

Things happen more quickly from now on. When next she sees Lord Warburton, Isabel chides him almost viciously about his profession of regard for Pansy and reprimands him for dallying about speaking to Osmond. But when Lord Warburton comes to call after a few days, it is only to say that he is about to return to England. Osmond manages to restrain his disappointment and wrath till Lord Warburton withdraws, and then he cruelly blames Isabel

[12] Ibid., Aug., 1881, p. 227.
[13] Ibid., p. 227.
[14] Ibid., Aug., 1881, p. 233.

for preventing Pansy's marriage, for thwarting him, and shows all the meanness of his nature.

And now Isabel admits to her friend, Henrietta Stackpole, who has been one of the doubting spectators of her marriage, the failure of it. She even tells Caspar Goodwood, who reappears, that if it will give him any comfort, he may now and then pity her. But to Ralph she refuses to give a sign, and Ralph, feeling that his end is approaching, decides to return to Gardencourt to die. As she bids him goodbye, Isabel promises to come to him if he sends for her at the last.

Madame Merle, meanwhile, has been out of town and she returns expecting to hear of Pansy's betrothal. When she is met instead by the news of Lord Warburton's departure, this well-poised woman for once loses her discretion and her self-control and blames Isabel. Isabel sees part of the truth—Madame Merle's interest is identical with Osmond's, Madame Merle married her, Madame Merle is wicked—but even now the good girl refuses to seek the reasons and connections of things and tries to dismiss them from her mind. She realizes her husband's indomitable will and cruelty when he sends Pansy, who has remained too interested in Rosier, back to the convent to think so that she will be ready for the next nobleman who appears.

In a short time a telegram comes from Mrs. Touchett saying that Ralph is dying and wishes to see her. Isabel goes to Osmond and tells him, only to be met by his demand that she remember her marriage vows and stay in Rome, announcing that if she goes, all will be at an end between them. And why shouldn't it be? For any person but Isabel it might have been, but she finds herself suddenly afraid, paralyzed. Marriage, conventional to Osmond, is a sacred thing to her.

Osmond's sister, the Countess Gemini, sees Isabel distraught, and reveals to her that she has no "duty" to Osmond, that Madame Merle is the mother of Pansy. Isabel hears it calmly and sadly, her duty still not apparent to her, yet her need to see Ralph a poignant ache which cannot be denied. She goes to the convent to say goodbye to Pansy, whom she pities more than ever and longs to help, and there she finds Madame Merle. The latter starts to explain her presence. Isabel stands aloof and silent. Madame Merle senses that her secret is known but that Isabel will never accuse her, never give her a chance to defend herself. Madame Merle takes it upon herself then to tell Isabel that the person who is most to blame for her unhappiness is Ralph, that he was responsible for the bequest in her uncle's will which made her "a brilliant match." Ralph—not Madame Merle—to blame? Isabel is amazed, then realizes it all with a rush of feeling for Ralph. He must have suffered too. How blind she has been, how unkind. If only she can reach Gardencourt before he dies.

Of course she does, for Ralph is waiting for her coming, clinging to life in order to see his vivid cousin once more. She arrives, sits by his bedside waiting till he is strong enough to speak; then the two face Isabel's story together. Never have they been so near, and both realize that, though one must die and the other live, live for a long, long time, the survivor will be helped by the consciousness of the love of the other and that life may have something of happiness in it yet.[15]

The end comes and Ralph is laid to rest beside his father. Isabel lingers at Gardencourt with Mrs. Touchett, wondering sometimes what she ought to do next, remembering she has promised Pansy not to desert her, but not wishing to move. Then Caspar Goodwood appears once more saying he has come to take her away with him, and at last she knows where to turn. There is a very straight path back to Rome and duty.

2. Criticism of The Portrait of a Lady

The outstanding characteristic of The Portrait of a Lady is its rich complexity—complexity of subject matter, plot, and treatment. Yet despite this, James placed his emphasis rightly, kept his material well in hand, and built up a story which, though complex, is so well made that it is quite as easy to follow as its simple predecessor. Never did the story or the characters get away from James; never did he go too far. His principle was not so much completeness of treatment, as it had been in The American, as adequacy of treatment, and he meant by this what the Greeks approved in their neither too much nor too little. He observed the mean, the just right, in every respect.

That he was able to do this was largely due to the way in which he approached and developed the story before he began to write it. The history of this he explained later to a certain extent in the pref-

---

[15] The scene is too tragic, and yet too beautiful, to remove it from the text for partial quotation. It is too long for complete quotation.

ace which he wrote for the novel when he assembled the *Collected Edition*. He said here that he had begun *The Portrait* with the character of his heroine whom he had had in mind for a long time, but had refrained from treating because of a pious desire to place his treasure right.[16] To her, as she stood isolated, had been added the other characters and the setting, and these characters, who seemed just to have come to him, had suggested her story.

I seem to myself to have waked up one morning in possession of them. . . . . I recognized them, I knew them, they were the numbered pieces of my puzzle, the concrete terms of my "plot." It was as if they had simply, by an impulse of their own, walked into my ken, and all in response to my primary question: "What will she *do?*" Their answer seemed to be that if I would trust them, they would show me; on which, with an urgent appeal to them to make it at least as interesting as they could, I trusted them.[17]

In all this, he admitted, he had been proceeding as Turgénieff proceeded, and he had gained confidence because Turgenieff had assured him that this was a legitimate way to build up a novel.[18]

But there had been the question of unity and emphasis. He was using a "small" person, and he was in for organizing an "ado" about her. That it could be done, he had been certain, for Shakespeare and George Eliot had often done it—there were Juliet and Hetty and Maggie and Rosamond and Gwendolen—but George Eliot and Shakespeare always eked out such persons with subplots, never let them matter enough, as much as they *might* matter.[19] With a weak agent, such as he had in Isabel, there was the danger that the story would become that of someone else, of Ralph, or of Madame Merle, of Osmond, even possibly of Lord Warburton or of Caspar Goodwood, or of all of these people together. To get around this danger, he had wisely determined that he must make it a view not of Isabel's relation to them, but of theirs to her.

There is always the escape from any close account of the weak agent of such spells by using as a bridge for evasion, for retreat and flight, the view of her relation to those surrounding her. Make it predominantly a view

---

[16] *Collected Edition*, III, xi, xii.

[17] Ibid., p. xvii.

[18] The extent to which James was dependent upon Turgénieff in this respect is to be seen also in the article written at the time of Turgénieff's death; see Chapter XIV.

[19] *Collected Edition*, III, xiii.

of *their* relation and the trick is played: you give the general sense of her effect, and you give it . . . . with the maximum of ease.[20]

While they were all interested in her, she must feel herself apart, think of herself as working out her destiny by herself. That had meant he would have to get into Isabel's mind, and this had suggested placing the *center* of the subject in Isabel's consciousness.

"Place the center of the subject in the young woman's own consciousness," I said to myself, "and you get as interesting and as beautiful a difficulty as you wish. Stick to *that*—for the center; put the heaviest weight in *that* scale, which will be so largely the scale of her relation to herself. Make her only interested enough, at the same time, in the things that are not herself, and this relation needn't fear to be too limited. Place meanwhile in the other scale, the lighter weight . . . press less hard, in short, on the consciousness of your heroine's satellites, especially the male; make it an interest contributive only to the greater one."[21]

Thus James envisaged in 1907 the problem which had confronted him when he wrote *The Portrait of a Lady*, showing where Turgénieff had reassured him, George Eliot and Shakespeare had warned him, and he *himself* had solved his "deep difficulty" by finding the most important way. But this is not all of the story.

Where, the critic is led to ask because of the great fondness of James for Isabel, had he obtained this "vivid individual?" Was she someone he actually knew—one of his many cousins? Had she grown out of the chance remark of a friend as Daisy had? Had he seen her in a boarding house? Had she come from his reading? The preface does not satisfy us on this point, and yet it gives a broadly general hint in the enumeration of the heroines of Shakespeare and George Eliot, who had been defrauded of mattering enough by their authors. And if one turns back to the critical article which James wrote in 1876 when *Daniel Deronda* completed its serial run,[22] the hint is confirmed. From James's article more than from George Eliot's novel, it is clear that Gwendolen Harleth was the prototype of Isabel Archer, for the points which James noted about Gwendolen are the points which a critic must note about his heroine.

Isabel is similar to Gwendolen in nature, in basic characteristics:.

"Gwendolen is a perfect picture of youthfulness—its eagerness, its presumption, its preoccupation with itself, its vanity and silliness, its sense of

[20] Ibid., p. xv.
[21] Ibid., p. xv.
[22] See Chapter XIV.

its own absoluteness. But she is extremely intelligent and clever, and therefore tragedy *can* have a hold upon her. Her conscience doesn't make the tragedy. . . . . It is the tragedy which makes her conscience, which then reacts upon it."[23]

If there is any difference between the two heroines, it is that of degree—an intensification in Isabel—and not of kind.

Isabel's story, broadly looked at, is the same as Gwendolen's:

"The universe, forcing itself with a slow, inexorable pressure into a narrow, complacent mind, and yet after all extremely sensitive mind, and making it ache with the pain of the process—that is Gwendolen's story. And it becomes completely characteristic in that her supreme perception of the fact that the world is whirling past her, is in the disappointment not of a base but of an exalted passion. The very chance to embrace what the author is so fond of calling a 'larger life' seems refused to her. She is punished for being narrow, and she is not allowed a chance to expand."[24]

Of course in the particulars and details of plot there are differences, but in each novel, a young woman affronts her destiny. In each case, her purpose is noble, exalted, and pursued with passion, and *The Portrait* is, as James said of *Daniel Deronda* as a whole, "the romance of a high moral tone."

Again Isabel and her story are presented in the same manner:

"Gwendolen is a masterpiece. She is known, felt, and presented, psychologically, altogether in the grand manner."[25] . . . . "Gwendolen's whole history is superbly told. And see how the girl is known, inside out, how thoroughly she is felt and understood. It is the most *intelligent* thing in all George Eliot's writing, and that is saying much. It is so deep, so true, so complete; it holds such a wealth of psychological detail, it is more than masterly."[26]

Truer words cannot be found to describe the portrait of Isabel and her history. Can it not be concluded that the desire, perhaps, too, the determination, to "do" thoroughly and completely, intelligently and feelingly, a similar heroine, had come to James in 1876 as he read and reviewed *Daniel Deronda*?

And the desire had been cherished and fostered. For this, James had experimented with American girls, trying out variations of the type, but hesitating to treat his "pious treasure" till he was sure of

[23] "Daniel Deronda: A Conversation," *Atlantic Monthly*, Dec., 1876. p. 692.
[24] Ibid., p. 692.
[25] Ibid., p. 687.
[26] Ibid., p. 692.

himself. For this, he had experimented with method, looking at his heroines through others, realizing that he must get at them and their minds directly if he was to do them justice, trying to on a small scale, but saving and storing up his energy for the service of Isabel.[27] Thinking of this, he had probably tried to imagine other characters who might help him, and one day these characters had suddenly stepped before him with Isabel's story in their hands. Some of these, like Isabel, are like people he had met in George Eliot—Osmond's refined and distilled brutality is like that of Grandcourt's; Ralph's helpless devotion is related to that of Will Ladislaw's in *Middlemarch*.[28] Others came from his own stories—Caspar is like Newman in his persistency; Pansy is like Aurora but with more delicacy due to her convent upbringing; Henrietta is related to Miranda Hope. Not a little of the greatness of *The Portrait* is due to the deep knowledge James had of all of his characters. He was thoroughly acquainted with them.

When, three years after writing the review, he turned to work on the portrait of Isabel, he probably had no consciousness of having borrowed her or her attendants. She was then *his* creature; like Gwendolen, to be sure, but there were many such in this world, and he had as much right to do her as he had to do Catherine, who was like Eugénie Grandet. Consider the following sentence from the review: " 'Gwendolen's history is admirably typical—as most things are with George Eliot: it is the very stuff that human life is made of.' "[29] What happened to Gwendolen often happened. James saw that it happened to American girls as well as to English—especially when they came to Europe with the desire to meet life, and the idea of their own competence to deal with it; then the universe forced itself in with a slow, inexorable pressure. James not only felt free to take a similar heroine, he felt impelled to, for he had discovered long

[27] In November 1878, Henry James wrote to William that he had been trying experiments in form using inferior subjects because he did not wish to waste or to use gratuitously big situations, and that he had learned to write and was coming to the big things. *Letters*, I, 66.

[28] When *The Portrait* was published in book form, W. C. Brownell reviewed it and noted briefly the parallelism of James's novel with *Middlemarch* in respect to the Lydgates and the Osmonds. (*Nation*, Feb. 2, 1882, p. 103). This likeness exists just as *Daniel Deronda* shows resemblances to *Middlemarch*, but James's review of *Daniel Deronda* gives such definite clews that, lacking a review of *Middlemarch*, we must conclude that the later novel was the more active influence. Ralph, however, resembles Ladislaw more than he does Deronda.

[29] *Atlantic Monthly*, Dec., 1876, p. 692.

before from George Eliot and others,[30] that it was the duty of the novelist to deal with the "very stuff" of life, and he had been proceeding with gradually increasing success ever since. He had even once tried a similar heroine of his own accord in Madame de Mauves.[31] There were no basically new subjects, for human nature was as old as the hills. The American side of it, however, had not yet been adequately done. The same conclusions are to be applied in regard to the resemblance of Osmond to Grandcourt and of Ralph to Will. Such people existed; such "refined and distilled brutality," such handicapped and silent devotion were only too characteristic of life. If Isabel was to face life, she must meet and feel—ah, so emphatically feel—both.

Accordingly James sought a plot, or rather took the one his characters offered, where this would be possible in the highest degree. It was not thus possible in George Eliot's novel where not only Gwendolen's story was thrust behind Deronda's but Gwendolen's hands were tied by poverty. James decided to give his American girl the center of the stage, and then he contrived by the device of the inheritance, which Ralph's love and interest made possible, to make her rich, thus putting it into her power to be magnanimous, to marry a poor man in the wish to help him. He made her, in her own opinion a free agent, and the most bitter part of her tragedy occurs when she finds that she has not been free, only blind, and that others have "made" her life.

What was in *Washington Square* on a small scale, is in *The Portrait of a Lady* on an enlarged and heightened scale. Isabel is intelligent and clever, but she is surrounded by people, two in particular, who are not only clever but wicked, and hence her defeat at their hands. It must not be overlooked, however, that defeated though she is externally, Isabel achieves a moral victory for herself.[32] Catherine did not; she sank into passive existence. Isabel, thus, is like Newman in *The American*.[33] Behind it all is the influence of Turgénieff and his use of failure,[34] now thoroughly absorbed by James as a dominating principle. When James wrote *The Portrait of a Lady*, he did not think of himself as working *under*

[30] See Chapters IV and V.
[31] See Chapter XI.
[32] See Chapter XII.
[33] See Chapter XV.
[34] See Chapter XII.

George Eliot and Turgénieff, but as working along *with* them, even, indeed, as the preface indicates, of working *above* them.

He treated his heroine not only intelligently and truly and feelingly, he treated her artistically. He let Isabel matter *enough*. He gave the whole novel to her. He not only placed her in the center, he placed the center in her consciousness, in her view of herself and of life. However, he did not stay in her mind all of the time, as he had stayed in Mallet's and Newman's, for Isabel, like Catherine, was not to see the conniving about her. But he looked at the others *only* as their plotting involved her, and except for Ralph, who was lovingly watching and seeing all, he stayed as much as possible out of the minds of those surrounding her. He kept everything focussed upon her; then he looked at everything as she saw it. The method which James used in *The Portrait of a Lady* was a combination of his method of using a mind as his glass and the direct approach which he used in *Washington Square*—it was his method made more flexible, adapted to his material, not ruthlessly applied despite the wisdom of the situation. James had control of it.

Then he put everything together, brought it out as he proceeded, built it up increasingly to a climax with an "architectural completeness" which only once again did he feel that he equalled.[35] In this regard, he mentioned in the preface, one thing which he regretted and another thing of which he was most proud. He regretted that he had brought in Henrietta, that "light ficelle" who runs beside Isabel, listens to her ideas, and often takes her to task, but plays no essential part in the story.[36] He was pleased with the way in which he had converted Isabel's sense of and for mild adventures into the very "stuff" of story.[37] By giving Isabel a premonitory feeling when she first sees Madame Merle that this grand lady is to play a part in her life, he had been able to produce "the maximum of intensity with the minimum of strain." He was proud, especially, of Isabel's vigil with herself half way through the book, when she spends the night viewing and reviewing the situation. That, brought in where it is, picks up and moves forward the action, accomplishes vividly in one chapter an account of three years of Isabel's life. "It was designed to have

[35] i.e., in *The Ambassadors*. See Collected Edition, III, xvi.

[36] Ibid., pp. xviiif. Henrietta is so much of a "light ficelle" that in giving the synopsis, it was impossible to indicate how often she is on the stage.

[37] Ibid., p. xviii.

all the vivacity of incident and all the economy of picture."[38] It *is* good, perhaps the best thing in the book, where everything is well-nigh superlative. No wonder James was proud.

There are details of treatment which James did not mention in the preface but left to the reader to discern from the book. The "architecture" which he was conscious of using enters on the first page and supports the novel through to the last. James set the stage for Isabel to appear—the spreading lawns at Gardencourt, the three men idly speculating—then brought her in, plunging her into a new world, a new kind of existence. What led to this, the antecedent action, he deferred for two chapters, and then recounted it rapidly securing thus an advantage artistically over *Washington Square* where he had followed Balzac. At the end, he left Isabel turning back to Rome to a scene which will be more unpleasant than any in the book, and he gave Henrietta the task of informing Caspar. Though it is stopped short by the author, Isabel's story is by no means finished; she must continue to live and suffer for many years, but there is no need for her story to be finished completely as James had felt compelled to finish the story of Catherine. The reader knows how Isabel will now act and feel, with her eyes opened and Ralph's love sustaining her and making life a bit more endurable. In the middle of the novel, James made everything lead to something else, and not only this, but intentionally gave Isabel premonitions of her unhappiness, vague foresight as to her future. The use of the direct approach not only enabled him to see the plotting of others, but it allowed him to look at Isabel from the outside as well as from the inside. The advantage of this he realized when he resumed Isabel's story after her marriage and wisely revealed the state of her mind indirectly by telling what others see and guess, before approaching it directly in the midnight vigil. All this shows the hand of an artist and a master as well, for though James trusted the stage to others temporarily, the glance of author, characters, and reader is kept focussed upon the mind of Isabel.

The finish of the novel is no less perfect than its architecture. It is narrative as James had never written it before—a blending of incident, dialogue, description—one running into the other so that the result is constant fluidity of motion.[39] The portions of straight

[38] Ibid., p. xx.

[39] James's approval of such a blending is given in "The Art of Fiction," *Longman's Magazine*, Sept. 1884.

narrative—for want of a word one must so distinguish what is not dialogue or description—run smoothly, but because the nature of the story demands it, often slowly, becoming quite analytical and expository in places. Still there is always, even in the most expositional of the parts, movement of a sort. James's concern was the *development* of a mind. The narrative portions frequently melt into dialogue, which easily assumes the burden of furthering the action, notably when Isabel and Osmond are conversing, or of telling what has happened, as in Isabel's facing Caspar after she has accepted Osmond. The dialogue operates still further in revealing character, both directly and indirectly. Much of the analysis of Isabel comes from the mouth of Ralph or of Henrietta—who looked at thus seems to have a function after all—as they talk with Isabel, criticize her, and lead her to expose herself. Because of this, little description of a pure, unmixed sort was needed, and there are no sustained passages of description, no large blocks of it such as James, following Balzac, had used in *Washington Square*. It is wrought into the dialogue, into the incident. One can say both that there is no description and that there is description on every page, achieved by a short remark, a phrase, or even one word as it accompanies dialogue or is worked into incident. The portrait of Isabel is the portrait of a mind rather than that of a person with physical form and body, and it takes the whole novel to give the complete portrait. The description of place is likewise wrought into the story, and the mention of place brings us to a discovery which is to be made in this novel as to the changing trend in James's interests.

Of place, only Gardencourt, because it serves as an opening setting, is done in any detail. Here the atmosphere is evoked by a short bit of pure description, and then by the attitude and talk of the three men over their tea, and then, most of all, by the effect of Gardencourt upon Isabel. When Isabel goes to Paris, to Florence, to Rome, however, except for Osmond's villa on the hill top, in which Osmond's personality expresses itself, James refrained from emphasizing in any way these cities which he had once thought it expedient to "do." He was now "doing" Isabel, and her story after it gets started, is not of what place does to her but of what people do. It is above place. It is also above time to a certain extent. Though laid in the mid-nineteenth century when "frail vessels" were beginning to go to Europe as the first step into a larger life, it deals really with the revelation of permanent traits of human nature and not of transitory ones, and James did wisely not to emphasize place and time any more than was necessary for location of the action. *Washington Square* shows James still interested in history in the Balzacian sense—limited by time and place; *The Portrait of a Lady* shows him interested in it in the George Eliot sense—the history of human nature at large. Though he was to retain both interests for a time, the second was eventually to dominate.

3. *The Conclusion.*

In conclusion, it must be observed that *The Portrait of a Lady* has art as well as life. James proved to his own satisfaction that it was possible to have both in a novel. To this perfect reconciliation of the two he had advanced from small beginnings. In the early days he had striven for first one and then the other and often both at once with results that had made him dubious at times as to whether he could ever adjust the two into an even balance. In *Roderick Hudson*, he had almost hit the mark. In *The American*, he had shot past it. Shortly after that, under the negative influence of French writers who failed to have it and the positive influence of a Russian and an English novelist who did have it, he had declared that life at any rate was indispensable, and that art, though desirable, was not necessary. It was better not to have it than to abuse it by forcing it to serve in unclean causes. The love of art, however, was as strong within Henry James, as the love of life. He had not been willing to relinquish his dream of reconciling the two, and he had begun all over again with a series of experimental studies in one phase or another of life and of art. And now at last in *The Portrait of a Lady*, he had triumphed, writing a novel that has as much life as those of George Eliot and Turgénieff and more art. For a while he was to remain here, still claiming when he wrote of the work of others or of the principles of fiction that if one had to be sacrificed, it had better be art, but in his own novels balancing the two. Gradually, by almost imperceptible degrees, the love of art, as it became more and more an easy thing for him to put into practice, was to encroach upon the love of life, and he was in time to come to look upon art as the *summum bonum*. Art then was to regulate life. This next and final development, however, is material for another study. My dissertation must end with James's first successful realization of his desire to write novels which should have abundantly both art and life.

BIBLIOGRAPHY OF THE EARLY DEVELOPMENT OF HENRY JAMES

As stated in the preface, the works of Henry James dealt with in this study are given with full bibliographical particulars in *A Bibliography of the Writings of Henry James* compiled by LeRoy Phillips, Boston and New York, 1906, pp. 3 to 23 and 87 to 140.

The following are the writings upon James which bear wholly or in part on his early life and works. This list is selective rather than exhaustive. The most important have been starred (*).

BEACH, JOSEPH WARREN: (a) *The Method of Henry James**, New Haven, 1918. (Interested primarily in the developed method, but pages 165 to 211 and 221 to 232 look back upon the early stories and novels.) (b) "Henry James," in *A History of American Literature*, vol. III, Cambridge, 1919.

BENTZON, T.: "Les Nouveaux Romanciers Américains: Henry James,"* *Revue des Deux Mondes*, May 1, 1883. (Important because an intelligent early interpretation from the pen of a Frenchman.)

BETHURUM, DOROTHY: "Morality and Henry James," *Sewanee Review*, July-September, 1923.

BRADFORD, GAMALIEL: *American Portraits*, Boston and New York, 1922.

BROOKS, VAN WYCK: *The Pilgrimage of Henry James*, New York, 1925. (Biographical; facts distorted by Brooks's idea that James's eventual settling down in England was the result of a nostalgia for Europe that had, as it were, been born in him.)

BROWNELL, W. C.: *American Prose Masters*.* New York, 1909. (Tone adverse.)

BUCHAN, R.: "The Modern Young Man as Critic," *Universal Review*, March, 1889.

BURTON, RICHARD: *Literary Likings*, Boston, 1903.

CARY, ELIZABETH L.: *The Novels of Henry James*, New York and London, 1905. (The first book devoted to a criticism of James's novels.)

CAIRNS, W. B.: "Meditations of a Jacobite," *Dial*, March 30, 1916.

CANBY, HENRY SEIDEL: *The Short Story in English*,* New York, 1909. (Good but brief, pp. 307–314.)

CHEVALLEZ, ABEL: *Le Roman Anglais de Notre Temps*. London, 1921. (English translation, New York, 1925.)

CHISLETT, WILLIAM, JR.: *Moderns and Near Moderns*, New York, 1928.

CROLY, HERBERT: "Henry James and his Countrymen,"* *The Lamp*, February, 1904.

DARGAN, E. P.: "Henry James, the Builder," *New Republic*, July 17, 1916.

DAVRAY, HENRY D.: "Un déraciné anglo-américain," *Mercure de France* February, 15, 1921. (Considers James's attitude towards French naturalism.)

EDGAR, PELHAM: *Henry James, Man and Author*,* London, 1927. (Restates the facts about James and his writings, but has little of an interpretative or critical nature.)

ELTON, OLIVER: *Modern Studies*,* London, 1907.

FAWCETT, E.: "The Novels of James,"* *Princeton Review*, July, 1884. (Excellent early summary of James's work up to 1881.)

FOLLETT, HELENE and WILSON: *Some Modern Novelists*, New York, 1918

FREEMAN, JOHN: *The Moderns*, London, 1916.

FRIERSON, WILLIAM C.: *L'Influence du Naturalisme Français sur les Romanciers Anglais de 1885 à 1900*, Paris, 1925. (Exaggerates the French influences upon James.)

FULLERTON, MORTON: "The Art of Henry James,"* *Quarterly Review*, April, 1910. (Points out the resemblances and differences between James and Balzac.)

GARNIER, MARIE-REINE: *Henry James et la France*, Paris, 1927.

GOSSE, EDMUND: *Aspects and Impressions*,* London and New York, 1922. (Mostly biographical.)

GUEDALLA, PHILIP: *Supers and Supermen*, New York, 1921.

HALE, E. E.: (a) "Novels and Tales of Henry James," *Dial*, March 16, 1908. (b) "Henry James," *Dial*, March 16, 1916.

HAPGOOD, NORMAN: *Literary Statesmen and Others*, Chicago and New York, 1897.

HARKINS, E. F.: *Little Pilgrimages among Men who have written Famous Books*, Boston, 1902.

HARVITT, HELENE: "How Henry James Revised Roderick Hudson," *PMLA*, March, 1924.

HAVENS, R. D.: "The Revision of Roderick Hudson," *PMLA*, June 1925.

HAYWOOD, J. C.: *How they Strike Me, These Authors*,* Philadelphia, 1877.

HIGGINSON, T. W.: *Short Studies of American Authors*,* Boston and New York, 1880. (Good, appreciative interpretation of early work.)

HOWELLS, WILLIAM DEAN: "Henry James, Jr."* *Century Magazine*, November, 1882. (In addition to criticism of James's fiction, Howells touches upon his relations with James as an editor and friend.)

HUEFFER, FORD MADOX: *Henry James*, London, 1913; New York, 1916. (Impressionistic and not always accurate.)

HUGHES, HERBERT LELAND: *Theory and Practice in Henry James*, Ann Arbor, 1926. (Poor.)

HUNEKER, J. G.: "The Lesson of the Master,"* *Bookman*, May, 1920.

KELLNER, L.: *Geschichte der Nordamerikanischen Literatur*, Berlin, 1913 (English translation, New York, 1915.)

LILJEGREN, S.: *American and European in the Works of Henry James.** Lund, 1920. (Treats the so-called international stories.)

LEACH, ANNA: "Henry James, an Appreciation,"* *Forum*, May, 1916.

LITTELL, P.: "Books and Things," *New Republic*, July, 30, 1919.

LUBBOCK, P.: "Henry James,"* *Quarterly Review*, July, 1916; also, *Living Age*, September, 1916. (Good, but deals mostly with later novels.)

MACY, JOHN: *The Spirit of American Literature*, New York, 1913. (Adverse.)

MATTHEWS, BRANDER: "Henry James, Book Reviewer," *New York Times Book Review*, June 12, 1921.

MICHAUD, REGIS: (a) *Mystiques et réalistes anglo-saxon d'Emerson à Bernard Shaw*, Paris, 1918. (b) *Le Roman Américain d'aujourd'hui*, Paris, 1926.

NADAL, E. S.: "Personal Recollections of Henry James," *Scribner's*, July, 1920.

O'BRIEN, E. J.: *The Advance of the American Short Story.** New York, 1923. (Considers briefly the influences upon James.)

PALACHE, JOHN G.: "The Critical Faculty of Henry James." *University of California Chronicle*, October, 1924.

PATTEE, FRED LEWIS: (a) *History of American Literature since 1870,** New York, 1915. (Adverse but good.) (b) *The Development of the American Short Story*, New York, 1923.

PHELPS, WILLIAM LYONS: *Howells, James, Bryant, and Other Essays*, New York, 1924.

POUND, EZRA: *Instigations*, New York, 1920.

PRATT, C. A.: "The Evolution of Henry James," *Critic*, April, 1899.

RANDELL, WILFRED L.: "The Art of Mr. Henry James," *Fortnightly Review*, April, 1916; also in *Living Age*, July, 1916.

READ, HERBERT: *The Sense of Glory*, Cambridge, England, 1929.

RICHARDSON, S. D.: "Henry James as a Novelist," *Harvard Monthly*, April, 1886.

ROBERTS, M.: *Henry James's Criticism,** Cambridge, 1929. (Chapters I and II deal with the early reviews and critical articles.)

SCHELLING, F. E.: *Appraisements and Asperities*, Philadelphia, 1922.

SCOTT, DIXON: *Men of Letters*, London and New York, 1917.

SHERMAN, STUART PRATT: *Our Contemporary Literature*, New York, 1917.

TILLEY, A.: "The New School of Fiction,"* *National Review*, April, 1883. (Follows Howells's article and considers James and Howells as new forces in fiction.)

VAN DOREN, CARL: *The American Novel*, New York, 1921.

VEDDER, HENRY CLAY: *American Writers of Today*, New York and Boston, 1910.

WAUGH, A.: *Tradition and Change*, New York, 1919.

WEST, REBECCA: *Henry James,* * New York, 1916. (A rapid survey of James's life and works bent around her idea that his inability to serve in the Civil War permanently affected his point of view.)

WILLIAMS, H.: *Modern English Writers*, London, 1925.

WISTER, S. B.: A Review of *Roderick Hudson, North American Review,* April, 1876.

WYATT, EDITH: "Henry James: an Impression," *North American Review,* April, 1916.

A SUPPLEMENTARY BIBLIOGRAPHY OF
MATERIAL COVERED BY THIS STUDY

Except for a few significant collections of the early tales, essays, and novels, no attempt has been made in Section I to list publications by James already included in the comprehensive *Bibliography of Henry James*, compiled by Leon Edel and Dan H. Laurence, London, 1957 which supplements the pioneer *Bibliography of the Writings of Henry James*, New York, 1906 by LeRoy Phillips. I wish to repeat here that this study of the early development of James depended upon the first appearance in print, as indicated by Phillips, of James's writings in the periodicals of the 1860's and 1870's. The many reprintings of the novels and tales in recent years have not always been dictated by any concern for, and in some instances by any indication of, the edition being reprinted—whether original magazine version, corrected first edition, or revised text. To include all such subsequent editions, irresponsible paperbacks as well as competently edited clothbound version, and to distinguish among them, calls for an extended supplement to the Edel-Laurence bibliography which will doubtless some day be forthcoming.

In compiling Section II, I have been guided by two somewhat opposite principles. In view of the importance—negative as well as positive—of many of the books on Henry James, it has seemed pertinent to list the outstanding ones from 1930 to 1964, even though other bibliographies have already recognized some of these books. Notable in this respect is the excellent checklist compiled by Maurice Beebe and William Stafford in the Henry James Number of *Modern Fiction*, Vol. III: 2, Spring 1957, and the earlier bibliography compiled by Lyon Richardson in *Representative Selections*, American Book Company, 1941. When it comes to the many critical articles on James published prior to 1957, I believe the selective bibliography by Beebe and Stafford is sufficient and most helpful for the student of the early period. I have endeavored to supplement this bibliography, however, by listing the most significant articles which have appeared since 1957, confining myself to those which deal with the early writings of James. Some of these later articles are, indeed, most important as the titles will reveal and add greatly to understanding the development of James as a novelist. Of recent importance to the future critic of James is the perceptive chapter in *Eight American Authors*, edited by Floyd Stovall, New York, 1956, 1963, wherein Robert E. Spiller reviews and evaluates the present state of Jamesian scholarship.

Urbana, Illinois, 1965   CORNELIA P. KELLEY

I. *Reprints of Early Writings by Henry James*

The American Novels and Stories of Henry James. Edited by F. O. Matthiessen, New York, 1947.

The Art of Fiction and Other Essays. Edited by Morris Roberts, New York, 1948.

The Art of the Novel, Critical Prefaces. Edited by Richard P. Blackmur, New York, 1934.

The Art of Travel. Essays edited by Morton Zabel, New York, 1958.

The Complete Plays of Henry James. Edited by Leon Edel, Philadelphia, 1949.

The Complete Tales of Henry James. Edited by Leon Edel, Philadelphia, 1962:

    Vol. I   1864-1868
    Vol. II   1868-1872
    Vol. III 1873-1875
    Vol. IV 1876-1882

Eight Uncollected Tales. Edited by Edna Kenton, New Brunswick, 1950.

Four Selected Novels (The American, The Europeans, Daisy Miller, The International Episode). Edited by Arthur Zeiger, New York, 1946.

The Ghostly Tales of Henry James. Edited by Leon Edel, New Brunswick, 1948.

The Great Short Novels of Henry James. Edited by Philip Rahv, New York, 1946.

Henry James: Autobiography. Edited by Frederick Dupee, New York, 1956.

Literary Reviews and Essays. Edited by Albert Mordell, New York, 1957.

The Notebooks of Henry James. Edited by F. O. Matthiessen and Kenneth B. Murdock, New York, 1947.

The Painter's Eye; Notes and Essays on the Pictorial Arts. Edited by John F. Sweeney, Cambridge, 1956.

Parisian Sketches. Edited by Leon Edel and Ilse Dusoir Lind, New York, 1957.

The Portable Henry James. Edited by Morton Zabel, New York, 1951.

Portraits of Places. Edited by George Alvin Finch, New York, 1948.

Representative Selections. Edited by Lyon N. Richardson, New York, 1941.

The Scenic Art, Notes on Acting and the Drama: 1872-1901. Edited by Allan Wade, New Brunswick, 1948.

Selected Letters. Edited by Leon Edel, London, 1956.

Selected Stories. Edited by Gerard Hopkins, London, 1957.

Short Novels. Edited by E. Hudson Long, New York, 1961.

The Short Stories of Henry James. Edited by Clifton Fadiman, New York, 1945.

Stories of Writers and Artists. Edited by F. O. Matthiessen, New York, 1944.

II. *Writings upon Henry James*

Books

A. Concerned Wholly With the Early Years

EDEL, LEON. *Henry James:* I, *The Untried Years*, 1843-1870, II, *The Conquest of London*, 1870-1881, Lippincott, Philadelphia, 1953, 1962.

LE CLAIR, ROBERT CHARLES. *Young Henry James*, 1843-1870, New York, 1955.

POIRIER, RICHARD. *The Comic Sense of Henry James; A Study of the Early Novels*, London, 1960.

B. Dealing in Part With the Early Years

ANDERSON, QUENTIN. *The American Henry James*, New Brunswick, N. J., 1957.

ANDREAS, OSBORN. *Henry James and the Expanding Horizon*, Seattle, 1948.

AUCHINCLOS, LOUIS. *Reflections of a Jacobite*, Boston, 1961.

BEACH, JOSEPH WARREN. *The Method of Henry James*, rev. ed., Philadelphia, 1954.

CANBY, HENRY SEIDEL. *Turn West, Turn East: Mark Twain and Henry James*, Boston, 1951.

CARGILL, OSCAR. *The Novels of Henry James*, New York, 1961.

COX, C. *Henry James and Stoicism*, London, 1955.

DUPEE, FREDERICK WILCOX. *Henry James*, New York, 1951.

———. *The Question of Henry James*, New York, 1945.

GALE, ROBERT L. *The Caught Image; Figurative Language in the Fiction of Henry James*, Chapel Hill, 1964.

GEISMAR, MAXWELL. *Henry James and the Jacobites*, Boston, 1963.

GRATTAN, C. HARTLEY. *The Three Jameses; A Family of Minds*, New York, 1932.

HARLOW, VIRGINIA. *Thomas Sergeant Perry: A Biography, and Letters to Perry from William, Henry, and Garth Wilkinson James*, Chapel Hill, 1950.

HOFFMAN, CHARLES G. *The Short Novels of Henry James*, New York, 1957.

HOLDER-BARELL, ALEXANDER. *The Development of Imagery and its Functional Significance in Henry James's Novels*, Winterthur, 1959.

HOLLAND, LAURENCE BEDWELL. *The Expense of Vision; Essays on the Craft of Henry James*, Princeton, 1964.

HOME, HELEN. *Basic Ideas of James's Aesthetics as Expressed in the Short Stories Concerning Artists and Writers*, Marburg, 1960.

HOWELLS, WM. DEAN. *Discovery of a Genius: William Dean Howells and Henry James.* Compiled and edited by Albert Mordell, New York, 1961.

JAMES, ALICE. *Alice James, her Brothers—her Journal*. Edited by Anna Robeson Burr, London, 1934.

KROOK, DOROTHEA. *The Ordeal of Consciousness in Henry James*, Cambridge, England, 1962.

LEAVIS, FRANK RAYMOND. *The Great Tradition; George Eliot, Henry James, Joseph Conrad*, New York, 1948.

LE CLAIR, ROBERT CHARLES. *Three American Travellers in England: James Russell Lowell, Henry Adams, Henry James*, Philadelphia, 1945.

LEVY, LEO BEN. *Versions of Melodrama; A Study of the Fiction and Drama of Henry James*, 1865-1897, Berkeley, 1957.

McCARTHY, HAROLD T. *Henry James: the Creative Process*, New York, 1958.

MARKOW-TOTEVY, GEORGES. *Henry James*, Paris, 1958.

MATTHIESSEN, FRANCIS OTTO. *Henry James, the Major Phase*, New York, 1944.

MATTHIESSEN, FRANCIS OTTO. *The James Family*, New York, 1947.

NOWELL-SMITH, SIMON. *The Legend of the Master*, London, 1947.

SHARP, SISTER CORONA. *The Confidante in Henry James; Evolution and Moral Value of a Fictive Character*, Notre Dame, 1963.

STAFFORD, WILLIAM T. *James's Daisy Miller: the Story, the Play, the Critics*, New York, 1963.

STALLMAN, ROBERT WOOSTER. *The Houses that James Built*, East Lansing, 1961.

STEVENSON, ELIZABETH. *The Crooked Corridor, a Study of Henry James*, New York, 1949.

STONE, EDWARD. *The Battle and the Books*, Athens, Ohio, 1964.

WEGELIN, CHRISTOF. *The Image of Europe in Henry James*, Dallas, 1958.

Articles

ADAMS, PERCY G. "Young Henry James and the Lesson of His Master Balzac," *Revue de Littérature Comparée*, XXXV, July-September, 1961, pp. 458-465. (Points out seven parallels: "La Vieille Fille" —"Poor Richard"; "La Peau de Chargrin"—"DeGrey"; "L'Enfant Maudit"—"Gabrielle de Bergerac"; "La Chef d'Oeuvre Inconnu"—"Madonna of the Future" and "The Sweetheart of M. Briseux"; "Le Lys dans la Vallee"—"Eugene Pickering"; "Eugénie Grandet"—"Washington Square.")

ALVAREZ, A. "Intelligence on Tour," *The Kenyon Review*, XXI:1, Winter 1959, pp. 23-33. (Travel sketches complement the novels.)

AUCHINCLOS, LOUIS. "A Strategy for James Readers," *Nation*, CXC:17, April 23, 1960, pp. 364-367. (Order in which James's stories and novels should be read.)

BEATTIE, MUNRO. "Henry James, Novelist," *Dalhousie Review,*
XXXIX:4, Winter 1960, pp. 455-463. (Recent criticism—psychological, aesthetic, allegorical—distorts James's novels by giving
one-sided interpretation. James's field not myth or epic but life.)

BERLAND, ALWYN. "Henry James and the Grand Renunciation," *The
Kansas Magazine,* 1958, pp. 82-90.

————. "Henry James and the Aesthetic Tradition," *Journal of the
History of Ideas,* XXIII:2, April-June, 1962, pp. 407-419. (James-
Ruskin-Arnold similar attitudes toward art.)

BEWLEY, MARIUS. "Henry James and 'Life'," *The Hudson Review,*
XI:2, Summer 1958, pp. 167-185. (Considers *Madame de Mauves,
Roderick Hudson, The Europeans.* Europe a testing ground for
American character.)

————. "The Verb to Contribute," *Spectator,* No. 6839, July 24, 1959,
pp. 114-115. (Like Arnold, James stressed moral seriousness of
art in early reviews.)

BLEHL, VINCENT. "Freedom and Commitment in James's *Portrait of a
Lady,*" *Personalist,* XLII:3, Summer 1961, pp. 368-381.

BOWMAN, SYLVIA E. "Les Héroines d'Henry James dans *The Portrait
of a Lady* et d'Ivan Tourguéniev dans *A. la Veille,*" *Etudes Angla-
ises,* XI:2, Avril-Juin 1958, pp. 136-149.

BUITENHUIS, PETER. "Henry James on Hawthorne," *New England
Quarterly,* XXXII:2, June, 1959, pp. 207-225. (James's appraisals
of Hawthorne.)

————. "Comic Pastoral: Henry James's *The Europeans,*" *University
of Toronto Quarterly,* XXXI:2, January, 1962, pp. 152-163. (Social
comedy inspired by Turgenieff.)

CAMBON, GLAUCO. "The Negative Gesture in Henry James," *Nineteenth Century Fiction,* XV:4, March, 1961. (Catherine Sloper's
withdrawal influenced by Hawthorne.)

CARGILL, OSCAR. "The First International Novel," *PMLA,* LXXIII:4,
Pt. 1, September, 1958, pp. 418-425. *(The American* developed
into a refutation of Dumas fils '*L'Etrangére,* seen by James in
February, 1876.)

CLAIR, JOHN A. "*The American:* A Reinterpretation," *PMLA,* LXXIV:
5, December, 1959, pp. 613-618. (Considers Mrs. Bread the true
mother of Claire. Newman "taken in" by Mrs. Bread.)

CRUTH, EDMUND. "Moonshine and Bloodshed: A Note on *The American,*" *Notes and Queries,* IX:3, March, 1962, pp. 105-106. Parallelism in appearance between Claire and Murillo's Madonna.)

DOVE, JOHN ROWLAND. "The Tragic Sense in Henry James," *Texas
Studies in Literature and Language,* II:3, Autumn 1960, pp. 303-314.

EDEL, LEON. "'A Tragedy of Error,' James's First Story," *New England Quarterly*, XXIX, September, 1956, pp. 291-317.

EDEL, LEON. "Who Was Gilbert Osmond?" *Modern Fiction Studies*, VI:2, Summer 1960, p. 164. (Challenges Stallman's identity of Gilbert Osmond as related to H. B. Brewster.)

EMERSON, DONALD. "Henry James and the Limitations of Realism," *College English*, XXII:3, December, 1960, pp. 161-166.

FOX, HUGH. "Henry James and the Antinomian James Household: A Study of Selfhood and Selfishness," *Arizona Quarterly*, XV:1, Spring 1959, pp. 49-55.

FUSSELL, EDWIN. "Hawthorne, James and 'The Common Doom',"' *American Quarterly*, X:4, Winter 1958, pp. 438-453. (Feeling of isolation common to both.)

GALE, ROBERT L. "Henry James and Italy," *Nineteenth Century Fiction*, XIV:2, September, 1959, pp. 157-170. (Italy provided scene after scene for James's fiction, and images for his description.)

———. "Henry James's Dream Children," *Arizona Quarterly*, XV:1, Spring 1959, pp. 56-63. (James's use of his childhood experiences in his stories.)

———. "A Note on Henry James's First Short Story," *Modern Language Notes*, LXXII, February, 1957, pp. 103-107.

———. "*Roderick Hudson* and Thomas Crawford," *American Quarterly*, XIII:4, Winter 1961, pp. 495-504. (Central character owes much to Crawford, American sculptor, whose wife James knew in Rome after Crawford's death.)

GARGANO, JAMES W. "*Daisy Miller:* An Abortive Quest for Innocence," *South Atlantic Quarterly*, LIX:1, Winter 1960, pp. 114-120. (Study of Winterbourne.)

———. "Foreshadowing in *The American*," *Modern Language Notes*, LXXIV:7, November, 1959, pp. 600-601.

GASS, WILLIAM H. "The High Brutality of Good Intentions," *Accent*, XVIII:1, Winter 1958. (*The Portrait of a Lady* James's first use of the theme of the evil of human manipulation.)

GLECKNER, ROBERT F. "James's *Madame de Mauves* and Hawthorne's *The Scarlet Letter*," *Modern Language Notes*, LXXIII:8, December, 1958, pp. 580-586.

GOLDSMITH, ARNOLD L. "Henry James's Reconciliation of Free Will and Fatalism," *Nineteenth Century Fiction*, XIII:2, September, 1958, pp. 109-126. (Relates Henry James to nineteenth century climate of opinion.)

GRENANDER, M. E. "Henry James's *Capricciosa*, Christina Light in *Roderick Hudson* and *The Princess Casamassima*," *PMLA*,

LXXV:3, June, 1960, pp. 309-319. (Christina Light develops naturally from *Roderick Hudson* to *Princess Casamassima* but becomes disillusioned, shopworn, petulant.)

GRENANDER, M. E., RAHN, BEVERLY, and VALVO, FRANCINE. "The Time-Scheme in *The Portrait of a Lady*," *American Literature*, XXXII:2, May, 1960, pp. 127-135. (Only one event dated— Ned Rosier's arrival in Rome, November 1, 1876, but everything before and after adjusted to that date.)

GRIFFIN, ROBERT F. "Notes toward an Exegesis: 'Four Meetings'," *University of Kansas City Review*, XXIX:1, October, 1962, pp. 45-49. (Negative moral judgment of the narrator on Caroline Spenser.)

HAFLEY, JAMES. "Malice in Wonderland," *Arizona Quarterly*, XV:1, Spring, 1959, pp. 5-12. (Compares Poe and James.)

HALPERN, MARTIN. "Henry B. Brewster," *American Quarterly*, XIV:3, Fall, 1962, pp. 464-482.

HARVEY, W. J. "Work in Progress I: Character and the Content of Things," *Essays in Criticism*, XIII:1, January, 1963, pp. 50-66. (*Portrait of a Lady* interplay of aesthetics and ethics.)

HOFTUND, SIGMUND. "The Point of View in Henry James," *Edda*, LXI:1, 1961, pp. 169-176. (Negative criticism of *The American*, technically and intellectually immature.)

HOPKINS, VIOLA. "Gloriani and the Tides of Taste," *Nineteenth Century Fiction*, XVIII:1, June, 1963, pp. 65-71.

JONES, LEONIDAS M. "James's 'Four Meetings'," *Explicator* XX:7, March, 1962, Item 55.

KAPLAN, CHARLES. "James's 'Madame de Mauves'," *Explicator*, XIX:4, January, 1961, Item 32.

KRAUSE, SIDNEY J. "James's Revisions of the Style of *The Portrait of a Lady*," *American Literature*, XXX:1, March, 1958, pp. 67-88. (Purpose of revisions to gain clarity, economy, concreteness, informality.)

MONTEIRO, GEORGE. "William Dean Howells: Two Mistaken Attributions," *Papers of the Bibliographical Society of America*, LVI:1, First Quarter, 1962.

MONTGOMERY, MARION. "The Flaw in the Portrait: Henry James vs. Isabel Archer," *University of Kansas City Review*, XXVI:3, March, 1960, pp. 215-220.

MOODY, A. D. "James's Portrait of an Ideal," *Melbourne Critical Review*, IV, 1961, pp. 77-92. (Ambiguous conclusion in *Portrait of a Lady* due to James's confusion about Isabel.)

Moore, John Robert. "An Imperfection in the Art of Henry James," *Nineteenth Century Fiction*, XIII:4, March, 1959, pp. 351-356. (Background of Newman insufficient—James's ignorance of the West, the Civil War, business.)

Namekata, Akio. "The Ordeal of Isabel in James's *The Portrait of a Lady*, *Essays*, No. 15, December, 1962, pp. 44-59. (In Japanese.)

Ohmann, Carol. "*Daisy Miller:* A Study of Changing Intentions," *American Literature*, XXXVI:1, March 1964, pp. 1-11.

Powers, Lyall H. "Henry James and Zola's *Roman Experimental*," *University of Toronto Quarterly*, XXX:1, October, 1960, pp. 16-30. (Influence of Zola and the French naturalists not discernible until the 1880's.)

———. "*The Portrait of a Lady*, 'The Eternal Mystery of Things'," *Nineteenth Century Fiction*, XIV:2, September, 1959, pp. 143-155. (Form determined by Isabel's going from Gardencourt to Rome to Gardencourt again—the pattern of redemption, the fortunate fall.)

Pritchett, V. S. "Babcockism," *New Statesman and Nation*, LIX, June 11, 1960, pp. 863-864. (James's comic approach in *The Europeans* and *The American*—the free and the fixed.)

———. "Birth of a Hermaphrodite," *New Statesman*, November 30, 1962, pp. 779-780. (The early Henry James and William James— "Confidence.")

Putt, S. Gorley. "James the First," *English*, XIV:81, Autumn 1962, pp. 93-96. (Early stories anticipate later: economy of phrase, contrasting and comic use of deliberate verbosity, love of Europe.)

Roberts, James L. "An Approach to Evil in Henry James," *Arizona Quarterly*, XVII:1, Spring 1961, pp. 5-16.

Rosenbaum, S. P. "Two Henry James Letters on *The American* and *Watch and Ward*," *American Literature*, XXX:4, January, 1959. (Letters to Osgood, 1877 about revisions.)

Rovit, Earl. "James and Emerson: The Lesson of the Master," *American Scholar*, XXXIII:3, Summer 1964, pp. 434-440.

Simon, Iréne. "Jane Austen and The Art of the Novel," *English Studies*, XLIII:3, June, 1962, pp. 225-239. (Interesting evaluation of George Eliot and Henry James—James interested in tragic irony of life; George Eliot in comic irony.)

Slabey, Robert M. "Henry James and 'The Most Impressive Convention in All History'," *American Literature*, XXX:1, March, 1958, pp. 89-102. (James and Catholicism.)

Snow, Lotus. "The Disconcerting Poetry of Mary Temple," *The New England Quarterly*, XXXI:3, September, 1958. (Compares imagery of *The Portrait* and *The Wings*.)

STAFFORD, WILLIAM T. "The Ending of James's *The American*," *Nineteenth Century Fiction*, XVIII:1, June, 1963, pp. 86-89. (The melodramatic early ending more appropriate than the sentimental later one.)

———. "Lowell 'Edits' James: Some Revisions in *French Poets and Novelists*," *New England Quarterly*, XXXII:1, March, 1959, pp. 92-98.

———. "William James as a Critic of his Brother Henry," *Personalist*, XL:4, Autumn, 1959, pp. 341-353. (William disliked Henry's choice of subject matter and his style.)

STALLMAN, R. W. "The Houses that James Built—*The Portrait of a Lady*," *Texas Quarterly*, I:4, Winter 1958, pp. 176-196.

———. "Who was Gilbert Osmond?" *Modern Fiction Studies*, IV:2, Summer 1958. (Probably Henry Brewster was James's model.)

STEIN WILLIAM BYSSHE. "*The Portrait of a Lady: Vis Inertiae*," *Western Humanities Review*, XIII:2, Spring 1959, pp. 177-190. (James and Henry Adams.)

TANNER, TONY. "James's Little Tarts," *Spectator*, No. 7019, January 4, 1963, p. 19. (Stories 1873-82 contain many Jamesian themes; also important as to use of observer-narrator.)

TARTELLA, VINCENT. "James's 'Four Meetings': Two Texts Compared," *Nineteenth Century Fiction*, XV:1, June, 1960.

TERRIE, HENRY L., JR. "Henry James and the 'Explosive Principle'," *Nineteenth Century Fiction*, XV:4, March, 1961, pp. 283-299. (James uses five basic principles of economy in his fiction: the functional handling of antecedent action, the double scene, the moment of recognition, the extended image, and the closely observed action.)

VAN DER BEETS, RICHARD. "A Note on Henry James's 'Western Barbarian'," *Western Humanities Review*, XVII:2, Spring 1963, pp. 175-178. (Suggests Mark Twain in *Innocents Abroad* served as source for Newman.)

VOLPE, EDMOND L. "James's Theory of Sex in Fiction," *Nineteenth Century Fiction*, XIII:1, June, 1958, pp. 36-47. (James looked through the sensible world to the moral world.)

———. "The Reception of *Daisy Miller*," *The Boston Public Library Quarterly*, January, 1958, pp. 55-59. (Questions the tradition that *Daisy Miller* was not well received by American critics. Finds the contrary.)

WARD, J. A. "Henry James's America: Versions of Oppression," *Mississippi Quarterly*, XII:1, Winter 1959-60, pp. 30-44. (America the land of oppression as well as land of innocence. Evil arises out of prohibition and restraint rather than out of any aggressive act.)

WATANAKE, HISAYOSHI. "Past Perfect Retrospection in the Style of Henry James," *American Literature*, XXXIV:2, May, 1962, pp. 165-181.

WRIGHT, NATHALIA. "Henry James and the Greenough Data," *American Quarterly*, X:3, Fall 1958. (Acquaintance with the Greenoughs influenced *Portrait of a Lady, Roderick Hudson, Wings of a Dove*— transplanted Americans with artistic consciousness.)

INDEX

4007

DATE DUE

PRINTED IN U.S.A.